Linguistic Simplicity and Complexity

D0763329

Language Contact and Bilingualism   1

Editor
Yaron Matras

De Gruyter Mouton

Linguistic Simplicity and Complexity

Why Do Languages Undress?

by
John H. McWhorter

De Gruyter Mouton

ISBN 978-1-934078-37-2
pb-ISBN 978-1-934078-39-6
e-ISBN 978-1-934078-40-2
ISSN 2190-698X

Library of Congress Cataloging-in-Publication Data

McWhorter, John H.
  Linguistic simplicity and complexity : why do languages undress? / by John
H. McWhorter.
    p. cm. — (Language contact and bilingualism; 1)
  Includes bibliographical references and index.
    ISBN 978-1-934078-37-2 (alk. paper) — ISBN 978-1-934078-39-6 (pbk. :
alk. paper)
  1. Complexity (Linguistics)   2. Second language acquisition.   3. Languages
in contact.   I. Title.
  P128.C664M39   2011
  417'.22—dc23   2011018843

Bibliographic information published by the Deutsche Nationalbibliothek

The Deutsche Nationalbibliothek lists this publication in the Deutsche Nationalbibliografie; detailed bibliographic data are available in the Internet at http://dnb.d-nb.de.

© 2011 Walter de Gruyter GmbH & Co. KG, Boston/Berlin

Typesetting: Apex CoVantage, LLC
Printing: Hubert & Co. GmbH & Co. KG, Göttingen
⊗ Printed on acid-free paper

Printed in Germany

www.degruyter.com

Contents

Acknowledgments

The chapters in this book other than the Introduction began as the following articles in order. Deepest thanks to the editors concerned for allowing me to reproduce them in this volume. They were:

- Tying Up Loose Ends: The Creole Prototype After All. *Diachronica* 28: 82–117 (2011)
- What the Creolist Learns from Cantonese and Kabardian (Review article of *Phonology and Morphology in Creole Languages,* ed. by Ingo Plag). *Diachronica* 23: 143–184. (2006)
- Review article of *Deconstructing Creole,* ed. by Umberto Ansaldo, Stephen Matthews and Lisa Lim. *Journal of Pidgin and Creole Languages* 23: 289–306. (2008)
- Oh, Nɔ́ɔ! A Bewilderingly Multifunctional Saramaccan Word Teaches Us How a Creole Language Develops Complexity. *Language Complexity as an Evolving Variable,* ed. by Geoffrey Sampson, David Gil and Peter Trudgill, 141–163. Oxford: Oxford University Press. (2009)
- Hither and Thither in Saramaccan Creole. *Studies in Language* 32: 163–195. (2008)
- Complexity Hotspot: The Copula in Saramaccan and Its Implications. *Proceedings of the Workshop on Linguistic Complexity in Interlanguage Varieties, L2 Varieties, and Contact Languages,* ed. by Bernd Kortmann and Benedikt Szmrecsanyi. Berlin: Mouton De Gruyter. (2011)
- Why Does a Language Undress?: Strange Cases of Indonesia. *Language Complexity: Typology, Contact, Change,* ed. by Matti Miestamo, Kaius Sinnemäki and Fred Karlsson, 167–90. Amsterdam: John Benjamins. (2008)
- Affixless in Austronesian: Why Flores is a Puzzle and What To Do About It. *Austronesian Undressed,* ed. by David Gil, Scott Paauw and John McWhorter. Berlin: Mouton De Gruyter. (2012)
- What Else Happened to English? A Brief for the Celtic Hypothesis. *English Language and Linguistics* 13: 163–191. (2009)

I also am grateful to Cathleen Petree and her colleagues at Mouton de Gruyter for accepting my proposal for gathering these articles into a book format, and Uri Tadmor, working at Mouton De Gruyter but also an Indonesian expert *par extraordinaire*, for helping to welcome me into the realm of linguists exploring the contact-rich sociohistory of the Austronesian language family and supporting this volume. This book would likely not exist if it were not for a chance encounter between Cathleen, Uri and myself at a Linguistics Society of America meeting that I happened to attend. Here's to making the best of serendipity.

Abbreviations

ABS	absolutive
ACC	accusative
AG	agent
AGR	agreement
APPL	applicative
ART	article
ASP	aspect marker
ASSOC	association marker
CAUS	causative
CL	classifier
COMP	complementizer
CONJ	conjunction
CPLT	completive
DAT	dative
DEF	definite
DEM	demonstrative
DET	determiner
DFP	different pivot
EMPH	emphatic marker
ERG	ergative
EVID	evidential
FOC	focus marker
FREQ	frequentative
GEN	genitive
HOR	hortative
IND	indicative
IMF	imperfective
IMP	impositive
INCL	inclusive
INF	infinitive
INJ	interjection
INST	instrumental
INT	interrogative marker
LOC	locative
NEG	negator
NI	new information

NMLZ	nominalizer
OBJ	object
PART	partitive
PASS	passive
PERF	perfective
PL	plural
POSS	possessive
PRES	present
PROG	progressive
PRET	preterite
PRT	particle
QUOT	quotative
R	realis
RD	reduplicated
REC	reciprocal
REL	relative
REV	reversive
RPAST	recent past
SP	same pivot
SPF	specificity
SUJ	subjunctive
TR	transitive
V	verbal
VN	verbal noun
2SOBJ	second person singular object
3S	third person singular pronominal
3SO	third person singular oblique pronoun

Introduction
The creole litmus test and the *NCSL* challenge

The chapters in this book, which with the exception of this one began as journal and anthology articles, are devoted to the exploration of a basic proposition. That is that the difference in complexity between languages' grammars is determined significantly by the extent to which second-language acquisition has played a role in their histories. This constitutes an expansion upon conceptions such as Thurston's (1987) distinction between *esoteric* and *exoteric* grammars, and Kusters' (2003: 41–4) demonstration of how amount of inflection and allomorphy varies according to whether languages are of Type 1 (mostly used as first languages) or Type 2 (mostly used as second ones).

A corollary of this framework is that grammatical simplification can be as significant a factor in languages born of second-language acquisition as grammatical mixture. That is, descriptions of creolization and other instances of language mixture as simply a matter of "feature selection" from the languages in a context are incomplete. Similarly incomplete according to my framework is a conception that any apparent simplification in a mixed language is always due to the choice of the least marked choice among the "features" available. There are cases, of which creoles are type, in which the choices made to encode most features are less "marked" than any that the source languages offer. The guiding principle, in other words, is simplification in a general sense.

1. Basic assumptions

The framework these chapters argue for consists of three main planks.

1. *The normal state of language is highly complex, to an extent that seems extreme to speakers of languages like English.* I propose that the natural state of human language is the extensive marking of fine shades of semantic and syntactic distinctions, plus rampant allomorphy and irregularity – typical of languages such as those of the Caucasus and Native American languages. Languages become accreted with this degree of complexity not for functional reasons, but because normal processes of sound change, grammaticalization and reanalysis ineluctably lead to such accretion, and human cognition happens to be able to acquire such systems when the brain is young. In

McWhorter (2007: 21–50) I outline a model of complexity that comprises the following three aspects:

Overspecification: Languages differ in the degree to which they overtly and obligatorily mark semantic distinctions, such as inalienable possession, the "fourth person" obviative, evidentiality, and definiteness.

Structural elaboration: An aspect of one grammar may differ from that aspect in another's in terms of the number of rules (in phonology and syntax) required to generate grammatical forms; examples include morphophonemic processes, concord, and heterogenous word order.

Irregularity: Grammars differ in the degree to which they exhibit irregularity and suppletion.

The Nakh-Daghestanian language Lak, then, is a "normal" language in its degree of overspecification and structural elaboration:

(1) *Insan-tura-l   arcu   žahil-minna-l   darcun-ni.*
      men-PL-ERG money.ABS young-NMLZ.CL1.PL-ERG steal-PAST.3
      'Young men stole the money.'

(Kazenin 2009: 401)

Lak marks ergativity; the modifier of an NP need not appear next to it, but if it does not, it takes a nominalization marker which varies according to noun class and number; the past marker varies for person. This degree of complexity is, under my analysis, that of a language that has undergone little or no second-language acquisition.

2. *Languages significantly low in this kind of complexity compared to their sisters owe this state to second-language acquisition in the past.* I propose that under ordinary conditions, languages lose a modest amount of complexity but maintain a basic level of it through the development of new complexities (cf. Chapter Seven, Section 2.2.). Under this analysis, languages that have not maintained this level have *always* been interrupted in their normal accumulation of complexity.

These languages include familiar ones such as English, the Romance languages, Persian, Mandarin Chinese, and Indonesian (McWhorter 2007). In these cases, grammatical mixture with other grammars is modest; what distinguishes them from their sisters significantly is degree of complexity. For example, in this light the "normal" Indo-European languages are Slavic, Baltic, Greek, Latin, Sanskrit, Pashto and Icelandic, while English, Dutch, the Mainland Scandinavian languages, the Romance languages and the modern Indo-Aryan languages show evidence of widespread second-language learning in the past.

I term languages of this kind Non-Hybrid Conventionalized Second-Language Varieties (NCSLs). Chapter Eight will suggest that some unusually analytic Austronesian languages of Flores and Timor also fit into this class.

3. *The languages evidencing the least complexity of all of the world's languages are creoles.* That is, where complexity has been lost to a radical degree, the language was born in a situation in which adult acquisition was universal or nearly so – namely, the languages termed creole languages. Because many creoles develop in close contact with older languages, while others are created by speakers of closely related older languages and thus maintain many complex features processible by all creators, not all languages termed creoles display the maximum degree of simplification that others do. However, there is a maximal degree of simplification that some languages display in comparison to their source languages that is unique, and all languages exhibiting this degree of simplification, despite the variation in that degree, are all ones born in rapid and widespread adult acquisition. That is, they are creoles.

As I will demonstrate via Saramaccan Creole in Chapters Four, Five and Six, creole languages of course have a degree of complexity: demonstrations of this, common since I first presented this hypothesis, do not qualify as refutations of my proposition. The point is that creoles are considerably *less* complex (according to the metric presented above) than older languages, including NCSLs, as will be demonstrated in Chapter Two.

An example is the contrast between a sentence in French and one in Haitian Creole:

(2) (a)   French:
  Ils n'ont   pas de   ressources qui puissent
  3P NEG.have NEG PART resource.PL REL can.SUJ.3P
  leur   permettre de résister.
  3P.OBJ allow   to resist

  (b)   Haitian:
  Yo pa   gen resous ki   pou pèmèt yo reziste.
  3P NEG have resource REL can allow 3P resist
                    (Ludwig, Telchid, & Bruneau-Ludwig 2001: 164)

The framework in this book cannot accommodate a claim that French's inflectional morphology, including irregularities such as *ont* and *puissent,* plus case-distinguished pronominal forms such as *ils* vs. *leur,* the partitive marker *de* and its very particular conditioning, and the occurrence of object pronominal *leur* in the clitic-climbing position before the verb, does not entail that more rules need to be applied to generate the French sentence than the Haitian one in which all of these traits are absent. Note also: I do not designate the plural -*s* on French's *ressources* as indicating more overspecification than Haitian's number-neutral *resous,* as it is not pronounced. Yet, morphophonemic liaison processes often preserve plural -*s* in spoken French whereas this process is absent in Haitian.

Equally unsuccessful would be an investigation as to whether Haitian exhibits complexity elsewhere in its grammar that leads it to match French in degree of complexity (cf. McWhorter 2005a: 102–41 on the comparison of Fongbe with Saramaccan and Haitian, and McWhorter 2007: 36–50 on such a comparison of Estonian and Saramaccan). The overall grammar of Haitian is markedly less complex than that of French, and the framework of these chapters will treat this as symptomatic of unusually prevalent adult acquisition.

2. Why these assumptions require statement

Few linguists would disagree with the basic proposition that second-language acquisition entails grammatical simplification.

However, there is a resistance in some quarters to the idea that such simplification could leave its mark on languages over time other than creoles. The languages I term NCSLs are commonly treated as having fallen into their lighter degree of complexity as a matter of chance (cf. Thomason & Kaufman 1988: 263–342 on English), or are attributed to a "drift" towards analyticity in Europe and the Middle East (the common take on Romance vs. Latin, or the colloquial Arabics vs. Classical). This leads to questions. What was it about earlier ages that conditioned the opposite "drift" into the complexity of ancient languages like Sanskrit, Latin, and Classical Arabic? What has made all of the subsequent stages of these languages "drift" towards analyticity together? And why no "drift" towards analyticity in Native American, Australian Aboriginal, Bantu, Uralic, Palaeosiberian, Dravidian or, actually, most languages on earth?

I propose that widespread second-language acquisition, an accepted source of grammatical simplification, was the cause. To wit, second-language acquisition can have effects on grammars more permanent than mere matters of individual speakers' interlanguage and post-critical stage fossilization, and less extreme than pidginization or creolization.

Meanwhile, while the influence of second-language acquisition on creoles is readily apparent to creolists, there is a resistance to the idea that it left a decisive enough impact on them to distinguish them from other natural language grammars. Plag (2008a, 2008b) argues carefully that creoles are indeed "conventionalized interlanguages of an early stage," but nevertheless rejects the entailment – which would seem inherent – that creole language grammars are simpler than older language grammars (cf. Plag 2008a: 130–1). This demonstrates an acute discomfort, typical among creole specialists, with the characterization of creoles as "simpler" (cf. Kouwenberg 2010: 173: "McWhorter's arguments that prototypical creoles converge on a set of properties which he designates 'simple' have won him few friends in the field"). The consensus would appear to be that whatever the effects of second-language acquisition on creoles, older languages can also fall into the same lesser degree of overall complexity as a matter of chance.

However, the languages in question have yet to be identified. There have indeed been a few attempts to specify older languages that display the three features of the Creole Prototype outlined in McWhorter (2005a: 9–37), as discussed in Chapter One. None of these go through, however, for reasons outlined in that chapter. In any case, the Creole Prototype is not intended as a condition of maximum simplicity, despite frequent misunderstandings on that score as evidenced, for example, by Kouwenberg's statement above. There is nothing inherently complex about tone or noncompositional derivation, for example. The Prototype refers to these features because of their being symptomatic not of complexity, but of a language's age.

The disproof that the least grammatically complex languages are creoles would be a language with no history of widespread adult acquisition that displayed as little complexity (according to the metric above) as a subset of creoles do. It is reasonable to hypothesize that such a language does not exist.

3. The Creole Litmus Test

In this chapter I will apply this framework to a little-known language, in order to illustrate the basic assumptions which will be examined more closely in the subsequent chapters.

I claim that creole languages are synchronically identifiable, even without recourse to information about their histories. That is, a creole is "a kind of language," not just a sociohistorical term. My stipulation – simplified here; cf. Chapter One for a more detailed presentation – is that a subset of languages show the following three kinds of indication that they were born recently of pidgins:

phonological: little or no use of tone to distinguish monosyllables or grammatical categories
morphosyntactic: little or no inflectional morphology
semantic: little or no noncompositional combinations of derivational markers and roots.

This proposition has been highly controversial among creole specialists, and in the years since I first proposed it, a conclusion would appear to have set in that, as Singler (2006: 159) puts it, "No linguistic litmus test of creole status exists – or could exist." However, I believe that one indeed could and does. The death knell sounded by Singler, as well as Ansaldo, Matthews & Lim (2007) and others is premature.

Chapter One will present a revision of the Creole Prototype hypothesis which will make its theoretical motivation clearer, and show that certain data thought to constitute exceptions to it in fact do not. Here, however, I will give a preview of how the Creole Prototype indeed constitutes a litmus test for creolization, with an examination of an isolating language that has not been considered a creole under any definition. This is a kind of language that could be seen as suggesting that even older languages can wend into a creole-like typology, and that there is therefore properly no synchronic essence limited only to creole languages. However, the language in question, isolating though it is, gives ample signs of its antiquity.

New Guinea, home to hundreds of languages spoken by small groups, is a setting that typically yields "normal" grammars in the sense specified above: robustly complex, most saliently in considerable morphological elaboration on the verb (Foley 1986: 12). An example is Amele:

(3) (a) *Ija hu-m-ig   sab j-ig-a.*
         I   come-SP-1S food eat-1S-RPAST
         'I came and ate the food.'

    (b) *Ija ho-co-min   sab ja-g-a.*
         I   come-DFP-1S food eat-2S-RPAST
         'I came and you ate the food.'

(Roberts 1988)

Amele displays various typical features of the languages termed, despite the multiple families it comprises which are unlinked to a reconstructed ancestor, "Papuan." SP and DFP stand for "same pivot" and "different pivot," the latter of which is a switch-reference marker. The subject is indexed with an affix on the verb corresponding to its person and number, which in addition differs according to the pivot marker. The *come* root is variable according to its affixation; such roots often vary even suppletively in Papuan languages. The past marker in these sentences refers only to the day in question, as opposed to a more distant past.

Things are quite different in Abun, of West Papua in the Northern Bird's Head peninsula. Abun is a rare thing: a largely isolating Papuan language:

(4) *Men ben suk   no   nggwe yo,   men ben suk   sino.*
    we   do thing LOC garden then we   do   thing together
    'If we do things at the garden, then we do them together.'

(Berry & Berry 1999: 23)

Isolating structure hardly bars extreme complexity, in itself. To assess whether Abun is identifiably less grammatically complex than a language like Amele, we must check whether it has free morpheme equivalents to the switch-reference markers or allomorphically variant subject-indexed suffixes. It, in fact, does not. Plus, not only is there no particle dedicated to the specific gradation of "earlier today" as there is in Amele – Abun does not mark tense overtly at all!

Here, then, is a language as isolating as a creole like Haitian – and, unlike isolating languages like Chinese and Yoruba, we see in (4) no tonal markings. In fact, Abun does have three phonemic tones. However, their functional load is quite light and Abun's grammarians venture that the distinction is on its way to extinction. Cases of three-way contrasts on monosyllables are rare: Berry & Berry (1999: 21) present but one, *šè* "flow," *šé* "flood," *še* "big." Even two-way contrasts are rare (*ndò* "good," *ndó* "bitter"), uncommon beyond an only slightly productive usage to indicate plurality (*an* "he, she, it," *án* "they," *ndam* "bird," *ndám* "birds" [ibid. 21]).

Yet, it would be infelicitous to treat this modest degree of contrastive tone as disqualifying Abun as a creole, because some creoles have marginally contrastive usage of tone as well. Saramaccan has *dá* "give" vs. *da* "be," *á* "not" vs. *a* "he, she, it," the future marker *ó* vs. the affective marker *o*. Principense Creole Portuguese has an HH pattern for some deverbal nouns contrasting with an LL one for the verbs, which does not correspond to the stress patterns: (*fálá* "speech," *fàlà* "to speak," *témá* "insistence," *tèmà* "to insist" [Maurer 2009: 26]).

In truth, all of these cases can be traced conclusively to developments after the genesis of the creoles, as will be discussed in Chapter One (which will also address similar data from Papiamentu). They are signs of the gradual accretion of complexity diagnostic of a language's transformation over time, but were not products of initial creolization itself. However, to the extent that this will seem a matter of special pleading to some – although it isn't! – we will proceed as if Abun's degree of tone is immaterial to assessing whether it is a creole.

In the same fashion, the fact that Abun has a transitivizing suffix on verbs (although it is used only on some) cannot disqualify it as a creole, given that Tok Pisin and its sister languages are readily admitted to the class despite departing from the Prototype with their transitivizing *-im* suffix (*Mi boil-im wata* "I boil water"):

(5)(a)   *Ji nyu.*
      I fear
      'I am afraid.'

  (b)   *Nu nyu-wa men o   nde.*
       2P fear-TR 1P   again NEG
       'Don't fear us anymore.'

                                    (Berry & Berry 1999: 27)

The distinction of ancient languages from creoles need not, then, rely on hair-splitting. Despite "flutter" such as the minimal tone and the transitive marker, there are two aspects of this isolating language that reveal it quite readily as ancient rather than as born of a pidgin recently – i.e. that disqualify it as a creole.

One is that as we would expect of an ancient language, combinations of derivational morphemes and roots have often drifted into noncompositionality. The noncompositionality in question is not the typical slight drifts from strict compositionality that derivation-root combinations undergo in all languages as the result of cultural conventions, such as the use of *transmission* to refer to an automobile part. Rather, what is diagnostic of antiquity is such combinations whose meanings are much more idiosyncratic and inexplicable synchronically than this, outright lexicalizations such as English's *understand,* or its verb-particle combinations such as *make out* or *put up with.*

In Abun, this kind of noncompositionality occurs in fact with the transitive suffix *-wa: kon* "cook," *kon-wa* "celebrate;" *bi* "give," *bi-wa* "pay for;" *ki* "say," *ki-wa* "ask for" (ibid. 29). Or, the original meaning of *ket* is directional, roughly "over to":

(6)   *Men tot ket   nden.*
     1P   cut LOC path
     'We cut across to the interior path.'

However, combined derivationally with roots, it can yield highly unpredictable meanings: *ye* "difficult," *ye-ket* "surprised."

The nature of such derivational morphemes in Abun can be demonstrated by their combination with the one verb *ki* "to say," yielding a wide range of idiosyncratic meanings:

wa "to, for"	*ki-wa* "ask for"
ket "to"	*ki-ket* "slander"
bot "through"	*ki-bot* "discuss"
gat "join"	*ki-gat* "speak persuasively"

The second Abun trait that reveals it as antique is that while it is isolating, it is nevertheless inflected. That is, it does not have bound inflection, but it has free morphemes that qualify as Inflection in a larger grammatical sense, along the lines specified by Kihm (2003). Creoles, too, have free morpheme Inflection: their tense-marking "particles," for example, are inflections which differ from inflectional affixes in the same function only in how they are handled by syntax (they Move rather than Merge, in Kihm's framework).

However, one aspect of the revision of the Prototype formulation in Chapter One is that languages born recently of rudimentary pidgins do not have, either bound or unbound, *paradigmatic* inflection: that is, allomorphic batteries of noun class markers, conjugation class markers, etc. Paradigmatic morphology is absent in a rudimentary pidgin, and from there, can only develop via grammaticalization or reanalysis over time. Abun, however, has paradigmatic morphology in the form of its battery of numeral classifiers. Such classifiers are analogous to noun class or gender markers (cf. Grinevald & Seifart 2004):

bo	fruit, motor
but	bundles
ge	person, animal
gwes	bamboo (cut pieces)
is	tuber
ka	person
ke	tree, house
koi	stick (cut pieces)
sak	cloth
wak	cloth

(Berry & Berry 1999: 42)

Therefore, the way that Abun reveals itself as ancient despite having almost no affixation and little contrastive tone is in having 1) noncompositional derivation, and also 2) "Inflection" of a kind – paradigmatic – that is absent in creoles. This absence makes sense if creoles were born a few centuries ago as makeshift pidgins created by adults. This is a reason to suppose that creoles were indeed born in this way – on top of the sheer empirical fact that relatively new creoles which emerged amidst ample documentation can be seen over time unequivocally emerging from rudimentary pidgins; namely, Tok Pisin and its sister creoles of Oceania.

Unsurprisingly, Abun also departs from creoles in having some over-specifications of a kind rarely encountered in them (cf. McWhorter 2005a: 72–101), such as a distinction between alienable and inalienable possession (Berry & Berry 1999: 79).

The numeral classifier issue is important. In earlier work I have stressed that noncompositional derivation crucially distinguishes analytic and tone-less older languages from creoles (cf. McWhorter 2005a: 16–18). However, numeral classifiers do as well, as they are typical in Southeast Asia which contains some of the only languages in the world with neither inflectional affixes nor tone, and are perhaps a handier metric. Few grammars devote much space to noncompositional derivation given that it is not, properly, grammar. Moreover, the alphabetical order of dictionaries means that they can only be searched easily for derivational morphemes' semantic contributions when the morphemes are prefixes, rather than suffixes. Numeral classifiers, like inflectional affixes and tones, are readily described even in briefer treatments.

Thus there can be, at present, no conclusive claim that a litmus test for creole status does not exist or would be theoretically impossible. Parkvall (2008) indicates that creoles are measurably less complex than older languages according to grammatical features tabulated in the *World Atlas of Language Structures*. Especially useful in this light is Bakker, Daval-Markussen, Parkvall and Plag's (2011) two comparisons. One is of creole languages and a range of older languages with "creole"-like profiles such as analyticity, according to the presence or absence of a substantial list of grammatical features examined in, again, the *World Atlas of Language Structures*. The other is of creoles and older languages according to the features tabulated in a wide range of creoles by Holm & Patrick's (2007) project comparing a range of creoles. Bakker, Daval-Markussen and Parkvall find that when the data is submitted to SplitsTree software, creole languages group together as a class – despite the sample including several analytic languages and African languages, two categories which we would expect to cluster with creoles according to the idea that there exists no synchronic class of creole language. All statements that there exists no synchronic distinction between creoles and older languages is, as of the publication of these articles, invalid without engagement with them.

Importantly, one kink in Parkvall and Bakker's result is that Hmong, a highly isolating Sino-Tibetan language, groups with the creoles. However, this is because they happen not to include numeral classifiers in their tabulation, these being rarely discussed as relevant to creoles because of their absence in them (as well as, probably, in the West African substrate languages associated with them). However, if classifiers were included, then Hmong, which has over 50, would no longer cluster with the creoles.

4. Abun as a NCSL

Even if Abun is identifiable as not the product of the recent pidginization and reconstitution of a language, the fact remains that it is notably less grammatically complex than the typical Papuan language. This is true not only in its analyticity but in overall degree of grammatical elaboration of the kind specified above, in a fashion that does not lend itself to quantification, but is starkly apparent nonetheless. Berry & Berry's (1999) Abun grammar reveals a language requiring a much briefer description than languages like Amele, Nasioi, Yimas, Iatmul, and the vast majority of the hundreds of Papuan languages – i.e. of the kind that might lead to a preliminary impression that it "seems like a creole" or is "creole-like."

4.1. The nature of the question

The question as to why is perhaps uninteresting from the perspective of the synchronically oriented linguist. To him or her, some languages are analytic, some are not, but all operate according to grammatical principles. From a diachronic perspective, however, the question is urgent.

Languages like Abun are sometimes approached according to an assumption that they simply "lost their morphology" as if this were a documented regular process of language change. However, it is not.

Why, after all, would a grammar over time lose not just some, but virtually all of its morphology? That is, precisely what would the process be? That such a thing seems even initially plausible to many linguists is perhaps an artifact of how English and some other Western European languages happened to develop. However, first, English and the Romance languages retain a goodly amount of inflectional and derivational morphology nonetheless, remaining fusional languages. Second, as noted above, even these developments are atypical of language change and constitute a challenge to diachronic theory (as addressed in McWhorter 2007). For example, under an assumption that losing almost of its morphology is an unsurprising pathway for a grammar to take, the languages of Australia are a stunningly intractable puzzle – there is not a single language on the continent that has somehow shed its affixation.

Moreover, we cannot propose that Abun never had affixation. Affixation develops as the result of ordinary processes of grammaticalization and re-analysis which are universally operant in human language. It is inconceivable that a human language could exist for as long as the 65,000 years often reconstructed as the length of human occupation of New Guinea without developing affixes of some kind. In fact, after this much time, we see from several hundred languages of the island that the norm is the development of considerable affixation. An Abun, then, is again a puzzle, not simply one possible pathway a language might ordinarily take.

We are faced, then, with the specific task of accounting for how a grammar goes from the state of Amele:

(7)   *Ija ho-co-min   sab ja-g-a.*
       I   come-DFP-1S food eat-2S-RPAST
       'I came and you ate the food.'

(Roberts 1988)

to the state of Abun:

(8)   *Men tot ket   nden.*
       we   cut LOC path
       'We cut across to the interior path.'

Crucially, we are faced not with how a language loses a single affix, or even one paradigm of affixes, such as through phonetic erosion or reanalysis. How does a language lose *all* of its affixation across the board – with no new affixes developing in the meantime?

4.2. Garden path explanations

More properly, as Paauw (2007) has noted, the relevant data set is several languages of the northern coast of Papua, including Tidore, Tobelo, Tehit, Moi, Maybrat, Meyah, Moskona, Ireres, Sougb, Hatam, and Mpur. Affixation is anomalously low for Papuan languages among this set, although Abun represents an extreme. The cause is not an analytic ancestor: although the classification of Papuan languages is at present incomplete, these languages belong to various families, with no sister relationships evident. In any case, if there by chance were such an analytic ancestor reconstructable, it would only relocate our question: how and why could there develop such a language at any time amidst richly inflected ones? That is, what would have exempted that language from submission to the otherwise universal processes of grammaticalization and reanalysis?

Among scholars of Austronesian and Papuan languages, it is common to suppose that analyticity of this kind is due to the use of Indonesian as a lingua franca. The idea seems to be that Indonesian, very light on inflection, would "infect" other languages with analyticity. This account, while plausible when applied to a single language, lacks explanatory power in a more general sense. Contact alone hardly requires that indigenous languages simplify. For example, for every Austronesian language treated as having shed complexity because of Indonesian, there are others with the same long-term and even threatening contact with Indonesian which remain typically complex languages, such as Tukang Besi of Sulawesi or, actually, most languages of Papua. Countless Niger-Congo languages in Africa have long been used alongside English and French; grammatically, they remain what they have always been. Certainly, Indonesian has certain simplifying effects on grammars, often as initial symptoms of language death (cf. Van Engelehoven 2003). However, Indonesian fails as an account of why Abun is analytic, as Paauw agrees.

4.3. Austronesian migration

A more promising explanation is the general spread of Austronesian eastward across the north of New Guinea to Oceania. Austronesian languages themselves remain scattered in the region as a sign of this movement. More important to our question, however, is that Abun and the other languages share features other than a tendency to low affixation: SVO word order in contrast to the SOV Papuan norm, and subject prefixes. Both of these are hallmark traits of Eastern Austronesian languages.

The Austronesian explanation beckons in particular because these analytic-leaning Papuan languages are spoken just where Papuans would have been in intimate contact with groups migrating from the islands westward across to Oceania. That is, if this "Sprachbund" were in the interior, the Austronesian explanation would be much less attractive.

It is generally assumed by Austronesianists that when Austronesian languages were brought to islands originally inhabited by Papuans, the Austronesian languages underwent both mixture and a certain degree of simplification (Klamer 2002), as the result of Papuans acquiring the Austronesian languages. This would presumably explain, for example, the lesser amount of affixation in Austronesian languages of the Central Malayo-Polynesian subfamily spoken in the Lesser Sunda Islands and the Moluccas. In most of these cases the Papuan languages no longer exist. However, it is unproblematic to reconstruct a similar process in cases on the island of New Guinea where the Papuan language survived. Austronesians' acquisition of it would have left behind evidence, in the form of both mixture (SVO, the subject prefixes) and the simplification typical in the wake of adult acquisition.

4.4. Situating Abun in a typology of language contact

As we have seen, Abun is not a creole – i.e. it does not display the radical degree of simplification compared to other Papuan languages that would mark
it as the recent product of a pidgin. The complexity differential is moderate
but substantial, and as such, Abun can be classified along with English, Persian and similar cases as what I termed a NCSL above. It is a language that
harbors symptoms of large-scale adult acquisition, without those symptoms
being extreme enough to put it in the creole class.

Abun, then, belongs in what can be seen as a kind of "black box" in the
typology of language contact. It is well known that languages can mix to various depths, ranging from mere lexical mixture to "intertwined" languages
like Media Lengua with Spanish lexicon and Quechua morphology and syntax. The signature study here would be Thomason & Kaufman (1988), and
the typology could be illustrated thusly:

Table 1. Degrees of language mixture

lexicon only	lexicon and syntax	lexicon, syntax, morphology, phonology
Germanic in Finnish	Romanian and other Balkan Sprachbund languages	Media Lengua Ancient language areas (Amazon, Australia)

It is also well known that some creoles are more mixed than others: the
usual terminology refers to greater substrate influence, ranging from the
highly Africanized Saramaccan Creole to a creole like Hawaiian Creole English, in which substrate influence on grammar is much less evident and,
pace an argument like Siegel's (2000a) pointing to Chinese influence, may
well be nonexistent.

Table 2. Degrees of language mixture in creoles

lexicon only	lexicon and syntax	lexicon, syntax, morphology, phonology
Hawaiian Creole Chinook Jargon creole	most creoles	Saramaccan Tok Pisin Berbice Creole Dutch

Then, creolists are also familiar with a class of contact languages often
termed semi-creoles, in which a lexifier language has been simplified to only

a moderate degree, with substrate influence similarly modest, such that the language is often thought of as a dialect of the lexifier rather than a different language. Examples include Afrikaans, which is Dutch as morphologically streamlined by contact with Khoi-San speakers, and Singapore English. Semi-creoles can be further classified according to whether mixture occurs only on the syntactic level or on the morphological and phonological levels as well. The latter occurs when the languages in contact are closely related, such as Shaba Swahili, which is less morphologically complex than standard Swahili but has, for example, some extra noun classes on the model of the other Bantu languages spoken by its creators (Kapanga 1993:447).

Semi-creoles, simplified to a moderate degree compared to creoles and varying in depth of language mixture, can be placed between older languages and creoles along a metric of simplification, such that we now have a typology grid referring to the axes of both mixture and simplification:

Table 3. Language contact typology integrating older languages, creoles and semi-creoles

	lexicon only	lexicon and syntax	lexicon, syntax, morphology, phonology
no simplification	1. Germanic in Finnish	2. Romanian and other Balkan Sprachbund languages	3. Media Lengua Ancient language areas (Amazon, Australia)
some simplification on all levels	4.	5. Afrikaans Réunionnais French Singapore English	6. Shaba Swahili, Kituba (Kikongo), Sango (Ubangian)
extreme simplification on all levels	7. Hawaiian Creole Chinook Jargon creole	8. most creoles	9. Saramaccan Tok Pisin Berbice Creole Dutch

The only remaining question is what fills Box 4. We would no more expect that nothing would than that we would expect there to mysteriously exist no element with the atomic number of 4 (beryllium) when there is one with the number 3 (lithium) and with the number 5 (boron). What kind of languages are only moderately simplified compared to their relatives, and are also not especially mixed grammatically at all? The answer is languages like English, the Romance languages, Persian, the colloquial Arabic dialects, Indonesian, and, as it happens, Swahili. Box 4 is the NCSL box.

Table 4. Language contact typology integrating mixture and simplification in all combinations

	lexicon only	lexicon and syntax	lexicon, syntax, morphology, phonology
no simplification	1. Germanic in Finnish	2. Romanian and other Balkan Sprachbund languages	3. Media Lengua Ancient language areas (Amazon, Australia)
some simplification on all levels	4. English, Persian, Indonesian, Mandarin, New Arabic, Swahili, Abun	5. Afrikaans Réunionnais French Singapore English	6. Shaba Swahili
extreme simplification on all levels	7. Hawaiian Creole Chinook Jargon creole	8. most creoles	9. Saramaccan Tok Pisin Berbice Creole Dutch

Chapter Eight will argue that an unusual assemblage of analytic Austronesian languages in central Flores should also be placed in Box 4, while Chapter Nine will show that in light of increasingly convincing evidence that English bears ample transferred structure from Celtic languages, it actually belongs itself between Box 4 and Box 5, and possibly in Box 5 entirely.

There will likely remain for many analysts a certain hesitation. All are comfortable with the basic association between second language acquisition and analyticity as a tendency. Fewer, however, are comfortable assigning the general typology of a language to widespread second-language acquisition, in view of the fact that affixes can erode over time and there is, certainly, a chance element in complexity differentials between languages. For example, one could presumably fashion a metric that would decide whether Korean or Hausa was the more complex grammar. I doubt that that difference would correlate meaningfully with sociohistorical factors.

With all of this acknowledged, however, a simple fact remains. There would appear to be:

1) no language maximally complex among its sisters with a history of widespread second-language acquisition, and

2) no language maximally complex among its sisters with no history of widespread second-language acquisition.

A crucial caveat: this does not apply to languages that were imposed on adults amidst widespread literacy, education, and language standardization. In these cases, a highly complex language can survive endless waves of second-language acquisition intact, as the original form of the language is always available and influential in print, the media, and schools. Russian is an example. English, the Romance languages, Persian, the colloquial Arabics, Mandarin, Swahili and other languages became NCSLs when used largely as oral languages, with reading and writing as largely elite activities and media as we know it marginal.

In any case, to contest the proposal of a "Box 4" NCSL language contact category, it is necessary to propose an exception to 1) and 2) above. This constitutes The NCSL Challenge. Otherwise, the time would seem to have come to allow pioneering work on this issue by Thurston, Kusters, Trudgill (1989, 2001), Dahl (2004) and others the status of canon rather than as "interesting" proposals, or as matters of "tendency" which, in itself, is distinctly *un*interesting.

5. The next level

My aim in this book is to work towards a typology of language contact with not only descriptive but deductive power. Grammatical analyticity can be of use in reconstructing population movements for which there is otherwise only fragmentary evidence, or even in directing researchers as to where to look for signs of population movements as yet uninvestigated.

There are four cases in Indonesia and its environs of languages that give the appearance of having drifted into states of unusually low complexity just as a matter of course, contradicting my hypothesis that only heavy second-language acquisition creates such languages. They are the colloquial Indonesians such as the Riau Indonesian that David Gil (2001) has proposed as such a case, the languages of central Flores, certain languages of eastern Timor, and certain languages of northern Papua such as Abun.

In subsequent chapters of this book, I show that the first three cases are all in fact due to extensive second-language acquisition. Chapter Seven argues that Riau Indonesian, and by extension all of the similarly analytic colloquial Indonesian varieties, is the result of the extensive use of Indonesian as a lingua franca by speakers of other Austronesian languages. In Chapter Eight

I show that the languages of central Flores and eastern Timor harbor evidence of creation by inmigrants from Sulawesi.

The fact is, however, that because these processes would have happened in societies where writing was rare to nonexistent, there will likely never exist the concrete documentation of the changes in progress of the kind available for languages with long traditions of writing (and therefore, also detailed historiography). There exist in Java no books in Indonesian written from century to century to show how the language of the Malay courts evolved step-by-step into the almost telegraphic colloquial Indonesian of Java today. The analytic Austronesian languages of Flores achieved this state in mouths alone; they are unwritten even now.

In the same way, at this point, there is no concrete evidence of the diachrony of Abun and never will be. Nor is there historiographical or archaeological evidence as of yet, and genetic evidence on the Austronesian-Papuan encounter at this point suggests only a fitful correlation between language family and ethnic origin (Friedlaender et al. 2008). Nor can even the linguistic evidence alone be considered conclusive in itself. Austronesian impact on the syntax allows that simplification went along with it but hardly requires that it did. Worldwide, languages *can* share syntax without becoming less grammatically complex overall, as is clear from Sprachbund cases in Australia (Heath 1978) and the Amazon (Aikhenvald 2001).

However, given that elsewhere, the degree of loss of complexity in all of these languages of Indonesia correlates so tightly with large-scale non-native acquisition, and that this is indeed *the only process known or even logically constructable for such loss,* we can reasonably propose that the typological anomaly contrast between these Flores languages and other Austronesian languages is itself evidence of a break in transmission in the past.

This is a logical upending of how linguists have usually reasoned on the relationship between grammatical complexity and sociohistory. Typically, we chart non-native acquisition in a language's history and argue that it caused its peculiar simplicity (something even creolists have traditionally been comfortable doing despite the resistance to the designation of creoles as "simpler" as a class). I propose that we venture, given the wealth of cases in which unusual simplicity can be responsibly linked to transmissional rupture, that radical analyticity and simplification compared to a language's close kin indicates that such rupture occurred, beckons investigation, and *is even a scientifically appropriate cause for supposing such rupture even if other evidence proves unrecoverable.*

As geologists treat cracked quartz as a sign of volcanic eruptions in the past, linguists might treat the strange simplicity of languages like Abun as evidence of social disruption in the past.

Section I
Creole exceptionalism

Introduction

Creole exceptionalism is a set of sociohistorically-rooted dogmas, with foundations in (neo)colonial power relations, not a scientific conclusion based on robust empirical evidence."

—(Ansaldo, Matthews & Lim 2007: 14)

The broken transmission and linguistic fossils dogmas have been "robustly disconfirmed by a range of comparative data and empirical and theoretical observations."

—(DeGraff 2003: 398)

Most people working on creole languages would seem to agree. Most linguists outside of creole studies tend to see creole exceptionalism as at least intuitive – but many creolists consider this a matter of regrettable ignorance. Kouwenberg (2010: 173), for example, characterizes typologists as "blissfully unaware of the controversies surrounding the idea of a creole prototype," notably with an implication that the controversy has conclusively demonstrated said idea as incorrect.

The question is whether creolists have actually disproven that creole languages harbor evidence of birth as pidgins. In the chapters in this section, I argue that they have not.

1. The nature of dogma

Refutation is not evaluated on the basis of page count. To qualify as refutation, writing, regardless of its volume, must carefully address the arguments it considers false. This has not happened sustainedly in the debate over whether creoles are a class of language. The opening statements above are, quite simply, untrue. They are founded upon only glancing engagement with the argumentation they oppose.

The vast bulk of work addressing creole exceptionalism flags the three features of the Creole Prototype without engagement with the details of its proposals in McWhorter (1998) and McWhorter (2001c), and treats the Complexity Hypothesis on the basis of mere quotation of the basic principle that creoles are "simple" (as opposed to simpl*er*) without, again, address of the justifications for that claim in McWhorter (2001a).

One senses that creolists of this mind consider arguments for creole exceptionalism to be so inherently implausible as to not require sustained engagement. This, at least, would be a coherent explanation for such confident dismissal of ideas so scantily examined. However, short of sustained *demonstration* that creole exceptionalism arguments are indeed unworthy of engagement, these claims and others in agreement can qualify only as assertion, in the wake of which impatience with other linguists' subscription to creole exceptionalism is unwarranted.

It is interesting, given that both of the opening quotes happen to settle upon the word *dogma,* that dogma can be analyzed as functioning in the work of opponents of creole exceptionalism as well. A useful example is Ansaldo (2008), who argues that Sri Lanka Malay is a compromise between Malay and Sri Lanka's Sinhalese and Tamil rather than the product of a break in transmission – i.e. that it is a "creole" under any traditional conception. He addresses three conceptions of creolization. He first argues that Sri Lanka Malay is not a creole in a sociohistorical sense, and secondly that it is not a relexification *à la* Lefebvre (1998).

Then thirdly, he argues that Sri Lanka Malay gives no appearance of being a young language in the sense that I have argued creoles are recently born of pidgins. However, he immediately also refers the reader to Michel DeGraff's work against creole exceptionalism as well as the then-forthcoming Ansaldo, Matthews & Lim volume (reviewed in this book in Chapter Three).

It's an odd moment in his argument. If the idea that creoles are a class of language is so dead in the water, then why does Ansaldo even venture it as a potential metric for typologizing Sri Lanka Malay? I submit that part of the reason is that, despite disagreement about particulars, Ansaldo feels on a certain level that the simple idea that a language can show signs of birth in widespread adult acquisition is hardly entirely incoherent.

The immediate references to oppositional work nevertheless – whereas he gives none for the first two schools of thought he refers to, despite ample literature of the sort – suggests a sense that one "must not" give more than the most fleeting hint of credence to a proposition that there is a such thing as a creole. We return, however, to the absence of sustained argument in the literature as a whole to justify this, as if it were a self-standing truth: a dogma.

2. "See no simplification, hear no simplification"

Yet in the same article, Ansaldo neglects evidence of exactly the kind of simplification that I argue is as key in language contact as just mixture. He concludes that "the restructuring process that occurs in S[ri] L[ankan] M[alay] in general can thus be captured in a modular view of grammar in which Malay lexical items and [Sri] Lankan semantics combine to form a new system."

This is incomplete. Only a subset of Sri Lankan (i.e., here, Sinhalese and Tamil) "semantics" are reflected in Sri Lanka Malay. To be sure, this language does mark a goodly amount of the semantic categories that, for example, Sinhalese does. An example is the use of the dative marker to mark experiencers and non-volition:

Sinhalese:

(1)   *Miniha-ṭə aliyawə peenəwa.*
      man-DAT elephant see
      'The man sees the elephant.'

                                                              (Gair 1998: 254)

Sri Lanka Malay:

(2)   *Derang-**nang** byaasa svaara hatthu su-dinggar*
      they-DAT   habit voice a   PERF-heard
      'They heard a familiar voice.'

                                                              (Nordhoff 2009: 334)

However, even the most thorough chronicle of Sri Lanka Malay grammar, Nordhoff (2009), presents only a partial reproduction of the full extent of Sinhalese verbal morphological categories, as demonstrated only partially here (Gair 1998: 17):

Table 5. Sinhalese verbal suffix categories

present	kərənəwa
past	kerua
emphatic	kəranne
past emphatic	kerue
conditional	kərətot
past conditional	keruot
hortative	kərəmu
volitive	kərannan

                                                              (*Continued*)

Table 5. Sinhalese verbal suffix categories (*Continued*)

involitive	kəraawi
permissive	keruaawe
infinitive	kərannə
present participle	kərətə
perfect participle	kərəla
gerund	keriimə

Moreover, the Sri Lanka Malay morphemes, mostly clitics, do not exhibit the degree of fusion with the root that their Sinhalese equivalents do, which makes for fewer morphophonemic distortions of the root and less outright irregularity. Also absent in Sri Lanka Malay are three conjugation classes that Sinhalese verb morphology occurs in.

Under my perspective, what all of this means is that Sri Lanka Malay can be readily identified as a language born amidst considerable abbreviation of the source language grammars. Ansaldo himself acknowledges that the Malay component was pidginized Malay of the kind commonly spoken throughout Indonesia. However, the Sinhalese/Tamil component is a reduced version of the original as well.

That is, in the typology of language contact introduced in the Introduction, Sri Lanka Malay would classify as a semi-creole, moderately simplified in comparison to its source languages, and specifically, as a semi-creole mixed in all modules (as per sources on Sri Lanka Malay). Sri Lanka Malay would belong, then, in Box 6 – but this would designate it not just as "combining modules" alone, but also as streamlining them.

There is a qualitative difference between the near reproduction of Quechua morphosyntax in Media Lengua and the rendition of Sinhalese and Tamil in Sri Lanka Malay. That difference is one of fidelity: in Sri Lanka Malay, substrate language grammar is reproduced with less fidelity than in Media Lengua and more than in Saramaccan Creole (cf. McWhorter 2005a: 104–22). Hence, see Table 6.

3. Taking "simplification" out of quotation marks

This typology seeks to taxonomize the results of language contact. An objection to the very endeavor of putting contact languages into boxes – literally and metaphorically – is incoherent minus an accompanying counterproposal of a particular kind. Specifically: amidst an "ecology" combining English and Portuguese with Fongbe, the result was a highly streamlined English/ Portuguese-Fongbe hewing much more closely to the Creole Prototype than any of the source languages do: Saramaccan Creole (Box 9). Saramaccan reproduces Fongbe grammar only in broad outline and retains only echoes of English or Portuguese grammar. There was also an "ecology" putting Finnish into contact with Germanic languages, during the last millennium of the B.C. period. It yielded Finnish with a lot of Germanic roots in it, with no simplification of Finnish in evidence (Box 1). If Box 9 is "socio-historically rooted dogma," then why is Saramaccan so much less grammatically complex overall than Finnish (cf. Chapter Two, 3.2)?

Table 6. Typologizing Sri Lanka Malay

	lexicon only	lexicon and syntax	lexicon, syntax, morphology, phonology
no simplification	1. Germanic in Finnish	2. Romanian and other Balkan Sprachbund languages	3. Media Lengua Ancient language areas (Amazon, Australia)
some simplification on all levels	4. English, Persian, Indonesian, Mandarin, New Arabic, Swahili, Abun	5. Afrikaans Réunionnais French Singapore English	6. Shaba Swahili **Sri Lanka Malay**
extreme simplification on all levels	7. Hawaiian Creole Chinook Jargon creole	8. most creoles	9. Saramaccan Tok Pisin Berbice Creole Dutch

Of course, here I could be accused of writing as if it were obvious that languages differ in overall grammatical complexity. However, frankly, isn't it? Over time, it is coming to the point that the only linguists vociferously resisting the open acknowledgment of this basic notion are creolists. Elsewhere, it is becoming accepted that discussions of grammatical complexity are hardly unworthy of sustained address, never suggest that the concept is invalid in itself, and are deeply connected with language contact (cf. anthologies such as Miestamo, Sinnemäki & Karlsson 2008 and Sampson, Gil & Trudgill 2009; articles by Wray & Grace 2007 and Lupyan & Dale 2010; and McWhorter 2007). Dixon's (1997: 75) observation, quite unconnected with debates over creole exceptionalism, is useful:

> While it is the case that all languages are roughly equal (that is, no language is six times as complex as any other, and there are no primitive languages), it is by no means the case that they are exactly equal. I have done field work on languages in Australia, Oceania and Amazonia and they were certainly not all equally difficult to describe. There is no doubt that one language may have greater overall grammatical complexity.

While observations that grammatical complexity is difficult to define, then, are valuable, less valuable is a corollary drawn from this that no language can be more complex than another – or more specifically, that there is something infelicitous in discussing complexity where creoles are concerned.

Anyone who claims that Saramaccan is as complex as Finnish, in ways that mysteriously have yet to be discovered, would feel quite differently if faced with learning, or even learning about, the grammars of the two. Finnish's morphophonemic consonant gradation processes and attendant irregularities alone are famous: *tupa* "hut," *tuvassa* "in the hut;" *parta* "beard," *parrassa* "in the beard," and a vast number of other regular alternations plus the exceptions. While Finnish does not have tone as Saramaccan does, the rules that Saramaccan's tone entails (including the sandhi rules) do not require anywhere near as much listing as the Finnish morphology situation does. There simply are not as many rules for Saramaccan tone as opposed to tone in an older language like Min Chinese (Hokkienese), where the tonal complexity could possibly compete with that of Balto-Finnic consonant gradations.

Observe Saramaccan compared to Finnish's sister Estonian, where there is a massive complexity differential, apart from the consonant gradations (which are even more prolific and riddled with irregularity than in Finnish), in the marking of an object in simple imperative, past-marked and negative past-marked sentences, requiring specific usages of partitive, genitive, and participial constructions (data from Tuldava 2004):

Estonian

(3) **Loe**   *raamat*   *läbi!*
read.IMP book.NOM through
'Read the book!'

(5) *Ma* **luge-si**-*n*   *raamat-**u*** *läbi.*
I   read-PAST-1S book-GEN through
'I read the book.'

Saramaccan

(4) *Lési dí   búku!*
read DEF book
'Read the book!'

(6) *Mi bi   lési dí   búku.*
I   PAST read DEF book
'I read the book.'

(7) *Ma ei*   **luge-nud** *raamat-**ut**.*   (8) *Mi*   *á bi*   *lési*   *dí*   *búku.*
    I   NEG read-PP   book-PART   I   NEG PAST read DEF book
    'I did not read the book.'   'I did not read the book.'

Saramaccan does differ from Estonian in the tone sandhi (not shown), breaking in these sentences between VP and object, and inapplicable to past marker *bi* as one of the closed class of words with inherent low tone.

But Estonian's genitive and partitive marking are allocated specifically according to mood (indicative) and polarity (negative), and marked according to intricate and exception-laden rules. For example, *raamat* is *raamat-ut* in the partitive only because it ends neither in a long vowel or diphthong (which would condition a *d* ending), nor a short vowel (which would probably mean that the genitive and partitive markers were identical, although the vowel would be unpredictable), nor *l, n, r,* or *s* (which would likely mean that *t* was appended with no preceding vowel), nor *-si* (which would condition the ending *-tt*), and does not happen to be one of the words where the partitive is marked by tripling the length of the vowel, or an outright exception, and does not happen to end in a consonant or consonant cluster subject to consonant gradations. Then, that the vowel in the suffix is *u* is unpredictable as well.

Significantly, the difference is not merely a matter of isolating vs. affixal structure. Saramaccan has words for marking the genitive (*fu* / *u*) and the partitive (*háfu*), and can create a resultative participle via reduplication (*lésilési* [having been] read, although this would be pragmatically unlikely). However, these features require vastly less rule listing in a grammar than the Estonian equivalents. Plus, Saramaccan does not recruit these strategies to obligatorily accompany objects and predicate negation.

Saramaccan does have, unlike Estonian, articles – but then Estonian's completive marking (with *läbi* "through") is more entrenched and obligatory. And so on. Comparisons like this mean something, and most linguists presented with the data would readily allow that Finnish and Estonian are more grammatically complex than Saramaccan. I, for one, have happened to have occasion to attempt to speak all three languages on a basic level, and can readily attest that Saramaccan was much, much easier to learn basic communication in. As to the idea that Saramaccan would be harder to acquire *further* competence in than Finnish and Estonian, this is a claim with no empirical basis. Neither linguistic analysis nor basic intuition has revealed a single language with the unusual characteristic of being difficult in its basics but bracingly easy to master the nuances of – a notion on its face incoherent, given the essence of the concept of nuance.

Upon which: certainly it is a reasonable proposal that Saramaccan is less complex than Finnish and Estonian because it was born within a context leading to a sharp diminution of grammatical complexity. Just as certainly, plantation slavery would seem to qualify, at least preliminarily, as a plausible setting for such. Can we really say that this way of looking at creole languages has been "robustly disconfirmed"? In fact, could it even be?

And most importantly, in claims that creole exceptionalism is mistaken, there is no address whatsoever of data from languages like Finnish and Estonian. That is a crucial and grave lapse in argumentation.

4. Redirecting stimulation

The fact remains that the general sense among creolists is that the Prototype and Complexity hypotheses are wrong. "Stimulating" perhaps – but usefully so only in "stimulating" people to demonstrate the fraudulence. I believe this verdict to be based on a misunderstanding of my argumentation. For example, the Prototype and Complexity hypotheses are not disconfirmed by oft-adduced observations such as that:

a)   Papiamentu has tonal processes
b)   Haitian Creole has derivational morphemes
c)   creoles do not have maximally unmarked sound inventories
d)   creole phonology can be modelled in Optimality Theory
e)   creole reduplication does not always have semantically predictable meaning
f)   creoles hew to the Prototype to differing degrees.

To the extent that these things are seen as counterevidence to treating creoles as identifiably young – and less complex – languages, there has been a failure of communication. I attempt to improve it in the following three chapters.

Chapter One is the Prototype hypothesis revised. Those seeking what is often termed a "metric" or "yardstick" for what a creole is will be disappointed – a necessary disappointment, as language contact processes are inherently scalar. The epistemological difference between quantum physics and language contact theory is vast. It is no more theoretically or empirically incoherent to judge one creole as more "prototypical" than another than it is to judge rabbits as more akin to mice than rhinoceroses (which they are, genetically) – the nature of the thing is a matter of degree. Those dismissing creole exceptionalism as flawed in its inability to starkly corral languages as "creole" or "not creole" are seeking a conception perhaps informed by syntacticians' parametric approach, which addresses a mere fragment of what language consists of, and one only fleetingly applicable to what distinguishes older languages from creoles (cf. McWhorter 2005a: 102–41). However, I hope to have couched the hypothesis in terms more commensurate with general linguistic theory.

Chapter Two is, too, a demonstration that arguments about the nature of creolization can no more be couched in binary terms than ones about evolution. Work showing that creole grammars have complexity are useful and have made creole studies a field with more connection points to other linguistic subfields. But there has never been a claim that creoles were not complex. The claim is that creoles are *less* complex – as is clear in all of the articles in a signature volume which, ironically, argues against the idea of creoles as less complex. That volume, highly inclusive, substantial, and well edited, is a useful springboard for an argument intended as applying to creoles as a whole.

Chapter Three addresses another volume taking issue with creole exceptionalism (a term I embrace: I most explicitly do propose that creoles are an exceptional kind of language). The arguments in this book largely argue past the ones I have proposed, in ways that seem endemic in a debate that qualifies more as a standoff than an exchange. As such, a review of the book is another useful spark for an address of the issues as a whole.

Chapter 1
The creole prototype revisited and revised

1.1. Introduction

The hypothesis that a subset of creole languages are identifiable as distinct from older languages synchronically (McWhorter 1998) has been subject to considerable criticism. This has led me to consider my Prototype hypothesis in the light of its reception over the past ten years.

My verdict is that the Creole Prototype hypothesis remains valid, but requires adjustments to account for the full range of data in both creole and older languages that such a hypothesis must cover. It has also become clear that a basic assumption of the Prototype hypothesis, that plantation creole languages began as pidginized varieties, needs justification for a wider audience than that addressed in the French-language rendition presented by Mikael Parkvall and myself (McWhorter & Parkvall 2002).

In this paper, I will first address the origin of creoles in pidgins – controversial among creolists despite the idea's familiarity outside of the subfield – and then revisit the three main planks in the Prototype hypothesis, aiming to make them account more precisely for the difference between an older language and one born recently from a pidgin variety.

1.2. The pidgin roots of plantation creoles

1.2.1. Are Atlantic creoles different?

The Creole Prototype hypothesis is based on an assumption that creole languages' features are traceable to the languages' origin as pidgins, specifically pidgins of a structurally reduced nature, typically termed "early" albeit stabilized, along the lines of Russenorsk and Chinook Jargon. In pidgins of this kind, there is typically (Sebba 1997: 39) no definite or indefinite article, no copula (in the present tense), little or no hypotaxis, no passive marking, few or no inflectional affixes, few or no marked sounds, simple phonotactics, no use of tone, and a preference for semantic transparency (on the latter, cf.

Mühlhäusler 1997: 180 on the relative paucity of derivational morphemes in pidgins).[1]

There is no disagreement that there have been instances in which pidgin-level varieties developed into creoles. Paradigm cases include Tok Pisin and its sisters (Mühlhäusler 1997, Tyron & Charpentier 2004), Sango (Samarin 1997, 2000) and Hawaiian Creole English (Bickerton 1981, Roberts 1998, 2000).

It would even seem evident that the difference between these creoles and their lexifiers is of a similar degree and type as that between Atlantic planta-tion creoles and theirs, such as in generalization of the infinitive, omission of copular morphemes, replacement of tense and aspect inflections with preverbal particles, elimination of grammatical gender, and replacement of postposed negators with preposed ones. That is, the untutored observer would readily hypothesize that Sranan Creole English and Tok Pisin were the results of similar processes affecting the acquisition of English: "I was going" in Sranan: *Mi ben e go;* in Tok Pisin: *Mi bin stap go.*

However, various researchers propose that despite this qualitative likeness, plantation creoles were not born as pidgins – i.e. that the developmental process that transformed *I was going* into Sranan's *Mi ben e go* was completely differ-ent from the one that transformed *I was going* into Tok Pisin's *Mi bin stap go.*

The most explicit arguments have been by DeGraff (cf. 2001), Chaudenson (1992), and based on the latter's formulation, Mufwene (cf. 1996). They argue that these languages are actually unbroken transmissions of the lexifier lan-guages, mediated by only slight grammatical abbreviation, such as the elimina-tion of some affixes, and that impressions that the creoles are radically different from their lexifiers are due to ignorance of the inflectional erosion in collo-quial varieties of the lexifiers. They also note that there is no documentation of pidgin stages of creoles like Sranan, Haitian Creole or Cape Verdean.

In fact, however, the absence of documentation of pidgin stages of such creoles cannot be taken, in itself, as proof that such stages did not exist. The plantation setting was one in which language was an oral phenomenon and

---

1 There are varieties termed pidgins in the literature with more grammatical elabo-ration than these, such as ones based on closely related languages, e.g. African ones like Sango and Kituba. Unsurprisingly, these varieties retain a robust degree of the complexity of their source languages, since such constructions would be familiar to all or most of the creators. My hypothesis is that creole languages emerged from pidgins of a less grammatically elaborated nature such as Chinook Jargon and Russenorsk. Henceforth in this article, I intend the word *pidgin* to refer to such "classic" cases rather than pidgins such as Lingala.

there did not yet exist scholars committed to transcribing socially despised vernacular varieties. Often, even creoles were only first committed to paper several decades or more after all evidence suggests that they had already emerged (e.g. Sranan in the first decade of the eighteenth century after emergence in the 1660s [cf. McWhorter 2000: 99–105] and Negerhollands Creole Dutch in the 1730s after emergence before 1700 [Hesseling 1905:20]).

If the creoles were preceded by a transitory pidgin-level competence, this stage would have been especially unlikely to strike any contemporary observer as worthy of committing to paper. Pidgin-level Tok Pisin, Sango, and Hawaiian Pidgin English were committed to writing because they existed for long periods and were used outside of isolated plantation settings.

My argument in this paper is that despite the lack of written evidence, the *linguistic* facts strongly suggest that Atlantic creoles arose as structurally reduced pidgin varieties. These creoles differ from their lexifiers in ways unknown in varieties unarguably the result of unbroken transmission; i.e. nonstandard dialects.

While I suppose that the pidgin-level variety emerged via starkly abbreviated acquisition of the lexifier language at the outset of contact between lexifier and substrate speakers, others prefer a "superstratist" analysis under which creoles developed from "approximations of approximations" of the lexifier grammar, the input signal diluting by degrees as new slaves were increasingly likely to learn from non-native varieties than from native speakers, until the result was a new language entirely, such as Haitian Creole.

I doubt that the latter scenario occurred, for reasons outlined in McWhorter (2000) and McWhorter (2005a: 142–59). However, as I have argued elsewhere (McWhorter 2005a: 32–4), the difference between the two scenarios is to an extent a matter of terminology, and the important issue for this argument is that a structurally reduced pidgin variety, however emerged, is the most plausible source for the traits I will discuss. As Siegel puts it (2006: 176), while superstratists "may be correct in saying that there was no stable pidgin in the history of some creoles, there were clearly 'pidginized interlanguages' being used by the slaves."

The following subsections will outline four features of Atlantic creoles that most usefully demonstrate this.[2]

---

2   The argumentation for three of the features in this section was first presented in French in McWhorter & Parkvall (2002). This section uses the original French text as a general model, but is vastly abbreviated from it and includes much new material (the original, for example, focused on French creoles rather than creoles

1.2.2. Generalization of the infinitive

The origin of Atlantic creoles in pidgins is suggested first in their generalization of the infinitive. For example, scholars of French-based creoles argue that the absence of verbal inflection in these languages is due not to pidginization, but to the fact that such inflections were already weakly represented in colloquial French varieties that slaves were exposed to (cf. Chaudenson 1992: 158–62). The idea is that with inflection only remaining in, for example, the second-person plural in the present tense in such varieties, the difference between French creoles' total lack of present-tense verbal inflection and the colloquial varieties' mere one inflection is hardly derivable from as catastrophic a process as pidginization. The relevant data are shown here:

Table 7. Verb conjugation in French and Haitian Creole

English	Standard French	Colloquial French	Haitian Creole
I talk	je parle	je parle [parl]	m pale
you talk	tu parles	tu parles [parl]	ou pale
he talks	il parle	il parle [parl]	li pale
we talk	nous parlons	on parle [parl]	nu pale
you (pl.) talk	vous parlez	vous parlez [parle]	nu pale
they talk	ils parlent	ils parlent [parl]	zot pale

Crucially, however, Haitian Creole did not generalize the zero-marked form as colloquial Frenches do, but one that ends in [e]. Given that there is no generally observed diachronic process that generalizes the second-person plural (change is more often based on the third- or first-person), it is clear that Haitian – and all French creoles – generalized the infinitive.

Crucially, the generalization of the infintive is common in pidginization. Examples include Tây Bôi Pidgin French of Vietnam (*Toi napas **savoir** monsieur*

---

in general). Yet, while I was the primary writer of the section treating these features in the French version, Mikael Parkvall contributed various data and observations during the rewriting process, of which some remains in this section. Also, Stéphane Goyette, in "checking" our French, in actuality recast and burnished the prose with a rhetorical artfulness that would have been quite beyond my capabilities in French. The spirit of a few sentences in this section began with Stéphane.

aller où? "You don't know where this man went?" [Schuchardt 1888, cited in Holm 1988: 360]), Burundi Pidgin French (*vous savoi'* "you know" [Niedzielski 1989: 91]), and Tirailleur Pidgin French of Senegal (Manessy 1994: 113).

A search for a colloquial French variety that generalized the infinitive would be futile. Wittmann (1998) notes that in colloquial Magoua French in Québec, rapid speech obscures the difference between inflected and infinitive forms of verbs of the *re* class – *prend, prendre* [prã], [prãn] – with the implication that the French of Magoua has drifted into the same state in its verbs as French creoles. However, in the other two French verb classes, the difference between inflected and infinitive forms is more phonetically robust, and is amply maintained in Magoua as in all colloquial French varieties: *parle, parler; dort, dormir;* etc. To wit, colloquial Frenches generalize the bare form. French creoles do not, and instead follow a pathway of change – generalization of the infinitive – unknown in unbroken transmission, but business as usual amidst pidginization. No vernacular, regional, or colloquial variety of French has ever been attested that categorically generalizes the infinitive.

Meanwhile, generalization of the infinitive is also the norm in creoles whose lexifiers are more robustly inflected than French even in their colloquial varieties. Palenquero Creole Spanish generalized the infinitive despite vigorous present-tense inflection in even the colloquial Spanish of the Colombian coast where it arose (Colombian Spanish data from Lipski 1994: 213–4; Palenquero data from Schwegler 1998):

Table 8. Verbal conjugation in Spanish and Palenquero Creole

English	Colombian Spanish (Pacific Coast)	Palenquero
I speak	yo hablo	i ablá
you speak	vos hablás	bo ablá
he speaks	él habla	ele ablá
we speak	nosotros hablamos	suto / ma hende ablá
you (pl.) speak	ustedes hablan	utere ablá
they speak	ellos hablan	ané ablá

(Note also that in the forms *hablo, habla* and *hablan*, the stress is on the first syllable.) Also relevant is that Portuguese is as richly inflected as Spanish, and yet whereas nonstandard varieties in Portugal are documented to over-generalize the third-person singular to varying extents (Naro & Scherre 2002), Cape Verdean, Guinea-Bissau Creole Portuguese, and the Portuguese creoles of the Gulf of Guinea generalize the infinitive.

No superstratist analysis of creole genesis has, to date, ever addressed this Iberian-based creole data.

1.2.3. Omission of the copula

Typically, creole languages do not preserve their lexifier's copular mor-phemes, or use them only variably and in fashions quite different from in the lexifier. For example, in Mauritian Creole French, the copula only ap-pears sentence-finally when the predicate is fronted: *Kot Pjer ete?* "Where is Pierre?" (Baker & Syea 1991: 159). The situation is similar in Haitian Creole. A copula *ye* appears sentence-finally after predicate fronting as in Mauritian; otherwise, while there is an equative copula *se,* derived from French *c'est,* this occurs only variably (i.e. *Bouki doktè* "Bouki is a doctor" is grammatical), while there is no copula in locative sentences (*Bouki* (*se) *anba tab la* "Bouki is under the table"). The facts are similar in all French plantation creoles.

Notably, there is no attested variety of French, regional or colloquial, in which sentences such as **Pierre sous la table* "Peter is under the table" or *Pierre médecin "Peter is a doctor" are grammatical. Even in African vehicu-lar varieties of French, despite some traits due to second-language acquisition, copular omission is rare (Lafage 1985; et cf. Manessy 1995 *passim*).

Rather, the omission of the copula is a natural and amply documented con-sequence of pidginization (Ferguson 1971, Sebba 1997). In fact, the copula is documented to be omitted by Africans in their first attempts to speak French (although even here, mostly before adjectival predicates; e.g. *lui petit petit* [Lafage 1985:140]), and it is significant that Manessy treats this level of acquisition as analogous to foreigner talk, which Ferguson (1971) famously equated with pidginization.

The omission of French copulas cannot be attributed to learners' failure to perceive them in rapid speech. Certainly the presence of first-person singular *suis* in *Je suis malade* "I am sick" could be difficult to perceive as rendered as [ʃy malad]. However, the third-person forms *est* and *sont* do not elide to this degree; rapid speech, it would seem, would obscure preceding subject pronominals while leaving the copular morpheme apparent, as in the rendi-tion of *Il est mon ami* as [lemõnami]. Here, it bears noting that third-person singular forms are most common in speech (cf. Hock 1991: 220–2): this would be a reason beyond phonetic robustness that these forms would be unlikely to disappear amidst unmediated transmission.

Moreover, the lack of acquisition of copulas is not a peculiarity local to French creoles and susceptible to an explanation concerning French alone or particularities of the contexts in which French creoles arose. Rather, this omission is a cross-creole commonplace. The Surinam creoles, of primarily English lexical base, have an equative and locative copula (Saramaccan *Mi da í tatá* "I am your father"; *Mi dé a wósu* "I am at home"), but neither is derived from English *be* verbs. Both developed from deictic morphemes after an initial stage in which the creole had no overt copula (McWhorter 2005a: 201–11; cf. McWhorter 2004b *contra* Migge's [2003: 64–78] argument that the copulas were substrate calques presumably present at the creole's birth). In creoles of other lexical bases as well, copulas are also often omitted and/or not derived from lexifier equivalents (cf. McWhorter 1992: 117–18).

Crucially, the absence of copulas in creoles is not modelled on their substrate languages. The West African languages that were substratal to most of the Atlantic creoles, for example, have regularly overt copulas (McWhorter 1997: 86), such as Fongbe:

(1) *Ùn nyí Àfiàví.*
    I   be Afiavi
    'I am Afiavi.'

(Lefebvre & Brousseau 2001: 144)

Under an analysis of creolization as grammar-internal change, the omission of copulas in creoles is a mystery. The disappearance of copular morphemes is hardly unknown in language change (Russian being the best-known example), but equally relevant is the near universal presence of copulas in European languages, so very few of which lack overt copulas despite eons of change in all levels of grammar, including phonetic erosion. Over almost two thousand years of the existence of English in Great Britain, for example, there has been no reported English dialect there that lacks copular morphemes, nor is the author aware of any such cases in dialects of French, Spanish, Portuguese or Dutch.

The *regularity,* then, with which lexifier copulas are absent in creoles suggests that something intervened in grammar-internal change. Under a pidginization analysis, the omission of copulas in creoles is predictable. This analysis is therefore preferable, and is a component of the argument that Atlantic creoles emerged as pidgin-level varieties.

1.2.4. Case Distinction in Pronouns

Creole languages tend strongly to eliminate the case distinction in their lexifiers' first-person pronominal, using the object or tonic pronominal across the board. Thus English-based creoles such as the ones in Surinam have *mi* and no reflex of *I* (Sranan *Mi waka* "I walk"); French creoles have a reflex of *moi* and none of *je* (Haitian *Mwen manje* "I eat"). Also relevant are the Portuguese creoles of Africa (of Cape Verde, Guinea-Bissau and the Gulf of Guinea) in which there is no reflex of Portuguese *eu*, with *n*, derived from the object pronominal *me* and oblique form *mim*, or Negerhollands Creole Dutch in which there was no reflex of Dutch subject pronominal *ik*, in favor of *mi* derived from Dutch object pronominal *mij*.

This tendency is unknown in colloquial English, French, Portuguese, or Dutch. That is, never in the history of these languages, even in varieties most removed from prescriptive tradition and most evolved away from the standard, is the first-person singular object pronominal form used in subject position (except with coordination; e.g. *Billy and me went to the store*). In dialect surveys of Great Britain, it is unknown that a sentence like "Me likes to walk instead of ride" is grammatical; similarly unknown are French varieties, in Europe or elsewhere, in which natural language change has led to sentences like "Moi aime marcher." *Moi, j'aime marcher* – yes, with *moi* as a topic. But why is it only creoles in which the *moi* reflex is a subject, while *je* is entirely absent?

Under an analysis of creoles as uninterrupted descendants from their lexifiers, this elimination of first-person subject pronouns is, again, a mystery. Rather, it much more plausibly submits to an analysis as evidence of the pidginization of the lexifiers – given that case distinction is notably rare in pidgins. The assumption that Atlantic creoles began as pidgins is based on just such facts.

The claim here is not that creoles entirely lack case distinctions in pronominals. Saramaccan, in the third-person singular, distinguishes subject *a* from object *ɛ̃* (as well as tonic *hɛ̃*), and there are similar instances in other creoles. Nor is it that lexifiers' subject pronominals never occur in creoles based on them: for example, Palenquero Creole Spanish has *i*, derived from Spanish subject pronoun *yo*. In addition, there are Romance dialects in which object pronominal forms have replaced subject ones in the first and/or second person, such as Aromanian and some Gallo-Italian dialects (Stephane Goyette, p.c.).

The question is specific: regardless of whether case distinction in pronouns is utterly unknown in creoles, what is the reason that so many of them lack it to such an extent, such as in the first-person singular? Colloquial varieties of the lexifiers *never* eliminate the case distinction in the first-person singular. Why do creoles do so so very much more? And as well in other persons and numbers? Where is *tu* as opposed to *toi* in French creoles? Or *us* in Surinam creoles?

Once again, pidginization lends a helpful account, given that pidgins tend strongly to eliminate case distinctions including in pronouns, retaining them if at all in the third person (cf. Mühlhäusler 1997: 148–9) (upon which the Saramaccan situation cited above is relevant). The replacement of *I* by *me* is robustly documented for cases such as Tok Pisin, in which the first-person subject pronominal is also based on the object form. Short of the identification of a regional French in which **Moi aime danser* "I like to dance" is grammatical, we see here a further justification for treating Atlantic creoles as born in pidgins, regardless of whether documentation of this stage in their development was ever transcribed.

1.2.5. Negator Placement

In English and Dutch, the predicate negator morpheme occurs after the verb; in French, the most phonetically salient of the two morphemes in the predicate negator construction, *pas,* occurs after the verb (*Je ne sais pas* "I don't know") and in colloquial varieties, preverbal *ne* is very often unpronounced. Yet in creoles with these lexifiers, the predicate negator occurs before the verb: "I don't know" is *Mi no sabi* in Sranan, *Mwen pa konnen* in Haitian, and was *Mie no weet* in Negerhollands Creole Dutch (cf. Dutch *Ik weet niet*) (Van Diggelen 1978: 71 cited in Holm 1988: 171).

There is no vernacular European model for the negator placement in these lexifiers: not even the most untutored regional English allows "You not have any money." It would be difficult to conceive of a process via which – or a reason why – these preposed negators emerged in so many creoles of assorted lexifier bases through stepwise grammar-internal change, especially given that no such processes are documented in historical records of the creoles in question. The preposed negators submit more gracefully to an analysis as results of the failure to acquire the lexifier negation strategy, and its replacement by a strategy typical of pidgins, a single negator external to the verb, usually (but not always) before it (cf. Mühlhäusler 1997: 146, Sebba 1997: 42).

Negation, then, stands as yet another creole feature which does not coherently lend itself to analysis as a close "approximation," as it is termed in the superstratist literature, of lexifier grammar. McWhorter & Parkvall

(2002) discuss some other creole features that are traceable to pidginization rather than unbroken transmission. However, the four presented here constitute a sufficient case, especially as they are intended as making the case not only individually, but in the sheer fact of their number. All of these features are, with no special effort necessary, explainable as results of pidginization. Pidginization is, therefore, the preferable explanation.

1.2.6. Implications

Certainly these features do not occur *only* in pidgins. These features' presence in creoles is significant given the diachronic relationship of these creoles with lexifier languages in which these features are opposite. This contrast between the lexifiers and the creoles vitiates a claim that the features in the creoles are unremarkable results of a few centuries of change – because no vernacular varieties of the creoles' lexifiers have happened into like developments of anything approaching the degree in creoles. Mandarin Chinese, for example, has categorically bare verb stems and a preverbal negator – but so did its Classical Chinese ancestor. French does not, which means that these same features in French creoles require explanation.

One reason that grammar-internal change has nevertheless often been thought a sufficient explanation is a mental schema of language change – common among linguists in general – based on Latin's development into the more analytic Romance languages, Old English's development into Modern English, and perhaps the development of Classical Arabic into the modern, more analytic colloquial dialects. However, besides that these developments did not entail the stark abbreviation and reinterpretation typical of pidginization, the sense of the development from Latin to French as typical is more problematic than traditionally realized.

I have argued (McWhorter 2002, 2007, and Chapter Seven) that all of the cases just mentioned and others were due to extensive acquisition of these languages by adults at certain points in their history, simplifying them to an extent that would have been unlikely or impossible if there had not been interference in transmission (cf. also Goyette 2000 on Romance). The argumentation for these cases would take us beyond what space limits allow. However, the reader is asked to consider the development of Proto-Slavic into, for example, Polish, Classical Aramaic into modern Aramaic dialects, the development of modern Algonquian languages from their reconstructed ancestor or Proto-Bantu into Swahili and Xhosa. In such cases the famous "drift" towards analyticity typical of a few subfamilies in Western Europe is not in evidence – and more to the point, worldwide, the kinds of cases just listed are typical of language change, rather than that of Latin to French. Note, for example, how little indication there would seem to be of analytic "drift" in the large body of Australian languages, home to hundreds of highly inflected languages for tens of thousands of years.

All can agree, in any case, that analytic drift is but one kind of change that occurs in language groups. If so, then the question is why creoles so regularly take that particular path, and to more extreme an extent than, for example, any Romance language (including even the most inflectionally eroded varieties of French; cf. Wittmann 1998). These can be seen as grounds, then, for assuming that plantation creoles emerged as pidgins just as Tok Pisin did.

It must also be noted that the traits I am ascribing to pidginization do not submit to explanation as transferred substrate language features. The analyticity of West African languages of the Kwa group and others corresponds to creoles' invariant verb stems, but does not account for the other traits I have discussed. For example, in Saramaccan's main substrate language Fongbe, verbs do occur in bare form. However, Fongbe has regularly expressed overt copulas, its first-person pronominal clitics occur in two forms distinguished by case, and one of its main negator morphemes is postposed to the verb (Lefebvre & Brousseau 2001: 143–9, 63, 128–9). Palenquero's main substrate language is Kikongo (Schwegler 1998); while Palenquero's verbs are uninflected, Kikongo is a heavily agglutinative Bantu language in which bare verb stems are ungrammatical.

In sum, a statement such as that the broken transmission hypothesis has been "robustly disconfirmed by a range of comparative data and empirical and theoretical observations" (DeGraff 2003: 398) is mistaken. No presentation from the superstratist quarter has addressed the four points adduced above, or at this writing, three relevant articles gathered in McWhorter (2005a: 72–159).

1.3. Motivation for revising the Prototype hypothesis

I have argued (McWhorter 2005a: 9–37) that we could know that a language was a creole with no knowledge of its sociohistory if it has:

a) *morphologically:* little or no inflectional affixation
b) *phonologically:* little or no use of tone to distinguish monosyllabic lexical items or morphosyntactic categories
c) *semantically:* little or no noncompositional combinations of derivational morphemes with roots.

The vast majority of the world's older languages depart from the creole prototype in having features a) and/or b). To my knowledge (after twelve years of investigating the issue and discussing it with other linguists) only three language groups are exceptions in having neither inflection nor tone: Polynesian languages, some Mon-Khmer ones, and a few languages of Indonesia such as the languages of Flores Kéo and Ngadha and the Papuan language Abun. The total of the languages in question is roughly fifty.

In these cases, the diagnostic of their age is evident in their harboring noncompositional derivation. For example, in the Polynesian language Rapanui, the abstract nominalizer *-Vŋa* is used compositionally in cases like *mate* "death," *mateiŋa* "dying," but also in cases like *papaku* "corpse" versus *papakuiŋa* "low tide" (Du Feu 1996: 179). In the Mon-Khmer language Chrau, the core meaning of the affix *ta-* is causative (*chuq* "to wear," *tachuq* "to dress"), but it also occurs in opaque lexicalizations: *dâp* "to dam up," *tadâp* "to fold or hem a shirt;" *chĕq* "to put, set," *tachĕq* "to slam down" (Thomas 1969: 102). In Kéo, there are many derivational morphemes with no synchronically perceptible meaning: *'adé* "ask," *'adé-'ona* "greet, converse" (Baird 2002:174).

However, even in these fifty-odd languages with neither inflection nor tone, there are reflections of age in morphology and phonology that distinguish them from creoles as readily as inflectional affixation and tone themselves would. It is these reflections that primarily motivate my revision of the Prototype Hypothesis.

1.4. Inflection

1.4.1. Inflection: bounded and free

While Polynesian languages are neither inflected nor tonal, they have particles that mark grammatical relations indicated in many languages via inflection. For example, Rennellese marks both agents and objects:

(2) *Kite e ia te baka.*
     see AG OBJ SPF canoe
     'He sees the canoe.'

(Elbert 1988: 108)

Rapanui is similar:

(3) *I   haka'emu i   te   vaka e   te   taŋata.*
     PAST CAUS.flood OBJ SPF boat AG SPF man
     'The boat was flooded by the man.'

(Du Feu 1996: 113)

Or, like many Polynesian languages, Tongan is ergative, and marks this with particles:

(4) *'oku   tamate 'e   he   fefine 'a   e   tangatá.*
    PRES kill   ERG DEF woman ABS DEF man
    'The woman kills the man.'

(Tchekhoff 1979: 409)

In Polynesian these particles have not become affixes – in languages which in the meantime also lack tone. However, the particles represent a stage between free content morpheme and inflectional affix, not bound to the roots with which they are associated, but having functions commonly carried out by affixes. Thus Polynesian languages lack inflection – but they have markers that differ from inflections only in boundedness rather than function.

Kihm (2003:336–9) provides a formal way to account for the likeness in question, observing that under the Minimalist paradigm, the difference between Portuguese *cantarei* "I will sing" and Guinea-Bissau Kriyol's *na kanta* "will sing" is merely one of Merge and Move. *Na kanta* requires only Merge: the functional feature T, represented by *na,* is interpreted in association with *kanta* without the items' being linked into a single word. *Cantarei* requires Move, where the head T is represented by an affix that must be raised and adjoined to the verb. Based on this and modifications that attempt to eliminate even the difference between these processes, Kihm argues that both languages have "inflection," – which I will henceforth capitalize when I intend Kihm's definition, as Inflection – the only difference being "the way they interface the lexicon with the morphological vocabulary, through syntax" (Kihm 2003: 358).

Under this analysis, we can analyze Polynesian languages' particles marking grammatical relations as Inflection – i.e. evidence of the reinterpretation of morphemes over vast periods of time into segmental markers of a distinction that a grammar can easily indicate via word order (or even context).

Crucially, creoles are among the grammars that tend strongly to mark subjecthood and objecthood via position and context. A very few have object markers, such as the Indo-Portuguese creoles, but these are used mostly with animates (e.g. in Sri Lankan Creole Portuguese). Even here, the creoles mark objects at the head of the implicational hierarchy according to which languages mark objects (cf. Aissen 2003). Animates are most likely to be marked while inanimates are less likely, such that while there are many languages that only mark animate objects (Spanish *Yo vi **a** Juan* "I saw John") it is rare that a language marks inanimate objects but not animates. That is, marking animate objects is the beginning of a process that ends in the marking of all objects, and as such, predictably no creole language has a grammatically obligatory patient marker.

Meanwhile, no creole is ergative, and as such, none distinguish with an overt marker the distinction between subject and agent. In creoles the interpretation of core grammatical relations depends largely on word order and context.

1.4.2. Numeral classifiers as Inflection

Mon-Khmer languages also demonstrate their age in terms of what can be termed Inflection. While these languages lack grammatical gender inflections, they typify the East and Southeast Asian areal trait of having batteries of numeral classifiers. Khmer, for example, has various numeral classifiers corresponding to animacy, shape, etc., such as *siəwphɨw muəy lou* "a dozen books," *kmaw-day pram daəm* "five pencils," *puəq-maaq pii nĕəq* "two friends" (Huffmann 1970: 69–70). The inflectionless and toneless languages of Indonesia also have numeral classifiers, as hallmarks of Austronesian languages of Asia. Kéo has twenty-four sortal classifiers (Baird 2002: 252–3).

Nor is grammatical gender itself alien to Mon-Khmer. Khasi of India and Bangladesh has only two classifiers, *ŋut* for humans and *tɨlli* for non-humans (Nagaraja 1985: 79). However, it has masculine and feminine grammatical gender particles that pattern broadly according to type and shape of object and assorted classes of abstract noun, but with a substantial degree of arbitrariness as well, paralleling the situation with gender marking in European languages (Rabel-Heyman 1977). Some examples:

Table 9. Grammatical gender markers in Khasi

masculine		feminine	
ʔu trnem	"hammer"	ka makhan	"butter"
ʔu prthat	"thunder"	ka ʔiktiar	"authority"
ʔu khllaay	"kidney"	ka khroŋ	"tax"

Numeral classifiers (and free grammatical gender-marking particles), albeit unbound, are a clear product of long-term grammaticalization, under which a nominal is reanalyzed into an abstract, grammatical usage. In giving overt distinction to noun classes, such classifiers can be seen as functionally similar to gender morphology (cf. Grinevald & Seifart 2004). Predictably, creoles' life spans have been too brief for such grammaticalization to have led to such morphemes.

The one example of classifiers in the creolist literature has been an oft-repeated claim tracing to Thompson (1958) that a pidgin, Chinese Pidgin English, had classifiers for humans (*fella*) and non-humans (*piece*), purportedly an abbreviated calque on Cantonese's wealth of classifiers. But in fact, Baker (1987: 180–1) reports that no *fella* classifier appears in any documentation of Chinese Pidgin English, and that only *piece* occurred, used with both human and non-human nouns. Thus it would appear that if Chinese Pidgin English had creolized, it would have had but one classifier, not indexing gender, but used invariantly with numerals, serving as a numerative marker. The contrast with the multiple classifiers typical in East and Southeast Asian languages is obvious.

Finally, no recorded creole marks grammatical gender. French-based creoles and some others mark biological gender, but this is a derivational rather than inflectional process.

1.4.3. Restatement

Thus there are many older languages which lack inflectional affixation but harbor unbound morphemes performing the same functions as affixes in other languages, and are products of the same kind of long-term grammaticalization. Under the assumption that Kihm's proposition on "Inflection" is valid, and the corollary one that restricting the Prototype hypothesis' address of inflection to bound forms would lack theoretical motivation, the Prototype stipulation on inflection must be recast.

It would be insufficient to stipulate simply that creoles lack both bound and unbound Inflection: creoles regularly have particles marking, for example, tense and aspect, which classify as unbound Inflection. Rather, creoles lack certain kinds of Inflection.

Booij's (1993) distinction of two kinds of inflection is useful in providing a principled account of what kinds of Inflection creoles lack and why. *Contextual* inflection is linked to syntactic context, and includes structural case and concord. *Inherent* inflection is (at least relatively) independent of syntactic context, and includes tense, aspect, gender and number markers.

Creoles lack contextual inflection bound or free. They do not lack inherent inflection – i.e. they have markers of tense, aspect and number – but they lack a type of it, gender marking. Gender marking is distinct amidst inherent inflection in a particular trait: its paradigmatic character, under the terminology of Moravcsik & Wirth (1986)'s typology of grammatical complexity.

Paradigmatic complexity involves the overt marking of subdivisions of semantic space such that the subdivision becomes denotationally arbitrary (declension classes in Latin).

Thus the proper formulation is:

> Prototypical creoles have 1) little or no inflectional *affixation* of any kind and 2) no *unbound* inflectional markers of a) contextual inflectional categories at all, and b) inherent inflectional categories of *paradigmatic* typology.

In other words, creoles have Inflection, but only unbound, inherent, and non-paradigmatic.

This reformulation is consistent with the central focus of the Prototype hypothesis, which is identifying signs of youth in creole languages.

1) *No inflectional affixation:* In a language born as a pidgin, and thus with little or no affixation, a few centuries later it will likely still have little or no affixation of either the contextual or inherent Inflection type, as the development of free morphemes into bound ones generally requires several centuries at least and often more time (cf. Hopper & Traugott 1993: 130–56).

2) *No contextual Inflection.* However, in the realm of *unbound* Inflectional categories, the difference between contextual and inherent Inflection is significant in terms of creole grammars. For one, to the extent that any pidgins have Inflection, it is much less often contextual than inherent (Roberts & Bresnan 2008).

In addition, whether bound or unbound, contextual Inflection is much less common in the world's languages. Many fewer than half categorically distinguish subject and object with overt markers: Iggeson (2005) documents that 100 out of 261 in his sample of the world's languages make no overt case distinction. This suggests that contextual Inflection is less central to human expression than inherent.

In that light, Kihm (2003: 359) notes that Universal Grammar, under the Minimalist framework, has syntactic heads for inherent inflectional categories but not for contextual ones, which again suggests that at least some inherent Inflection is fundamental to the human language endowment, whereas contextual Inflection is but a possible development that may arise over time via the emergence of overt marking of peripheral distinctions not encoded in our innate syntactic toolkit as, for example, tense presumably is.

3) *No paradigmatic inherent Inflection.* In this light, virtually all languages mark certain *inherent* Inflectional categories at least in unbound

fashion – i.e. all but a very few languages mark tense and aspect, and all known creoles do. However, *paradigmatic* rendition of Inflection usually requires more time to arise than monomorphemic expression. This is because it requires two developments. First must emerge a tendency to overtly distinguish semantic distinctions hitherto left unmarked (i.e. gender) or the conventionalization of paradigms distinguished by phonetic commonalities (i.e. in part, Latin's declensions). Then, encoding such distinctions entails the emergence and conventionalization of not just one morpheme but several, including the time required for phonetic erosion.

On gender, then, Corbett (2005) finds that out of 256 of the world's languages, many more than half (144) have no gender distinctions. Gil (2005a) documents numeral classifiers in just 140 of 400 languages in a worldwide sample. Pidgins – that is, the rudimentary makeshift varieties I stipulate that creoles *give evidence of* emerging from (cf. Section 2) – do not have paradigmatic inflection of any kind.

Table 10. Contextual and inherent morphology in an ontogenic perspective

Primary Condition	Secondary Conditions
	Inherent with paradigmatic complexity – Spanish *Yo vi y compré el libro.* I see.PAST and buy-PAST the book 'I saw and bought the book.'
Primary Condition	Secondary Conditions
Inherent: Saramaccan *Mi bi bái dí búku.* I PAST buy the book 'I bought the book.'	Inherent with paradigmatic complexity; contextual – Hebrew *Ani matz-ati ve kan-iti et ha sefer.* I find-PAST and buy-PAST OBJ the book 'I found and bought the book.'
	Inherent and contextual with paradigmatic complexity – Russian *Ja uvid-el i po-kup-il knig-u.* I see-PAST and PERF-buy-PAST book-ACC 'I saw and bought the book.'

The *paradigmatic* manifestation of inherent Inflection can be seen as an accident of how items may or may not transform over time. As such, it is predictable that *paradigmatic* Inflection would be lacking in languages born just recently from pidgins since pidgins do not mark, for example, grammatical gender. Note also that Chinese Pidgin English, if it had developed into a creole, would have conformed to our prediction. It would have had not a *paradigmatic* expression of gender Inflection expressed by two or more numeral classifiers, but a mere expression of a *single* category, the numerative, via its single classifier.

That creoles, with their unbound, non-paradigmatic inherent Inflection represent a typology closer to a pidgin than older languages is illustrated here, on the basis of the reasoning above. Note that in the second-column sentences, morphemes of like denotation vary according to paradigm, such as the first-person past markers in Spanish.

Thus Polynesian and Mon-Khmer languages are not different from creoles solely in having noncompositional derivation-root combinations. They also have Inflection, of an unbound type. They have drifted into a state typical of ancient languages, but unexpected of languages recently born as pidgins.

1.5. Tone

1.5.1. Register

The Mon-Khmer family's best-known members are Vietnamese and Khmer (Cambodian); most others are small and obscure. While some are tonal, more are not. However, in the proper sense, there is more than numeral classifiers and noncompositional derivation to distinguish them as ancient in terms of the Prototype hypothesis, if adjusted slightly.

This is because most Mon-Khmer languages that do not have tone have register distinctions instead, such as between clear (i.e. "normal"), creaky, and breathy voice. Thurgood (2002: 346) notes that register and tone are based on similar aspects of vocal production, such that register systems differ from tonal ones largely in which of several interacting phonological aspects – such as pitch, intensity, duration, voice quality – have become most salient.

As variations on an articulatory theme, register and tone tend to carry out like functions in grammars. Thus like tone, register often distinguishes minimal pairs, as in Bruu of Thailand, in the transcription of which the accent signifies breathy voice: /tuup/ "to be thick (e.g. of cloth)," /tùup/ "to bury" /luup/ "to leap over," /lùup/ "to pat fondly" (Thongkum 1981: 230–1).

More precisely, in Mon-Khmer register and tone occupy a pathway of phonetic transformation, in which consonants condition register distinctions that become phonemic when the consonants change quality or wear away, with the register distinctions then perhaps later transforming into ones of pitch, i.e. tone. For example, Premsrirat (2001) gives an array of dialects of Khmu that demonstrate steps along this kind of transformation. In pairs distinguished by voicing of the initial consonant in Eastern Khmu, in one Western Khmu dialect, after devoicing only a distinction on the vowel between breathy (̤) and tense (´) remains as phonemic. This then evolves into a pitch distinction (Western Khmu 3), through an intermediate stage in which both pitch and aspiration are phonemically distinctive (Western Khmu 2) (Premsrirat 2001: 54).

Table 11. Register and tone in Khmu dialects

	Eastern	Western 1	Western 2	Western 3
"cut down a tree"	bok	po̤k	phòk	pòk
"take a bite"	pok	pók	pók	pók
"weigh"	jaŋ	ca̤ŋ	chàŋ	càŋ
"astringent"	caŋ	câŋ	cáŋ	câŋ

Another example is the Chamic languages, which are Austronesian, but so deeply impacted grammatically by Mon-Khmer that their very classification has been a challenge. They display various stages in the process whereby register can then develop into tones. The Western Cham variety has register while the Tsat variety has a five-way tonal distinction, while Haroi and Phan Rang Cham represent intermediate stages along the pathway from Western Cham to Tsat (Thurgood 1999: 214–36).

The distinction between creoles and older languages in terms of tone, then, must be amended. More precisely, creoles make little or no use of tone *or register* to encode lexical or morphosyntactic distinctions. Creoles can be assumed to lack register in these functions for the same reason that they lack tone in the functions.

That is, it is reasonable to assume that pidgins eschew monosyllabic lexical and morphosyntactic tone because they are difficult for second-language learners to acquire quickly under untutored conditions. A useful source is Salmons (1992: 31–2, 56–63, 140–2) on the fate of tone under contact conditions, in Proto-Indo-European and its descendants as well as African contact varieties like Songhay).

Even if the learners themselves speak tonal languages, the differences in how tone is used between the lexifier and the native languages would preclude their transfer into a general lingua franca. That is, if [ga] with high tone means "flutter" in the lexifier and "yesterday" in the learner's language, then the learner will be unlikely to carry [ga] with high tone into the pidgin or creole in the "yesterday" meaning, since this would be incomprehensible to lexifier speakers – as well as to fellow learners speaking other tonal languages in which [ga] meant, say, "horse" in one and "warm beverage" in another. Relevant is that tone can even disappear amidst levelling between dialects, such as Kajkavian Croatian, atonal despite its source dialects all being tonal (Magner 1966).

The result in creole genesis would be tone itself cancelled out entirely (e.g. French-based creoles) or largely relegated to more general areas of grammar where its use can be readily conventionalized and understood between speakers of different native languages with the assistance of contextual factors, such as the suprasegmental or in encoding variant denotations of reduplication (e.g. in Atlantic English-based creoles as documented by Carter 1987, James 2003, Gooden 2003). Subsequently, the development of tonal distinction of monosyllabic lexical and morphosyntactic contrasts results, for example, from erosions of consonants and other phonetic transformations over time (Matisoff 1973, 1991).

We can assume that register distinctions would be precluded in creoles for similar reasons. An objection might be that we cannot be certain that rapid acquisition eliminates register as opposed to tone, given that there are no examples of a group acquiring a Mon-Khmer language in pidgin form and expanding it into a creole, nor are there any recorded examples of Mon-Khmer speakers creolizing any other language (Tây Bôi Vietnamese Pidgin French never went past the pidgin stage). To be sure, there are examples of more gradual language mixture involving Mon-Khmer languages, such as Chamic, in which register has indeed been recorded to survive. But Chamic emerged amidst long-term bilingualism of the kind that led to the Balkan Sprachbund. We lack an example of a pidgin-to-creole life cycle in the Mon-Khmer area.

However, there are other indications of how register would fare in pidginization and creolization. Creoles have emerged among speakers of languages with a trait analogous to register contrasts, ATR (advanced tongue root) harmony. Here, vowels occur in complementary pairs distinguished by a phonational contrast in articulation, such as that in Akan between /i, e, ä, o, u/ and /ɪ, ɛ, a, ɔ and ʊ/ (Stewart 1967). Yet despite the decisive substrate impact that Akan has been argued to have had upon creoles like Jamaican patois (LePage & DeCamp 1960) and Negerhollands (Stolz & Stein 1986), neither these – nor any creole to my knowledge – displays ATR harmony to anything approaching the extent in Akan and many other Niger-Congo languages. Also relevant is Nubi Creole Arabic, whose substrate languages included Nilo-Saharan ones like Mamvu and Bari that have vowel inventories hingeing on an ATR contrast. Nubi, however, essentially has a basic five-vowel contrast with two long vowels of marginal occurrence (Owens 1991:10).

1.5.2. Mon-Khmer languages without register

1.5.2.1. Heavy proliferation of vowels in Mon-Khmer

But there remain some Mon-Khmer languages that have lost register rather than transformed it into tones. These include Khmer, some languages in the Bahnaric and Aslian subfamilies, and some in the Khmuic one (for example, Western Khmu dialects have register and/or tone, but Eastern Khmu lacks both [Premsrirat 2001]). Yet even these languages are easily distinguishable from creoles in the synchronic sense.

This is because their vowel systems contrast sharply with creole ones, because of what the loss of register leaves behind. Specifically, the development of registers regularly conditions a proliferation in vowel distinctions, which remain after register falls away. For example, Thurgood (1999: 179–80) notes that breathy voice tends to centralize vowels as a lower larnyx conditions a longer vocal tract and thus lower formants and lower F2. As a result, Mon-Khmer vocalic inventories contrast with creole ones in tending to have central vowels, sometimes at all three heights.

In contrast, phonemic schwa is rare in creoles, one exception being Korlai Creole Portuguese of India, which inherits it from its substrate language Marathi (Clements 1996: 61). Register also tends to condition diphthongization, lending Mon-Khmer vocalic inventories a weight of nucleic diphthongs foreign to creoles. Mon-Khmer, in fact, has the largest known vowel inventories in the world, many languages having as many as three dozen distinctions (including phonemic length-based ones).

Thus the Mon-Khmer languages without register or tone do not have the typologically ordinary seven to ten vowel distinctions typical of creole languages. For example, Khmer had register in earlier stages, but has since lost it rather than developing tones. However, register left behind a "footprint" in the form of thirty vowels (Ferlus 1992):

Table 12. Khmer vocalic inventory

iə	iə	uə			
ii	ïi	uu			
ee	əə	oo	e	ə	o
ɛe	ʌə	ɔo			
ɛɛ		ɔɔ	ɛ	ʌ	ɔ
aɛ	aʌ	aɔ	ĕa		ɔ̆a
	aa	ɑɑ		a	

Less dramatic but typical examples are Loven of the Bahnaric subfamily, which has 23 vowels, a number closely paralleling most members of its West Bahnaric branch (Jacq & Sidwell 2000: 25):

Table 13. Loven vocalic inventory

ii	ïi	uu	i	ɨ	u	iə	iə	uo
ee	əə	oo	e	ə	o	iɛ		ua
ɛɛ	ʌʌ	ɔɔ	ɛ	ʌ	ɔ			
	aa			a				

or Khmu dialects, which have 22 (Premsrirat 2001: 50).

1.5.2.2. Vowels in creoles

There exists no creole language with three dozen vowels (phonemic or phonetic) or anything close, and overall, creole vocalic inventories are compact compared to the Mon-Khmer norm. Smaller ones include that of Tayo Creole French of New Caledonia, with five oral and two nasal vowels (Corne 1999: 21), and Berbice Creole Dutch of Guyana's six (the basic /a e i o u/ and a lax ɛ) (Kouwenberg 1995: 239). Inventories this small are by no means a norm among creoles, and are even hardly unusual cross-linguistically: but the fact remains that there appears to exist no Mon-Khmer language with this few vowels.

On the upper end of the scale among creoles are some where nasal variants of the basic set of vowels increase the tally. Saramaccan would be an example, with the five basic vowels, two lax mid vowels (ɛ, ɔ), and then nasal renditions of all seven, bringing the count to 14. Bakker, Smith and

Veenstra (1995: 170) suggest a higher count by designating length contrasts on the basis of cases such as *bɛ* "red," *bɛ́ɛ* "belly," and *bɛ́ɛ* "bread," but this analysis is questionable: the articulatory nature of such words strongly suggests sequences of nuclei, this even more likely given that tone assignment and sandhi apply to such words according to their behavior elsewhere with nuclei. In general, where phonemic length contrasts exist in creoles, they are weakly contrastive, as in Annobonese Creole Portuguese as described by Post (1995: 193–4), in which short of counting the marginal length contrasts, there are the five basic vowels plus three diphthongs. Similarly, while lax vowels are robustly contrastive in Saramaccan, in Cape Verdean they occur relatively infrequently, only occasion compact sets of minimal pairs, and are absent in many dialects (Veiga 2000: 85–6, 94).

Importantly, my claim is not that creole languages' phonemic inventories are uniquely small in the cross-linguistic sense. As I have noted elsewhere (McWhorter 2001a: 151), while I do believe that the world's least complexified languages in terms of morphology and syntax are creoles (although because of the sociological vagaries of language labelling and the clinal nature of language reduction and mixture, not all languages termed creoles are less grammatically complex than any older language), there are a great many older languages with much smaller phonemic inventories than any creole. For example, there are no creoles with the dozen-odd phonemes typical of Polynesian languages. In reference to vowels specifically, there is no creole analyzable as having a mere pair of vocalic phonemes as are some Caucasian languages.

My point is more specific: Mon-Khmer languages display a proliferation of vowels beyond the moderate degree in creoles and unusual compared to other languages in the world, and this is diagnostically indicative of great age. To wit, vocalic systems of this kind in Mon-Khmer are analyzed (e.g. by Thurgood 1999) to have arisen as the result of disruptions caused by vocalic and suprasegmental transformations over time.

Interestingly, according to the data available to me, even the Mon-Khmer languages with the fewest vowels hover a step above creoles like Saramaccan in their tally. Chrau, for example, has seventeen phonemic vowel distinctions (Thomas 1971: 44–5) (including two central phonemes according to Thomas' analysis), and its South Bahnaric sisters Stieng, Köho and Mnong hover closely around this number (the latter two have one fewer phoneme) (Sidwell 2000). In North Bahnaric, Bahnar retains 15 vowels, divided between a short and a long set (Smith 1972: 5):

Table 14. Bahnar vocalic inventory

ĭ		ŭ		i	ɨ	u
	ɔ̆			ê	ə	ô
ĕ	ă	ŏ		e	a	o

1.5.3. Restatement

Thus stipulation 2) of the Prototype hypothesis must be restated. The motivation for stipulation 2) is to refer to a readily evident result of age on the level of the sound system, as opposed to morphology (the inflection stipulation) and semantics (the compositionality stipulation). Tone alone, however, undershoots the purpose. Rather:

> Prototypical creoles have little or no distinction of monosyllabic lexical items or morphosyntactic distinctions via tone or register, and do not have vocalic inventories of typologically unusual proliferation.

The stipulation on vowels cannot, in any scientifically responsible or logical sense, refer to a precise number. There is no principled reason why Saramaccan's 14-vowel inventory is the largest possible that a language with a pidgin history could have, especially since creoles have existed for centuries, during which a certain number of phonemes can naturally arise (the creole ancestral to Saramaccan and its sister creoles Sranan and Ndyuka, for example, did not have the nasalized series of phonemic vowels, which arose via the erosion of final nasal consonants). Also, as noted above, Mon-Khmer languages can have vowel inventories only slightly larger than 14. Possibly a creole will be discovered with 17 vowels, while presumably there are Mon-Khmer ones with just 14 or fewer.

The designation "typologically unusual" does not and can not begin with a particular number of vowels: our data is human language, not the periodic table of the elements. However, the essence of my stipulation is that no creole has as many vowels as Mon-Khmer languages *can*. The number of vowels in a language like Khmer is a result of the drift of phonetic material over time. However, pidgins could not, as I have argued, harbor register distinctions by nature – and if creoles begin as pidgins as I have proposed, then the pidgin would not lend a phonetic seedbed poised to drift into unique vocalic proliferation by now. Thus, a language like Khmer, despite its analytic typology, reveals itself as not a creole first in its numeral classifiers, but also in its unusual number of vocalic phonemes.

1.5.4. The Prototype hypothesis does not stipulate "no tone"

It must be clear that my claim is not that creoles "do not have tone," especially given an increasingly copious literature revealing that tone plays a greater role in many creoles than was hitherto acknowleged, such as in Saramaccan (e.g. Good 2004a), Papiamentu (e.g. Rivera-Castillo & Pickering 2004) and Principense Creole Portuguese (Maurer 2009). My claim has been that creoles show their youth not in "lacking tone," but in not using tone to distinguish, for one, morphosyntactic categories, and also monosyllabic lexical items.

1.5.4.1. Monosyllabic vs. disyllabic

The latter stipulation, which I have motivated above, may seem a mere stunt designed to rule out bisyllabic tonally contrasted minimal pairs such as Saramaccan's various examples such as *bígi* "large" vs. *bigí* "begin." However, the fact is that in most cases in creoles, high tone correlates with stress. Specifically, the creole is a compromise between tonal systems spoken natively by its creators and the stress-based ones of the lexifier language. In the Saramaccan pair above, for example, the contrasting occurences of high tone correlate with the placement of stress in the source words *big* and *begin*.

As I have outlined elsewhere (McWhorter 2005a: 13), this represents a *phonetic* use of tone, which is quite plausible even in a pidgin: i.e. even in the first attempts at the use of a lexifier, speakers of a tonal language could easily render stress with high tone in accompaniment (cf. Goldsmith 1987 on the tendency for the two to gradually coincide in language change, amidst a discussion by Salmons 1992 [56–63] on how language contact can accelerate same). However, for the reasons noted above, they could not transfer monosyllabic items distinguished only by tone into the pidgin, since these would be incomprehensible to speakers of the lexifier or even to speakers of other substrate languages – even if these were tonal as well.

However, there is now work demonstrating disjunctions between stress and tone in disyllabic items in various creoles, interpretable as contradicting the Prototype hypothesis in showing contrastive rather than phonetic tone. These cases, however, do not represent these languages' phonological systems at their outset, which is the focus of the Prototype Hypothesis – which 1) in no way denies that creoles will depart from their state at genesis as time passes, and 2) requires that such departures can only be identified as such with appeal to plainly demonstrable evidence of latter-day development (McWhorter 2005: 20).

1.5.4.2. Papiamentu

For example, Papiamentu data can be presented in a way that suggests that stress and tone are independent in a fashion that contradicts my hypothesis, as in Rivera-Castillo & Pickering (2004: 265), as with the form /mata/. The participial verb form "killed" is /ma'tá/ and the noun "plant" is /'máta/. In these, stress and high tone co-occur – but the base form of the verb "kill" is /'matá/, with stress on the first syllable and high tone on the final one.

However, in a more general sense, this is the *only* regular disjunction between stress and high tone in this creole. As Rivera-Castillo & Pickering (2004: 266) show, in nouns, trisyllabic verbs, and in monosyllables, stress and high tone correlate, as we would expect of a language created by speakers of tonal languages encountering a stress-based one. Moreover, this exception is not problematic but predictable within my hypothesis. The Prototype hypothesis requires that creoles with ample long-term exposure to their lexifiers will depart from the prototype. Papiamentu is just such a creole, and my stating this is not an ad hoc feint designed to sweep away otherwise inconvenient data.

Holm (1989: 314–5) refers, for example, to the "unusually high degree of European influence on the creole," its "historical movement towards Spanish," the "importation of Spanish morphology," and the fact that "many features of Papiamentu are more like those of a European language than an Atlantic creole." Holm's statements are typical of the literature on Papiamentu, in which it is agreed that the language has been significantly influenced by Spanish.

As such, we can plausibly suppose that Papiamentu began with verbs based on the infinitive – as most creoles do, as noted in Section Two – which in Spanish has final-syllable stress. This would have occasioned co-occurence of stress and high tone: /ma'tá/. However, third-person singular verbs in Spanish have penultimate stress, and if Papiamentu was steeped in Spanish influence after its emergence, then – given that language change so often generalizes from the third person, given its heavy usage – a natural process would be for stress on verbs used finitely to migrate to the penultimate. Crucially, it would be natural for this reassignment of stress to occur while high tone remained on the final syllable: hence /'matá/.

Meanwhile, Spanish influence has also meant that Papiamentu, unlike most creoles, has a reflex of the Spanish participial form, in which stress occurs on the final syllable of the root (/ma'tado/), rendered in Papiamentu with a typical confluence of stress and high tone on that syllable. That is, /ma'tá/ remains in the grammar alongside /'matá/.

Thus the /'matá/ form constitutes a single departure from the "prototypical" in Papiamentu, predictable from its heavy influence from Spanish.

1.5.4.3. Principense

Another example where departure from the Prototype is demonstrably a result of subsequent development is Principense, in which there are also disjunctions between stress and tone. A tonal pattern serves the derivational purpose of distinguishing verbs from nouns (*fálá* "speech," *fàlà* "to speak," *témá* "insistence," *tèmà* "to insist," (Maurer 2009: 26) and this pattern does not correspond to stress in Principense or Portuguese (e.g. Portuguese *falar* /fa'lar/). Moreover, a couple of dozen nouns have two low tones but syllable-final stress (/sà'pè/ "hat") (ibid. 19).

However, Principense is one of four varieties of creole Portuguese in the Gulf of Guinea, which are assumed to be related (namely, an early variety of Sao Tomé was the father to the other three; cf. Holm 1989: 277–9). In the other varieties, tone (or pitch-accent, the most widespread analysis of Sao Tomense) corresponds to stress (cf. Ferraz 1979, Maurer 1995); e.g. Sao Tomense *flá* "to speak," /ɔ'pɛ/ "foot," compared to Principense's LL *òpè* (Sao Tomense data from Ferraz 1987).

The Principense trait, given its historical relationship to Sao Tomense, would be due to a rightward assimilation pattern applying to both high and low tone: *fálà > fálá, *fálá > fàlà. This would also have happened unpredictably to yield the LL items such as *sàpè* "hat."

Crucially, this analysis would be scientifically implausible (i.e. arbitrary) if Principense did not contrast with three living close relatives in which tone correlates with stress as in Saramaccan. To be sure, one other Principense stress-tone disjunction does not submit to this analysis, at least in terms of available evidence: an HL tonal sequence, evidenced in about 50 words, occurs almost only in cases where the Portuguese source had a liquid-final first syllable: /'létà/ "alert" > *alerta*. This creates a few minimal pairs; here, with /'létá/ "letter" (Maurer 2009: 19). This suggests that perhaps at an earlier stage of Principense, the liquids persisted in some form and blocked, for some reason, rightward assimilation. However, there is nothing to my knowledge in the phonology or phonotactics of Sao Tomense, Fa D'Ambu (Annobonese) or Angolar to confirm this reconstruction.

However, these HL cases are, after all, ones where synchronically, tone *does* correlate with stress, and the disjunctions between stress and tone elsewhere in the language are analyzable as derived from an original stress/tone correlation preserved in Principense's close relatives.

In sum, while the Prototype hypothesis does stipulate "little or no inflectional affixation," it does not state that creoles have simply "little or no tone," but something much more specific, motivated by what we would expect of languages born recently of pidgins.

1.6. Noncompositional derivation: The reduplication question

A derivational process unmentioned in my previous discussions of the Prototype hypothesis is reduplication. It has been pointed out that creoles have reduplicated forms in which the relationship between the root and reduplicated form is not predictable according to any of the various meanings that reduplication has in the creole or in languages worldwide (e.g. intensification, iterativity, approximation). Baptista (2003: 180), for instance, shows in Cape Verdean forms such as *peli* "skin," *peli-peli* "stark naked," *buli* "gourd," *buli-buli* "to shake," and *bóka* "mouth," *bóka-bóka* "in secret." Kouwenberg, LaCharité & Gooden (2003: 108–9) give similar forms in Jamaican Creole; cf. also Ladhams, Hagemeijer, Maurer & Post (2003: 171) for similar examples in the Gulf of Guinea Portuguese creoles.

One interpretation of these data is to suppose that because my stipulation that (a subset of) creoles are unique among the world's languages in lacking noncompositional derivation-root combinations was incorrect, stipulation 3) is entirely untenable and leaves the Prototype hypothesis without a third of its justification.

However, the issue is actually more specific. A claim that Cape Verdean forms like *peli-peli* contradict my thesis requires that pidgins lack such noncompositional instances of reduplication, such that we could say that their presence in creoles is a contradiction to tracing creole structure to pidgin origin. In fact, however, pidgins *do* have noncompositional reduplication.

The relevant issue is not whether pidgins have *productive* reduplication processes: they barely do, as noted by Bakker (2003). What they do have is lexicalized reduplicated forms (cf. also Mühlhäusler 1997: 179), and this includes noncompositional cases. Examples include *pil* "blood," *pilpil* "red" in Chinook Jargon (Grant 2003: 322) and Pidgin Hawaiian's *naminami* "to speak, tell" from *namu* "to mutter unintelligibly" and *panipani* "to have sexual relations" from *pani* "to close, shut" (Roberts 2003).

Therefore: noncompositional cases like Cape Verdean's *peli-peli* occur in pidgins as well, and thus pose no problem for the Prototype hypothesis.

This certainly means that my initial stipulation that noncompositional derivation is unknown in pidgins was inaccurate: one kind of noncompositional derivation indeed is. However, the validity of the hypothesis as a whole is predicated upon whether creoles have features indicating a recent birth as pidgins.

I argue that virtual absence of (certain types of) inflection and particular uses of tone are just such features, because these are absences inherent to pidginization. Since noncompositional reduplication, too, *does occur in pidgins, its presence in creoles is predictable,* as long as we restate stipulation 3) as:

> Prototypical creoles have little or no noncompositional combination of *nonreduplicative* derivational morphemes with roots.

The presence of noncompositional reduplication even in pidgins suggests that a certain degree of noncompositionality is natural to reduplication as soon as a language hits the ground, in contrast to other derivational processes. Nothing inherent to cognition would lead speakers of a language to immediately, or even quickly, combine *under* and *stand* to connote mental comprehension. A word like *understand* can only emerge via a gradual, probabilistically determined acceptance by an increasing subset of a speech community of a particular metaphorical extension out of many possible that could yield a word meaning "to comprehend."

Reduplication, however, is semantically linked to a vast array of connotations in the world's languages and quite often within single ones: plurality, intensification, diminutiveness, approximation, similarity, result, etc. Amidst all of these functions, the one unifying aspect is that reduplication yields an item that has, in some fashion, the character of the unreduplicated root meaning. Since likeness, in all of its generality and multifariousness, lends itself to the metaphorical creativity inherent to human consciousness even in a synchronic sense rather than just the diachronic one, it is perhaps unsurprising that even pidgin varieties include reduplicated forms departing from the basic semantics of the root form.

That is, we might expect that even in a pidgin like Chinook Jargon, that when a word for *red* was needed, "blood-blood" was recruited despite its unpredictability. This process, based on an extension founded upon immediately intuitive likeness, could plausibly occur very quickly. It could occur more immediately than a much less immediately intuitive metaphorical interpretation of the semantic combination of the particular connotations of *under* and *stand.* In that case, after the reinterpretation has happened, synchronically one is left asking "How is one standing 'under'?" – and it bears mentioning that etymologists have no account of how *understand* emerged.

In any case, in terms of the specific issue of whether or not a case like *pelipeli* makes stipulation 3) of the Prototype hypothesis untenable, the simple fact is that similar cases occur in pidgins, and thus are commensurate with the Prototype analysis.

1.7. Falsifiability

The cleanest possible refutation of the Creole Prototype hypothesis would be the identification of an older language that exhibits all three of its features. There have been four such attempts since the Prototype idea was published in 1998.

The claim by Ansaldo & Matthews (2001) that Chinese is such a case is perplexing. The contrast of monosyllables with tone is fundamental to Chinese, and thus conclusively disqualifies it from the Prototype. Ansaldo and Matthews appear to suppose that the fact that many creoles make some use of tone means that we are faced with an insignificant difference of degree, but section 5.4 in this paper should suffice to reveal the flaw in this approach.

Sampson's (2006: 370–2) argument that Old Chinese exhibited all three prototype features founders upon derivational morphology. Sampson cites three derivation-root pairs such as **ak* "bad" and **aks* "to hate" and notes that the contribution of the derivational morpheme (here, the reconstructed suffix-*s*) is semantically unpredictable only to a modest degree. Sampson's thrust is to liken Old Chinese in this regard to my characterization of creoles, in which I allow that even in them, derivation-root combinations drift from strict compositionality to a modest degree, of the type termed *institutionalizations* in Matthews (1974: 193–194,) such as *transmission* referring to part of a car. This kind of conventionalization, inevitable of language usage in the real world, is not strictly "predictable," although not unrecoverably opaque as are cases such as *understand.*

Sampson, however, undercovers the relevant data in Old Chinese. Another trait of derivation in older languages that I have referred to is that derivational morphemes' contribution can vary so widely across the words to which it is applied that a single meaning is no longer gleanable. This, too, is a result of semantic drift over a long period of time. An example I have cited elsewhere is another from Chrau, the prefix *pa-* (Thomas 1969:103, Thomas 1971: 153):

Table 15. Chrau derivational morpheme *pa-*

gaň "go across"	*pagaň* "crosswise"
le "dodge"	*pale* "roll over"
lôm "lure"	*palôm* "mislead"
lăm "set, point"	*palăm* "roll"
joǫ "long"	*pajoǫ* "how long?"

Sampson's brief sample of a few isolated cases of Old Chinese derivation obscures that its derivational morphemes were of the above type. Typical was the semantic contribution of the morpheme reconstructed as originally-*s*, transcribed at the stage of the language in this table as-*h* (from Norman 1988: 85):

Table 16. Old Chinese derivation

grang "to walk"	*grangh* "behavior"
drjuan "transmit"	*drjuanh* "a record"
ram "salt"	*ramh* "to salt"
ljang "to measure"	*ljangh* "quantity"
djangx "ascend"	*djangh* "a top"
təp "reply to a greeting"	*təbh* "reply to a person"
ʔak "to be evil"	*ʔagh* "to hate"

There is no single function attributable to this morpheme, nor to another derivational process accomplished via voicing an initial consonant (ibid.). Scholars of the history of Chinese regualrly note the irregular nature of the recoverable derivation in Old Chinese, and suppose that it was the product of long-term semantic drift. In this, Old Chinese, despite its lack of inflection or tone, was identifiable as an old language.

Henri Wittmann's argument on the CreoList in 1999 that the Mande language Soninke has all three Prototype features also fails, for reasons this paper has made especially clear. As I have noted elsewhere (McWhorter 2005a: 369) Soninke has, most importantly, a goodly degree of inflectional morphology. In the terms explicated in this paper, we can further specify that this includes inherent Inflection with paradigmatic complexity, including three allomorphs of a plural marker, applied arbitrarily to roots (i.e. yielding what can be treated as declension classes). Wittmann claimed that these Soninke markers are clitics rather than affixes. However, for one, they lend themselves much more plausibly to affixal analysis; e.g. they often cause morphophonological alterations on roots (ibid.). Then, to the extent that one might analyze them as clitics, then under the terms proposed in this paper, they still qualify as Inflection – as they would even if analyzed as free morphemes. Structurally reduced pidgins do not have allomorphic paradigms of plural marking, bound or not. My argument is that a language with such a feature – bound or not – was not recently born.

Only David Gil (2001) has shown a language that actually has all of the features of a Prototype creole and is arguably less complex than most or all of them. I predicted that it would turn out to have a sociohistory including a break in transmission. The history of this variety is indeed one such, and I have argued that Riau Indonesian (and similar vernacular varieties of Malay/Indonesian) can be analyzed as creoles (McWhorter 2001b, 2007).

Is this a feint rather than a scientific argument? That is, "Show him an older language like that and he just says it's a creole"? This is a reasonable question, but my reasoning is more constrained than that. If Riau Indonesian were spoken by a group with no evident history of extensive migration and population mixture in the recent past, then no such analysis as a creole would have been possible. However, Malay has been a lingua franca for millennia, learned more as a second language than as a first one, often for utilitarian reasons such as trade. The question would be why there would not be pidginized and creolized versions of it, given that plantations are hardly the only setting creoles have emerged in (Nubi Creole Arabic in the military, Unserdeutsch Creole German in an orphanage, Hawaiian Creole English in Honolulu amidst schoolchildren, etc.).

Unsurprisingly, there are grammatically reduced varieties of Malay across Southeast Asia, and equally unsurprisingly, they have long been treated as products of irregular transmission. Grijns (1991) analyzes Jakarta Malay as conventionalized second-language acquisition. Assorted analysts derive vernacular, grammatically reduced renditions of Malay from a pidgin; namely, Bazaar Malay (e.g. Adelaar & Prentice 1996). With no objections, Baba Malay of Malaysia is even traditionally classified as a creole.

Riau Indonesian differs from standard Malay in qualitatively similar ways as Jakarta, Baba and other vernacular Malays do. As such, my argument that Riau Indonesian is the product of a break in transmission is simply continuing a tradition, and is fleshed out in McWhorter (2007: 222–37) with ample comparison with the Malayic group and Austronesian as a whole.

1.8. Conclusion

Upon which I present the Creole Prototype hypothesis ten years later, recast with a finer-grained engagement with grammatical detail:

> A natural language is a creole (i.e. born recently from a pidgin and thus emerged from broken transmission) iff it has:
> 1) *morphologically:* little or no inflectional affixation, and among un-bound inflectional markers, none of contextual inflection, or of inherent inflection of the paradigmatically complex sort,

2) *phonologically:* little or no distinction of monosyllabic lexical items or morphosyntactic distinctions via tone or register, and no typologically unusual proliferation of vowels, and

3) *semantically:* little or no noncompositional combination of nonreduplicative derivational morphemes with roots.

This is not an arbitrary grab-bag of features, but ones carefully vetted according to what we would expect in the very specific case of a *language born recently as a pidgin.*

The larger intent of the presentation has been to demonstrate that creole languages are the result of neither:

a) unbroken grammar-internal development with merely moderate abbreviations from adult acquisition – the thrust of superstratist analyses, nor:

b) largely just mixture of two or more languages' features – the thrust of Lefebvre's (1998) relexification hypothesis and other work depicting creoles as simply grammatical compromises; e.g. Aboh & Ansaldo (2007).

Rather, the evidence suggests that creoles are languages which emerged from structurally reduced pidgins, and bear hallmarks of that origin in their current structural makeup.

Chapter 2
Comparative complexity: What the creolist learns from Cantonese and Kabardian

2.1. Introduction

In *Phonology and Morphology of Creole Languages,* Ingo Plag gathers papers intended to fill a gap in the discussion of creoles until recently: that of phonological and morphological processes. The need is urgent. Back in 1994, Pieter Muysken (1994a: 105) noted that in the first fourteen issues of *Journal of Pidgin and Creole Languages,* there were exactly three articles on phonology and two on morphology out of 78, and six years later, Lefebvre (2000: 134) showed that in the twelve issues since Muysken had written, there had been but five more articles on phonology and none on morphology.

There had been perhaps an unhealthy excess of attention paid in the past – including by myself – to a certain small class of grammatical features germane to addressing two prominent issues, multilectal variation and Derek Bickerton's Language Bioprogram Hypothesis. The focus on, for example, tense and aspect markers, serial verbs, and copulas taught much, but had a way of discouraging sustained attention to creole grammars as a whole.

Thus this volume is a breath of fresh air, full of valuable information on creoles that often remain unevenly described despite hefty bibliographies. However, the book is also grounded in a particular subtext. The guiding aim of many of the papers, and the original impetus for the volume, is less description for its own sake than addressing certain controversial claims. One is that creole languages are a synchronically identifiable class rather than just sharing a type of social history. Another is the related observation that the distinctness of the class lies partly in these languages being less structurally complex than older ones.

These controversies were sparked, as it happens, by work of mine, the first paper of which (McWhorter 1998) specified that creoles were identifiable in combining certain phonetic and morphological traits: 1) little or no tone contrasting monosyllables or encoding morphosyntax, 2) little or no inflectional affixation and 3) little or no noncompositional combinations of derivational morphemes and roots (such as *understand*). My claim was that these three features all take long periods of time to develop, from stages of a grammar in which they initially do not exist, and that creoles, as products of pidgin languages that eschew features unnecessary to communication, have not existed long enough to have accreted these three traits – and are therefore identifiable as a type of grammar. In later work (McWhorter 2001), I expanded this idea into an argument that throughout their grammars, creoles are less complex than older languages – although hardly devoid of complexity – for the same reasons that they hew to the "Prototype" described in the 1998 paper. Much, or most, complexity is grammars is, I have argued, the result of gradual drift over time, leading to features that grammars elsewhere do without with no problem: declension classes, alienable possessive marking, consonant mutations. Creoles are new languages recently born from pidgins, and thus have not drifted as far into needless elaboration as older languages.

Most creolists' response to these claims have been highly skeptical, such that a significant strain of creolist work since has endeavored to highlight creoles' structural complexities. In itself, this is welcome. This work has built bridges between the creole studies and linguistics as a whole in a way that much previous creolist work could not.

However, I am unable to conclude that the work in question refutes my basic argument that creole languages are, as new languages, less needlessly elaborated than older ones. In my assessment, these articles leave standing a basic claim that creoles are a structurally unusual type of language that resulted from a particular kind of language contact, which therefore have interesting implications for second language acquisition, diachronic theory, typology, and even generative linguistics.

Plag's volume, gathering between two covers so many authors arguing otherwise, many of whose work represents years of their and others' responses to the Creole Complexity hypothesis, provides a useful opportunity for a constructive reply. The book gathers papers originally presented at a conference in Siegen, Germany in 2001, but as it happens, four of the papers presented there were published in *Yearbook of Morphology 2002*. As such, I will also refer to these four papers in this review article, as they are equally germane to the topic and include some especially insightful and crucial ones.

2.2. There's complex and there's complex

A major strain in these articles is an implication that to the extent that creoles' grammars can be shown to submit to analysis according to generative formalisms, their status as less complex than older languages is refuted. When reading these articles I revel in seeing so many creoles described in such detail with the tools familiar to linguists elsewhere. However, my argument is not that creole grammars lack complexity, but that they evidence *lesser* complexity than languages that have existed for millennia. My assumption is that all natural languages are based on Universal Grammar and can be described according to schemas of abstract and systematic mental representation. What I question is that such demonstrations reveal creoles as equally complex to Hausa, Navajo, Polish, or Khmer.

2.2.1. Inflection and complexity

Alain Kihm's article is one of the richest of this group, and thus demands substantial address. Kihm starts with observing that under the Minimalist paradigm, the difference between Portuguese *cantarei* "I will sing" and Guinea-Bissau Kriyol's *na kanta* "will sing" is merely one of Merge and Move. *Na kanta* requires only Merge: the functional feature T, represented by *na,* is interpreted in association with *kanta* without the items' being linked into a single word. *Canterei* requires Move, where the head T is represented by an affix that must be raised and adjoined to the verb. Based on this and modifications that attempt to eliminate even the difference between these processes, Kihm argues that both languages have "inflection," – which I will henceforth capitalize when I intend Kihm's definition, as Inflection – the only difference being "the way they interface the lexicon with the morphological vocabulary, through syntax" (358).

The implication of Kihm's perspective is that because *na kanta* and *cantarei* differ only in which of two elementary processes created them, there are no grounds for viewing inflectional affixation as adding complexity to a grammar. A ready interpretation of this would be that abstract generative analysis reveals a seeming difference in complexity as a mere parametrical alternation. I would find such a discovery massively stimulating in itself. However, in this case, I cannot help sensing that a fuller range of data would yield a different picture.

To be sure, inflectional affixation is not *necessarily* more complex than free forms in the same functions. For example, Swahili's encoding the past with the inflection *-li-* is no more or less complex than Saramaccan encoding it with free morpheme *bi.* In terms of tempo of articulation, there is not even any appreciable difference between how quickly *mi bi ké* "I wanted" goes by in running Saramaccan speech as opposed to *ni-li-taka* "I wanted" in Swahili. Only the fact that other auxiliaries can intervene between Saramaccan's *bi* and the verb distinguishes *bi* as free.

However, I think it would be misrepresenting both creole and older language data to leave the issue there. The issue is less whether creoles have

Inflection than how much Inflection, and what effect it has on roots – because these are aspects of grammatical complexity.

For example, we might imagine an argument that where Russian for *I will want* is *xočú* and Saramaccan's version is *mi ó ké*, that Saramaccan's future marker *ó* is a functional head equivalent to Russian's *-u* affix, the one having Merged and the other having Moved. Obviously, however, there is more to the case than this.

Table 17. Future marking in Russian and Saramaccan Creole

Russian (infinitive: *xotet'*)				Saramaccan (infinitive: *ké*)			
1S	ja xočú	1P	my xotím	1S	mi ó ké	1P	u ó ké
2S	ty xóčeš'	2P	vy xotíte	2S	i ó ké	2P	ũ ó ké
3S	on xóčet	3P	oni xotját	3S	a ó ké	3P	de ó ké

Of course both languages have Inflection. But there are also clear qualitative differences in how Inflection is manifested:

1) Russian's future-marking functional head varies in its manifestation according to person and number. Saramaccan's does not.
2) Russian has an infinitive inflection (which varies according to conjugation class and other factors); Saramaccan has neither this nor a free morpheme in the function (such as English's *to*).
3) In Russian the final consonant of the root is altered in the singular forms, from [t] to [č]. Saramaccan's *ó* may well be analyzable as "Inflection" – but here is Inflection that does not distort the roots it applies to phonetically.
4) In Russian the 1S suffix takes stress but the 2S and 3S suffixes do not; then, the plural suffixes do. Saramaccan's *ó* is not variably stressed according to person or number. We can analyze both future markers as functional heads – but these functional heads submit to different phonological complications.
5) Even within the first conjugation in Russian, there are verbs whose suffixes other than the first person one do take stress. But when this happens, there is also a vowel change: "you want" *xóčeš'*, but "you give" *dajóš'* (**dajéš'*). Saramaccan's Inflection does not entail paradigmatically conditioned vowel alterations (and incidentally, Russian's *give* verb is irregular as well: the infinitive is *davat'*, which loses its first vowel and middle consonant in its present-tense inflected forms – but then in many other reflexes, not).

6) *Degree* of inflection varies enormously among languages. Even under Kihm's analysis of Inflection, Saramaccan has but a handful of Inflections (presumably, including its tense, aspect and mood markers). Russian Inflects nouns, pronouns and adjectives in six cases, with these occurring then in three declensions, all of them with subclassess and irregularity, and its verbs occur in two conjugations of a very similar nature to the nominal declensions. Even creoles with somewhat more Inflection than Saramaccan never even approach Russian's *degree* of Inflection: e.g. older languages range from isolating to polysynthetic, but creoles are always either isolating or very close to it.

Kihm has an answer for that previous observation, starting from Booij's (1993) distinction of two kinds of inflection. Contextual inflection is linked to syntactic context, and includes structural case and concord. Inherent inflection is (at least relatively) independent of syntactic context, and includes tense, aspect, gender and number markers. Kihm proposes that creoles "maximize the role of syntax as an interface between the lexicon and the morphology," (359) such that contextual inflection is filtered out because, under the Minimalist model, case markers are not generated as heads inserted into a syntactic frame. Meanwhile, amidst inherent inflection, only tense, aspect and mood marking make it into creoles because they are represented by heads, while gender and number are lexical processes that do not involve syntactic projections.

This is a clever formulation, but clearly suffers, firstly, from an assumption that the syntactic tree of the Minimalist school is a mental reality. We are to presume that tense is privileged in creoles because it is generated as the head of its own syntactic projection – but this is just something that Minimalism happens to stipulate. Things get messier when we recall that proposals of additional projections like NumP are common in the notoriously heterogenous realm of Minimalist work. Kihm suggests, assuming that there is no NumP projection, that his formulation explains why plural marking tends to be linked with definiteness in creoles: definiteness is a syntactic projection DP, and thus number can "piggyback" upon it. But under some of the more copiously headed trees some Minimalists assume, NumP would presumably allow plural marking of more independent and thus wider application, as in European languages. At present there is no consensus among Minimalists as to how many such heads Universal Grammar includes.

Meanwhile, Kihm's argument can be seen as simply leading to the same questions that found my positions on complexity. Kihm goes so far as to suggest that maximization of syntax is possibly a "principled description of what creoles consist in" (359). This is a conclusion which, in entailing the concept of *maximization,* would likely be warmly received by creolists uncomfortable with the notion that creoles contain *less* of something. But this brings us to a question: why do creoles "maximize syntax" more than older languages? The question is especially urgent when we acknowledge that the result of this maximization, despite the enlargening implication of that term, is that the grammars in question have much *less* of something than a language where syntax is less "maximized" – inflectional affixes.

More specifically, a possible reading of Kihm's argumentation is that "maximization of syntax" is shorthand for a description of isolating languages in general. Although Kihm states that "maximization of syntax" applies to creoles specifically, his article does not address older isolating languages, which leaves a possible assumption that creoles' maximization of syntax does not define them as a class, but merely places them amidst those languages among the world's 6000 that happen to have drifted into being uninflected. This would dovetail with claims such as Veenstra's (1996) and DeGraff's (1999) that creoles differ grammatically from their lexifiers primarily because of factors falling out of their eschewal of inflectional afiixes. Creoles, then, would merely fall into the class occupied by languages like Thai.

But the reality is that older isolating languages display more overt manifestations than creoles do of categories encoded with inflectional affixes in European languages. In many ways, older isolating languages are "unravelled" versions of synthetic ones. Around the world, isolating languages use free morphemes to encode ergativity, elaborate focus mechanisms, evidentiality, grades of pragmatic implication, and so on (McWhorter 2005a: 72–101). Especially common are numeral classifiers, often occurring in great number, which are functionally similar to grammatical gender affixes and can be seen as their diachronic source (Grinevald & Seifart 2004).

Certainly, Minimalists do not usually assign focus, evidentiality beyond core modal concepts, and pragmatic distinctions to their own functional projections. As such, a potential objection might be that such things would not qualify as Inflection as Kihm has it. But this would lead to the question as to why older isolating languages nevertheless have so much more inflectional affixation, if not Inflection, than creoles – a question that remains valid even if many of the inflectional affixes happen to fall beyond the purview of what Minimalism stipulates as occurring as heads of syntactic projections. It would appear that my questions about complexity address linguistic features which fall outside of the highly constrained purview of Minimalist inquiry – but certainly the features remain on view, begging explanation. There is little more tense or aspect Inflection in Cantonese than in Saramaccan, for example – but Cantonese has a vast battery of numeral classifiers and pragmatic particles that no creole does. Polynesian languages do not have any especially prolific battery of tense and aspect particles – i.e. Inflections – but they usually have particles marking agent and patient which are functionally equivalent to inflectional affixes marking such distinctions in other languages, often even distinguishing ergativity.

Why, then, do creoles "maximize syntax" to so exclusive a degree? To wit: why is there no creole that "maximizes syntax" in having free particles marking tense and aspect, but beyond the realm of functional categories expressed by their own projections, happens to also have numeral classifiers, regular case marking with free morphemes (as, for example, the isolating Fongbe [Niger-Congo] does with its free genitive and objective particles as described in Lefebvre 1998: 101–10), or the like?

That is, among the countless isolating languages in the world, the vast majority of them do *not* largely restrict surface appearance of morphology to the verbal subclass of Booij's inherent subclass of morphology. If creoles are unique in this, then whether they have Inflection or not, we cannot agree with Kihm's assessment that the controversy over creole inflection is "pointless" because "having little or no morphology is simply not a sensible description when predicated of a grammar as a whole" (358). This only coheres if we assume that a grammar's "maximization of syntax" is a mere random variation with no qualitative or diachronic implications – as if we were treating red versus green.

In actuality, extreme "maximation of syntax" is, in the cross-linguistic sense, a deeply peculiar state for a grammar to be in. It entails a strange paucity of inflectional *categories, affixed or not* – classifiers, pragmatic particles, evidential markers, etc. – a paucity unknown in older languages and begging explanation. Here is a sentence from an isolating language: note its ergative marking and its evidential and quotative marker:

Akha (Sino-Tibetan):

(1) *Àsjhaŋ sjháŋ nɛ   shḿ-thö nɛ   bzö séq ŋà   djé   nà-bɔ́ áŋ   nɛ.*
    A.   S.   ERG awl   INST hole kill EVID QUOT ear   LOC INST
    'Asjhang Sjhang killed her with an awl through her ear.'
                                           (Hansson 1976:16)

Devoid of Kihm's Inflection, this language nevertheless marks categories that no creole does, and it is by no means unusual as isolating languages go.

It would seem that one reason creoles might maximize syntax to such a degree – if we accept this formulation – is that it is the nature of grammars' aging to drift away from this relatively unmediated expression of Universal Grammar.

However, I suspect that Kihm's analysis will be more promising than Bakker's article in *Yearbook of Morphology 2002* (henceforth YM) attempting to point up a hitherto unknown degree of "inflection" in pidgins rather than creoles. Making his point requires Bakker to assume that all languages that happen to have come to be called "pidgins" form a typological class of some kind. But contact varieties between closely related languages or dialects that are well inflected are often rather inflected themselves, since the retention of the inflections does not impede communication, such as the Bantu-based "pidgins" like Sango and Lingala. There is a long-standing question as to the usefulness of treating these languages as "pidgins" at all compared to cases of indisputably massive structural reduction in pidgins like Russenorsk and Chinese Pidgin English; not for nothing have they often been classed as koines or, especially among Francophone linguists, "vehicularized" languages.

Besides, as to the implication that the pidgins that plantation creoles came from may have been more inflected than we know, there are three things that must be kept in mind. First, we would wonder why this would be when for all but a very few of the plantation creoles, most of the languages their creators spoke were isolating. Second, we will never have empirical data of the pidgin stages. Third, if the pidgin stages were by chance mysteriously well inflected, then our question would still remain as to why the creoles tossed the inflection overboard and retain little or none of it. A good example would be Cape Verdean and Guinea-Bissau Kriyol, many of whose creators spoke well-inflected West Atlantic languages like Manjaku and Balanta: if the pidgin was even moderately inflected, then why are the creoles almost completely isolating? This would only return us to the interesting issues that Kihm addresses.

2.2.2. Complexity in phonology

Whereas Kihm attempts to demonstrate creoles as indistinguishable from older languages in terms of "maximization of syntax," Thomas Klein shows that Haitian Creole's phonology demonstrates complexity of a kind that submits itself to meticulous rule ordering within the Optimality Theory format.

His presentation joins a growing body of work suggesting that creoles' phonological complexity is robust enough that one could not distinguish whether a language was a creole based on its sound system. Other examples include Good's (2004a) demonstration that Saramaccan's lexicon is split between a pitch-accent component and a truly tonal one, Rivera-Castillo's

(1998) analysis of the complex interaction in Papiamentu between stress and tone, and Nikiema & Bhatt's analysis in the volume under review of Haitian Creole (returned to below).

As it happens, in my previous work I have noted that creoles' segmental inventories, for one, are by no means the least numerous among the world's languages. No creole has the notoriously sparse inventories of many Polynesian languages, for example (McWhorter 2005a: 375). However, I have largely refrained from addressing phonological processes per se given that until recently, there were relatively few analyses allowing a cross-creole verdict on complexity. As of recent years, that is no longer the case, and I openly acknowledge that phonology alone would not motivate a thesis that creoles were especially simplified compared to older languages.

However, given that such a thesis is more plausible in terms of morphology and syntax, it bears mentioning that creoles' phonology, while "complex," remains complex to a distinctly moderate degree. The analyst who argues that phonological complexity in itself refutes my claims about creoles' manifestation of signs of their youth is responsible for spelling out why creole phonology appears never to be as maximally complex as some older languages' phonologies are.

2.2.2.1. Complexity in Haitian Creole phonology

Klein's article is a useful example of the issue at hand. The Haitian determiner occurs in various allomorphs. *La* occurs after consonants (*liv la* "the book"). After final [a], the allomorph is *a* (*papa a* "the father"). After final front vowels, the form is [ja] ([papje ja] "the paper") and after final back rounded ones, [wa] ([bato wa] "the boat").

Klein notes that *la*'s occurrence after consonants is, in fact, a challenge to Optimality Theory, which stipulates that open syllables with onsets are unmarked, through the constraints NoCoda and Onset. That is, Optimality Theory treats sequences of CV syllables as fundamental, while Haitian's *la,* occurring after final consonants, inherently forces consonant sequences (*liv la*) while the occurrence of the *a* allomorph entails vowel hiatus (*papa a*).

Klein then gives an account of how Optimality Theory could model the generation of the allomorphs, with the assistance of some supplemental OT-style mechanisms of his own creation. *La* carries a lexical violation of the preference for open syllables. Thus it cannot occur after, for example, *papa* because [papa la] would allow the unmarked CVCV pattern that it is specified to flout. In Optimality Theory terms, this would allow *la* to surface devoid of its requirement that a coda precede it, and thus run up against the MaxIO faithfulness constraint that input is "faithfully" represented in the output. This leaves the *a* allomorph as the preferred alternative even though it yields a syllable with no onset [papa a], which the constraint ranking takes care of by ranking ONSET lower than the "structure-preserving" MAXIO.

Meanwhile, we might imagine that the grammar might pull the output back towards the unmarked pattern of CVCV phonotactics by resyllabifying, such that, for example, [liv a] could surface as [li va]. Klein has the grammar block this with the OT constraint that requires the right edge of the stem to be the right edge of the syllable, R-ALIGN-STEM-SYLL.

The result is a typical Optimality Theory-style table (221), with its highly particular terminology and format. One senses from Klein's argumentation that the sheer casting of the allomorphy in this kind of schema is intended, in itself, as a demonstration that Haitian determiner allomorphy is "complex":

Table 18. Optimality Theory account of Haitian's determiner *la*

Input 1: /liv+la/				STEM-FINAL-NOCODA
				*
Input 2: /liv+a/				
Candidates:	R-ALIGN-STEM-SYLL	MAXIO	ONSET	STEM-FINAL-NOCODA
☞a. [liv.+la]$_{input1}$				*
b. [li.v+la]$_{input1}$	*!			*
c. [li.v+a]$_{input2}$	*!			*
d. [liv.+a]$_{input2}$			*!	*

But if Klein's intention is to argue that because creole phonology submits to constraint rankings, creoles are "complex," then the argument is predicated upon an assumption that I have argued that creoles are not natural languages. I am aware of no language whose describers would find that its phonology requires no rule ordering, a fundamental of human language sound systems. However, my argument is a relative one: that creoles are *less* complex than older languages. As such, it is germane that in plain language, the above table can be seen as indicating – simply – "*la* after consonants whether you like it or not; otherwise *a* – and no resyllabification."

To be sure, there is also the glide insertion. But Klein treats it as "another creole pattern of interesting complexity" (211), whereas actually, a linguist might almost be surprised if such glides did *not* occur. As ordinary grammars go, the emergence of such intervocalic glides, matching in placement the preceding vowel, are unremarkable results of rapid speech. Klein himself later concurs, noting that "homorganic glide insertion is quite widespread in the languages of the world" (224). Thus the glides certainly show that "creoles have phonology" – which has not been denied. But "interesting" phonology?

A better case for this might be if, for example, [j] were inserted after back vowels and [w] after front ones. This would be phonetically eccentric, and would likely trace to the erosion of an underlying segment or morphological affix, which might emerge on the surface only in certain contexts and thereby increase the complexity of the grammar in ways familiar to scholars of uniquely challenging phonological and morphophonemic systems. Haitian glide insertion, in contrast, is a sort of process that one might illustrate to help teach beginners in linguistics the basic concept of manner of articulation.

In that light, while Klein intends his presentation as proof that Haitian phonology is "complex," one of the essential challenges in phonological analysis of grammars is charting the pathway from the phonemic representations that end up in fascinatingly altered form on the surface. Crucially, Klein's presentation exhibits a pathway from underlying to surface representation that would hardly strike phonologists as distant or analytically challenging. The formalism of terms like R-ALIGN-RIGHT-SYLL and MaxIO, after all, refers to what are basically simple stipulations to "keep it the way it is." In OT terms, they are faithfulness constraints, rather than markedness constraints. Markedness constraints are perhaps somewhat infelicitously named, as what they work towards is unmarkedness. They discourage departures from unmarked fundamentals and thus, when highly ranked, tend to recast and thus distort underlying forms, working against any markedness they contain in order that surface manifestation will be as unmarked as possible.

Crucially, ranking faithfulness constraints high, as Haitian does in its generation of determiners, is but one configuration a natural language phonology may evince. As often as not, phonological constraints absolutely marginalize "keeping it the way it is."

2.2.2.2. Complexity in older languages' phonology

In the Northwest Caucasian Circassian language Kabardian, for instance, the distance from phonemic to phonetic form is typified by the sentence "we gave it to you," in which /ø-w-a-d-tə-aɣ-ś/ is pronounced as [wötʰˌtʰáːś] (Colarusso 1992: 45). Importantly, this does not represent allegro speech phenomena, but ordinary transformations. Two dozen phonological and morphophonemic rules operate in complex ordering to produce these surface forms. For example, for "he gave it to me," we begin with the phonemic representation, which with glossing is:

(2)   ø- q'ə- s- a-   y- ə- tə- aɣ-   ś
  he HOR me DAT it NP give PST AFF
  "He gave it to me."

(ibid. 38)

For the record, HOR stands for what Colarusso describes as a pragmatic horizon-of-interest morpheme, conveying a degree of emotional stake in the proposition. No creole known to me is documented with a morpheme *regularly* marking such a fine shade of pragmatic denotation. Certainly creoles have their emotive pragmatic particles (e.g. Saramaccan's "softener" *o*). But none have the thirty such particles that Cantonese uses in prolific combination, in sentences such as:

(3)   *Kéuih ló-jó* *daih* *yāt mìhng **tìm ge** **la** **wo.***
  she take-PERF number one place too PRT PRT PRT
  'And she got first place too, you know.'

(Matthews & Yip 1994: 345)

in which *tìm* is evaluative, *ge* is assertive, *la* denotes currency, and *wo* newsworthiness. I submit that this is because Cantonese is ancient and creoles are young.

  In any case, the Kabardian string first goes from: / ø - q'ə - s - a - y - ə - tə - aɣ - ś / to / ø - q'ə - **z** - a - y - ə - **t** - afi - ś /. (Changed segments or morphemes are in boldface.) The following rules have applied:

a. The first s > z because of a voice assimilation rule that operates before morpheme boundaries.

b. The schwa of the root [tə] is elided by a morphophonemic rule that elides /ə/ before morpheme boundaries followed by [a].

c. ɣ > fi because of a morphophonemic rule that sonorizes past tense markers' codas.

After this, the string becomes / ø - q'ə - z - **y** - ə - t - afi - ś / because of a rule deleting vowels before glide onsets. Next: / ø - q'ə - z - ə - **y** - t - afi - ś / because of a metathesis rule between glides and vowels that occurs after non-syllabic morphemes. Finally, surface form is [q'ɪz̧zi:̧tʰá:ś] because, other than that voiceless stops (here, /t/) are underlying aspirated:

a. Syllables often (but not always) create a coda by copying the following syllable's onset (and thus the first of the two [z]'s)
b. Codas color vowels in surface form, the two underlying ones being [ə] and [a].
c. Loss of a glide (including h's) causes compensatory lengthening in vowels, and hence the long vowels.

And so, we return to Klein's "complex" rule: "*la* after consonants; otherwise *a* – and no resyllabification."

Importantly, however, Haitian does, elsewhere in its phonology, exhibit deeper transformations than Klein shows. Emmanuel Nikiema and Parth Bhatt argue that a great many words in Haitian have underlying final consonants deleted on the surface that appear in derivationally related forms, such as (abridged from the source, 50):

Table 19. Phantom consonants in Haitian derivational affixes

mèg	"thin"	mègri	"to get thin"
règ	"rule"	règle	"to rule"
mas	"mask"	maske	"masked"
dirèk	"direct"	direktèman	"directly"

Thus the phonemic representation of *mèg* is /mɛgʀ/, and so on. That most linguists (and many Haitians) are aware that the etymology of, for example, *mèg* is the French *maigre* is artifactual: within the mental representation of Haitian alone, as Nikiema and Bhatt note, we must posit these underlying consonants, on the pain of specifying multiple derivational affixes such as [ʀi], [le] and [ke], which would, in any case, be arbitrarily lexically specified. Here, then, is the kind of morphophonological complexity that founds the phonologist's discipline, analogous to the loss of word-final stops in the Nilo-Saharan language Baale because of contact with relatives that lack such stops, where because the stops are retained before suffixes, the result is morphophonemic rules that did not exist before: *mὲὲlέ* "axe," *mὲὲlέ-k-ká* "axes" (Dimmendaal 2001: 362).

However, Klein's presentation demonstrates nothing of this kind. Rather, he implies that his argument refutes mine in showing simply that Haitian phonology is "complex" – when my interest is in "how complex?" And it must be said that this question also applies even to Nikiema and Bhatt's presentation, which is clearly not of the order of derivational complexity that Kabardian requires in every sentence a speaker utters. Klein's and Nikiema and Bhatt's articles certainly show that phonologically, creoles are real languages – but I have endlessly insisted on this very fact in my own work. The fact remains that no creole has the depth of phonological complexity of Kabardian – or any Caucasian language I am aware of, or of any of countless older languages for which similar facts could be adduced, as they so often are in introducing linguistics students to the challenges of phonological analysis.

I submit that this is not a random fact: it is due to that no young language could exhibit such derivational complexity in its phonological module, because the development of such requires a great deal of time during which the ravages of erosion and transformation lead, blindly but decisively, to such distortive generative processes.

Norval Smith's presentation supports this point, examining the contrast in Surinam creoles' reflections of English consonant clusters. Sranan retains them (*bro* "blow"), Saramaccan eliminates the second segment and inserts a vowel copy (*bɔɔ́*) while Aluku does both the former and alternatively, for emphasis, inserts an archaic liquid between the vowels (*bo[l]ó*). Smith presents an analysis under which each creole makes different allowances within an X-bar model of the syllable. Indeed, then, Surinam creoles' phonologies can be represented according to structured abstract mental representations. However, the analysis is predicated upon a parent creole to all of these (Early Sranan) which reanalyzed English words according to a CV syllabic structure with no non-nasal codas. Here is one case where what the phonologist most readily processes as unmarked is also less complex. Early Sranan, with its phonotactics similar to Japanese, had less complex phonotactics (i.e. fewer syllable types) than English, Portuguese, or its substrate languages (Fongbe has syllable-initial clusters; Kikongo has syllabic consonants).

The upshot is that creolization itself – i.e. as represented in the language that emerges directly from the contact situation – results in simplification, while complications blow in afterwards (but after a few centuries, are not yet on the order of the phonology of Kabardian). Emmanuel Schang's treatment of syllable structure in the Portuguese creoles of the Gulf of Guinea similarly reconstructs a template of CV sequences as the source of today's variation.

2.2.2.3. Tonal complexity

The issue of relative complexity also applies to tone. I have argued that it is rare for creoles to use tone to distinguish lexical items (by itself) or to mark morphosyntax. This means that when Winford James shows that Tobagonian Creole uses tone, then the verdict in terms of complexity will address the fact that James identifies a single morphemic tone: *kyà* "can" versus *kyá* "can't." Otherwise, high tone distinguishes emphatic usage of pronouns from neutral ones – arguably a universal of human language – and tone varies on a few items according to their syntactic position, but in this, does not carry the functional load in conveying meaning (*dì bwáí wán* "the boy [who is] alone; *mì wàn-bwáí* "my only boy"). The difference between this and the high functional load of tone in Tobagonian's West African source languages is obvious. Similarly, it is useful when Shelome Gooden shows that tone patterns differently in Jamaican reduplicatives depending on whether they signify the intensive ([jélójélò] "very yellow") or the distributive ([jélójèlò] "yellow all over") (Gooden also presents acoustic demonstration). But then analysts will differ as to whether this is a morphosyntactic distinction, and in any case, again, the functional load is minor compared to that of segmental and affixal material in the creole.

An especially innovative piece on tone is Good's in YM showing that in Saramaccan, tone marks the occurrence of serial verbs when the two verbs are separated by an NP object. In a previous classic analysis of shared-object serials in Saramaccan, Rountree (1972) argued that the two verbs merely sandhi with one another and "skip" the intervening object, as in (4) where the bolded segments are ones that are low-tones in isolation but are raised to high by sandhi:

(4) Mi *ó*   *nákí dí   lògòsò kúlé gó a   mí wósu.*
     I   FUT hit   DEF turtle   run go LOC   my house
     'I will hit the turtle and run to my house.'

(Rountree 1972: 325)

But there is a subclass of Saramaccan words marked with unchangeable low tones that are insensitive to sandhi, and Good shows that in serial verb constructions with verbs of this subclass, stipulating mere sandhi between the verbs is insufficient: a first serial verb without unchangeable low tones sandhis "phantom style" even when the second one has unchangeable low tones and thus cannot, such as *bɔsɔ* "loosen":

(5) *A nákí dí   tatái bɔsɔ.*
     he hit   DEF rope loosen
     'He hit the rope and loosened it.'

and also that the first syllable of a second verb without unchangeable low tones is marked high even when the first verb is one with such unchangeable low tones, such as *bà* "carry":

(6)   *A bà   wátá bébé éside.*
      he carry water drink yesterday
      'He carried water and drank it yesterday.'

(ibid. 110)

However, what I stipulated in the Creole Prototype hypothesis is that creoles do not use tone to mark morphosyntax, and verb serialization is not a morphosyntactic distinction. Good's analysis fleshes out an amply documented point that Saramaccan sandhi is sensitive to syntactic structure. This is a definite example of complexity in a creole – but it is also germane that Saramaccan sandhi is much less complex overall than its substrate model in Gbe languages (Ham 1999, McWhorter 2005a: 111–2). Importantly, the fact that sandhi breaks between verbs and NP objects – which is true whether there is a following serial verb or not – does not qualify as tonal marking of the accusative, i.e. as a morphological marking. The break occurs more generally, at left edges of maximal projections, such as between verbs and PPs (*kumútu a dí wósu* "exit from the house," where the final syllable of the verb does not raise and leaves the following adposition *a* with its low tone).

2.2.2.4. *Markedness versus complexity*

Klein actually intends his presentation as showing that in its imperative toward structure preservation (faithfulness constraints), Haitian phonology creates markedness on the surface. The observation is well taken, but the overlap between markedness and complexity is, in fact, slight. In McWhorter (2005a: 63–5), for instance, I specify that complexity cannot be equated with markedness in terms of syntactic parameter settings: i.e., that a language could have no inflections, have SVO word order and obligatory subject pronouns (i.e. widely analyzed syntactic parameters set "off") and still have vast batteries of pragmatic particles, seven tones, deeply transformative morphophonemics and morphotonemics, and dummy verbs – which are complexities under the metric I have specified in various sources. In terms of phonology, the fact that grammars are colored to varying extent by shades of distaste for sequential consonants or vowels is unrelated to issues of complexity: there is nothing "complex" about uttering two consonants or vowels in juxtaposition, regardless of how rarely or commonly grammars allow it to occur.

Anne-Marie Brousseau in her article is more aware that markedness is of marginal import to complexity, in her demonstration that Haitian's accentual system is a compromise between French and Fongbe in terms of markedness, rather than a less marked system. She presents several interesting observations, such as that the reason French-based creoles never have tone or pitch-accent even when their substrates were tonal is that because French stress occurs at the end of phrases, tone language speakers are not able to re-analyze word-based stress patterns as tonal. But her interest is not in whether Haitian's markedness is "complex," but in examining how the Haitian system complies with predictions of the Full Transfer/Full Access Mode hypothesis of second language acquisition (Schwartz & Spouse 1996).

Markedness also applies to the issue of segmental inventories. The difference between older languages and creoles extends to this: for instance, Kabardian's /ś/ is alveopalatal while /š/ is palatoalveolar; no creole has as copious and fine-grained a consonantal system as Kabardian, and while Kabardian has only two underlying vowel phonemes, the rules conditioning their surface appearance as several more allophones create a complexity of generation of surface vowels unknown to me in any creole language. Similarly, an underlying /w/ often surfaces in Kabardian not as, say, /v/ or /u/, but /p/ – still labial, but distant in a fashion that phonologists analyzing Haitian do not present for that creole.

Christian Uffmann's article interestingly shows that in their, at most, moderately copious segmental inventories, creoles switch from the faithfulness tendency they hew to in their phonologies to a higher ranking of markedness constraints. Crucially, while markedness constraints occasion generative complexity in phonological processes, in generating segmental inventories they simplify. Thus Ndjuka's main two substrate languages were Gbe and Kikongo. Gbe mid vowels have ATR distinctions (e/ɛ, o/ɔ) and include a schwa, while Kikongo has a basic five vowel system ([a, e, i, o, u]). Ndjuka reproduces the Kikongo vowels, not the Gbe ones, ranking the markedness constraint *[-ATR] higher than the faithfulness one (IDENT(ATR)):

Table 20. Optimality Theory account for the recruitment of source language vowels in Ndjuka

/ɛ/	*[-ATR]	IDENT(ATR)
[ɛ]	*!	
☞ [e]		*

Creoles, then, discourage the surface appearance of marked vowels, such that segmental inventories remain modest in distinct contrast to older languages like Kabardian – or French, whose three front rounded vowels, schwa, and back [ɑ] are absent in Haitian Creole, as Uffmann notes.

This is significant because it is further evidence that creolization will not reduce to a matter of the prioritization of qualitatively equivalent structural parameters, such as contextual over inherent morphology or, in this case, faithfulness over markedness constraints. If creoles preferred faithfulness across the board in their sound systems, then they would have relatively shallow phonological processes but richer segmental inventories: we could imagine, for example, a Haitian with unremarkable derivational depth in terms of determiner allomorphs, but a segmental inventory reproducing its substrate language Fongbe's. But this is not what happens. Instead, the essence of creolization would appear to be simplification, accomplished via whatever permutation of Universal Grammar's alternations will create it, even when this requires a different alternation in one part of the grammar than in another.

2.2.2.5. Emergent versus entrenched complexity

Finally, both Klein's paper and another one on Haitian phonology by Albert Valdman and Iskra Iskrova show something common in creole grammars: the more saliently complex aspects tend strongly to be optional rather than obligatory – which can be taken as evidence that they have only existed for a few centuries (cf. McWhorter 2005a: 115–20). Klein notes that in some Haitian varieties, glides are inserted between noun and determiner only after tense vowels (thus "the glass" is [vɛ a] rather than [vɛ ja]). However, this is a variable feature across Haitian dialects. One can imagine a future Haitian in which glide insertion is obligatorily indexed to vocalic tenseness – but it does not exist at present.

Similarly, Valdman & Iskrova posit underlying nasal phonemes in Haitian to distinguish minimal pairs like [pan] "breakdown" and [pãn] "to hang," and chart a progressive nasalization rule for forms whose codas vary when derived: [vãn] "to sell" would be underlyingly /vãd/, with the coda nasal when the root occurs alone, but not when it is followed by an affix that resyllabifies the root's coda as an onset of the second syllable ([vã.dɛz] "saleswoman"). But in Haitian nasalization processes beyond this, Valdman and Iskrova stipulate a degree of optionality that suggests that Haitian Creole in 2500 AD may be a language with an intricate battery of regressive and progressive nasal assimilation rules both phonological and morphophonological, but which today exist only as a series of tendencies: [fanal] ~ [fãnal] "lantern," [padõ] "pardon" > [padõnɛ̃] ~ [padone] "to pardon," etc. Valdman and Iskrova even note that early documents of Haitian have much less of this nasalization, showing that it is indeed a change in progress (another indication of which is that the variation is not dialectal, but intra-speaker). They also tell us that the nasalization fails to occur in twice as many words as it does – in other words, at present the tendencies are rather weak.

Or: Sabine Lappe and Ingo Plag discuss word-final epenthesis in Sranan and its conditioning by vowel harmony, showing that one in four cases of epenthesis flout the harmony: *musu* "must" but *busi* "bush," *waka* "walk" but *dagu* "dog." Predictably they show that documentation proves that even this degree of structure in the system arose only over time. Lappe and Plag are mainly committed to examining whether a connectionist model produces fewer overgeneralizations of the harmony than a rule-based account, and find that in fact it makes little difference. The lesson would appear to be that Sranan is indeed "a real language" in having data to submit to connectionist analysis – but an obvious contrast remains between this emergent and partial vowel harmony and the more regularized and morphophonemically sensitive harmony systems in older languages. Igbo ATR vowel harmony is categorical within words except for a very few exceptions: *ugo* "eagle," *ụdị* "sort," and it is sensitive to morphological categories in applying to inflections – *si-ghi* "did not cook," *sị-ghị* "did not tell" – but not to (most) aspect markers *i-bi-kọ-rị-ta* INF-live-ASSOC-APPL-DIREC "to live together to one another's advantage" (Zsiga 1997: 233–4). Creoles "have phonology," but never of this type.

2.3. Finding chaos amidst order?

There are also cases in which authors' analyses of creole grammars' complexity could be countered by less elaborated and arbitrary treatments of the same data. As in many of the above cases, while complexity itself is clearly on view, the issue is whether we are faced with complexity of such an extent that the creole could be mistaken as an older language. Nicholas Faraclas' piece on Tok Pisin is a crucial example.

2.3.1. Tok Pisin adjectives

His presentation, quite valuable in itself, shows that conventional analyses of Tok Pisin's *-pela* morpheme as merely rendering stative verbs as attributive adjectives is a vast oversimplification. A superficial conception of *-pela* is that it simply marks adjectives when used attributively, as in *kol-pela ples* "cold place," and is not affixed in predicate position (*ples i kol* "the place is cold").

But Faraclas argues that in fact, property items in Tok Pisin fall into five classes (276–7):

1. Some occur either before or after the noun, but when occurring before, are optionally affixed with -*pela:* "cold house" is *haus kol, kol haus,* or *kolpela haus.*
2. Some occur only before the noun and must appear affixed with -*pela:* *bikpela haus* "big house" (**bik haus,* **haus bik,* *haus bikpela)
3. Some do not take -*pela* and occur only before the noun: *liklik haus* "small house"
4. Some do not take -*pela* and occur only after the noun: *haus nogut* "bad house"
5. Some do not take -*pela* and occur either before or after the noun: *mau banana / banana mau* "ripe banana"

Faraclas' main point is that the behavior of -*pela* has been Eurocentrically misanalyzed, such that Tok Pisin has no adjectives but instead uses -*pela* as a nominalizer, in a fashion presumably "complex" to a degree hitherto unnoticed. One argument for this is that -*pela* can be used to form abstract nouns: *longpela* "length." Then, he sees support in that Tok Pisin's substrate languages have a morpheme that is more obviously an associative linker between nominals that also occurs in the same range of functions as -*pela*. Thus Kuanua's *na,* for example, associates two nominals:

(7)   *mapi na   davai*
       leaf   LINKER tree
       'tree leaf' (276)

but also uses the item with preposed property items:

(8)   *pua   na   pal*
       white LINKER house
       'white house' (275)

and to nominalize (*lolovi-**na*** "length" [273]).

For one, if -*pela* were a nominalizer, then this would not be, necessarily, "complex" – it would just mean that Tok Pisin grammar were different, in an interesting fashion, from English. But actually, the data that Faraclas presents do not conclusively demonstrate his intended case that Tok Pisin has no true adjectives. To the extent that nominals with -*pela* like *longpela* are intended as an important demonstration, this usage is quite marginal, comprising only three forms, all of measurement (Verhaar 1995: 18) (-*pasin* from *fashion* is the usual abstract nominalizer, as in *gutpasin* "goodness" [Mühlhäusler 1985: 625]).

Then, elsewhere the nominalizer argument becomes rather strained. For example, -*pela* is also used to pluralize pronouns: *mi* "I," *mipela* "we (exclusive)," *yu* "you," *yupela* "you (pl.)." Faraclas would subsume even these usages of -*pela* under the nominalizing one, here "denoting an abstract or generalized instantiation of the item to which it is attached" (274). But this implies that *mipela* "we," based on *mi* "I," parses along the lines of, perhaps, "*I*-ness" or "a larger conception of the 'I'." But the question would then be what independently motivates this analysis rather than the more immediately plausible one of treating -*pela* as a simple marker of plurality in this usage. I am aware of no treatments of such numeral morphemes in other grammars as "nominalizers." If the *longpela*-type forms are intended as justifying this rather athletic notion of nominalization, then we return to the fact that Tok Pisin only uses -*pela* as a nominalizer in three words. Reasonable linguistic analysis, even fully watchful for the biases conditioned by Standard Average European, will treat this usage of -*pela* as marking plurality; it is no more likely as a nominalizer than -*teen* is in English, where its contribution is obviously that of connoting "ten." Thus the pronominal reflex of -*pela* is distinct from the attributional one. (Crowley 1990: 285 is skeptical of Faraclas' treatment of -*pela* in this vein, given that the cognate -*fala* in Tok Pisin's close sister creole Bislama behaves quite differently from morphemes like Kuanua's *na*.)

But as to the behavior of -*pela* elsewhere, Faraclas' presentation leaves plausible that it is indeed, primarily, a marker of attributive adjectives, which would also take in the numerals (*paippela haus* "five houses") and demonstratives (*dispela man* "this man") that he would also analyze as underlyingly nominal (presumably, "a fiveness of houses," for example).

Where his argument bears upon complexity, then, is in the fact that -*pela* appears only when adjectives are preposed rather than postposed to the nominal, and then often only variably, or even not at all, in which case then, adjectives are stipulated as either preposed, postposed, or both. The issue would seem to be, specifically, a degree of lexical stipulation for affixation and placement that we would not expect according to my hypothesis that creolization decreases complexity. Faraclas' description of the five classes of adjectives implies that their affixation and positioning is arbitrary to a degree reminiscent of, say, broken plurals in Arabic, in which it is unpredictable which of about eight nonconcatenative patterns most nouns form their plurals with, requiring lexical storage (*qalam, 'aqlām* "pen, pens," *bayt, buyūt* "house, houses," *kalb, kilāb* "dog, dogs," *kitāb, kutub* "book, books," *šahr,* *'ašhur* "month, months" and so on).

But in fact, the appearance of *-pela* and the placement of adjectives is not unconstrained to anything approaching that degree in Tok Pisin. Faraclas' analysis, intended as showing that Tok Pisin has complexity, in fact neglects regular grammatical conditioning of the morpheme's appearance. Supplementing Faraclas' description with four others (Hall 1943, Mihalic 1971, Wurm & Mühlhäusler 1985, Verhaar 1995), the basic picture is this:

1) The default is that adjectives can occur either before or after the noun: *aipas man* / *man aipas* "blind man."

2) The affixation of *-pela* is conditioned by phonotactics. If the adjective is bisyllabic it takes *-pela* only if neither syllable has a coda: thus *hevipela* "heavy," *arapela* "other," but *lapun* "old," *longlong* "crazy," *wankain* "same," *planti* "many," etc. (Sources often simply say that disyllabics in general do not take *-pela* [Hall 1943: 25, Mihalic 1971: 19]; to acknowledge complexity as much as possible I am presenting what appears to be the actual conditioning.) Then trisyllabic adjectives never take *-pela* regardless of coda: *namabawan* "first rate," *namabatu* "second rate" (Verhaar 1995: 14).

3) When it is licensed by syllable number and type, *-pela* is obligatorily affixed when an adjective occurs before the noun: *ples kol* / *kolpela ples* "cold place"). (Faraclas is unique among the sources in listing *-pela*'s occurrence on preposed adjectives as only optional, and in giving monosyllabic *mau* "ripe" as not taking *-pela* [e.g. Verhaar 1995: 16 lists *mau* as preposed and taking *-pela*]).

4) Some adjectives occur only preposed. With monosyllabic and light bisyllabic ones, this means that the form marked with *-pela* is the only one; these are high-usage items like *bikpela* (**bik*) "big." About a dozen other adjectives too heavy to take *-pela* also occur only preposed, such as *liklik* "small." Verhaar (1995: 172–3) gives a few items of this type that are monosyllabic (*fri* "free," *las* "last," *neks* "next") or light bisyllabic (*holi* "holy," *mama* "mother") and yet do not take *-pela,* but they are all neologisms borrowed from English, thus falling outside of the native lexicon, except for *mama* whose usage is indistinguishable from compounding. Among heavier adjectives, *liklik* is the sole outlier in that it takes *-pela* (*liklikpela*) (Mihalic 1971: 19, Verhaar 1995: 172–3, *contra* Faraclas' data), likely because of its heavy usage.

5) There are some monosyllabic adjectives that do not take -*pela,* and therefore always occur postposed. The membership of this class varies from source to source; for example, Mihalic, Wurm & Mühlhäusler and Verhaar include *wail* "wild" and *wel* "oily," but these occur with -*pela* in online sources. Surely, this is symptomatic of the fact that Tok Pisin varies greatly according to region, register, period of elicitation, pidgin or creole status, etc. However, all sources indicate that there is such a class in the grammar. There are also a few disyllabic adjectives that only occur postposed.

Faraclas' description, it would appear, presents five "classes" where a more graceful analysis is a phonotactic rule – -*pela* only affixes monosyllables and light disyllables – plus a morphosyntactic one – -*pela* only occurs when the modifier is preposed – and then two groups of exceptions: a group of adjectives that only occur preposed, and a group that only occur postposed.

As to complexity, Faraclas' presentation is useful in showing that Tok Pisin indeed has some. The -*pela* affix's conditioning by phonotactics is reminiscent of the similar conditioning of the -*er* comparative versus the *more* comparative in English (*bigger, heavier,* but **reliabler,* *comfortabler). That some adjectives can only occur either preposed or postposed is similar to the fact a small class of Romance adjectives, in languages in which adjectives are reguarly postposed, can occur preposed as well, and so on.

Faraclas, then, demonstrates that affixation and placement are not strictly regular for Tok Pisin adjectives. Yet, it is unclear that Faraclas has demonstrated that, as he has it, -*pela* signifies that Tok Pisin has a "rich, nuanced and multifacteted morphosyntax." If we allow that just possibly a single morpheme might be so multifarious in its behavior that it alone could constitute a "rich, nuanced and multifaceted morphosyntax," then -*pela,* its complexities acknowledged, is not the best candidate for an example.

2.3.2. Finnish: a truly rich, nuanced and multifaceted morphosyntax

Let's compare it, for example, with the marking of a single category in an older language: the partitive in Finnish (data from Karlsson 1999). The basic pattern is that the marker is -*a* after most short vowels, -*tta* after -*e,* and *ta* elsewhere (including long vowels and diphthongs): *talo-a* "house," *kone-tta* "machine," *ajatus-ta* "thought," *maa-ta* "country."

However, this sensitivity to phonology goes further: the allomorphs occur in alternate forms according to vowel harmony, in which if the stem has no back vowels, an alternate allomorph occurs: *païvä-ä* "day," *perhe-ttä* "family," *syy-tä* "reason."

But – *-ta,* the "elsewhere" morpheme, also occurs with many stems that end in short vowels, because the partitive is actually generated from the stem as it occurs with the genitive marker, and in many cases is built on that stem with an elided *e* that leaves the consonant before it as the final segment and thus conditioning *-ta: kieli* "language," but not **kieli-ä* because the genitive is *kiel-en,* and thus the partitive is *kiel-tä.* Then, there are exceptions that must be stored by rote: despite ending in *-e, itse* "self," *kolme* "three," *nukke* "doll," and many proper names ending in *-e* take *-a* instead of *-tta.*

Thus – *-pela*'s appearance is sensitive to phonotactics, and appears only variably on some adjectives. The Finnish partitive marker always appears when the semantics stipulate it, but varies allomorphically according to segment class and vowel quality, is conditioned partly by underlying root forms that never surface, and then, like *-pela,* requires some rote storage as well.

Meanwhile, there are further complications when the partitive occurs with the plural suffix *-i.* Most basically, with plural marking, *-a* appears after stems ending in short vowels and *-ta* after stems ending in long vowels – with the vowel harmony still applying, and morphophonemic rules changing *i* to *j* between vowels and shortening the long vowel with plural affixation:

talo "house," talo-j-a "houses"
perhe "family," perhe-i-tä "families"
maa "country," ma-i-ta "countries"

But this leaves a question as to which allomorph appears when the stem ends with a consonant. In fact, all such stems are transformed into vowel-final ones in the genitive, and properly, the partitive is based on these inflected stems. Thus for consonant-final roots, the plural allomorph is assigned on the basis of whether the *inflected* stem ends in a short (i.e. conditioning *-a*) or long (i.e. conditioning *-ta*) vowel. Thus *nainen* "woman," genitive *naise-n,* partitive plural *nais-i-a,* but *rikas* "rich," genitive *rikaa-n,* and thus partitive plural *rikka-i-ta.*

Then syllabicity comes into play just as in Tok Pisin, as well in conjunction with arbitrary lexical specification and variability. *Some* nouns with three or more syllables take *-ta* in the plural even though they end in a short vowel: *lukija* "reader," *lukijo-i-ta* "readers," (in which the stem-final *-o* is conditioned by a morphophonemic rule activated by an assortment of features that hardly constitute a natural class, but which needs not concern us here). However, with many such words, *-a* is possible as well. Meanwhile, all of this applies only to nouns; trisyllabic adjectives behave in the normal way.

Finally, while with pronominals *-pela* is affixed to singular forms with no phonetic distortion, the Finnish partitive with pronominals is riddled with irregularity: *minä* "I," partitive *minua, se* "it," partitive *sitä,* and so on.

Importantly, I have by no means chosen the most baroque comparison possible. Partitive marking in Finnish's close sister Estonian is so much more elaborate in terms of complex interaction with its notoriously complex consonant gradations plus rampant irregularity that its very learnability seems almost questionable. Partitive marking in Finnish is useful here because despite its complexity, it lends itself relatively well to brief description. This, it would seem, is "rich, nuanced and multifaceted morphosyntax" – or at least, of a degree incontrovertibly more than some adjectives occurring only before or after the noun and *-pela*'s being not used above a certain syllabic weight total.

The question, then, is what creole displays complexity of the degree of partitive marking in Finnish. Here, the question as to whether it is inappropriate that I use an inflectional category as a comparison is inapplicable, because attributive *-pela* is itself an inflection. If creoles are as complex as older languages, then why does *-pela* not occur in various allomorphs, occasioning assorted distortions of the stems to which it is affixed and creating true "classes" of adjective in the paradigmatic sense, rather than there being small, closed sets of adjectives that exhibit specific behaviors?

2.3.3. Tok Pisin's substrate languages: more truly rich, nuanced and multifaceted morphosyntax

Faraclas also argues that the equivalents of *-pela* in Tok Pisin's Austronesian and Papuan substrate languages are more regular in their behavior, such that *-pela* qualifies as more complex than its sources. But if that happens to be true with this one morpheme, Faraclas elides that the grammars of those ancient languages are, overall, visibly more complex in myriad ways than Tok Pisin. For example, one substrate language that Faraclas includes for comparison is the Oceanic language Kwaio. Kwaio's pronominals are indexed to number to a cross-linguistically superlative degree, with dual, paucal *and* plural forms (Keesing 1985: 28):

Table 21. Kwaio pronouns

	singular	dual	paucal	plural
first person (inclusive)	(i)nau	('i)da'a	('i)dauru	gia
first person (exclusive)		('e)me'e	('e)meeru	('i)mani
second person	(i)'oo	('o)mo'o	('o)mooru	('a)miu
third person	ngai(a)	('i)ga'a	('i)gauru	gila

To be sure, Tok Pisin and its sister creoles Bislama and Solomon Islands Pijin have inclusivity distinctions in their plural pronouns, such as *yumi* "we (inclusive)" versus *mipela* "we (exclusive)." However, none of them are even remotely as overspecified in this regard as Kwaio. Keesing referred to Kwaio as a principal substrate language of Solomon Islands Pijin, and the pronominal issue was one of many contrasts between the two languages that led Keesing (1988) to argue that Solomon Islands Pijin (and by extension its sister creoles) incorporated substrate features in simplified form.

Or, Faraclas makes brief mention of Tok Pisin's genitive/associative marker *bilong,* as in *pikinini bilong Sipik* "child of the Sepik" (282). But Kwaio overtly marks much finer shades of this relation than Tok Pisin and its sisters do. For example, Kwaio has an equivalent of *bilong, na,* likely cognate with the Kuanua *na* that Faraclas focuses on: *oga-na boo* 'pig-GEN belly' "a pig's belly." But this is only used in Kwaio if the part is attached. There is another marker assigned to detached parts of an object, that changes morphophonemically according to the final vowel of the referent (Keesing 1985: 15–6):

Table 22. Kwaio genitive marking

oga	oga-'e boo	"a belly section of pork"
fote	fote-'e	"shoulder blade of"
lasi	lasi-'i	"head of"
lodo	lode-'e	"seed of"
nunu	nunu-'i	"shade of"

Note that with *o*-final nominals, alteration extends to the stem as well, with the final *o* changing to *e*. But then, this is suspended in the specific case that the preceding nominal is deverbal: *bulo* ("twist"): *bulo-'e firi* "rope of domestic tobacco."

In any grammar of the various Papuan and Austronesian languages that can be treated as substrate languages of Tok Pisin, there are ample instances of this kind that are unknown in Tok Pisin or its sisters. These older languages are rife with paradigmatic specifications sensitive to phonology and assorted fine-grained semantic categories, elaborated additionally by irregularities. Tok Pisin, in contrast, has some phonotactically conditioned affixation and a modest degree of lexically specified head-modifier order. The reason for this is that while Tok Pisin is a young language, its substrate languages are ancient.

2.3.4. Nubi Creole Arabic: the nature of arbitrariness

The same argument applies to Kihm's depiction of Nubi Creole Arabic as displaying six different ways of encoding the plural, including two fossilized triconsonantal root patterns, some fossilized dual-marking, and three suffixes. Kihm implies that this creole distributes pluralization strategies randomly across nouns, when in fact, one of them, suffixation of -*á,* is the productive construction while the others are compact numbers of exceptions to be learned by rote (Heine 1982, Owens 1991: 14, Owens 1997: 153, Luffin 2005: 134–56). Kihm's statement that the creole's plural formation is "even more unpredictable than it is in the lexifier" cannot stand, given that in all colloquial Arabic varieties including Nubi's lexifier Sudanese Arabic (Kaye & Rosenhouse 1997: 283–4), pluralization applies in truly unpredictable fashion in several different "broken plural" strategies with none of them the default. It is no accident that of the strategies Kihm lists, the -*á* suffix is the regular one: it is typical of creolization in replacing the arbitrary and marked with the regular and unmarked – here, a simple suffix. Scattered exceptions amidst a general pattern occasion a degree of complexity greater than pure regularity, but not one as extreme as arbitrary distribution across multiple patterns.

2.3.5. Plural inflections: calques on the ancient or signs of the new?

Marlyse Baptista's article on plural inflections in creoles is another example where it can be argued that complexity is being claimed where others would see confirmation that the languages in question are recent products of pidgins. Against my Prototype characterization of creoles as lacking inflectional affixation, Baptista shows that many creoles variably use the plural suffix of their lexifier languages. She refers to examples such as Cape Verdean, where there are even cases of head-modifier agreement in this marking (318–9):

(9)   *Rapariga-s   txiga   sedu.*
       young.woman-PL arrive early
       'The young women arrived early.'

(10)   *Ah! Ke-s   djenti-s   la.*
       Oh DEM-PL person-PL there
       "Oh! Those people."

She shows similar plural affixation as attested in Guinea-Bissau Creole Portuguese, Palenquero Creole Spanish, and Ghanaian Pidgin English.

Yet it is germane that these are all creoles that have always been spoken in diglossic relationships with their lexifier languages. Baptista considers one Cape Verdean dialect she cites from as disqualified from that analysis because its speakers have been isolated from the rest of Cape Verdean society – and presumably Portuguese – since 1940 (317). However, the creole has existed for five centuries, and thus the social history of this group does not rule out that their speech variety was influenced by Portuguese until 1940, and there is no reason to suppose that the plural marking would drop out of the grammar over the succeeding sixty years.

I have specified (e.g. McWhorter 2005a: 29–32) that creoles can be divided into those that have existed in diglossic relationships with their lexifiers and thus are drawn somewhat from the Prototype and those that have emerged and thrived apart from the lexifier. In the volume under review, Veenstra presents a useful contrast in this vein. Louisiana Creole French has developed in contact with the vernacular French of white descendants of Acadians (Cajun French), and thus has a verbal alternation between short and long forms for tense in most verbs (from Neumann 1985: 196):

(11)(a)   *Sop-la   frem a sez-er.*
          shop-DET close at six-o'clock
          'The shop (always) closes at six o'clock.

   (b)   *Sop-la   freme a sez-er.*
          shop-DET close at six-o'clock
          'The shop closed at six o'clock.'

But in Mauritian Creole, which has developed in a much less intimate relationship with French, the short/ long distinction occurs in only a certain subset of verbs rather than most, and is linked not to a semantic distinction (or, for the generativist, functional category) but conditioned by a syntactic wrinkle. The short form occurs when the verb is followed by a subcategorized element within VP, and otherwise the long form occurs: *Pye ti manz min* "Peter ate Chinese noodles;" *Pyer ti manze Rozil* "Peter ate at Rose Hill" where a PP adjunct follows the verb rather than an argument (Veenstra in volume under review, 305). And then again, this is only evidenced in some verbs: most Mauritian verbs are invariant in all contexts.

Even here, however, we are dealing with the French plantation creoles, which all developed in diglossic relationships with French. Creoles that developed completely independently of their lexifiers retain even less reflection of Indo-European apparatus. To return to plural marking, for instance, the Surinam Creoles and the Portuguese creoles of the Gulf of Guinea have no vestige of lexifier plural marking – or any regular inflection. Thus it is reasonable to attribute the plural inflections Baptista calls attention to as, indeed, contact phenomena.

Nevertheless, Baptista also specifies that in all of these cases, the markers are used not in all cases of plurality, but when the referent is either animate, definite, or both. She intends this as evidence that the plural marking is systematically conditioned by semantics – i.e. that creoles have "grammar" and thus complexity. But this conditioning, quite consistent across the creoles she notes and also typical of unbound plural markers in other creoles, actually has implications for the issue of creoles' youth.

For a plural marker to be restricted to animates and/or definites is not just one of many possible configurations, but primal in the developmental sense. Across languages, plural marking typically first becomes conventionalized in exactly this realm, and only later becomes obligatory for all plural entities as in European languages. For example, at one extreme, languages mark plurality in pronouns – the quintessence of animacy and definiteness – but usually not with nouns, such as Mandarin Chinese (Comrie 1989:190). Inanimates are the last members in the implicational hierarchy of plural marking's extent in grammars (Dixon 1979: 85). Definiteness is also at the top of an implicational hierarchy, at the bottom of which is nonreferential indefinites (generics) (Croft 1990: 116).

That is: there are apparently no languages that pluralize inanimate indefinite nouns but not animate definite ones; rather, some languages give overt plural marking to a particular subset of possible cases, animates and definites, while others mark increasingly larger subsets to the point of covering all possible cases (with allowances made for grammars' different impositions of count vs. mass distinctions in cases such as English *hair* and French's *cheveux*). As usual, creoles hew to the more abbreviative end of that continuum.

Baptista herself notes (328) Mühlhäusler's (1981) observation that Tok Pisin's plural marker *ol* was first used to mark humans, and later spread to non-animates. This pathway is typical, in fact, of noun phrase modifiers in general, an example being the incipient indefinite article in Syrian and Egyptian Arabic (Classical Arabic does not have one), which currently is used only with humans (Brustad 2000: 18–43).

Baptista, however, proposes that the creoles she refers to have the animate/definite distinction not as a preliminary stage in the spread of plural marking, but as an inheritance from their substrate languages (328–9), which implies that the creoles' youth is not why they restrict their plural marking as they do. She demonstrates this by noting that, for example, Malinke, a substrate language of Cape Verdean, has similarly conditioned plural marking. But this brings us to a common muddy area in arguments about the source of creole structures, in which substrate languages have features which, in their equivalents in the creoles, happen to also be analyzable as results of pidgin origins.

A typical example is analyticity: it is often claimed that creoles with isolating substrate languages like Twi, Fongbe and Yoruba are analytic because they are modelled on those languages, whereas others would argue that the resemblance there is accidental, and that the creoles are analytic because they were born as pidgins. Another example is that those same African languages have serial verbs. Many argue that creoles created by their speakers have serial verbs because of transfer, but Bickerton (1981), Byrne (1987) and Veenstra (1996) have argued that the resemblance is, again, accidental, and that the creoles have serialization as a way of encoding case relations and aspectual concepts in the face of the minimal number of grammatical items they inherit from their pidgin stages.

In the case of analyticity, however, Palenquero has always stood as a suggestion that the pidgin analysis is correct for that feature. Palenquero's sole substrate language was Kikongo (Schwegler 1993, 1996), a highly agglutinative language, and yet Palenquero is an analytic language except for its (variable) plural suffixation inherited from Spanish with animates and definites; otherwise it retained a single Kikongo inflection, the plural one, again used with animates and definites, and as a clitic. In that light, Palenquero is also decisive in deciding whether this animate/definite plural marking in some creoles is modelled on the substrate's grammar. The case is likely impossible to decide conclusively with Cape Verdean and Guinea-Bissau Creole Portuguese, because their substrates include Malinke and close relatives like Mandinka that restrict plural marking to animates and defintes; similarly, Ghanaian Pidgin

English is spoken by people whose indigenous languages are isolating ones like Twi and Gã that also use plural marking restricted in that fashion.

But regarding Palenquero, plural marking in Kikongo and Bantu languages in general is not linked to animacy or definiteness. Rather, Kikongo's plural marking is more general, as we would expect of a language where the plural marker is bound, suggesting long-term heavy usage during which it would be surprising if plural marking had not spread beyond the initial phase of optionally marking animates and definites. Thus:

(12) *N-sumba-nga o* **ma**-*ki.*
      I-buy-PROG ART PL-egg
      'I am buying eggs.'

(Bentley 1887: 608)

where *maki* is marked for plural despite being neither animate nor definite, or with an adjectival:

(13) **M**-*ambote kaka n-zol-ele.*
      PL-good   only I-want-PERF
      'I only want good ones.'

(ibid. 556)

It is true that of Kikongo's fifteen noun classes, in three, singular and plural marking are identical such that plural marking can be treated as neutralized. However, this is an unlikely model for Palenquero's plural marking. For one, *complete absence* of marking in Kikongo would not properly explain its restriction in Palenquero to *specifically the animate and definite*. In addition, while there is a fair share of animates in the two of the three Kikongo classes that contain count nouns (the other contains abstract concepts), there are just as many inanimates in them – *nzo* "house," *nkunga* "song," *nxinga* "string," *mvu* "year" – and crucially, the most animate of animates, humans, occupy not these three classes but two others, in which they do have plural markers: *mbunji, abunji* "little brother, little brothers;" *mundele, mindele* "white man, white men." Finally, even the nouns in classes invariant for plural take modifiers that must be plural-marked, as here, where *nti* and *mvuma* take no plural marking but the modifiers do:

(14) *Nti* **mi**-*awonso* **mi**-*nkwa mvuma* **za**-*mpembe.*
      tree PL-all   PL-having flower PL-white
      'all trees which have white flowers'

(ibid. 563)

There is, then, no model for Palenquero's animate/definite plural marking in Kikongo, which is overall a grammar in which plurality is marked redundantly regardless of animacy or definiteness.

Therefore, the data Baptista presents show not simply that "creoles have inflection," but that creoles in long-standing contact with their lexifiers have inherited their plural inflections but use them in much more restricted fashion than the lexifier does. Moreover, this restricted usage is not just a calque on the same feature in ancient substrate languages, such that we would be seeing a mere transfer of grammar – i.e. "complexity" – from substrate to creole. The reason that when creoles have -*s* plural suffixes they only use them with a small subset of plural referents is because they are marking plurality in a fashion that is typical cross-linguistically of *incipient* plural marking, in pidgins, creoles, and even older languages.

In this vein, Tonjes Veenstra's article treats the vestigial French inflections in creoles like those above as evidence that creoles are born from the stage called The Basic Variety (Klein & Perdue 1997), exemplified by French learners who often pass through (or stop at) a stage alternating between inflected and uninflected verb forms with no functional distinction. Mauritian is different from fully aqcuired French, then, in that at a certain point learners in Mauritius took the Basic Variety as the target and assigned structure to its materials, and hence the conditioning of the -*e* inflection in Mauritian Creole. Veenstra, correctly in my view, notes that this characterization contradicts ideas such as that creoles are simply relexifications of substrate languages (Lefebvre 1998), and squarely treats creolization as a kind of second language acquisition. The plural marking that Baptista points to can be subsumed under exactly the same analysis.

2.4. Clarifications necessary

Finally, there are articles in which it appears that I have not been sufficiently clear in my exposition. A key example is Maria Braun and Ingo Plag (henceforth BP) in YM, who take issue with my point that creoles only develop complexity over time by showing that even in its earliest documentation, Sranan has derivational affixes, compounding, and semantic opacity.

The problem is that my thesis does not treat any of those three features as arising only over time.

2.4.1. No language is purely compositional,
        and all languages have "semantic opacity"

I do not, for example, claim that creoles have no affixes, but that they tend to have few or no *inflectional* affixes; as early as McWhorter (1998), the article that began the creole complexity debate, I readily note that Haitian Creole and others have derivational affixes. Rather, my claim is that in creoles, derivational affixes have yet to devolve into noncompositional contributions to their combinations with roots, as in the English *understand* or the Russian *najti* "to find," composed of the prefix for "to" plus the root for "to be."

Thus, BP's listing of early Sranan's derivational affixes is well-taken, but applies to my thesis only in whether it includes semantically opaque affix-root combinations. It does not: all of the examples that they give with *-man* (*helpiman* "helper"), abstract nominalizers *-sanni* (*lau* "be mad," *lausanni* "folly"), and *-fasi* (*pori* "to spoil," *porifasi* "depravity") and *-tentîn* ("teen" as in *tutentîn* "twenty") are semantically predictable: as we would expect of a language that was brand new and based on a pidgin. Similarly, Margot Van Den Berg's demonstration in the volume under review that Sranan's *-man* emerged not as an element in a compound but as an affix from the outset can be taken as implying that creoles have derivation at their birth – which is thoroughly consonant with my claims about creole morphology.

Crucially, the diagnostic is cases of truly opaque lexicalization: there is no claim that a human language can exist in which affix-root combinations' meanings are not often somewhat narrower than the compositional semantics alone imply, given that languages are spoken amidst living cultures and refer to the real world (cf. Matthews 1974: 193–4 on *institutionalization*). Thus I cannot agree with Patrick Steinkrüger's assessment in his chronicle of derivation in Chabacano Philippines Creole Spanish that its reduplication and compounding are "in many cases" "semantically opaque." There are no cases in his lists that bypass ordinary institutionalization: *kaminá* "to walk," *kamina-kaminá* "to stroll;" or *kanto-y-pláya* "seashore" vs. *kánto del apláya* "edge of the beach." As welcome as data on this long under-documented creole are, for instance, it is unclear to me that the *y*-compound is semantically "opaque" to any degree even if it falls slightly closer to the lexicalization pole than the one with *del*.

Similarly, in YM Claire Lefebvre treats as "unpredictable" diminutive forms such as *ti-devan* DIM-front "genitals" and *ti-bourik* DIM-donkey "rude person." Certainly we cannot *predict* that all or even most human languages will render a rude person as a small donkey. But the equation of compositionality with pure predictability is an artifact of the stringently constrained purview of generative grammar, which Lefebvre works in. This is sufficient for answering the questions relevant to that realm, but inadequate and misrepresentative of the questions posed in a thesis such as mine, which refers to diachrony and the gradient degrees of *analyzability* (Bauer 1988: 61) inherent to it. It is not *analyzable* that comprehension is denoted by a combination of *under* and *stand* in English: here is opacity. In contrast, it is quite *analyzable* that a rude person might be referred to 1) as a donkey rather than, say, a rabbit, and 2) with a diminutive – since pejorativity is one of the prototypical cross-linguistic uses of the diminutive (Jurafsky 1996) (in English, *Why, that little. . .!*). Otherwise Lefebvre presents examples of noncompositionality with Haitian prefix *de-*, which I discuss at length in McWhorter (2005a: 25–8) and treat as evidence that Haitian has been colored by ongoing contact with its lexifier language, an old one in which affixes like this have had millennia to drift into true noncompositionality.

Meanwhile, I have not addressed compounding at all in my work on creoles – for the simple reason that all languages have it, including the most analytic ones (in which, in fact, it tends to be especially prolific). One could say that to list a language's compounds is rather like documenting that an animal moves. Pidgins are full of compounds; so, then, would even early creoles be.

More pertinent to my claims are BP's examples of what they present as noncompositional derivation-root combinations. An example is the trio of words *faddom* "fall (down)," *liddom* "lie (down)" and *siddom* "sit (down)." BP's data show that if *-dom* was perceived as an affix at all, it was in compositional fashion: unlike in the modern language, *dom* "down" was still current, and all of the verbs have semantics clearly based on its meaning. BP, however, point out that the "roots" in these cases, *fa, li,* and *si,* did not exist independently, and thus would have been semantically opaque.

However, it is not true that a root is semantically opaque simply because it does not occur in isolation. In the English word *ruthless,* the root *ruth,* while listed in large dictionaries, is an archaism, long extinct in the living language. However, the meaning of *ruthless* – "without mercy" – is well-known, and as such, the root *ruth* is not semantically opaque. English speakers are quite aware that since the derivational suffix's denotation is "without," the meaning of the root is *mercy,* based on cases like *hopeless, worthless,* and so on where the root survives in isolation. In the same way, to the early Sranan speaker, the semantic contribution of *fa, li* and *si* would be clear.

Then, today, *dom* (*don* in modern orthography) no longer survives on its own in Sranan. But similarly this does not license supposing that *-don* now qualifies as semantically "opaque," as productivity cannot be equated with analyzability as a morpheme of consistent denotation (cf. Aronoff 1976: 38, Bauer 1988: 61). If *-don* in today's *fadon, lidon* and *sidon* is processed as morphological, then the semantics of all three verbs so clearly include downward movement that it is reasonable to assume that *-don,* as the element they have in common, is processed as conveying that part of these words' meaning – whether it is productive or not. The analogy is with *-ity* in English, barely productive (**spuriosity*) but readily processible as a nominalizer where it occurs (*credulous, credulity; opaque, opacity*).

Beyond this, BP call attention to various cases where sequences of segments in monomorphemic items happen to be identical with words of unrelated semantics, such as that while *nemsheki* is "namesake," *sheki* also means "shake," or that in reference to the term *Saramakka, makka* also means "thorn." These are less opacities than unremarkable results of the fact that in any language, the finiteness of phonetic, and therefore syllabic, inventories means that chance resemblances of this kind will inevitably be a part of any human language. A claim that any human language could be devoid of semantic opacity of this kind would require that there are human beings whose language does not allow, for example, word play.

That chance homonymies are inherent to language also applies to BP's claims of noncompositionality in reduplication, which itself does classify as derivational. For example, "wasp" is *wasiwasi* because one of the regular denotations of reduplication in Sranan is of objects or creatures usually encountered in groups. It happens that *wasi* alone means "wash," but it is questionable that this qualifies as semantic opacity in a structural sense, because to the speaker, the relationship between *wasi* and *wasiwasi* is less opaque than nonexistent. The English speaker, presented with the oddity of a word like *understand,* comes up short in being able to explain what is being "stood under," because *under* has but one connotation, and even its more metaphorically extended one – e.g. in words like *undergo* – does not apply to *understand.* Crucially, there is no alternate meaning of *under* that refers to, for example, an animal, a tool, paint, or ennui. The Sranan speaker, apprised that *wasiwasi* means "wasp" and *wasi* means "wash," will not wonder what wasps have to do with washing. Rather, they will process this as a chance homophony – which I have never claimed creoles would lack. A structurally opaque case here would be if *wasi* meant, for example, "frog," another living creature that is small and locomotes through the air – in which case there would be some cognitive motivation for supposing a morphological relationship between *wasiwasi* and *wasi* that was quizzically unclear.

Similarly, if *wirriwirri* means "hair, grass, leaves," then this is another example of reduplication indicating things occurring in plurality. The fact that there is a word *kappewirri* for "thicket" where *wirri* occurs alone is not "noncompositional," but a case where a morpheme usually encountered reduplicated because of its semantic nature happens, in this instance, not to be. Reduplication in this "aggregate" usage has low functional load: the morphological process itself does not create the denotation of the word, but instead is a process that happens to often be applied to words that already have that denotation inherently. While my thesis refers to distortions of meaning, the early Sranan speaker processed the *wirri* in *kappewirri* as referring to the same entity as *wirriwirri* did. The wrinkle here is one of grammatical, rather than semantic, exception – a morphological process has failed to occur, but leaves semantic denotation clear. It is questionable that "opacity" is at issue.

BP also treat a few reduplicated forms like *gobbogobbo* "peanut" and *busibusi* "cat" as noncompositional because the unreduplicated items do not occur at all in isolation. But the same argument applies: reduplication does not create the aggregate denotation, but merely reiterates it. Peanuts are rarely encountered alone. *Busibusi* is more idiosyncratic: cats are given to coming to one when called with repetitive sibilant utterances, which in English have for time immemorial often been manifested as the set vocative "Here, pussy-pussy!" But this is not noncompositionality: the fact that the unreduplicated root denotes a cat is clear to a Sranan speaker in a way that the semantic contribution of *under* in *understand* is not to a modern English speaker. To wit: the Sranan speaker, asked what a *busi* is, will say that it is a cat except that the word is *busibusi* (as I have ascertained asking the question of speakers of Sranan's source and sister creole Saramaccan in which *cat* is denoted with a similarly reduplicated cognate). The English speaker, asked what is being stood "under" in *understand,* draws a blank.

A true exception would be a reduplicated form referring to an entity that does not have the semantics of any derivational process that reduplication is indexed to. BP do present one, *woijowoijo* "market." There is nothing inherently plural or hypocoristically vocative about a marketplace (unless *woijo* means "booth" which there is no indication of), and so this is certainly a queer instance. But it is also the sole one. Languages leak.

2.4.2. Why don't true lexicalizations get "caught in the net"?

Yet even here, a question might remain about creoles and opaque derivation. Now and then I have been asked at conference presentations why a creole might not incorporate a lexifier's noncompositional derivation-root combinations and therefore display a good portion of the quotient of them that the lexifier does. To wit, we might ask what rules out that an English-based creole would take in semantically noncompositional verb-particle combinations with *up* like *turn up, show up* (as in to embarrass in competition), *put up* (overnight), *take up* (a hobby), *make up* (a face) and others, where the semantic contribution of *up* is neither its core directional one nor the more abstract one of completion (*cook up* [some eggs], *finish up, sew up*).

The answer is that pidgins do not adopt anything but a sliver of a lexifier's lexicon. When a pidgin incorporates some mere hundreds of lexical items (Sranan contains at most about 600 English-derived lexical items [Koefoed & Taranskeen 1996]) – and the vast majority are monomorphemic core concepts most likely to have been perceived by non-native speakers learning the language orally – then sheer chance ensures that only a few examples of any derivational morpheme's combinations with roots will be incorporated. As such, there are not enough occurrences of the morpheme for a learner to perceive a range of its usages from the compositional to the ambiguous. To untutored learners, the morpheme becomes a mere phonetic appendage, likely unnoticed as a unitary phenomenon by most speakers.

Notice, then, that Sranan does *not* include that vast class of verb-particle combinations with *up*. Instead, its derivational apparatus is mostly an internal development. While *-man* has its analogue in English words like *mailman,* more important is that Sranan lacks a reflex of agentive *-er* and uses *-man* even on roots that would take *-er* in English, such as *helpiman*. We might accept Van den Berg's case that this is a substrate transfer from Fongbe. But then, *sanni* (< *something*) and *-fasi* (< *fashion*) are clearly not derivational morphemes in English. Sranan speakers mostly created a new derivational apparatus because the small lexicon it inherited from English was not large enough for derivation to be abstracted from it. (Also, Sranan's derivation is not simply modelled on Fongbe's; it would not submit to point-for-point likeness to Fongbe derivational markers as Lefebvre in YM proposes for Haitian, and in fact I am skeptical that Haitian's derivation corresponds as closely to Fongbe's as Lefebvre claims [McWhorter forthcoming]).

Where we have documentation of pidgins becoming creoles, the internal emergence of derivation is obvious and uncontested, such as in Tok Pisin (Mühlhäusler 1997: 195–7). I propose that in cases like Sranan, even though we will always lack documentation of its original state, the very fact that it uses English words but with largely self-innovated derivation is one of countless indications that it arose in the same way as Tok Pisin – as a pidginized English (cf. McWhorter & Parkvall 2002 for more argumentation that most creoles were born as pidgins). Of course, in the case of creoles that develop and live on in diglossic relationships with their lexifiers, an additional proportion of the lexifier's words will enter the creole over time, and there is no reason that noncompositional derivation, in enough examples to be identifiable within the synchronic representation of the grammar, would not be included in the influx. This is why, for example, French-based creoles like Haitian have some such cases, although all evidence from their gram-mars, histories, and sociohistorical documentation shows that they arose from pidgins as Sranan did (McWhorter & Parkvall 2002, McWhorter 2005a: 27).

An illuminating case on this issue is Bislama, which indeed has incorpora-tions of roots (usually verbs) appended with *-ap* from *up*. Crowley (1990: 305–6) actually presents these as evidence against creoles' "simplicity" (as it happens, addressing passing claims on this score up through the eighties, rather than my claims which I had not published until long afterward). But when he states that "it is almost impossible to make any kind of semantic generalizations about its meaning" (305), Crowley appears to suppose that the only regular denotation of *up* as a verb particle is its vertical one, as in forms like *hangem* "hang," *hangemap* "hang up." However, another more abstract but thoroughly regular denotation of *up* as a particle in English is that of accomplishment or completion (Quirk, Greenbaum, Leech & Svart-vik 1985: 1162; Huddleston & Pullum 2002: 304–5). This reflex of *up* cannot be treated as "irregular" simply because its meaning is more grammatically abstract, and thus less immediately processible especially to the layman, than the one indicating verticality.

This accomplishment/completion denotation is the meaning of *-ap* in al-most all of the cases Crowley presents (this also being the case in his later coverage of the issue in his Bislama grammar of 2004) such as:

Table 23. Lexemes with suffix *-ap* in Bislama

laenem "line up"	laenemap "line up"
miksim "mix"	miksimap "confuse"
fiksim "repair"	fiksimap "repair"
wil "wheel"	wilimap "wind up"
hip "pile"	hipimap "pile up"
ful "full"	fulumap "fill up"

Crowley (1990: 305) presents *fomem / fomemap* as meaning "form a com-mittee," presumably semantically unpredictable, but then in the 2004 source translates it more generally as "establish," in which case it falls under the ac-complishment/completion usage. This also applies to *folem* "follow," *folemap* "take a course, follow a radio show," which simply shows that the morpheme is at least somewhat productive in the language, again encoding a completive concept.

As I noted above, English indeed has a class of truly opaque usages of *up* contrasting with the semantically regular ones encoding accomplishment (cf. Quirk, Greenbaum, Leech & Svartvik 1985: 1163). However, amidst the examples Crowley gives in both sources, I find a sole one: *wekemap* – to suppose that *-ap* here refers to the vertical movement that generally follows waking up would be strained, and to awaken is already an accomplishment or completion, such that *-ap* cannot be read as contributing that facet of the semantics in any synchronic sense. Again, languages leak. But overall, it appears that Bislama almost exclusively selected the particle *up* in cases that lent themselves to regular semantic interpretation. This is what my characterization of creole languages predicts.

2.5. Conclusion

Responses like those in this volume and YM to the thesis that creoles are less complex than older languages eloquently demonstrate that creoles are complex. However, I am less sure that this work makes a conclusive case against a claim that the least complex languages in the world are all creole languages. Ample reference to a wide sample of the languages of the world is not just optional, but crucial to seriously assessing the complexity thesis. Too often, responses to it lend an impression that the only relevant languages for comparison to creoles are, roughly, English, French, Spanish, Portuguese, Dutch, Fongbe and Kikongo.

Of course one might argue that these languages, as older ones, should suffice as comparanda. But for one, authors neglect the degree of difference in complexity between even these and creoles. Kihm, for example, in his conclusion passingly tips his hat to myself in acknowledging that as to creoles, "what morphology they have is rather simple, never based on such processes as apophony, suppletion, etc." (357) – but neglecting that this observation would seem to entail that the difference between Guinea-Bissau Creole Portuguese and Portuguese itself is vaster than a mere matter of Move versus Merge. Also relevant is that while papers in this volume addressing Fongbe only refer to its phonology, and Lefebvre in YM treats its derivational likenesses to Haitian, Fongbe's grammar *overall* conclusively surpasses both Saramaccan (McWhorter 2005a: 122) and Haitian (ibid. 139) in complexity.

And the fact remains that older languages beyond Western Europe and West Africa shed equally crucial light on the issue. That in isolating languages like Akha and Cantonese, free morphemes mark assorted categories absent in creoles refutes attempts to define creoles as simply prioritizing Merge over

Move. Then, inflected languages like Kabardian and Kwaio show that there is a vast degree difference in amount of inflection between languages and the complexity it occasions, such that the fact that creoles often have a touch of inflection cannot be taken as refuting a complexity thesis as if we were dealing with a simple either/or parametrical difference between inflected and isolating.

Languages like Akha, Cantonese, Kabardian and Kwaio are what I view as evidence that creolization creates fascinatingly unusual languages. We must value articles showing that creoles "have phonology" or "have morphology" as evidence that creoles are natural languages. But older languages' phonology and morphology can be much more elaborate and arbitrary than that in any documented creole language – and very often is. This is evidence that creoles are not just hybrids, but are human language a few centuries past rebirth.

Chapter 3
Reconstructing creole: Has "Creole Exceptionalism" been seriously engaged?

3.1. Introduction

In *Deconstructing Creole* (ed. by Umberto Ansaldo, Stephen Matthews and Lisa Lim [Amsterdam: John Benjamins, 2007]), primary editors Umberto Ansaldo and Stephen Matthews assign themselves the task of combatting what they regard as an erroneous strain in creole studies, i.e. the assumption that creoles constitute a distinct type of language, that resulted from unusual sociohistorical circumstances.

The editors are, one senses from the scholarly yet quietly aggrieved tone of their introduction, dismayed that certain creolists have attracted considerable attention with an assumption that there was something unusual about how creole languages emerged, which resulted in creoles being less grammatically complex than older languages, reflecting more closely than older languages the basic core of the human language capacity. Ansaldo and Matthews are committed to an alternate view, that creole languages are distinct only in being the results of contact, and that they are no more or less complex than older languages.

To Ansaldo and Matthews the principal question is this: why would we expect creoles to be a synchronically distinguishable class of languages? The implied answer in their introduction and some of the articles in the volume is that only colonialist biases could lead anyone to suppose that Haitian Creole is identifiably newer – and therefore, less grammatically complex – than Hungarian. More pacifically, they assume that the problem is one of insufficient familiarity with the inner workings of creole grammars, such that a closer look at same will reveal hitherto unknown complexities.

However, one could turn this epistemology upside-down and ask just why would we *not* expect creoles to be identifiable as a synchronic class. Only when technology allowed the relocation of vast numbers of persons from one continent to another permanently did the circumstance ever arise in human history in which vast numbers of adults with a wide assortment of language backgrounds had to 1) quickly acquire an unfamiliar language for everyday use for the rest of their lives, and 2) use their rendition of the new language as the lingua franca of a new community within a community, in which interaction with native speakers of that language was occasional and socially distant.

Certain creolists have assumed that the result under such circumstances would be a pidgin that subsequently expanded into a full language – a creole. However, this creole presumably was not yet accreted with the bells and whistles that millennia of gradual morphing leave on an old language. Ansaldo and Matthews, in contrast, assume that the result in such circumstances would evidence no "break in transmission," as the in-house jargon has it, and that the natural language the slaves created by the slaves would be one just as accreted with arbitrary complexities as Hausa or Albanian. More specifically, Ansaldo and Matthews would appear to suppose that slaves basically learned the new language pretty well, merely mixing in some features from their native languages and leaving out a just a few of the less frequently encountered marginal complexities of the new language.

Okay – but read a grammatical description of, say, the Portuguese-based creole Angolar (Maurer 1995) and then one of Portuguese itself. In doing so, one cannot escape the conclusion that Ansaldo and Matthews' assumption is the counterintuitive and peculiar one, which would require careful and persuasive argumentation to even begin to float. Why would new languages not be identifiable as new? Why, precisely, would new languages not be less complex than old ones – given that old languages are replete with complexities that are agreed to have resulted from changes over the passage of time? Why, precisely, would people creating a new language not start with a structurally more elementary one and build from there?

Ansaldo and Matthews introduce *Deconstructing Creole* as a book that will actually get across the tantalizingly counterintuitive argument that new languages arise, voilà, indistinguishable in any scientifically valid way from older languages, and that those who have argued otherwise are either naive, professionally ambitious, or unknowingly ethnocentric. I learned much from the book, but in the end, the articles in *Deconstructing Creole* are, together, one more argument in favor of the "exceptionalist" conception of creoles that so alarms the authors.

3.2. The Language Bioprogram Hypothesis: addressed or misread?

This becomes clear, first, in the introduction (which is less a mere curtain-raiser than a piece as substantial as the other articles in the volume). Ansaldo and Matthews designate two "exceptionalist" hypotheses, Derek Bickerton's

Language Bioprogram Hypothesis and my own Creole Prototype hypothesis, as conclusively refuted, but this verdict is based on what must be deemed insufficient familiarity with the creolist literature.

For example, they claim that Sarah Roberts' work on the emergence of Hawaiian Creole English has refuted Bickerton's entire Language Bioprogram Hypothesis argument. However, their impression that Roberts' work has shown that "HCE emerged gradually over a couple of generations and from a pidgin that already contained a number of features found in HCE" is a rather eccentric interpretation of Roberts' work. Roberts is a careful scholar and makes clear that Hawaiian Creole English was not as radically clean a break from Hawaiian Pidgin English as Bickerton once claimed. However, the main thrust of the papers by Roberts that Ansaldo and Matthews cite was that the creole was indeed created by children, and was in no sense a mere predictable evolutionary step from the pidgin. If a second generation of children added some features to the creole, the fact remains that the first generation created something quite strikingly unlike the pidgin: they created a full language where there had first been none. To wit: on this point, Derek Bickerton is correct, and the same process of children creating a full language has also been identified in the birth of Nicaraguan Sign Language.

Ansaldo and Matthews are correct that Bickerton's idea that the creole was created by children who heard only pidgin English and had no recourse to the languages spoken natively by their immigrant parents has not held up. Roberts has shown that the children who created the creole were bilinguals who were, in addition, hearing standard English in school five days a week. Nevertheless, the fact remains: they created a creole that had not existed before, a language that no specialist in the history of the English language would view as a typical diachronic development of English grammar like the English of Manchester or Cleveland. Nor is the difference between Hawaiian Creole English and other English varieties traceable to contact with Chinese and other languages plantation workers in Hawaii spoke: the article by Jeff Siegel (Siegel 2000b) that they cite covers some possible Chinese-derived features in the language which, taken together, hardly explain the utterly stark difference between Hawaiian Creole English's grammar and that of Cockney or African-American Vernacular English. Something interesting happened in Hawaii: something "exceptional."

Ansaldo and Matthews' impression that Bickerton's Language Bioprogram Hypothesis has been vanquished entirely, and that the birth of Hawaiian Creole English was a mere matter of a new dialect emerging gradually, is not one that could be founded on a purely empirical engagement with the issue. The authors appear to have approached the issue with certain expectations already set. This is, of course, inevitable of scientific work. However, I suggest that in this case, the result is a misreading of the evidence.

3.3. Are creoles just mixtures of languages?
Selective data set

This problem continues in the volume's various arguments to the effect that creole genesis is simply a matter of languages mixing with no remarkable simplification involved, and that any impression otherwise is an artifact of the fact that the creoles have often been the result of contact between isolating languages.

For example, as noted, in their introduction Ansaldo and Matthews also sound the death knell for my Creole Prototype hypothesis. That hypothesis argues that when a language has little or no inflection, little or no use of contrastive tone to distinguish monosyllables semantically, and little or no non-compositional derivational morphology, it is a creole – i.e. a new language born as, and then expanded from, a pidgin state. The introduction, however, points us to a forthcoming paper which will present a principle that "Creoles with clearly isolating morphology have long existed in intimate contact with isolating superstratal or adstratal languages." This is intended as an argument that creoles only exhibit what I have described as their "prototype" because their creators spoke morphologically isolating languages.

Never mind that this leaves unaddressed that my Creole Prototype also addresses the semantic nature of derivation, rather than the presence or absence of bound morphemes. More to the point, the idea that creoles have isolating morphology only because their source languages do is, simply, wrong. Guinea-Bissau Creole Portuguese is the result of contact between Portuguese and various West Atlantic languages; all are well-inflected (cf. Kihm 1989). Yet Guinea-Bissau Creole is very low on inflection. Palenquero Creole Spanish has very moderate inflection, and yet it is the product of contact between two languages, Spanish and Kikongo, which are both highly inflected. Another one: the pidgin Chinook Jargon was creolized on the Grande Ronde reservation, and yet it was a typically analytic creole (Grant 1996), despite the fearsomely elaborate bound morphology in all of the Native American languages spoken by its creators. In the South Pacific, New Guinea and Australia, sister varieties Tok Pisin, Solomon Islands Pijin, Bislama and Australian "Kriol" have long been used by people speaking inflected languages natively.

Many creoles, then, have arisen from, and co-existed among, heavily inflected languages and remained isolating. I argue that this is because creole genesis entails radical simplification of source languages' grammars. It is unclear to me what counterargument Ansaldo and Matthews could present that took in the creoles their introduction makes no notice of.

In the same vein, in one article in the volume Enoch Aboh and Ansaldo present a case for this conception of mixture. Their prime demonstration is that the configuration of the noun phrase in Surinam creoles can be analyzed as combining features from English and Gbe languages. They follow this with showing that Sri Lankan Malay has case markers derived from those in Sinhala and Tamil, with the implication that Sranan and Saramaccan can be analyzed as products of the same process of mixture that has yielded Sri Lankan Malay.

The problem with this analysis is that if we pull the camera lens back, so to speak, mixture alone cannot account for the difference between contact languages they address and their source languages. To be sure, Aboh and Ansaldo stipulate that a certain degree of grammatical elision – termed by them as "altered" replication – will occur in "a highly multilingual environment with low normative tendencies." This, for them, explains why Surinam creoles lack inflection: English is rather moderately inflected as Indo-European languages go, and Gbe languages largely lack it entirely. Hence in a contact situation between these languages, inflection would have been especially unlikely to survive in the new hybrid language.

However, this analysis fails for other creoles. For example, the Gulf of Guinea Portuguese creole Angolar arose amidst contact between Portuguese and the West African languages Edo and Kimbundu. Edo is an analytic language, but Portuguese and Kimbundu are well-inflected, and based on the richer lexical contribution of Kimbundu to Angolar than to its sister creoles Sao Tomense, Principense and Annobonese, we assume that the contact situation that yielded Angolar was one in which Kimbundu was a crucial presence.

Yet verb roots in Angolar are invariantly uninflected. Portuguese has grammatical gender marking while Kimbundu, as a Bantu language, has ample noun class marking – and yet Angolar nouns are bare. Clearly, this is not the result of mere mixture – why would the Edo typology win out so consistently if the issue were a matter of a hybrid "ecology"?

Consider also the French creoles of the Indian Ocean Mascarenes, such as Mauritian. Spoken French is moderately inflected; the Bantu languages such as Makhuwa and Yao that slaves of these islands spoke are highly inflected. The result – an alternation between short and long forms of verbs derived formally from French but not functionally, and reflecting nothing of Bantu grammar at all. This is a hybrid of French and Bantu? Obviously not: it is a vast simplification of French structure, within which Bantu played no part at all.

"Inflection may be acquired when it is associated with some semantics," Aboh and Ansaldo mention in reference to these long and short forms of verbs in such French creoles. But why just this? Surely the tense and aspect-marking inflections in Bantu have "some semantics," and yet there are no such inflections in Mauritian and its sister creoles. Among the creators of Angolar, surely Portuguese's plural inflections had some semantics, not to mention Kimbundu's noun class markers, which correlate roughly but robustly with real-world taxonomy.

A case based on Surinam creoles and a case of language contact between older languages such as the one that yielded a Sri Lankan-flavored Malay cannot stand as an argument about creolization in the larger sense. One cannot, in the scientific sense, characterize creolization as a process via address of a single creole or two. Surely, some consider this appropriate out of an assumption that creolization is simply a matter of the same contact processes that resulted in Romanian, Yiddish or Sri Lankan Malay. This, however, is a mere assumption, and my arguments have proposed that the assumption is not valid. These arguments can only be usefully addressed with a view towards creoles as a whole.

Examples continue. One example: Nubi Creole Arabic is low on inflection, when its creators spoke Arabic, very highly inflected, and assorted Nilotic languages which are also well-inflected. Aboh and Ansaldo's chapter suggests little familiarity with the range of data appropriate to valid statements about creole genesis – ironically, a charge authors in this volume often level at those adhering to the paradigm I have suggested.

Hans Den Besten, as it happens, shows that Cape Dutch Pidgin, modelled largely on Khoekhoe, was not a direct relexification of that language, but a "stripped" one entailing a great deal of abbreviation of Khoekhoe structures. In treating a pidgin rather than a creole, and one which he stipulates was not the direct precursor of today's creolized Khoekhoe Afrikaans, this article can only relate diagonally to the issue of what creoles are like. However, to the extent that we accept that creoles can be born from pidgins, it is germane that when a pidgin is a creole's source (or one of them), it does not mirror substrate language grammar, but reduces it (a lesson most comprehensively imparted by Keesing 1988).

3.4. How to disprove the Creole Prototype hypothesis: or not

My arguments about the Prototype and complexity are often met with demonstrations that creoles do exhibit complex features, along with statements about the Uniformitarian Principle, isolating typology, August Schleicher, I-language, etc. However, curiously few analysts seem to have understood that the proper way to refute my thesis is to present an older language which exhibits the same unusually moderate degree of grammatical complexity that creoles do. The metric to follow would be along the lines of the comparisons between Saramaccan and two older languages in McWhorter (2005: 48–57), or for those who would prefer a more detailed conception of what I consider grammatical complexity to entail, cf. McWhorter (2007: 21–50). To put a point on it, to the extent that this language is not presented, I consider my thesis unrefuted.

On the claim that the Mande language Soninke is such a language, see Chapter One, Section 7, to which it should be added that outside of the Prototype issue, a thorough grammar of Soninke (Diagana 1995) makes it amply clear that it is also, according to the perspective I have presented in various sources (e.g. Chapter Two), an older language, replete with elaborated features clearly the result of millennia of accretion.

Other than this, the only linguists contributing to *Deconstructing Creole* on the Prototype question who appear to understand the actual task involved in constructively addressing what I have written are Anthony Grant and David Gil. Grant's paper is on the Chamic languages of Southeast Asia. The Chamic group are Austronesian languages which have lost Austronesian's battery of morphology (i.e. as well-known in Tagalog and Malay) and become isolating, as the result of long-term contact with isolating Mon-Khmer languages. Grant's argument is that the Chamic languages have drifted into having the same cluster of Prototype features as creoles without any break in transmission, implying that the Prototype is merely a typology that may result from contact with isolating languages.

However, I have already presented why that idea undergenerates the full range of creole data, and in any case, Grant does not cover the full range of what my Prototype Hypothesis stipulates. Like many analysts, Grant appears to suppose that inflection and tone are more important to cover in addressing the Prototype hypothesis than the compositionality of derivation-root combinations. He mentions very briefly, twice, that these combinations are compositional in Chamic, but without substantial discussion, referring only to a marker or two.

In this light, it must be noted that Grant's sources for the Chamic languages are mostly word lists and brief grammars. The fact is that typically, only more complete grammars of languages actually address noncompositional derivation, and often it is only identifiable from substantial dictionaries. Sources of this kind are barely available for Chamic (the fine book-length study Thurgood 1999 is not concerned with data that would shed light on the topic). As such, as thorough as Grant's analysis is overall, he does not (possibly because at the current state of research he *could* not) tell us the extent to which derivation-root combinations are noncompositional in Chamic.

This is crucial, because, as I have noted elsewhere (cf. McWhorter 2005a: 16–18), there are older languages which have neither inflection or tone, and which only reveal themselves as older according to the Prototype metric in their derivational noncompositionality. I have called especial attention to this phenomenon in the Mon-Khmer language Chrau of Vietnam, for which a decent grammar happens to exist and charts derivational morphemes whose meaning is so inconsistent that no single one is gleanable. Grant has not given us any indication that the Chamic languages are not ones of this kind.

In general, Grant is especially interested in isolating typology, whereas while this is surely a crucial issue in language contact in Southeast Asia, noncompositionality of derivation-root combinations has nothing to do with analyticity. For one, such combinations can be opaque even when derivational morphemes are free rather than bound: in Lahu, *te* is a causativizer, but with *tâ?* "to carry" the result means "to carry along," not "to make carry" (Matisoff 1991: 432). In any case, a language could be replete with dozens of derivational bound affixes and yet, if all of them made compositional contributions to the words they created, then this would qualify as a Prototype feature.

Another aspect of Chamic that is noteworthy within the context of this discussion is the overall grammatical complexity of Chamic languages. The main focus of this volume, when addressing my own work, is the Creole Prototype hypothesis (Ansaldo also explicitly focuses his review of McWhorter 2005a in *Journal of Pidgin and Creole Languages* 22:1 on it), rather than my more general subsequent proposal that creole languages are less grammatically complex than older languages, and in much more than degree of inflectional affixation. In the end, I am more interested in the general complexity issue than the narrower one of whether or not there is a diagnostic test for creolization, such that I have written much more on the complexity issue than the Prototype one since 1998 and have even written a monograph on complexity as applied to older languages worldwide (McWhorter 2007).

In this light, Grant usefully acknowledges that the Chamic languages bear complexities of a kind that creoles do not. For example, their contact with Mon-Khmer languages has lent them numeral classifiers, which can be analyzed as an incipient form of gender marking (Grinevald & Seifart 2004), and Mon-Khmer's hallmark elaborated phonemic inventories, again unknown in creoles.

Thus while Chamic parallels creoles in lack of inflectional affixation and, in some varieties, lack of contrastive tone, not only are we currently ignorant as to the extent of its derivation's noncompositionality, but we know that overall, Chamic languages display a degree of structural complexity that creoles do not, just as Mon-Khmer languages do even when lacking inflection and tone. Chrau, for example, has 39 numeral classifiers, obligatory in usage (Thomas 1971: 130–4). I propose that creoles lack these things because simplification is central to their birth. It is unclear what Ansaldo and Matthews would propose as the reason, other than serendipity.

Meanwhile, David Gil has argued in various articles that the Riau dialect of Indonesian is radically simplified compared to standard Indonesian simply by chance, such that there is no need to link this degree of simplification to non-native acquisition and a break in transmission. I have argued (most comprehensively in McWhorter 2007: 222–34 and Chapter Seven) that the history of Riau Indonesian and a comparison of it, Standard Indonesian and relatives of Indonesian in the region make it inescapable that Riau Indonesian is indeed the product of heavy use as a lingua franca by speakers of other languages – i.e. a break in ordinary transmission. Gil takes a novel approach and argues that two of these relatives, Sundanese and Minangkabau, are as radically simplified as Riau Indonesian despite there being no evidence that they are the product of a break in transmission.

Specifically, Gil examines the freedom of interpretation of items under association. In a language like English, association is highly constrained by rules such as subjects normally preceding objects, such that if an English-speaking subject is presented with the sentence *The bird is eating* and then shown one picture showing a bird eating and the other showing a cat eating a bird, he or she will point to the former picture. However, if a Sundanese speaker is given the equivalent sentence *Manuk dahar* 'bird eat,' then they will accept both pictures as illustrating the sentence, because it could also mean "He (the cat) eats the bird." The absence of case or inflectional affixation constraining the interpretation makes this possible in Sundanese.

Testing sixteen sentences, Gil shows that of eleven languages, Minangkabau and Sundanese have the freest association according to this metric – and, by implication, parallel Riau Indonesian, whose freedom of associational semantics Gil has examined elsewhere.

However, this associational freedom is but one aspect of what grammatical complexity can consist of, and in many other areas of grammar, Minangkabau and Sundanese surpass Riau Indonesian. For example, they parallel Standard Indonesian's battery of derivational morphology complete with morphophonemic complications in their surface realization. Meanwhile,

Minangkabau surpasses even Standard Indonesian in grading distance more finely and in the number of numeral classifiers (Moussay 1981). Sundanese has the same traits, as well as productive infixation, a negative existential marker, a high yogh vowel along with the typical vowel inventory of languages of its Malayo-Javanic group, and other features (Müller-Gotama 2001).

Thus I accept Gil's argument that his study shows that a language can drift into extreme simplicity in a particular grammatical feature – as well as that in this case, Minangkabau and Sundanese clearly surpass even creoles like Saramaccan. However, in that my interest is in overall complexity, it would seem that the study does not, in itself, demonstrate that Minangkabau and Sundanese have by chance drifted into the *overall* degree of simplicity of Riau Indonesian.

And in the meantime, I remain somewhat bemused at the fact that over ten years after the Prototype article (McWhorter 1998), so few have come forward with older languages that can be shown to be as "prototypical" as creoles not just in isolating typology or tonelessness, but in compositionality of derivation, demonstrated with a modest but representative sampling of the morphemes and the meanings they create.

On the one hand, I sense that for many grammarians, noncompositional derivation seems rather inconsequential in falling outside of systematic, productive grammar itself. However, it happens to be exactly the kind of thing that happens to a language's lexicon over time, and thus is every bit as crucial to a diagnosis according to my metric as inflections and tones.

On the other hand, I can't help thinking that if a linguist had found a language of this kind, surely by now it would have been brought to my attention, eagerly presented as refuting the hypothesis many find so disconcerting. Is it possible that no such languages have been encountered? If so, this is, of course, support for my hypothesis.

3.5. What qualifies as "broken transmission"?

Another theme in the volume is a claim that creoles are the result of unbroken transmission rather than pidginization or any substantial degree of grammatical reduction under any guise. For example, in one article Ansaldo and two co-authors cover the emergence of Baba Malay, a creole Malay with Hokkien Chinese admixture. They note that the Chinese people who created this variety had no experience linguistically or socially that could be associated with a break in linguistic (or cultural) transmission. Their implication is that this bodes ill for the general idea that a break in transmission is a necessary component of creole genesis.

I, for one, would agree, given that I have argued that Riau Indonesian and other similarly reduced Malay varieties qualify as creoles, despite David Gil proposing them as ordinary older languages that have drifted into a uniquely grammatically streamlined state by accident. I have always suspected that a ready riposte to that argument would be that these varieties did not emerge amidst forced population displacement and stark social subordination. As such, Ansaldo and his colleagues' point about Baba Malay is well taken.

They do leave a question unanswered, however. They are striving towards a characterization of creoles as simply the product of mixture between competing grammatical features in a heterogenous context. However, Baba Malay is not solely a mixture of Malay and Hokkien: it is a highly simplified mixture of both. Hokkien is a variety of Min Chinese, which is a strikingly complex language (despite being analytic; too much discussion of complexity focuses on affixation rather than complexity more generally). If Baba Malay were solely a mixture of Hokkien and Malay, then it would have, if not seven or eight tones like Min, then at least three or four, a healthy array of serial verb constructions, multiple semantically specific negators, multiple complementizers linked to particular shades of meaning, and so on. Meanwhile, we might also expect some reflection of Malay's rich battery of voice- and valence-marking derivational affixes (McWhorter 2007: 199).

This is not a mere guess, as there exist analogous varieties. The Western Cham variety of Chamic, a hybrid of Austronesian and Mon-Khmer languages, has five tones. Acehnese, the "black sheep" of the Chamic family spoken in Sumatra at a great distance from the others, is replete with Mon-Khmer-derived sounds and affixes modelled largely on Austronesian. As often in this book, a broader perspective on the languages in question (here, the Austronesian family and, specifically, the many varieties of vernacular Malay/Indonesian) suggests significantly different conclusions.

Baba Malay, then, not only demonstrates that creoles need not emerge under plantation-type circumstances, but also that creoles are indeed less grammatically complex than their source languages, whether this be on a plantation, in an army (Nubi Creole Arabic), in an orphanage (Unserdeutsch) or among a successful immigrant merchant class (Baba Malay).

Jeff Siegel's article does take a wide-lens perspective, as his work so consistently does, and pointedly, his conclusions are somewhat at odds with the volume's central assumptions. He makes the valuable observation that the debate over whether creoles emerge via a break in transmission of a lexifier language is actually based on a mere issue of semantics. The superstratist argument of linguists such as Robert Chaudenson and Michel DeGraff stipulates that rather than emerging from pidgins, plantation creoles were actually the end result of a gradual dilution of lexifier input as slave populations got larger. The first slaves, existing in roughly equal numbers with whites on what began as small farms, would have acquired a relatively complete rendition of the lexifier, moderated only slightly by the effects of second language acquisition. The next wave of slaves would be exposed to this moderately incomplete rendition, but the effects of second language acquisition would have made their rendition even less faithful to the lexifier itself, and so on, until the result was a creole. Hence there was no point at which there was a significant break in transmission.

Siegel notes that there were, however, documented cases in which a pidgin was the initial phase in a creole's birth, such as Hawaii and the South Seas. It is also germane that there is ample evidence that even at the small farm phase in many colonies, creole languages were already spoken. Siegel mentions the "mermaid text" from Martinique, while McWhorter (2005a: 145–9) covers this and many other cases. I am unaware of a sustained engagement with these facts in superstratist work.

More importantly, the superstratists readily acknowledge that second language acquisition was central to the process even they describe in places like the French Caribbean. At this writing, it has become widely agreed that the features of the Basic Variety level of acquisition described by Klein & Perdue (1997) are directly relevant to the birth of creoles. Thus while the superstratists "may be correct in saying that there was no stable pidgin in the history of some creoles, there were clearly 'pidginized interlanguages' being used by the slaves." As such, as Siegel puts it, "One side [those arguing for a break in transmission] believes that normal transmission entails only the thorough acquisition of a language as a mother tongue through enculturation. The other side [superstratists] believes that normal transmission can also entail the partial learning of a language as a second language."

I, for one, am unconvinced that plantation creoles emerged as the result of what has been termed "approximations of approximations," for reasons outlined in McWhorter (2005: 145–9); there is, for example, no evidence that the Surinam creoles began as lightly abbreviated renditions of English and all indication that they did not. It also bears mentioning that while because there are no French creoles as divergent from their lexifier as Sranan and Saramaccan are from English, the idea that Haitian Creole is "a type of French" makes a certain intuitive sense, that idea is rather starkly counterintuitive for the Surinam Creoles: few would accept that Sranan is, in any sense, a kind of English. It is a new language entirely.

However, the nature of the sociohistorical evidence is such that there will likely never be a smoking gun confirming absolutely my view or that of the superstratists. Their objection, then, that there is no evidence of pidgins preceding plantation creoles is like treating the absence of a fossil of a creature ancestral to both humans and the great apes as confirmation that humans are not descended from primates. Primate fossils are rare and fragmentary in the relevant locations, such that the exact ones we seek may have never been preserved. In the same way, no one on early plantations was concerned with writing down the way slaves spoke – the evidence is simply not there. Our reconstructions, therefore, must be based on extrapolation from other lines of evidence, such as comparison with language contact situations and diachronic development patterns worldwide.

In that light, my conclusion is that a "French" with no grammatical gender, no inflectional affixation elsewhere, no sign of French's deeply entrenched partitive marking, bare verbs, no subjunctive, virtually no irregular verbs, no clitic climbing, and frequent zero copula displays ample hallmarks of being the product of something other than the ordinary stepwise morphing that other French varieties have been undergoing over the roughly two millennia of French's existence. Moreover, it is unclear to me that the idea that non-native acquisition in non-prescriptive circumstances simply accelerates ordinary tendencies of internal grammatical changes explains this difference. No French variety anywhere in the world, or for that matter any Romance variety, shows any signs of even being on the way to a cluster of developments like these.

However, it would appear that many will remain convinced that the "approximations of approximations" idea is valid, possibly in part because of sociological discomfort with presumed implications of the "exceptionalist" idea that the mental sophistication of African slaves is somehow compromised. If so, the important thing is that the end result contrasts with the lexifier to a degree unknown in diachronic developments, even amidst language contact, outside of those entailing rapid acquisition of a language by adults for permanent use as a primary language. Moreover, it contrasts not solely in evidencing mix-ins from other languages. It contrasts in being streamlined in terms of complexity in comparison to older languages, including the lexifier that seeded it.

3.6. That creoles have morphology: novel observation?

Joseph Farquharson's paper is in the vein of several elsewhere seeking to revise the tradition of creolists supposing that creole languages have what is often termed "little or no morphology," either derivational or inflectional.

I am not certain that creolists have been as dismissive of the presence of creole morphology as we are often told: after all, there are decades' worth of grammatical descriptions of creoles in which the authors, generally creolists themselves, readily document morphology. In fact, when interpreted from my own work, the conception of creoles having "little or no morphology" of any kind which seems to so arouse analysts is typically based on a reading of some passages in McWhorter (1998: 793) referring to pidgins, which, despite unremarkable traces of morphology in pidgins here and there, are based on a valid generalization few would dispute based on pidgins such as Chinook Jargon, Ndjuka-Trio Pidgin or Russenorsk. The observation has come to be cited divorced of its context which treated creoles as derived from pidgins, in an article in which I readily acknowledged and discussed the *derivational* morphology which readily develops even early on in *creoles*.

In this light, at the end of Farquharson's discussion, the simple fact remains that creole languages tend strongly to have little or no inflectional affixation, a factor I attributed to recency of emergence. Farquharson contributes as-sorted observations intended to disassociate low inflectional affixation from age, but it is unclear that they succeed.

I am afraid that evidence that a single speaker of Sri Lanka Malay is docu-mented to have begun using a pronoun as a clitic eons after the language emerged does not constitute evidence that a community-wide grammar can develop an inflection in an instant. Meanwhile, the fact that sign languages like American Sign Language have had what can be analyzed as inflectional affixation since their birth is apparently a function of the manual modality (McWhorter 2005a: 321–3). The question is which spoken pidgin language is documented to have emerged with inflectional affixation, other than those spoken by speakers of closely related inflectional languages, in which case their very classification as "pidgins" has always been controversial in any case (ibid., McWhorter 2005a: 157–9).

Meanwhile, Farquharson cites Alain Kihm's clever argument (2003) that under the Minimalist paradigm, free morphemes can be analyzed as "inflec-tions" just as affixes can, the only difference being that free morphemes are generated via Merge and the affixes by Move. As I have discussed in Chapter One, however, Kihm's analysis neglects the fact that boundedness has phonological effects that lead typically to morphophonemic alternations, changes in stress rules, and irregularities – which constitute added complex-ity. To suppose that there is no difference in the complexity of past marking between Saramaccan's Merge-generated "I saw," *Mi bi sí* versus Russian's affixal Move-generated *Ja videl* neglects that past-marking "inflection" in Russian entails paradigms of affixes marking person, number and gender, conditioning assorted stress phenomena, in two conjugational paradigms, and amidst considerable irregularity.

3.7. Sidebars

Other articles in the volume propose that valid theories about creole genesis must take sociological circumstances into account more diligently. Nicholas Faraclas and several co-authors note that the different linguistic results in the Caribbean under different plantation powers cannot be reduced solely to linguistic factors and that sociohistorical ones must also be taken into account.

It is somewhat ticklish for this author to comment on this article. There has reigned an idea, based on Cuba and Puerto Rico, that the reason there are so few Spanish-based creoles was because the small-farm stage lasted so long on these islands that once slaves were brought in larger numbers, relations between blacks and whites were, while fraught, less implacably distant than on plantations in Surinam or Haiti, and that amidst this social context a very lightly Africanized Spanish itself was too well-established to be transformed by newcomers.

However, I have written a book (McWhorter 2000) arguing that there were Spanish colonies, little discussed in the creole genesis literature, in which slaves vastly outnumbered whites early on and interracial relations were distant and brutal. I propose that these colonies – Colombia, Mexico, Venezuela, Peru, and Ecuador – contradict the idea that there was a particular Iberian-type slavery context that discouraged the formation of creoles. More to the point, under the traditional analysis, we would expect that mines and plantations in these mainland Spanish colonies would certainly have yielded creoles as removed from Spanish as Sranan is from English or Angolar is from Portuguese.

Faraclas and his co-authors' article briefly mentions my book, but does not engage with its argument, instead presenting a case which, while an extended and considered one, is essentially a continuation of ones traceable to work of the sixties and seventies by scholars such as Sidney Mintz. I can only say that Colombia, Ecuador, Venezuela, Peru and Mexico stand as challenges to the Faraclas article's verdicts. I would be interested to see what he and his co-authors would conclude upon, perhaps, engaging with those colonies in the future.

Meanwhile, Roxy Harris and Ben Rampton make some suggestions for couching creole analysis within a broader contextual frame including conversational analysis and issues of cultural identity. I understand their sense that the competing schools of thought on creole genesis, reducing the languages to some scratches on paper and positing historical reconstructions on the basis of fragmentary evidence, neglect that creoles are, in the end, systems of communication used by human beings interacting dynamically with their environment. It is beyond my purview to engage at any length with this thoroughly valid observation. However, I maintain that the systems of communication that creolophones use to express their identities and the layered renditions of consciousness that this requires do so in a code which is less heavily accreted with needless grammatical complexity than people do when expressing their identities in the Caucasus Mountains, and that this is simply because the creolophone's code is newer.

3.8. Does any creolist not believe in Creole Exceptionalism in unguarded moments?

Since I first presented my ideas about the Creole Prototype and creole complexity, it has come to my attention that I needed to spell out my terms more carefully. I have attempted to do so, and at this point, my closest and most comprehensive engagement with precisely what I intend by "complexity" in creoles and in other languages is Chapter Two of this book. I have also presented further thoughts on older languages giving the superficial appearance of being "prototypical" in the Introduction and Chapter One, as well as a chapter on what grammatical complexity consists of in McWhorter (2007) referring to languages throughout the world.

While articles demonstrating that creole languages have complexity are always interesting, it is unclear to me that it has been demonstrated that the claim that creoles are less grammatically complex than older languages is a mere misimpression from the fact that creoles tend not to have as much inflectional affixation as European languages.

Joseph Farquharson's contribution, for example, is quite scholarly in tone, and yet he does announce himself as working against what he terms a "prejudice" towards viewing creoles as devoid of morphology. That word is indicative: its pure meaning is simply that of working with a preconception. However, it also has a sociohistorically rooted rhetorical flavor suggesting preconceptions of a particularly unsavory nature.

It must be observed that a statement that, for example, Saramaccan is less grammatically complex than Russian can, in the logical sense, be founded not in prejudice of any stamp, but a simple engagement with the data. It could be asserted, in fact, that to propose that there is no difference in complexity between Saramaccan and Russian grammar is, itself, one which might well involve a degree of "prejudice," here intended solely in its dictionary definition.

For example, Corne (2000: 312), after an examination of the origins of Tayo Creole French in New Caledonia, observed, with no indication of considering it a controversial or even noteworthy statement, that its grammar is "less complex than that of any given ancestral language." Creolist writings have always been replete with statements of this kind by well-respected figures on the basis of sustained comparative analysis of creoles and their source languages (cf. Keesing 1988 as another example), and are received without complaint. Is Corne's conclusion about Tayo, readily clear from a comparison of it with its Melanesian substrate languages in discussions such as Corne (1995), founded in "prejudice" of any kind? It also bears mentioning that neither Tayo nor its substrate languages are addressed in any of the articles in this volume.

It would appear that a distinct discomfort arises at the prospect of proceeding from statements of this kind about individual creoles to a more general one – i.e. a basic logical induction – that simplification is a central aspect of creole genesis. Books could be written as the result of said discomfort, and *Deconstructing Creole* is one of those that have been. In any case, the book teaches us, despite the intentions of its editors and authors, that creoles are the product of, indeed, the "deconstructing" of grammar followed by its reconstitution over what has so far been a brief period of time – such that signs of the deconstruction are still very much on view.

Section II
Creole complexity

Introduction

Communication is inherently partial and treacherous. We each of us see the world through a lens that no one else does.

For me, nothing has more starkly illustrated this fundamental solitude of the human condition than the fact that a community of creolists are under the sincere impression that I, as a working linguist who has spent a twenty-year career writing about creole languages, think that creoles have no grammatical processes.

This is the conclusion that one must draw from the plethora of articles in response to the creole exceptionalism position, urgently demonstrating that creoles have grammar. The implication is that someone, such as myself, was unaware of this.

I accept some blame for this impression. Until the past ten years or so, little of my published work, on issues such as substrate influence and my Afrogenesis Hypothesis (McWhorter 2000), suggested interest in grammatical operations per se. Likely this is part of why a critical mass of creolists have supposed that I, confronted with creoles' lack of inflection and their lack of centrally contrastive tone in the vein of Chinese, perceived no grammar to speak of. Certainly, then, for me to start writing about creoles' lesser complexity and relative youth would seem hasty, suspect, callow.

The three chapters in this section are intended as a demonstration that creole exceptionalism, whether it is judged convincing or not, is not based on ignorance of, or lack of interest in, grammar. The original articles appeared in scattered places, and there has been no reason to expect anyone to encounter all or even any of them. However, here they are together. They examine three grammatical features of Saramaccan, all showing that the grammar exhibits all manner of complexity.

Saramaccan is spoken in the Surinamese rain forest by approximately 20,000, and developed among slaves escaped from coastal plantations in the late seventeenth century. In terms of its grammar, it is an offshoot of a "father" creole, Sranan, today the vernacular lingua franca of Surinam. Sranan also spawned another Surinam rain forest creole, Ndjuka. Saramaccan's vocabulary is derived mostly from English and Portuguese, with significant contributions also from Dutch, Kikongo and Fongbe. However, its phonology and grammar are so deeply influenced by Fongbe, the African language spoken by most of its creators, that it is in no way a dialect of any European language in the way that creoles like Jamaican or Gullah can be analyzed as "types of English."

The chapters are written according to an assumption that it is not sufficient, when demonstrating that a creole "has complexity," to simply show that its determiners have a few conditioned allomorphs, that it has derivational processes, or that its phonology requires rule ordering. These things are common across the world's languages. If these things alone are anything approaching the sum total of what complexity is in creoles, then my point is neatly demonstrated that creoles are the world's simplest languages. If all creoles have is this, then they are, compared to Turkish, Aramaic or Dyirbal, unusually simple and that's all there is to it. But there is a great deal more.

In that vein, I have been interested in analyzing complex aspects of creoles of three qualities:

1) They are features manifesting a more complex rendition of a given construction or semantic concept than in English or related languages. They thus make heuristically clear that creoles are complex just as older languages are – in overshooting strict necessity here and there, a lesson clearest when the features are not those in English or French that happen to overshoot necessity (such as determiner allomorphy or rule ordering). Saramaccan's new information marking, for example, surpasses in overspecification (cf. the complexity metric in the Introduction) any overt, regularized mechanism in any Western European language (Chapter Four).

2) They are the kinds of features that creolists have supposed may be "hidden." That is, they are aspects of complexity not as obvious as inflections but crucial to an evaluation of creole complexity regardless. Chapter Five, for example, shows that a construction typically lumped into a list of "serial verb constructions" in Surinam creoles, when mentioned at all, is actually at the heart of a more complex system of indicating direction than in Western European languages, conditioned according to transitivity. None of the features treated in these chapters have been analyzed elsewhere, including the full range of allomorphy of the Saramaccan copula (Chapter Six). That is, while I retain my evaluation of Saramaccan as less complex than the vast majority of the world's languages, I do not render that judgment viewing Saramaccan as anything approaching maximally simple. One can see complexities of a kind in Saramaccan

and still analyze it as less complex overall than Estonian. Or Fongbe, Kikongo, Portuguese, Dutch or English.

3) They are not indicated with inflectional affixes. One of the ironies of the opposition to creole exceptionalism is that despite the accusations of Eurocentrism and antique notions of colonial superiority, so many of the presentations are concerned with exploring the extent to which pidgins and creoles have inflectional affixes. Cf. Farquharson (2007), or work such as DeGraff (1999) seeking to parse creole genesis as essentially a resetting of the strong inflection parameter, implying that the grammatical difference between Haitian and French is no different from that between Chinese and French, such that no conclusions about complexity or signs of youth could cohere.

There are two problems with this inflection fetish. One is the guiding idea that such affixes are a *sine qua non* of grammatical complexity, when in fact they are but one of legions of ways that a grammar can evidence complexity, vastly undershooting an evaluation as to whether creoles can be analyzed as young languages (the central point in McWhorter 2005: 72–101).

Second, the idea that humans are genetically programmed with a sensitivity to grammatical parameters such as one for inflectional affixation is vastly unlikely to pass the test of time (cf. Newmeyer 2005, Culicover & Jackendoff 2005), such that creolist theory focusing on it risks obsolescence. This is already clear in work of eighties vintage such as Bickerton (1984) and Byrne (1987), seeking to characterize Saramaccan as Universal Grammar with all settings marked "off."

These chapters also, inherently, contest another assumption underlying the work stressing that creoles have grammar. This point is typically made as if it alone constitutes a refutation of the idea that creoles are less complex than older languages. That is, the logical calculus is:

A. Creole exceptionalism claims that creoles are less complex than older languages.
B. But creoles have grammatical processes.
C. Thus creoles are as complex as older languages.

The only way this makes sense is under a tacit assumption that all languages are equally complex, or that the question as to whether that is true is so hopelessly treacherous that it would be futile to even address it.

However, as I argued in the Introduction to the first section, neither of those tacit assumptions is valid. In fact, in all of the cases in these three chapters, we see that while creoles, as natural languages, evidence grammatical complexity, they do not evidence *superlative* grammatical complexity.

Where a creole's construction is complex, typically the source language equivalent is more so – and in all cases that I know, the creole does not manifest that trait in *as* complex a fashion as many older languages do.

One of the most bemusing comments I ever experienced after a presentation on creole complexity was when one specialist – in a civil and almost playful vein, yet sincere nonetheless – complained that whatever complex creole trait someone brought up, I always seem to bring up some more baroque rendition of it in some other language. He said this with an air of finding it frustrating, as if I cheat at some kind of game.

All I can say is that if I'm cheating, then I wish creolists convinced that creoles are unexceptional would cheat along with me in making their case. Creole exceptionalism is a position made on the basis of the world's languages. It can only be refuted upon the same basis.

If you don't think it's right to designate creoles as a kind of language, then bring me a language not thought of as a creole that looks just like Saramaccan in terms of the three traits – no paradigmatic inflection, no seriously contrastive tone, and no lexicalized derivation-root combinations. Really – bring it.

It's neither Soninke, Mandarin (sorry, Ansaldo and Matthews) nor Old Chinese (sorry, Greg Sampson) (cf. Chapter One). I challenge those opposed to put up, and it's a fair challenge. Which language do you know of that conforms to the Creole Prototype? Which language do you know of that seems oddly uncomplex and yet has never been learned by foreigners much?

Put up – or consider that my hypothesis may be less "provocative" than simply apt.

Chapter 4
Oh nɔ́ɔ!: Emergent pragmatic marking from a bewilderingly multifunctional word[1]

4.1. Introduction

I have argued (cf. McWhorter 2005a) that creole language grammars exhibit less complexity than grammars of older languages, as the result of creoles' origins as radically reduced pidgin varieties. It is natural to human languages to accrete complexity as a matter of course over the millennia. Creoles, born as radically reduced pidgins and having existed as full languages for only a few centuries, have not had time to accrete the volume of complexity that Russian or Navajo has.

Arends (2001) has argued that creole grammars have not been sufficiently examined for it to be certain that they lack the complexity of older languages, a conviction common in responses to my thesis. This observation leads, it must be said, to a question as to why older languages' complexity is evident even in briefer grammatical descriptions, such as inflectional paradigms, heterogenous word order, ample irregularity, multiple tones indicating lexical and grammatical contrasts, and the like. The complexity of Polish and Chinese is evident immediately, after all, in a Berlitz phrasebook.

However, that question left aside, Arends was correct that for too many creoles over which great quantities of rhetorical ink have been spilt over the years, the degree to which their grammars have been described is modest enough that complexity may well reveal itself with further research. In this paper, I will show that this is indeed true in the case of the development in Saramaccan Creole English of a conventionalized system for marking new information, conditioned according to position, tense, and aspect.

My presentation will also elucidate, however, that this feature – like so many complexities in creole grammars – was not present in the language at its emergence, such that it would support a thesis that, simply, the immediate product of the creolization of a language is a grammar indistinguishable in

---

1 Title in salute to my erstwhile colleague Jim Matisoff's fabulous title for his paper on a distinctly analysis-resistant marker *ve* in Lahu (Matisoff, James A. 1972. Oy, ve! Lahu nominalization, relativization, and genitivization. In: John Kimball [ed.], *Syntax and Semantics*, Vol. I, 237–57. New York: Seminar Press).

complexity from Korean. Rather, as I have often noted, complexity in creoles grows over time from an original state in which the language had much less. Moreover, as the growth process has occurred over a few centuries rather than millennia, creoles' complexities are not *maximally* elaborated in comparison to equivalent features in older languages.

Finally, the discussion will also serve as a corrective to a tendency in studies of grammatical complexity – in creoles and beyond – to conceive of complexity as essentially a shorthand for inflectional morphology. A great many of the world's languages have little or no inflectional morphology, and yet display complexity in various other aspects of their grammars. In focusing on incipient inflectional morphology in creoles as evidence of their accretion of complexity, we miss much.

The Saramaccan data in this paper was gathered by myself and graduate student assistants at U.C. Berkeley from native speakers unless otherwise noted.

4.2. Emergent versus original complexity

I must make clear at the outset that the claim is not that at their emergence creoles lack complexity completely. They emerge with a certain degree of complexity already (albeit much lesser than in older languages; cf. McWhorter 2005a: 102–41).

A great deal of this complexity is due to the tranfer of a feature from a source language. For example, Saramaccan tone sandhi is sensitive to syntax, breaking at the left edge of maximal projections:

(1)   /mi wási koósu butá a dí sónu/ → [mi wásí # koósu bútá # a dí sónu]
      I   wash clothes put in the sun
      'I washed my clothes and put them in the sun.'

(Rountree 1972: 325)

The principal creators of Saramaccan spoke the Niger-Congo language Fongbe, in which there is a similar tone sandhi system:

(2)   /é sà àsɔn wè/ → [é sâ # àsón wê]
      he sell crab two

(Wiesemann 1991: 77)

Thus this feature can be assumed to existed in Saramaccan from the beginning of its history.

However, most features in Saramaccan that are markedly complex were not modelled on Fongbe, and have arisen grammar-internally.

4.3. New information marking in Saramaccan: synchrony

The word *nɔ́ɔ* in Saramaccan is used clause-initially with great frequency, often translated as "then":

(3)   ***Nɔ́ɔ*** *mi ó   kándi   a   míndi* wósu.   ***Nɔ́ɔ*** i *butá   wã̌ kódjo,*
      NI   I   FUT   lie.down LOC middle house   NI you put a cudgel a
      wã̌ kódjo   a   bándja.
      cudgel LOC side
      Nɔ́ɔ i   *kái woló kɛ́ɛ́!* . . .
      NI   you call alas cry
      'I'm going to lay down in the middle of the house. Then you put a stick, a stick off to the side. hen you wail out 'Alas'! . . .'

However, the "then" translation is inexact. In the first sentence of the example below, *hɛ̃̌* "then" already conveys sequentiality (more precisely the collocation *hɛ̃̌ wɛ* which includes focus marker *wɛ* and is Saramaccan's closest equivalent to English's "then" in the sequential sense), such that at best, a "then" meaning for *nɔ́ɔ* would be redundant.

(4)   ***Nɔ́ɔ*** *hɛ̃̌   wɛ   wã̌ mujɛ́ɛ   bi   dé a   dí   kɔndé naándɛ́.*
      NI   then FOC   a   woman PAST   be LOC   DEF village there
      Nɔ́ɔ *dí   mujɛ́ɛ,   a   palí dí   míi   wã̌ dáka.*
      NI   DEF woman she bear DEF child one day
      'So, then [in the wake of certain events described]: there was a woman in the village there. The woman, she bore a child one day.'

Of course, no language lacks redundancy. However, *nɔ́ɔ* is used with such frequency in spoken Saramaccan that a "then" meaning would imply a usage rate of "then" so peculiarly high as to seem an almost compulsive dedication to overtly marking chronological posteriority despite context and utterance order almost always making it quite clear.

Nɔ́ɔ has a more specific function than this, gracefully demonstrated by the following contrast. An informant once said to me in reference to a planned conversation in the near future:

(5) *A búnu.* ***Nɔ́ɔ*** *mi ó   tá   háika i.*
    it good NI   I   FUT IMF listen you
    'Good. So I'll be listening for you (waiting for your answer).'

He prefaced the second assertion with *nɔ́ɔ*. Shortly thereafter, he repeated:

(6) *A búnu, mi ó   tá   háika dí   kái fii   tidé   néti.*
    it good I   FUT IMF listen DEF call POSS.you today night
    "Good, I'll be listening (waiting) for your call tonight."

but this time, without the *nɔ́ɔ*. This was because the impending phone call
was now no longer new information within our discourse.

The function of *nɔ́ɔ* is marking new information. Saramaccan's speakers
use it as a foregrounding strategy, to point to shifts in a narrative. Each *Nɔ́ɔ*
indicates, so to speak, a new camera angle in the "film" of the utterance.

The foregrounding function of *nɔ́ɔ* is clear when we revisit the first citation presented in this paper above, shown in context after preceding material.
The animal subject of the folk tale is talking to his wife about a famine they
are suffering under, and starts using *nɔ́ɔ* to foreground his plan for getting
food (which is to play dead, wait for the animals of the area to come mourn
him, and then wake up and club them to death):

(7) *Já   sí hángi dɛ́ ku u? Wá   sondí u njã̌. Mi ó   pɛɛ́*
    you.NEG see hunger be with us we.NEG thing for eat I   FUT play
    wã̌ kɔ́ni,
    a trick
    'You see the hunger we are suffering from? We don't have anything to
    eat. I'm going to play a trick,

    mi ó   pɛɛ́, mi ó   ganjã̌ dɛ́dɛ. ***Nɔ́ɔ*** *mi ó   kándi   a   míndi*
    I   FUT play I   FUT pretend dead NI   I   FUT lie.down LOC middle
    wósu. ***Nɔ́ɔ*** *i   butá*
    house NI   you put
    I'm going to play, I'm going to pretend I'm dead. I'll lay down in the
    middle of the house. You put

    wã̌ kódjo, wã̌ kódjo a   bándja, wã̌ kódjo a   bándja. ***Nɔ́ɔ*** *i   kái*
    a cudgel a cudgel LOC side   a cudgel LOC side   NI   you call
    woló, kɛɛ́ . . .
    alas cry
    a stick, a stick to the side, a stick to the side. Then you call "Alas!," you cry . . .'

Nɔ́ɔ comes in when the speaker starts describing what he is going to do, i.e.
presenting a new "camera shot" within the utterance. In a film, one could

imagine his description depicted in the hypothetical as a vignette while he narrated on the soundtrack.

Nɔ́ɔ is especially conventionalized in marking matrix clauses that occur after preceding adverbial complements, the matrix clause containing the new information. This is the case with temporal complements:

(8) *Té mujɛ́ɛ sí Kobí,* **nɔ́ɔ** *de tá kulé.*
    when woman see Kobi NI they IMF run
    'When women see Kobi, they run.'

(9) *Dí mi bi kó lúku de,* **nɔ́ɔ** *de bi duúmi kaa.*
    when I PAST come look them then they PAST sleep already
    'When I came to see them, they were asleep.'

and concessive ones:

(10) *Ée dí míi á dú ɛ̃,* **nɔ́ɔ** *dí m'má ó náki ɛ̃.*
    if DEF child NEG do 3SO NI DEF Mom FUT hit 3SO
    'If the child doesn't do it, then the Mom will hit him.'

New information marking is sensitive to tense when occurring on matrix clauses after temporal adverbial complements. In the past tense, *nɔ́ɔ* is superseded as a new information marker by *hɛ̃́:*

(11) *Dí a bi tá duúmi,* **hɛ̃́** *mi gó kumútu dɛ́.*
    when he PAST IMF sleep NI I go leave there
    'When he was sleeping, I left.'

(12) *Dí mi bi jabí dí dɔ́ɔ,* **hɛ̃́** *mi sí dí gṍɔ̃́ munjã́.*
    when I PAST open DEF door NI I see DEF ground wet
    'When I opened the door, I saw the ground wet.'

This word is derived etymologically from "then" and is usually translated as such. However, more precisely, "then" in the sequential sense is usually rendered, as noted above, by *hɛ̃́* in conjunction with focus marker *wɛ* as *hɛ̃́ wɛ:*

(13) *Dí mujɛ́ɛ-míi tá fɔ́ pindá, tá fɔ́ pindá ku táti a*
    DEF woman-child IMF beat peanut IMF beat peanut with pestle LOC
    máta.
    mortar
    'So one day, the girl was beating peanuts, beating peanuts with a mortar-and-pestle.

> *Hɛ̃́ wɛ Anási wáka dóu dé.*
> then FOC Anansi walk arrive there
> Then Anancy approached.'

Hɛ̃́ in isolation is a foregrounder (although there is also a homonym, the tonic third-person pronoun: *A táa "Hɛ̃́!* "He said, 'Him!'"). Its translation in this function as "then" is processible, but in my view distracts from its actual function, an abstract pragmatic one.

Nɔ́ɔ, as the marker of new information applying most widely in the grammar, bleeds into the domain of unbounded semantics in co-occurring optionally with *hɛ̃́* in the configuration *nɔ́ɔ hɛ̃́:*

(14) *Mi dɛ́ a   dí   wósu báka,*
      I   be LOC DEF house back
      ***nɔ́ɔ hɛ̃́** mi sí wɑ̃́ mujɛ́ɛ,   hɛ̃́   mi sí dí   wómi náki dí   mujɛ́ɛ.*
      NI   I see a   woman then I see DEF man hit DEF woman

  'I was behind the house, then I saw a woman and saw the man hit the woman.'

(15) *Dí   a   boóko dí   báta kaa, **nɔ́ɔ hɛ̃́** a léi   mi.*
      when he break DEF bottle CPLT NI   he show me
      'When he broke the bottle, he showed it to me.'

The order of occurrence between these two markers is fixed: **hɛ̃́ nɔ́ɔ*.

Only when applying to full clauses does new information marker *nɔ́ɔ* occur clause-initially. Otherwise, it is postposed, as to dependent clauses:

(16) *Té wɑ̃́ óto pási báka **nɔ́ɔ**, i   tɑ̃́   búnu.*
      until a other time again NI   you stay good
      'Till another time, be well.'

and to arguments and adjuncts:

(17) *A búnu e – amanjɑ̃́   **nɔ́ɔ** mi ó   jéi fii.*
      it good INJ tomorrow NI   I FUT hear for.you
      'So very good – tomorrow I'll listen for you (wait for your call).'

The following sentence usefully shows *nɔ́ɔ* used in both positions while also nicely exemplifying the essence of the foregrounding function. *Nɔ́ɔ u nɔ́ɔ* is a fronted nonverbal predicate (lit. "Us, this is" [in certain contexts, in Saramaccan the copula is deleted when the predicate is fronted]):

(18) **Nɔ́ɔ** u **nɔ́ɔ**, dísi kaa.
     NI us NI this CPLT
     'This is *us*.' (This is the way we are.)

The first *nɔ́ɔ* foregrounds the whole proposition amidst a larger discourse. The second, postposed because it modifies an argument rather than a clause, presents as new information the "us" whose traits have just been described. The meaning of the sentence within the context is "Consider the *new* realization that what I have just described constitutes not a random assortment of traits, but the essence of 'us,' *new* to your knowledge."

Sentences without overt new information marking via *nɔ́ɔ* or *hɛ̃́* are not ungrammatical:

(19) Ée i   bi   láfu mi, mi bi ó   féti ku i.
     if you PAST laugh me I PAST FUT fight with you
     'If you'd laughed at me, I'd have fought with you.'

However, the markers are used much more frequently than not. Informants asked for translations of English sentences use them most of the time in their answers; spontaneous utterances are replete with them. They are considerably *entrenched,* in the terms of Langacker (1987), if not strictly *obligatorified,* in the terminology of Lehmann (1985) on grammaticalization.

Certainly *nɔ́ɔ* and *hɛ̃́* have been acknowledged and translated. However, they have not been parsed as marking, in systematic fashion, an aspect of grammar common to all languages but marked overtly by only a subset. In entailing two markers conditioned by tense, aspect and position, the marking of new information in Saramaccan is more complex than in, for example, English.

An indication of the "evolved" nature of this new information marking is that the main marker *nɔ́ɔ* no longer has lexical content; it is a pure function word just as, e.g. imperfective marker *tá* and focus marker *wɛ* are. Anglophone students of linguistics must be taught the concept of new versus old information via illustrations of topicalization, clefting and intonation. Saramaccan students of linguistics could simply be taught that "new information" is that which is marked by *nɔ́ɔ*.

4.4. New information marking in Saramaccan: diachrony

4.4.1. *Nɔɔ́*

Saramaccan has wrested its principal foregrounding marker from, rather counterintuitively, the adverb *nɔɔ́mɔ,* derived from *no more.*

4.4.1.1. From no more to new information marker

Nɔɔ́mɔ lives elsewhere in the grammar in clause-final usage, having drifted semantically from the compositional meaning of *no more* into connoting, first, the pragmatic assertion "definitely":

(20) *Mi ó   gó téi   ɛ̃   **nɔɔ́mɔ.***
      I   FUT go take 3SO   definitely
      'I'm definitely going to get her (romantically).'

(21) *Mi ó   dú   ɛ̃   **nɔɔ́mɔ.***
      I   FUT do 3SO   definitely
      'I'm definitely going to do it.'

Presumably, the semantic derivation is based on a usage of *no more* to assert "That's all (and no more)," "That's all there is to it."

   In a further semantic extension, *nɔɔ́mɔ* also can connote "always," "continuously":

(22) *Nɔɔ́ léti fuu   u mú' súku   **nɔɔ́mɔ.***
      NI   right POSS.us we must look.for always
      'We must always look for the right way for us to be.'

The "definitely" meaning, intensifying an assertion, has been extended into an intensification of a durational nature. (*Nɔɔ́mɔ* cannot, in the modern language, express its original compositional meaning of "no more.")

   Neither of these meanings appear relevant to a foregrounding marker on their face. However, the source of new information marker *nɔɔ́* as *nɔɔ́mɔ* is supported by various facts. For one, the phonetic derivation is supported by the fact that *nɔɔ́mɔ* was also the source for a homonym of new information marker *nɔɔ́,* which connotes "only" – intuitively derived from *no more,* given its restrictive connotation. This homonym occurs clause-finally, unlike the new information marker. This difference in position, in fact, determines which meaning is conveyed: when *nɔɔ́* occurs clause-finally rather than clause-initially or after an argument, it connotes "only":

(23) *Mi lési téni baáti u dí búku* **nɔ́ɔ**.
I read ten page of DEF book just
'I've only read ten pages of the book.'

(24) *Mɛ́ sá' fá u táki ɛ̃* **nɔ́ɔ**.
I.NEG know how we talk 3SO just
'I just don't know how we say it . . . !'

Confirming that *nɔ́ɔ* as "only" is derived from *nɔ́ɔmɔ* is that the "only" usage still occurs occasionally as *nɔ́ɔmɔ:*

(25) *A táa téi dí pási akí nángó* **nɔ́ɔmɔ**.
he say take DEF road here IMF.go only
He said 'Just go down this road.'

(Price & Price n.d.: 170)

The derivation of "only" from *no more* is semantically obvious, but crucially, this diachronic pathway shows that the source of the *nɔ́ɔ* new information marker in *nɔ́ɔmɔ* is phonetically plausible.

Yet while the *nɔ́ɔmɔ > nɔ́ɔ* evolution is phonetically plausible, a semantic evolution from "definitely" or "continuously" to a new information marker is distinctly less graceful. One tempting solution is to suppose that the new information marker has a different etymological source, such as "now." This account beckons in Saramaccan especially given that the word for "now," *nɔ́unɔu* (reduplicated from an original *nɔ́u*), has the lax vowel that *nɔ́ɔ* has.

However, one problem with this account is that *nɔ́unɔu* does not occur in a clause-initial sequential or foregrounding usage. And in any case, comparative data indicate that the new information's source was indeed *nɔ́ɔmɔ*, its original compositional "no more" meaning drifting differently than it did in the usages of *nɔ́ɔmɔ* clause-finally.

Crucial indication that this was the case are in Saramaccan's sister languages, Sranan and Ndjuka. A proto-creole in late seventeenth century Surinam yielded three main ones today: Sranan, Surinam's lingua franca; Ndjuka, a direct offshoot of Sranan spoken by descendants of slaves who established communities in the interior, about as similar to Sranan as Swedish is to Norwegian; and Saramaccan, also spoken in the interior by descendants of escaped slaves, which retains most of the grammar of Sranan and Ndjuka but has a vast amount of relexification from Portuguese and a higher component of lexical items from Fongbe and Kikongo.

In modern Sranan and Ndjuka, for example, the etymon from *no more* is used both in the clause-final semantic evolutions in Saramaccan and in a

function clearly similar to that of Saramaccan's clause-initial new information marker *nɔ́ɔ*. Here, for example, is Ndjuka's usage of its *naamo* to mean
"continuously":

(26)   *Ai   fufuu **naamo***
       he.IMF steal continuously
       'He keeps stealing'

(Shanks 1994: 137)

And here is Sranan's cognate, *nomo,* used as "only":

(27)   *Mi go wan leisi **nomo** na   Nickerie.*
       I   go one time only LOC   Nickerie
       'I've only been to Nickerie one time.'
                    (Languages of Suriname Sranan-English online dictionary)

Then, note that Sranan uses the same etymon clause-initially, in neither a
"continuously," "only," or "definitely" meaning:

(28)   *M tek ontslag a   bas, a no wan pai moro,*
       I   take dismissal LOC boss he NEG want pay more
       da   m n   e-wroko dj ên   moro.
       then I NEG IMF-work give 3SO more
       ***Nomo** den   sma   tai mi tak: W   a   no   sraften,*
       then   DEF.PL person talk I   COMP well he NEG slavery.time
       j   a   leti.
       you have right
       'So I let the boss fire me; he didn't want to pay me anymore, so I didn't
       work for him anymore. The people told me 'It's not slavery time any-
       more; you're right.' (Voorhoeve 1962: 71; running translation mine
       [Voorhoeve did not give one])

Voorhoeve translates *nomo* here as "then," but in fact, *nomo* is a rare rendition of "then" in his data, in which "then" is almost always expressed as
da(n) (from Dutch *dan* "then") or *ne* (from English *then,* as will be discussed
below). Note the *da* in the first sentence of the above passage, or the *da* and
ne in this one which also includes a *nomo* usage:

(29)   ***Da** m gw a   masra Engels, go aksi masra Engels tak:*
       then I   go LOC Mister Engels go ask Mister Engels COMP
       M wan moro moni.
       I want more money

Mi no   kan wroko f â   mon   dati.
I   NEG can work   for DEF money that
***Nomo** masra Engels e-ko   tak,*
then   Mister Engels IMF-come say
*mj om   go tai mi brada. **Ne** m taki:*
I   must go talk my brother then I say
M n   a   neks   e   make nanga m brada.
I   NEG have nothing until make with my brother

Then I went to Mr. Engels, went and asked him 'I want more money.
I can't work for that money.' Then Mr. Engels was up and saying I have
to talk to my brother. Then I said 'I don't have anything to do with my
brother.' (Voorhoeve 1962: 70; running translation mine)

In Voorhoeve's data, *nomo* is not merely a chance variant used to mean
"then." Instead, it is used to draw attention to an event of especial, decisive
dramatic prominence: above, Mr. Engels' condition for a raise in salary, or
in the example before that, the speaker's friends' approval of his quitting.
While Voorhoeve had no reason to attend to this nuance in his translations, it
is *da(n)* and *ne* that are mere markers of the sequential; *nomo* has a different
function, foregrounding new information.

Because English provides no single word serving to mark new information, predictably translations of this usage of *nomo* in Sranan and its cognate *na(a)mo* in Ndjuka are various (whereas translations of *da[n]* and *ne* as
"then" are more consistent among sources). Voorhoeve (1962) prefers "then,"
while the Languages of Suriname Sranan-English dictionary translates it as
"however" or "but":

(30) ***Nomo** di   a bigin taki, a   trawan ati   bron.*
      but   when he begin speak DEF other   heart burn
      'But when he began to speak, the other one got mad.'

Then, Shanks (1994) translates the Ndjuka cognate as "meanwhile":

(31) ***Namo**,   ne a si   wan olo.*
      meanwhile then he see a   hole
      'Meanwhile, he saw a hole.'

(Shanks 1994: 137)

I suggest that the variation in these translations reflects the fact that this
usage of the item has no true equivalent in English, and in fact has no semantic meaning at all, but a pragmatic one of flagging the information structure

of running discourse. These usages of *nomo* (in Ndjuka *na*[*a*]*mo*) are, under a more graceful analysis than that indicated by the multifarious translations, new information markers.

Their foregrounding function is not as conventionalized in Sranan and Ndjuka as *nɔ́ɔ* is in Saramaccan, classifying as sentential adverbs rather than the pragmatic particle that Saramaccan's *nɔ́ɔ* is. Moreover, there is no tense-sensitive division of labor in Sranan and Ndjuka between *nomo/namo* and the *then*-derived forms (*ne* in both, with *neen* as an alternate in Ndjuka). *Nomo* and *namo* can be assumed to reflect an earlier stage in the process that yielded, in Saramaccan, a phonetically abbreviated and grammatically conventionalized new information marker. In the terminology of Dahl (2004), the marking of foregrounding is more *mature* in Saramaccan, albeit not entailing the increased phonetic boundedness that Dahl's argument stresses.

Thus we can assume that Saramaccan's new information marker *nɔ́ɔ* is derived from an erstwhile usage of *nɔ́ɔmɔ* in clause-initial position, confirmed by the fact that the full form *nɔ́ɔmɔ* does occur as a new information marker on occasion, both clause-initially and after arguments:

(32) **Nɔ́ɔmɔ** *déé   mbétimbéti túu kái ɛ̃.*
     NI   DEF.PL animal.RD all call 3SO
     'So all of the various animals called him.'

(Price & Price n.d.: 120)

(33) *Nɔ́ɔ de tá píki   táa   ná   panyã̌ mi, hɛ̃* **nɔ́ɔmɔ** *i   músu téi.*
     NI they IMF answer COMP NEG grab me 3SO NI   you must take
     Then they were answering 'Don't grab me, it's him you should take.'

(ibid. 148)

The evolution of *no more* into a marker of new information would seem, on its face, slightly absurd. However, in fact, the connotation inherent in the semantics of *no more* of drawing a boundary is a plausible source for a marker setting off what has come before as separate, and thus foregrounding the subsequent material.

That is, a clause-initial discourse marker with negative semantics does not necessarily connote a negative meaning. Mendoza-Denton (1999) has documented that in the speech of many modern American English speakers, the use of *no* as a turn-initial discourse marker can convey not denial but agreement:

A: Why don't you do it like this, it's better that way.
S: No, yeah, you're right.

(Mendoza-Denton 1999: 282)

In the same way, it is common in many current dialects of English for turn-initial *no* to serve as a way of introducing novel observations, such that there is a *no* with each new "camera shot," as in this recent exchange the author was in:

J: So you spent six years in New York, nine in L.A., and then . . . Toledo.
T: (laughter) No, it was really hard at first, but after a while the low cost of living starts to become really attractive.

Nɔɔmɔ can be assumed to have become a new information marker in like fashion, the negative semantics of *no more* bleaching into a pragmatic guide-post marking a new development in a narrative or conversation.

4.4.1.2. New information marker nɔɔ as a post-emergence development

Our question at this point is whether new information marker *nɔɔ* was present in Saramaccan at its origins, thus supporting an idea that creolization alone can yield deeply conventionalized marking of pragmatic nuance, and that increasing complexity is not a significant aspect of the morphing of creoles over time.

First, given that a *no more* derivant has a foregrounding function in all three creoles today, we assume that this feature was present in their parent: the usage of *no more* in this particular function is too idiosyncratic (i.e. found in no other creole language or even older language known to me) to suppose that it emerged independently in all three.

That this was the case is supported by the fact that *no more* already has this function in our earliest detailed description of Sranan, a dictionary of 1783 (Schumann 1783). Alongside citations showing that the clause-final usages of *no more* have already lexicalized into their current functions:

"definitely":

(34) *Killiman musse dedde, **no morro**.*
      kill-man must die   no more
      'A murderer has to die, no questions asked.'
      (trans. from German: *Ein Mörder muss partout sterben, da hilft nichts davor.*)

"only":

(35) ***No morro** tu   jari, **no morro** passa, sinse mi kommotto*
      no more   two years no more   pass   since I exit
      janda wantron.
      there one-time

'It's only two years so far since I left there.'
(trans. from German: *Es sind nur erst 2 Jahr, es ist noch nicht ueber 2 Jahr, seitdem ich von dort weg bin.*)

We find a citation in which a clause-initial *no more* has no ready translation (i.e. is left untranslated into German), would be incoherently translated as "definitely" or "only," and thus, given the modern connotation of *nomo* in exactly this position, can be treated as serving in a foregrounding function, such that I include in the English translation an initial *so* marking the utterance as new information:

new information:

(36)   **No morro** *hulanga   tem ju   sa   libi dea?*
no more   how-long time you FUT live there
'So how long are you going to live hereabouts?'
(trans. from German: *Wie lange wirst du dich hier aufhalten?*)

In Saramaccan sources of the same period, there is no indication of a foregrounding function of *no more*. However, its modern clause-final usages are already in place, as in these sentences from Johannes Riemer's 1779 dictionary (Arends & Perl 1995: 326):

"definitely":

(37)   *A tann go kai* **no morro**.
he IMF go fall no more
'He definitely will fall.'

"always":

(38)   *Ju   tann siki* **no morro**.
you IMF sick no more
'You are constantly ill.'

"only":

(39)   *Mi killi wan pingo,* **no morro**.
I   kill one pig   no more
'I only shot one pig.'

This means that the grammaticalization of *no more* had proceeded apace clause-finally, and it is reasonable to assume that it had also done so clause-initially. Given that the sources for Saramaccan in the 1700's consist of two rather brief dictionaries which consist, more precisely, of one dictionary and a second modelled upon it, it is reasonable to assume that the absence in them of a foregrounding usage of *no more* is accidental.

Yet at this point we could theoretically surmise that early Sranan, the parent creole to all three of today's, may have had a new information marker *no morro* at its outset, when it formed after the English settled Surinam in 1651. Two things speak against this.

First, the usage of *no more* as a new information marker is hardly compositional, and in fact appears at first glance counterintuitive. This means that its usage in such an abstract, pragmatic function would have been the product of reinterpretation over a long period of time, such as that between 1651 and the late 1700s when substantial attestations first appear.

Second, the only way around the simple fact of the time requirements of grammaticalization would be if this usage of *no more* were, like Saramaccan's tone sandhi patterns, inherited from Fongbe at the language's birth. However, despite the rich contribution to these creoles' grammars from Fongbe, there is no evidence that the foregrounding system is a Fongbe inheritance – neither in its incipient form in Sranan and Ndjuka or in its more developed form in Saramaccan.

There is no item in Fongbe cognate to *nɔ́ɔmɔ* used both as a marker of new information and as an adverb expressing conviction and/or duration (cf., e.g. Höftmann & Ahohounkpanton 2003, Lefebvre & Brousseau 2001; Anne-Marie Brousseau, p.c. May 2007). Fongbe does not mark foregrounding overtly in any fashion as conventionalized as in Saramaccan or even in Sranan and Ndjuka. For example, the spoken Fongbe text in Lefebvre & Brousseau (2001: 539–42) indicates none such, despite the frequency of *nɔ́ɔ* even in brief citations of spoken Saramaccan.

Thus the process most fully realized in Saramaccan has its roots in a grammar-internal morphing that began in the creole spoken on Surinamese planations in the late 1600s, before the slaves escaped who went on to develop the offshoot creoles Saramaccan and Ndjuka. To the extent that all of the Atlantic English-based Creoles, including the Surinam trio, have been argued to trace back to a single one born in West Africa, St. Kitts or Barbados (Baker 1999, McWhorter 2000), we can assume that the new information marking described here began in Surinam rather than tracing to an earlier stage of the creole spoken elsewhere. This is because there is no cognate mechanism in other Atlantic English-based creoles (although *no more*'s clause-final usage as "only" is a shared feature among them).

4.4.1.3. Sidebar: nɔ́ɔ and multifunctionality

In a broader sense, in Saramaccan *no more* has made an awesomely multifarious contribution to both the grammar and lexicon of the language. There is even one further development from *nɔ́ɔmɔ,* presumably via the "only" homonym of *nɔ́ɔ:* an interrogative marker *nɔ́:*

(40)   *Tío   dédɛ **nɔ́**?*
       Uncle dead INT
       'Is Uncle dead?'

However, the interrogative is just as often marked in Saramaccan with a derivant of *nɔ́, ɔ:*

(41)   *I   ábi   tjiká ɔ?*
       you have suffice INT
       'Do you have enough?'

The *ɔ* marker always has a neutral interrogative function; *nɔ́,* on the other hand, can serve in that function as in (40) (presumably because it arose in that function), but just as often today exists in a contrastive relationship with *ɔ,* lending a gentler tone to an interrogation. A minimal pair:

(42)   *I   kɛ́   baláki ɔ?*
       you want vomit   INT
       'Do you want to throw up?'

(43)   *I   kɛ́   baláki **nɔ́**?*
       you want vomit   INT
       'Now, is it that you need to throw up, sweetie?'

Nɔ́ retains a degree of the specific minimizing connotation of its source word *nɔ́ɔ*"just, only," while its descendant *ɔ* has settled into a purely grammatical function of marking interrogation.

In sum, then, *no more* has yielded six items in Saramaccan: a new information marker, an intensifying pragmatic adverb "definitely," another adverb "continuously," an adverb "only," and two interrogative markers. This is a useful demonstration of how creole languages wrest the full, nuanced lexical and grammatical equipment of a natural human language from the limited lexicon resulting from pidginization, given that the Surinam creoles are based on a mere 600 English words (Koefoed & Taranskeen 1996: 120).

> *nɔ́ɔ* new information marker

nɔ́ɔmɔ "no more" > *nɔ́ɔmɔ* "definitely" > *nɔ́ɔmɔ* "continuously"
> *nɔ́ɔ* "only" > *nɔ́* interrogative marker >
> *ɔ* interrogative marker

4.4.2. The diachrony of *hɛ̃́*

The usage of *hɛ̃́* as a new information marker in the past tense also emerged independently of the languages spoken by Saramaccan's creators. There has been a suggestion otherwise, which does not stand up to scrutiny.

In its phonetic aspect, *hɛ̃́,* albeit traditionally translated as "then," is not a predictable reflex of English's [ðɛn]. According to the regular rendition of English words in Saramaccan, one would expect [d] rather than [h] (e.g. *dísi* < this). Meanwhile, it happens that *hɛ̃́* is identical phonetically to the tonic form of the third person singular pronoun. Boretzky (1983: 110–1) suggested a reason for this that would explain the anomalous [h]: namely that *hɛ̃́* is not a reflex of *then* at all. He suggested that the homonymy between the pronoun and the "then" word is modelled on a similar likeness between the words for "he" and "and then" in Ewe (*éyeé*) and Yoruba (*òun*).

However, Boretzky wrote at a time when research on slave shipments and correspondences between creoles and individual African languages were not as advanced as they have since become. It was once thought, for example, that Saramaccan's grammar had been created by speakers of as many as a dozen West African languages (cf. Byrne 1987). However, subsequently neither historical research on the provenience of slaves in Surinam, etymological study of Saramaccan's lexicon, nor examination of which African languages its grammar corresponds with most closely have identified Ewe and Yoruba speakers as having played a significant part in the development of Saramaccan. Rather, all indications have been that Fongbe was the primary model, and there is no homonymy between "him" and "and then" in Fongbe.

In fact, the Ewe and Yoruba accounts are not necessary. *Hɛ̃́* is a plausible development from [ðɛn] albeit not following the more general *Lautgesetze.* The steps would have been the following:

1. [ðɛn] > [dɛn] (*this* > [disi])
2. [dɛn] > [nɛn] (In Sranan and Ndjuka, copula *da* > *na;* also, in Ndjuka, "then" is *neen* from original [den]; a short form is *ne,* which we have seen in Sranan, where it is the only form).

3. [nɛn] > [ɛn] (in Saramaccan, heavily used grammatical items can lose initial alveolar consonants; e.g. original locative marker *na* > *a*, *na* now surviving largely as a morphophonemic alternate; copula *da* > *a* in sentences with a fronted possessive *U mí a dí búku* 'POSS ICOP DEF book" "The book is mine").

4. [ɛn] > [hɛn] (analogously to a prothetic [h] in various vowel-initial English words as rendered in Saramaccan: *hánsi* "ant" < *ants*, *hógi* "evil" < *ugly*.

(This analysis leaves to speculation at which point in Saramaccan word-final nasal consonants eroded and left behind nasality on the preceding vowel as phonemic, a phenomenon the timing of which is obscured in documentation by orthographical conventions.)

Thus *hɛ̃́* is not, as the Boretzky analysis suggested, a sequential marker that Saramaccan got "for free" when speakers of West African languages were inclined to use the phonetic shape of the third person pronoun as a word meaning "then" as well. *Hɛ̃́* developed independently of West African influence as a natural phonetic evolution from English's *then*, and took its place as a tense-specific new information marker unknown in English or Fongbe. *Hɛ̃́* was part of Saramaccan's development of complexity grammar-internally.[2]

4.4.3. But *How* Complex?

Despite that Saramaccan's new information marking is certainly an interesting complexity in the grammar hitherto unacknowledged, another lesson that it teaches is that just as creoles do not emerge with the mass of complexity of a grammar millennia old, they do not accrete such a mass in just a few centuries. Where creoles exhibit complexity, it is not in a *superlative* degree in the cross-linguistic sense. This is not accidental: it is a symptom of youth.

For example, the overt tracking of information structure in Saramaccan is analogous to the obligatory focus tracking in languages of the Philippines like Tagalog, which obligatorily marks focus on a sentential constituent with both a trigger particle *ang* and affixal markers that vary according to the constituent in focus (Schachter 1987: 941) (AT = agent trigger, PT = patient trigger, DT = dative trigger, BT = benefactive trigger TG = trigger marker, AC = actor, DR = directional):

---

2 This stands as a revision of my muted but permissive enthusiasm for the Ewe derivation in McWhorter (2005a: 374).

(44) actor:

    (a) ***Mag-**aalis*   ***ang*** *tindero*   *ng bigas sa sako*
        AT.PROG-take out TG storekeeper PT rice   DR sack
        para sa babae.
        BEN   woman
        'The storekeeper will take some rice out of a/the sack for a/the woman.'

patient:

    (b) *Aalisi-**n***   *ng tindero*   ***ang*** *bigas sa sako*
        PROG.take out-PT AC storekeeper TG rice   DR sack
        para sa babae.
        BEN   woman
        'A/the storekeeper will take the rice out of a/the sack for a/the woman.'

directional:

    (c) *Aalis-**an***   *ng tindero*   *ng bigas **ang** sako*
        PROG.take out-DT AC storekeeper PT rice   TG sack
        para sa babae.
        BEN   woman
        'A/the storekeeper will take some rice out of the sack for a/the woman.'

benefactive:

    (d) ***Ipag-**aalis*   *ng tindero*   *ng bigas sa sako **ang** babae.*
        PROG.take out-DT AC storekeeper PT rice TG sack TG woman
        'A/the storekeeper will take some rice out of the sack for a/the woman.'

However, the Tagalog system includes allomorphic variation of the affix according to grammatical relation, and entails marking the focus with two morphemes. The system is, therefore, more complex than Saramaccan's system. Foregrounding is also more obligatory in Tagalog than in Saramaccan: in Tagalog it is completely grammaticalized, whereas in Saramaccan it is better described as pragmaticized. This is to be expected, given that Tagalog has existed for countless centuries longer than Saramaccan, and is the descendant of the presumably unbroken transmission of an ancient language over tens of thousands of years.

Other features that have arisen in Saramaccan over time demonstrate in the same way that the language "has grammar," but are not powerful as demonstrations that a creole's grammar is, overall, indistinguishable in complexity from Yoruba's or Bengali's. For example, Saramaccan's two copulas can subdivide the semantic domain of nonverbal predication more finely than Fongbe does – but at present, only optionally, while other languages can subdivide the same domain between more morphemes than two (McWhorter 2005a: 117–8, 125–6). Saramaccan's original predicate negator *ná* has split into two that subdivide the domain of negation differently, but not in more *complex* fashion, than Fongbe's two, while, again, many languages subdivide the negation domain between many more morphemes, such as Southern Min Chinese's nine (Chappell 2001: 346):

Table 24. Negator morphemes in Souther n Min Chinese

bô	perfective
m̄	imperfective
(iá) bē	negation of expectation
boē	negation of ability
boâi	negation of perfective desiderative ("didn't want to V")
m̄mài	negation of imperfective desiderative ("don't want to V")
mài	negative imperative
m̄mó	negative hortative
m̄bién	negation of necessity

Or, Saramaccan has morphed into a modest assortment of morphophonemic rules – but they are not only modest in tally but phonetically shallow (McWhorter 2005a: 116–21).

However, it is hardly impossible that in several centuries, *nɔ́ɔ* may become a suffix (perhaps [-*na*]) obligatorily appended to foregrounded arguments. Meanwhile, *hɛ̃́* could easily lose its initial consonant and nasalize the vowel in the pronominal following it, perhaps yielding a paradigm of subject pronouns phonetically colored by nasalization used exclusively in matrix clauses after adverbial subordinate ones. The *nɔ́ɔ hɛ̃́* configuration could become frequent enough that in a future stage of Saramaccan, the past-tense new information marker could be perhaps [nɛ̃] or [nwɛ̃] contrasting with non-past *nɔ́ɔ,* and perhaps constituting the beginnings of a paradigm of foregrounding morphemes indexed to tense or aspect or other grammatical contrasts.

These are, of course, speculations. The main point is that Saramaccan is well positioned to morph into such directions, and already has an overt marking of a feature left largely to intonation and context in its source languages – as well as countless other languages of the world.

4.5. Complexity and inflection: a highly partial overlap

This Saramaccan feature is also a demonstration that grammatical complexity involves much more than inflectional affixation. Surely this is known to all linguists in the intellectual sense. However, there is habit of mind that encourages linguists to think first of inflections when the topic of complexity is at hand.

This is partly because inflectional affixation is so readily documented even in brief grammars, is subject to the tidiness of counting, and has been so amply analyzed in linguistic science (hence inflection is the topic in Kusters' [2003] foundational monograph on comparative complexity in grammars). The focus on inflection is also a conditioned reflex driven by our familiarity with well-inflected European languages. The problem is that this focus can distract us from what grammatical complexity is in a broader sense. For example, if the new information markers in Saramaccan actually were already inflections, they would long ago have been highlighted as evidence that creole languages "have grammar."

A Chinese variety, Xiang, marks at least eleven tense and aspect categories overtly (compared to Mandarin's five):

Table 25. Aspect markers in Xiang

da	past
ga	perfective
gada	perfect
kelai	experiential
zai(*goli*)	progressive
da	durative stative
ji	durative as continuative background
can	durative as "vivid" continuative background
reduplication	brief delimitative
can	delimitative compared to another event
(*da*)*zhe*	trial or "for just a little while" delimitative

This paradigm encodes subtle differences such as that between simultaneous events whose conjunction is unremarkable versus those whose conjunction is pragmatically unexpected:

(45)(a)   *Zhan¹ San¹ da²   **ji**   kou³sau⁴   zou³lou⁴*
          John   make ASP whistle   walk
          'John walked while whistling.'

  (b)   *Zhan¹ San¹ kan⁵   **can**   (kan⁵   can)   ku²   gada.*
        John   watch ASP watch ASP cry   ASP
        'John cried while watching.'

(Zhou 1998: 12–3)

Ngadha, an affixless Austronesian language of Flores, makes ample use of modal particles to convey pragmatic meanings, in a fashion similar to German's. Certainly all natural languages can convey such pragmatic meanings, but where grammars develop entrenched monomorphemic indications of such beyond ordinary mechanisms of intonation or phrasal collocations, it qualifies as a grammatical overspecification. For example, here is *dzaö laä* "I go" modified with just a few of the particles:

Table 26. Some Nghada modal particles (Arndt 1933: 27; trans. from German mine)

*dzaö **mu** laä*	'I'm going, whatever happens.'
*dzaö **mu le** laä*	'I'm keeping on walking along, whatever happens.'
*dzaö **mu mara** laä*	'I'm going whatever happens, and I'll deal with the circumstances.'

It is urgent that cases such as these be kept in mind when assessing creoles' development of complexity. The current tendency is to operate under a tacit assumption that the complexity to watch out for in creoles is the development of inflectional affixation and/or marking of the categories typically associated with it. The problem is that this has often yielded less than promising results.

DeGraff's (1993) argument that subject pronouns in Haitian Creole are actually null subject syntactic clitics implied that Haitian was a step away from displaying subject prefixes like, for example, Bantu languages. Yet Déprez (1992), Cadely (1994) and Roberts (1999) have conclusively refuted this argument. See also Kihm's problematic argument on Arabic plurals and Nubi Creole Arabic (Chapter Two, Section 3.4).

The development of inflectional affixation is but one of legions of directions a grammar may wend in over time. It is hardly the case that all analytic languages show signs of developing inflections any time soon, as is clear from Chinese languages and countless other Sino-Tibetan, as well as Mon-Khmer, Thai, and Niger-Congo, languages. Creoles tend strongly to be analytic, and there is no a priori reason to elevate inflectional affixation as the most likely or interesting complexity that they may develop. Other complexities common in analytic languages include ergativity (e.g. in many Polynesian languages, indicated via particles), alienability distinction in possession (also incipient in Saramaccan [McWhorter 2005a: 116–7]), evidential marking, and numeral classifiers (which can be analyzed as a kind of grammatical gender marking).

Here, for example, is a sentence from an analytic language, Akha, a Sino-Tibetan language of Southeast Asia (a language also mentioned in Chapter Two, because in the case that the reader happens not to read that chapter, sentences like this one are too central to the issue of creole exceptionalism to miss):

(46) *ŋà nɛ àjɔq **áŋ** áshì thì **shì** biq **ma**.*
I ERG he ABS fruit one CL give EVID
'I gave him one fruit.'

(Hansson 2003: 243)

There are no inflectional affixes in Akha. Yet in the sentence above, we see ergative and absolutive marking, a numeral classifier (one of an entire paradigm in Akha), and an evidential marker, this one used to mark conviction exclusively in the first person (!) (evidential markers often occur in first and non-first person shapes in Akha). Russian, as complex as it is, marks none of these distinctions overtly.

It is in this light that we must view the emergence of a system of new information marking via particles in Saramaccan. This system is distinctly un-Indo-European, and yet in the cross-linguistic sense, it qualifies as an accreted complexity. To tacitly suppose that Saramaccan's future stages – or other creoles' – will be ones more like English and Dutch is arbitrary, and focuses on an abbreviated conception of the multifarious nature of what grammar actually is across the world's 6000 languages. Saramaccan could just as easily morph into a language like Akha.

Chapter 5
Hither and thither in Saramaccan Creole

5.1. Introduction

This chapter will examine two serial verb constructions encoding movement in Saramaccan Creole[1] that have received little attention, with the aim of demonstrating their implications for ongoing controversies over the place of creole languages in language contact typology. The grammaticalized usages in Saramaccan of *túwɛ* "throw" and *púu* "pull" shed useful light on certain issues curently under debate:

a)   creoles' relative complexity compared to older languages
b)   whether creoles' commonly remarked appearance of relative simplicity is due to inadequate description
c)   the corollary question of the extent to which creoles emerged via the word-by-word relexification of their creators' native, and unquestionably "complex," grammars.

This paper is intended as an attempt to outline my positions on these issues with reference to two specific constructions in one creole, to complement a previous presentation that addressed certain creole grammars as a whole (McWhorter 2005a: 102–41).

5.2. *Túwɛ* "throw"

5.2.1. Syntactic and semantic behavior

The meaning of the Saramaccan verb *túwɛ* as an independent lexical item is "to throw."

(1)   *Mi túwɛ dí súndju a   dí   can.*
      I   throw DEF dirt   LOC DEF trashcan
      'I threw the dirty thing into the trashcan.'

---

1   All Saramaccan data were elicited by the author and graduate student assistants from native consultants except examples 71 and 72 (at which citation is given). Special thanks to consultants Rohit Paulus and Gerda Menig.

While phonetically obscured today, the etymology is more apparent in the cognate item in Saramaccan's progenitor creole Sranan, *trowe,* as well as the earlier Saramaccan form documented in the late eighteenth century, *trueh* (Arends & Perl 1995:361), intermediate in phonetic evolution between Sranan *trowe* and today's *túwɛ.*

Predictably, the verb is also used in various semantic extensions of the core concept of throwing, such as "to drop":

(2)   *A   túwɛ dí   báta wáta a   dí   wómi hédi.*
      he throw DEF bottle water LOC DEF man   head
      'He dropped the bottle of water on the man's head.'

and assorted idiomatic usages such as *A táki túwɛ* 'she talk throw' "She is talking not to anyone in particular." This is but one of many idiomatic usages of *túwɛ,* a semantically central and fecund word in Saramaccan with an efflorescence of related meanings just as, for instance, *put* has in English.

Of interest in this paper is the occurrence of *túwɛ* as the second verb in serial verb constructions. There is a smallish set of verbs regularly used in this slot in Saramaccan that have grammaticalized considerably, such as *dá* "to give" which expresses the benefactive:

(3)   *Gaãtangi fu dí   i   lúku   dí   mií   **dá** mi.*
      thank.you for that you care.for DEF child give me
      'Thank you for looking after my children for me.'

5.2.1.1. Range of usages

In the case of *túwɛ*'s occurrences of this kind, an initial impression might be that the meaning is merely the core lexical one, occurring sequentially after the first verb. For example:

(4)   *A ba   pɔtɔpɔtɔ túwɛ a   wáta.*
      he carry mud   throw LOC water
      'He carried mud to the water (and threw it in).'

In this sentence, we imagine someone first carrying the mud and then throwing it into the water, with *túwɛ* indicating a discrete action.

But this kind of interpretation is harder to support for other V2 occurrences of *túwɛ.*

(5) *Kobí tɔ́tɔ dí   wómi túwɛ.*
Kobi push DEF man   throw
'Kobi pushed the man down.'

This sentence does not refer to the oddly particular notion of Kobi first pushing the man and then afterwards embarking upon the new action of throwing him. In fact, informants often translate this sentence and similar ones along the lines of "Kobi pushed the man and the man fell down." We might propose, then, that in the V2 slot, *túwɛ* has taken on the meaning of "to make fall" (i.e. to fell), which would seem plausible given the short semantic step to this meaning from the core "throw" one. This analysis could apply to further usages such as:

(6) *A kóti dí   páu túwɛ.*
he cut DEF tree throw
"He cut the tree down."

(7) *Mi súti dí   píngo túwɛ.*
I   shoot DEF pig   throw
"I shot the pig (and hit him)."

But other usages render even this proposed semantic contribution oddly redundant. *Túwɛ* is also used as V2 in cases where making the object fall is already not just an intuitive result, but the core semantics, of the matrix verb:

(8) *De kándi té túwɛ a   kiíki.*
they pour tea throw LOC creek
"They poured tea into the creek."

Especially illustrative is the equivalence between the following two sentences: if *túwɛ* can mean "to pour" used by itself, then what is the function of its use as a second verb in a serial construction with another verb meaning "to pour"?

(9)(a) *A **túwɛ** dí amána fátu a dí   bṍṍ   hɛ̃ a paajá híi dí   táfa líba.*
he pour DEF syrup LOC DEF pancakes then it spread all DEF table top

  (b) *A **kándi** dí   amána fátu **túwɛ** a dí   bṍṍ hɛ̃ a paajá hii dí   táfa líba.*
he pour DEF syrup throw LOC DEF flour then it spread all DEF table top
'He poured the syrup on the pancakes and it spread all over the table.'

Moreover, *túwɛ* can even be accompanied after the object by *kaí* "to fall," again curious under an analysis of V2 *túwɛ* as a causative-marked *fall*:

(10)   *A súti dí   pátupátu túwɛ gó kaí a   wáta.*
       he shoot DEF duck   throw go fall LOC water
       'He shot the duck and it fell into the water.' (not that *he* fell in)

Crucially, there are cases where the *fall*-related semantics are simply inapplicable:

(11)   *A jáka déé   ganíã   túwɛ gó a   dɔ́ɔ.*
       he chase DEF.PL chicken throw go LOC outside
       "He chased the chickens outside."

5.2.1.2. A unified analysis

A unified analysis of the use of *túwɛ* in all of these sentences except ones where a discrete throwing action is clear (i.e. [4]) is that *túwɛ* does not encode a discrete lexical meaning, but serves a grammaticalized function: marking the end of a pathway of movement. Hence, for example, the above sentence, in which the birds were not made to fall in any way: *túwɛ* serves to indicate that the birds ended up outside, at the end of an action designed to chase them out of an enclosed space.

This analysis is preferable to the rather vague semantic contribution that we would have to posit otherwise:

(12)   *Hái mi túwɛ a   dí   wáta kó.*
       pull me throw LOC DEF water come
       'Pull me in onto the shore.'

(The *come* verb in this sentence indicates direction towards, with the locative *a* directionally neutral, rather than indicating movement towards the water as one might suppose given the semantics of Romance items such as French's *à* and Portuguese's *a*). Here again, this is not a peculiar request to be first pulled in and then thrown down; *túwɛ* indicates that the pulling is to achieve the person's ending up on the shore, marking the trajectory with an end point.

(13)   *Vínde ɛ̃ túwɛ gó naandɛ́.*
       throw it throw go there
       "Throw it over (onto) there."

Here, the use of *túwɛ* seems curiously redundant if intended to specify that throwing something also entails its falling eventually. As a marker of the object's landing and coming to rest, the use of *túwɛ* is coherent. Certainly, redundancy is hardly alien to any grammar: but a significant body of *túwɛ* occurrences submit to an analysis of the item as a grammatical one, such that the redundance that certain occurrences at first glance suggest qualifies as impressionistic.

Importantly, there are indeed cases in which *túwɛ* is used as a second verb in a serial construction in which it does retain its core lexical meaning. This is the case with, for example, the previously cited:

(14) *A   ba   pɔtɔpɔtɔ túwɛ a   wáta.*
      he carry mud   throw LOC water
      'He carried mud to the water (and threw it in).'

This is typical of the fact that in grammaticalization, original usages typically persist alongside derived ones, often indefinitely. But most uses of *túwɛ* as V2 in a serial construction are of the grammaticalized variety.

As such, *túwɛ* has developed into what can be termed a path satellite in the terminology of Talmy (1985). For example, its semantic domain overlaps partially with English *down* as in *I cut the tree down* or *I shot the pig down.*

Besides its grammatical rather than lexical semantic contribution, a further indication of its grammaticalized nature is that it cannot cleft with copy, as lexical verbs in Saramaccan can. This construction encodes contrastive focus, as in:

(15) *Nɔnɔ́, **jéi** mi **jéi** dí   a   tá   kó.*
      no   hear I   hear COMP he IMF come
      'No, I *hear* him coming.'

When the more grammaticalized verb in a serial construction retains a semantic contribution that corresponds to a concrete, lexical concept, then it can be clefted with copy just as the modified verb can, such as *gó* "go" when used to indicate direction towards:

(16) ***Kulé** Kobí **kulé** gó a   wósu.*
      run   Kobi run   go LOC house
      'Kobi *ran* to the house.'

(17) ***Gó** Kobí kulé **gó** a   wósu.*
      go   Kobi run   go LOC house
      'Kobi ran *to* the house.'

However, *túwɛ* as the second verb in a serial does not allow this:

(18)   ***Túwɛ** mi súti   dí   píngo **túwɛ**.*
       throw I shoot DEF pig   throw
       'I shot the pig and got him.'

(19)(a)   ***Fáa** Kobí **fáa** dí   páu túwɛ.*
          fell Kobi fell DEF tree throw
          'Kobi *cut* the tree down.'

   (b)   ***Túwɛ** Kobí **fáa** dí   páu **túwɛ**.*
         throw Kobi fell DEF tree throw
         'Kobi cut the tree *down*.'

Note, incidentally, that *fáa* means precisely "to make fall," and yet *túwɛ* occurs as V2. In its usage as a second serial verb, *túwɛ* is in most cases purely a piece of grammar, functionally equivalent to an inflection: it no longer has a discrete lexical connotation that would submit naturally to focus.

5.2.2. *Túwɛ* and creole complexity

Túwɛ is firstly useful in clarifying my hypothesis in previous work that creoles, as new languages born from pidginization, are structurally simpler than older languages (McWhorter 2005a: 9–141).

This claim has engendered a number of arguments demonstrating that various creoles indeed display "complex" features. This is welcome in itself. However, this work also tends to be predicated upon a tacit that I have perhaps implied that creoles are the simplest possible languages, and this has been by no means my intention.

5.2.2.1. *Túwɛ is complex beyond its mere status as a "serial verb"*

For example, according to the frameworks under which Saramaccan has most often been documented, the grammaticalized rendition of *túwɛ* qualifies as but one of many verbs that happen to be used in serial verb constructions. Serial verbs have figured so largely in work on Saramaccan partly because of their models in West African languages, and partly within arguments that they constitute default expressions of Universal Grammar (Bickerton 1984: 179, Byrne 1987, Veenstra 1996). Be this as it may, there is nothing identifiably either "simple" or "complex" about serial verbs, and thus one might suppose that serial *túwɛ* has no implications for the complexity issue.

But in fact, we might imagine a hypothetical linguistics field in which most linguists natively spoke languages with serial verbs rather than European languages, compared to which serialization naturally appears exotic. In this alternate universe, no one would be moved to devote articles and sections of grammars to "serial verbs," as this would seem the "natural" way that a language patterned. More interesting would be the grammatical distinctions that verbs happened to mark, "serially" or not.

In this hypothetical world, the serial use of *túwɛ* would more likely be seen as showing that the acquisition of Saramaccan requires mastering the explicit marking of the *completion of movement trajectories,* with a path satellite that is also restricted to *transitive sentences. Túwɛ* is not used, for example, to mark completion of trajectories in intransitive sentences. For example:

(20) *A lolá kaí *(túwɛ) a   gõ̃ó.*
      it roll fall   LOC ground
      "It rolled to the ground."

Learning the language, one might easily work from transitive sentences like *Mi kóti dí páu túwɛ* "I chopped the tree down" and assume that the Saramaccan version of *It rolled to the ground* would include *túwɛ* as well – and immediately reveal oneself as a second-language learner overgeneralizing. In transitive sentences, the semantics of the main verb in the *túwɛ* serial often inherently entail that the object would achieve the end of a trajectory, and yet the redundant appendage of *túwɛ* to confirm the end point is allowed nonetheless. But in intransitive sentences the *fall* verb, for example, is allowed to contribute its implied end point without reinforcement by *túwɛ* or a like element; hence the above example and others such as:

(21) *Dí   sikífi-papái kumútu   kaí a   gõ̃ó.*
      DEF pen   come.out fall LOC ground
      'The pen fell (off) to the ground.'

(22) *Dí   sikífi-papái tómbi kaí a   dí   táfa líba.*
      DEF pen   spill fall LOC DEF table top
      'The pen rolled off of the table.'

Diachronically, this is an epiphenomenon of the agentive semantics of *throw,* naturally lending itself to usage within transitive constructions in which an object is acted upon by an agent. When a pen rolls off of a table, it is an experiencer moving on its own steam; even if the movement is initiated by an actor, this fact is pragmatically backgrounded and thus is not expressed in the syntax. Hypothetically, in a future stage of Saramaccan, *túwɛ* will have been extended to intransitive sentences, its evolution into a path satellite being thereby complete in being valency-neutral. But at the present stage of the language, synchronically, *túwɛ*'s serial usage is conditioned by argument structure, hardly elementary in the acquisitional or cross-linguistic sense.

Note also that *túwɛ* as V2 is only fitfully translatable into English (or most languages). It corresponds to the English satellite *down* in some usages such as with felling trees or killing animals (*Mi súti dí píngo túwɛ* "I shot the pig [dead]"). Elsewhere it corresponds to the connotation of *-to* in *into* and *onto*. In reference to the latter, *I pushed him in the water* is technically ambiguous between indicating that the pushee fell into the water and that the pushee and I were wading in the water and I shoved him. But *I pushed him into the water* can only mean that the pushee started on dry land and ended up in the water. *Túwɛ* as V2 marks this distinction.

But in other cases, one would be hard pressed to give any English equivalent to the connotation:

(23) *A jáka déé   ganíã túwɛ gó a   dɔ́ɔ.*
      he chase DEF.PL chicken throw go LOC outside
      'He chased the chickens outside.'

In the English rendition, *outside* expresses that the birds were chased out of the house; what separate piece of meaning expressable in English, then, does *túwɛ* correspond to?

In general *túwɛ* as V2 contributes a fine, abstract, and ultimately unnecessary nuance of meaning, of the kind that native speakers of the language, for example, are not consciously aware of. Asked what *túwɛ* "means" in such usages, consultants first give the core lexical meaning of "throw." But if queried further, given the observation that the sentence does not seem to depict throwing, they typically pause and shake their heads – just as linguistically untutored English speakers would if asked what, for example, *out* means in verb-particle complexes like *tapped out, worn out,* or *Simpsoned-out*. If Saramaccan were a maximally simple language, then we might expect that it would only encode a central core of grammatical concepts that speakers of almost any language would comprehend – as is true of pidgins regardless of their source languages. But this is not true of Saramaccan.

5.2.2.2. Túwε's complexity has been missed because of biases in grammatical coverage

Saramaccan's use of *túwε* is also relevant to a common opinion among creolists that a verdict on creoles' complexity is premature until there are more detailed descriptions of the languages, a view given by, for example, Arends (2001: 181). I feel that this view was more appropriate up to about the 1990s than it is today. While substantial grammatical descriptions of more creoles are still necessary, the number of solid grammars now available, combined with the weight of four decades of journal and anthology articles, are such that creolists are no better, but no worse, off than workers in most language areas. Very few area specialists, after all, have the blessing of the vast amount of description available to the Romance, Germanic, or Slavic specialist – and even these regularly rue the paucity of descriptions of nonstandard dialects.

Yet, it is undeniable that among specialists on Surinam creoles, contingent interest in a certain range of topics such as serial verbs and tone sandhi has distracted many specialists from attending to, for example, the grammatical nature of *túwε* and its cognates. Byrne (1987), despite its ample attention to serial verbs, made no mention of the *túwε* serial construction, as it would be of little import to a thesis concerned with issues of Government-Binding theory. Migge (1998), despite being a dissertation on substrate influence in Ndjuka, does not mention the serial construction with *towe*. Sebba (1987: 47–8) on Sranan serial verbs treats serial constructions with *trowe* only in passing, and as occurring in contexts where the actor has no control over the result. This appears to be motivated partly by the source of the item in *throw away,* and is based largely on a constrained number of sentences from written texts rather than the living language. But a sentence Sebba gives like the following does not submit gracefully to an analysis as devoid of control:

Sranan

(24) *Philip naki   a   kapten trowe   na   gron.*
Phillip strike DEF captain throw LOC ground
'Phillip strikes the captain to the ground.'

(Sebba 1987: 48)

This analysis is also difficult to support in Saramaccan sentences like:

(25) *De kándi té   túwε   a   kiíki.*
they pour   tea throw LOC creek
'They poured tea into the creek.'

I intend no criticism of these authors' work: to treat a language with a focus on its implications for theoretical issues rather than exhaustively tabulating all of its grammatical machinery is thoroughly valid in the intellectual sense. Sebba, for example, was interested in issues of syntactic configuration, and as such would not be expected to have addressed the particularities of a serial verb construction that does not happen to encode a grammatically central distinction such as the benefactive, comparative, or instrumental as other Surinam creole serials do.

However, the fact remains that the result of the particular interests of Surinam creole specialists such as those above was that they left an impression that Saramaccan and its sisters did not have a *transitive end-of-trajectory path satellite*. This has indeed been a "hidden" complexity of Saramaccan.

5.2.2.3. Túwɛ *and complexity: Relative versus superlative complexity*

However, I also assert that neither this feature nor others in Saramaccan belie my claim that creoles are less complex than older languages overall. There is a tacit implication in many presentations of "complex" features in creoles that the feature presented is but the tip of an iceberg, such that a comprehensive address would reveal that Saramaccan Creole is as complex as Ojibwa or that Cape Verdean Creole Portuguese is as complex as Georgian – if only a scholar happened to take a good long hard look and present the data.

But this has yet to be proven. I remain struck by the simple fact that creoles as a group never display complexity to a *superlative* degree in the cross-linguistic sense. Saramaccan, for example, inherited rather involved tone sandhi specifications from Gbe languages – but in a less complex rendition (Ham 1999). Indeed, Kramer (2004) argues that the system has features that Fongbe's does not – but Fongbe's system remains more complex overall.

Or, Saramaccan's marking of the end-of-path trajectories is reminiscent of, for example, the distinction in Slavic languages' motion verbs between indeterminate and determinate movement, where the latter expresses focus upon movement towards a goal. Here is a distinction in Russian, indicated with root alternations:

Indeterminate:

(26)   *Ptits-y   letaj-ut*
        bird-PL fly-3PL
        'Birds fly.'

Determinate:

(27) *Vy   let-ite   v Moskv-u?*
  you.PL fly-2PL to Moscow-ACC
  'Are you flying to Moscow?'

The indeterminate verb form is, in the infinitive, *letat'*, while the determinate one is *letet'*. One might propose that this means that Russian expresses a distinction roughly equivalent to the one that *túwε* does but with verbal root alternations rather than a serial verb.

But this would be a vast oversimplification. For one, Russian surpasses Saramaccan in complexity in the sheer irregularity that the motion verbs evince. The difference between indeterminate and determinate verbs must be learned by rote; there are neither suffixes nor root alternations that encode the difference in regular fashion: *letat'* / *letet'* for *fly*, but *begat'* / *bežat'* for *run*, and then there is the suppletive distinction *xodit'* / *idti* for *go*. Saramaccan has no overt distinction between types of motion verb, either affixal or analytic.

And then there are morphophonemic rules that add extra wrinkles to appending the person- and number-marking concordial suffixes: in the determinate *letite* "you (PL) fly" but *leču* "I fly." The motion verbs, typically of items of heavy use, tend to also to be outright irregular in their conjugational patterns. Saramaccan, like all languages, has morphophonemic processes. However, they are mostly only modestly distortive in the phonetic sense (McWhorter 2005a: 119–20), and apply to a compact set of grammatical items (such as *fu* "for," which varies according to the personal pronoun it occurs with: 1S *fu mi* > *u mi*; 2S *fu i* > *fii*; 3S *fu ε̃* > *fε̃ε̃*). As to their occurrence with motion verbs, while morphophonemic distortions riddle all of Russian's motion verbs, there is but a single one in Saramaccan's: when *gó* "to go" occurs with preverbal progressive marker *tá,* the result is *nángó.* Moreover, the very category of irregular verb is virtually nonexistent in Saramaccan: other than the aforementioned, there is a single other case, in that identificational *be*-verb *da* cannot take the past marker *bi,* instead replaced in the past by the main other *be*-verb *dέ.*

Then, the contrast between indeterminate and determinate occurs within the realm of the imperfective – but Russian verbs also occur in perfective forms. This means that motion verbs occur in three renditions: the indeterminate and determinate forms within the imperfective, and then also perfective forms, prefixing *po-*, such that *poidjom* means "Let's go," as opposed to *idjom* which would only encode the indeterminate imperfective (roughly, "we are going [somewhere]").

And this only scratches the surface of Slavic verbs of motion, notoriously challenging both to analysts and to second-language learners. *Túwɛ* shows that Saramaccan has complexity, but *túwɛ*'s behavior will not motivate a century's worth of treatises offering competing accounts for its occurrence and nuances, as Slavic motion verbs have.

5.2.3. *Túwɛ* and the Relexification Hypothesis

5.2.3.1. *A basic match between Saramaccan and Fongbe*

According to the Relexification Hypothesis promoted by Lefebvre (most summarily, 1998), we expect that serial *túwɛ* was created as a calque on an identical usage of the *throw* verb in its main substrate language.

The principal substrate language of Saramaccan was the Kwa Niger-Congo language Fongbe of Togo and Benin, as is clear from the fact that Saramaccan parallels this language very closely in syntax and borrowed many lexical and even grammatical items from it. Predictably, Fongbe indeed can mark the end of trajectories with the verb *throw:*

(28) *Kòkú sò sìn ò kòn **nyì** àyí.*
       Koku take water DEF pour throw ground
       'Koku spilled water on the floor.'

However, this usage of *throw* is marginal in Fongbe and only slightly conventionalized. Much more common is the use of the verb *put* in the function; it is here that Fongbe has a model for the general pattern shown for the usage of *túwɛ* in the previous section:

(29) *Kòkú sò mɛ ò zín ɖó àyí.*
       Koku take person DEF push put ground
       'Koku made the person fall.'

(30) *Kòkú sò àmì ò kòn ɖó gò mɛ̀.*
       Koku take oil DEF pour put bottle in
       'Koku poured the oil in a bottle.'

                                                (Lefebvre & Brousseau 2001: 412)

(31) *Kòkú nyì yòvózên ò ɖó xàsùn ò mɛ̀.*
       Koku throw orange   DEF put basket DEF in
       'Koku threw the orange into the basket.'

                                                                (ibid. 426)

5.2.3.2. *Discrepancies between Saramaccan and Fongbe*

However, while the source of Saramaccan's end-of-trajectory marking in Fongbe syntax is clear in the general sense, a relexificationist perspective is fraught with problems.

First, Saramaccan's creators reproduced a construction Fongbe expresses with *put* by means of a construction expressed with *throw*. In fact, Saramaccan does use its own *put* verb, *butá,* as a second verb in a serial construction in a function broadly similar to *túwɛ*'s:

(32) *Mi tá tjá wáta gó butá a dí gbóto déndu.*
     I   IMF carry water go put LOC DEF boat inside
     'I am carrying water into the boat.'

(33) *Mi sáka dí búku butá a dí táfa líba.*
     I   put.down DEF book put LOC DEF table top
     'I placed the book on the table.'

But Saramaccan's *butá* "put" is not a grammaticalized end-of-pathway marker as Fongbe's *ɖó* is. It is restricted to contexts in which its lexical connotation of placement is still easily recoverable. Note the following contrast:

(34)(a) *Mi sáka   híi soní butá, hɛ̃ mi kulé.*
        I   put.down all thing put   then I   run
        'I dropped everything, then I ran.'

   (b) *Mi sáka   híi soní túwɛ kulé.*
       I   put.down all thing throw run
       'I dropped everything and ran.'

Butá is used when the person lets the things drop as a discrete and premeditated action before running; *túwɛ* is used to describe a more immediate and less deliberated occurrence. Fongbe's *put* verb *ɖó* is not semantically restricted in this way: Fongbe data on this verb such as that in Lefebvre & Brousseau (2001) and elsewhere indicate a more deeply grammaticalized marker of much less selective occurrence.

This returns us to the fact that Saramaccan accomplishes this function with a *throw* verb, while Fongbe's *throw* verb *nyì* is used this way only marginally. *Nyì*'s syntactic placement also diverges from *túwɛ*'s. As shown in (28), Fongbe's *nyì* "to throw" occurs in a triverbal construction in which the main verb is the second, while *só* "to take" occurs first, in a rendition grammaticalized from its lexical meaning, bordering on serving as an accusative marker, as known in various related languages such as Yatye (Stahlke 1970). The *take* verb in Fongbe occurs widely in such usages (Lefebvre & Brousseau 2001: 409–15), but Saramaccan's *take, téi,* is used in serial constructions only in more literal, descriptive contexts (cf. Veenstra 1996, McWhorter 2005a: 109–11):

(35)   *Kobí téi   dí   matjáu kóti dí   bɛ́ɛ́.*
       Kobi take DEF axe   cut DEF bread
       'Kobi cut the bread with an axe. / Kobi took an axe and cut the bread.'

Meanwhile, in Fongbe the main verb and *nyì* are adjacent, contrary to *túwɛ*'s occurrence after an object shared with the main verb as in the sentences I have cited.

Thus while it is incontestable that Saramaccan's *túwɛ* and *butá* are modelled in a general way upon Fongbe structures, it must be noted that Lefebvre's (1998 and other works) mechanism for relexification, described as the replacement of lexical and functional items of the substrate language by phonetic strings from the lexifier language, cannot account for their behavior. To wit, a Saramaccan string in which a Fongbe sentence like (36) is relexified by phonetic forms from English (or in the case of *tutú,* from Kikongo [cf. Daeleman 1972: 14 for etymology]) would be ungrammatical:

(36)   Fongbe   Kɔ̀kú   sɔ́   sìn   ɔ́   kɔ̀n   **nyì**   àyí.
                      Koku   take   water DEF   pour   throw   ground
       Saramaccan   *Kokú   téi   dí   wáta   tutú   túwɛ   a gṍṍ
       'Koku spilled water on the floor.'

(A correct Saramaccan rendering: *Kokú tutú dí wáta túwɛ a gṍṍ.*)

Similarly, Saramaccan's creators did not simply replace their use of *ɖó* "put" with a phonetic string from Portuguese (*botar* "to put"): usages of *put* typical in Fongbe would be ungrammatical in Saramaccan:

(37)   Fongbe   Kɔ̀kú nyì   yòvózên ɔ́   **ɖó**   xàsùn ɔ́ mɛ̀
                     Koku throw orange DEF   put   basket DEF in
       Saramaccan *Kokú túwɛ dí   fóu-fátu butá a dí   mánda déndu
       'Koku threw the orange into the basket.'

(A correct Saramaccan rendering would be *Kokú vínde dí fóu-fátu túwɛ a dí mánda déndu.*)

Lefebvre's hypothesis is couched in a highly constrained, schematic mechanism, which is laudable in casting her findings in as scientific a fashion as possible. But creole genesis is not tidy enough to conform to the predictions of one-to-one correspondence between lexifier and substrate lemmas that Lefebvre's conclusions tend to imply.

5.2.3.3. The Fongbe substrate as retained in a different creole

Túwε is also revealing in a cross-creole context. Lefebvre's hypothesis is illustrated via the comparison of Haitian Creole and Fongbe, with the thesis that Haitian is Fongbe morphology and syntax with French lexical items (or, in Lefebvre's terminology, labels). However, Haitian Creole has not a hint of the use of serial verbs to mark the end of changes of location. I am aware of no description or treatment of the creole that mentions such, nor does Lefebvre in the 1998 work or in any of her articles on Haitian over the decades.

To be sure, Lefebvre's hypothesis includes various explanations for the discrepancies between Haitian and Fongbe. For example, one of Lefebvre's main stipulations is that Haitian lacks Fongbe features for which there was no readily perceptible equivalent in French, such as a logophoric pronoun.

Clearly, however, this was not the case regarding a Fongbe construction which simply utilized two semantically central verbs with obvious equivalents in French. Haitian did, after all, incorporate French's *jeter* "to throw" and *mettre* and *poser* "to put" as lexical items, and also incorporated verb serialization itself. The question, then, is why Haitian does not use its *jeter, mettre,* and/or *poser* cognates as Saramaccan used *throw away* and Portuguese *botar.* Lefebvre (1998) does not address the absence in Haitian of Fongbe's serial verbs marking ends of pathways.

Lefebvre also proposes that discrepancies between Haitian and Fongbe can be explained as the result of dialect levelling between different renditions of the early version of the creole by speakers of different varieties of the Gbe complex. An example she gives is that Haitian presumably lacks a calque of Fongbe's habitual marker because the Ewe variety of Gbe happens to lack one (Lefebvre 1998: 139). According to this analysis, Ewe-speaking slaves would have developed an early Haitian Creole without a habitual marker, and their version happened to win out in a competition with the Fongbe-modelled variety as the creole jelled.

In fact, since there is no historical documentation of distinct early Haitian varieties, Lefebvre's analysis is inevitably speculative. But in the case before us in this article, this account fails in any case, as Ewe uses its *put* verb just as Fongbe does:

Ewe

(38) *tsɔ́ nú* **da** *ɖé   anyí*
      take thing put reach down
      'to put down'

                                                    (Westermann 1930a: 234)

Finally, Lefebvre treats various features that Haitian has that Fongbe does not as "innovations," with explanations in each case as to why the creole departs from its substrate source. However, here we encounter not an innovation in Haitian, but an abbreviation – and a reason for the discrepancy must also be able to explain why Saramaccan did incorporate the very construction that Haitian did not.

Our problem, then, is this. Lefebvre's hypothesis proposes that in Haiti, Fongbe speakers created a creole by substituting French labels for Fongbe ones, and that where Haitian does not copy Fongbe, it is because assorted factors made doing so impossible. Yet, at roughly the same time in Surinam, Fongbe speakers created another creole with mostly English and Portuguese words, that reproduces (or reflects) several Fongbe structures that Haitian does not, with the barriers to calquing that Lefebvre surmises for Haitian's creators mysteriously suspended. Lefebvre's hypothesis is argued strictly on the basis of Haitian Creole: other creoles and substrates are not a part of the argumentation.

Relexification was certainly a central process in creole genesis, but an empirical and scientific account must be able to explain "minimal pair" discrepancies between two creoles based on one and the same substrate language. Neither a relexification model nor the various corollary processes Lefebvre stipulates meet this standard regarding end-of-path satellites.

5.2.3.4. The degree of Fongbe's retention was determined by availability of the lexifier

Indeed, the absence of *túwε*-style serial verbs in Haitian is not an isolated contrast between Haitian and Saramaccan. Rather, it is one of a great many Fongbe features in Saramaccan that are foreign to Haitian, such as CV phonotactics, tone, grammatical uses of reduplication, and wholescale borrowings of lexical and grammatical items (Saramaccan's words for *what* [*andí*] and *who* [*ambέ*] are Fongbe retentions, as is its focus marker *wε*) (cf. Smith 2001 for a similar argument). Saramaccan also makes much greater use of serialization than Haitian; the end-of-path serial construction is but one of many that Saramaccan has that Haitian lacks.

It would appear, then, that we are faced not with explaining a single discrepancy, but a general pattern under which Saramaccan is further removed from its lexifier grammatically than Haitian is (cf. Muysken 1994b). Sociohistory provides a useful explanation.

Saramaccan developed in a rain forest culture removed from any substantial contact with Europeans, and most importantly, speakers of its main lexifier English left Surinam less than twenty years after they founded it, in the 1660s, after which the colony was run by the Dutch. Haitian Creole developed among slaves working on plantations run by French speakers, and in a country where Haitian has always existed in a diglossic relationship with French itself.

Certainly the typical field slave in Haiti had little substantial contact with French speakers – otherwise, a creole would have been unlikely to develop. But as is well known, blacks occupied a hierarchy on plantations, with some slaves having much closer contact with whites than others. If we accept Le-Page and Tabouret-Keller's *Acts of Identity* (1985), depicting Caribbeans as controlling a dynamically fluid and variegated multilectal speaking competence, as a classic work of sage analysis, then there is a certain infelicity in simultaneously supposing that the black community in colonial Haiti had no significant relationship with French regardless of individuals' circumstances or the multifarious manifestations of social networks.

Also germane here is DeGraff's assertion (e.g. 1999, 2001) that Haitian Creole is less the product of pidginization than a continuation of French mediated by moderate effects of second-language acquisition. While I have argued in various articles that DeGraff's claims on this score are unduly extreme (cf. the first five chapters in McWhorter 2005a, and McWhorter & Parkvall 2002), DeGraff does refer to ample data showing that Haitian Creole has, and has always had, a closer relationship to French than Saramaccan has to English or Portuguese. Incontestable, for example, is that Haitian Creole inherited most of French's battery of derivational affixes, while Saramaccan inherited possibly none of English's or Portuguese's.

Facts such as these suggest that it is an oversimplification to assume that there is no qualitative difference between the relationships of Saramaccan and Haitian to Fongbe simply because both creoles emerged among Africans in plantation colonies. Relexification occurred in creoles to varying degrees. It is reasonable to suppose that the sociohistorical circumstances of the Saramaka, living in isolation from Europeans and maintaining a culture deeply imprinted by African folkways, would render their new language further removed from its lexifier(s) and more intimately patterned upon its substrate than in the case of Haitian.

We can make our way from supposing to knowing with a test case: a creole 1) created in a context in which the lexifier was largely unavailable as was the case in the emergence of Saramaccan, and 2) whose substrate has the same end-of-pathway construction as Fongbe. São Tomé Creole Portuguese was created by speakers of the Nigerian language Edo and the Bantu language Kikongo (Ferraz 1979); historical data suggest that Edo was the main contributor (Hagemeijer 2005), and the creole's ample structural parallels with Edo – and scant ones with Kikongo – make this even clearer. The creole emerged in the early 1500s, but the Portuguese began abandoning the island in the 1580s. As such, it has not developed in a diglossic relationship with Portuguese; socially, the poverty-stricken islands of the Gulf of Guinea are notoriously isolated from the larger world.

São Tomense has a serial verb construction similar to Fongbe's, in which a *put* verb marks the end of trajectories:

São Tomense

(39)   *Omali klaga lodoma zuga* **pê** *ple.*
         sea   carry bottle   throw put beach
         'The sea threw the bottle on the beach.'

(Hagemeijer 2005)

(40)   *N ga   zuga kupi* **pê** *son.*
         I ASP throw saliva put ground
         'I spit on the ground.'

(Hagemeijer 2005)

This is modelled on Edo, which has similar constructions. There is an element in Edo typically described as a preposition that is a grammaticalized and slightly phonetically altered reflex of the *throw* verb (cf. Ogie 2003: 15):

Edo

(41)   *ọ* **fi**   *ígho* **fii**   *otọ.*
         he throw money onto ground
         'He threw money onto the ground.'

(Agheyisi 1986: 45)

(42)   *ọ de **fii** ẹzẹ.*
       he fall into river
       'He fell into the river.'

(ibid. 46)

In Edo's close sister language Emai, the cognate item is maintained as a verb in the V2 position in the serial construction:

Emai

(43)   *òjè súá ólí údò   **fí**   ò   vbí   úkpódè.*
       Oje push the stone throw CL LOC road
       'Oje pushed the stone onto the road.'

(Schaefer & Egbokhare 2002: 67)

Then there is an Edo equivalent of Fongbe's *ɖó,* the element *yè,* translated as a verbal item "to put" by Hagemeijer on the basis of descriptions and aspects of its syntactic behavior:

Edo

(44)   *I   rhi-ɛre **y**-eva.*
       1S-take-3S put-there
       'I put it there.'

(Melzian 1937: 228 cited by Hagemeijer 2005)

Overall, this calque of a construction saliently divergent from Romance or Germanic structure appears only in creoles with distant relationships to their lexifiers. No French creole has it – and no French creole has developed in the kind of isolation that Saramaccan has. Meanwhile, the other two main Surinam creoles – which like Saramaccan jelled after English, the main lexifier of all three creoles, was no longer available – do have it.

Sranan, which developed on coastal plantations while Saramaccan took root in the interior, has cognates of both *túwɛ* and *butá,* in the latter case using the English-derived *poti* (< *put*):

Sranan

(45)   *Philip   naki   a   kapten **trowe**   na   gron.*
       Phillip strike DEF captain throw LOC ground
       'Phillip strikes the captain to the ground.'

(Sebba 1987: 48)

(46) *Mi sa   opo yu **poti** na   abra   a   liba.*
      I   FUT lift you put   LOC across DEF river
      'I shall lift you to the other side of the river.'

                                                    (Sebba 1987: 47)

Ndjuka, an offshoot of Sranan created by other escapees into the rain forest, also has cognates of both items:

Ndjuka

(47) *Den e   tyai en **poti** a   boto.*
      they PROG carry it put   LOC boat
      'They were bringing it and putting it into the boat.'

                                              (Huttar & Huttar 1994: 505)

(48) *Anga ala fa Winta á   poi wai   mi **towe**.*
      although   Wind NEG can move me throw
      'Although Wind cannot blow me over.'

                                                    (ibid. 231)

(49) *A fiingi a   pen **towe** go na   a   sutu tapu.*
      he throw DEF pen throw go LOC DEF chair top
      'He threw the pen on top of the chair.' (elicited from a consultant by the author)

   The lesson from this data is that a simple proposal that creoles developed via substituting lexifier phonetic strings for substrate words does not account for the cross-creole range of data. It does not explain why Haitian lacks Fongbe's end-of-trajectory marking by serial verbs. It does not predict that Saramaccan reproduces this feature of Fongbe's but only in a remodelled fashion. In general, while seeming plausible when only Haitian is adduced, it does not include the fact that the degree of relexification in creoles differs – and vastly – according to degree of contact with the lexifier.

5.3. *Púu* "to pull"

5.3.1. Description

The lexical source of *púu* is *pull,* but its core meaning is a semantically narrower evolution from this, "remove" (the meaning "to pull on," as a rope, is *hái* [< *haul*]):

(50) *De tá púu lái a bóto.*
they IMF pull cargo LOC boat
'They were unloading the boat.'

Púu is also used in various specialized meanings, being a semantically fertile word in the language just as *túwɛ* is. It is the word for "to row," and can also be used to indicate *choose:*

(51) *De púu mi gó kóti údu tidé.*
they pull me go cut wood today
'They chose me to cut wood today.'

Púu is also used as the second verb in serial constructions, where it indicates movement away from, off of, or out of:

(52) *A gó féki dí keéti púu a dí bɔutu.*
he go dust.off DEF chalk pull LOC DEF blackboard
'He's going to wash the chalk off of the blackboard.'

(53) *A hái ɛ̃ fínga púu a dí baáku déndu.*
he pull his finger pull LOC DEF hole inside
'He pulled his finger out of the hole.'

Púu does not require a following PP:

(54) *Hái ɛ̃ púu!*
pull it pull
'Pull him!'

(55) *A hái dí hédi u mi púu, hɛ̃ a butɛ̃ɛ̃ a dí táfa líba.*
he pull DEF head for me pull then he put.it LOC DEF table top
'He pulled my head off and put it on the table.'

Also, the aspect of the semantics of English *pull* specifying that the agent acts from outside of the location (object of the PP) is lost in the V2 usage, which has bleached to the basic perspective-neutral concept of removal. Thus the action depicted can also be exerted at the location from which the removal occurs (that is, it can refer to pushing as well as pulling):

(56) *A pusá dí miíi púu a dí nési.*
it push DEF child pull LOC DEF nest
'It pushed the child out of the nest.'

(57) *A tɔ́tɔ ɛ̃ púu a dí sípi.*
he push him pull LOC DEF ship
'He pushed him off the ship.'

(58)   *Mi jáka de púu a   dí   wósu.*
     I   chase them pull LOC DEF house
     'I chased them out of the house.'

In its serial usage, then, *púu* can be described as an ablative marker, in the literal sense of the term traditional in, for example, Uralic grammatical description: movement away from. Finnish ablative marking is inflectional: *pöytä* "table," *pöydä-ltä* "off the table." Saramaccan expresses the same concept with a serial verb construction.

5.3.2. *Púu* and relexification

As it happens, this serial ablative marking is not documented in Fongbe in any form. Fongbe does not use a *pull/remove* verb, such as *dɔn,* as a grammaticalized second verb in a serial construction. Fongbe instead has a preposition, *sín,* meaning "from / out of." (No Fongbe source I have consulted documents such a usage, such as Höftmann & Ahohounkpanton (2003) or Kihm & Lefebvre (1993), or most usefully, Lefebvre & Brousseau (2001: 423–4) where *dɔn* itself is discussed in the chapter on serialization, but not as V2.)

5.3.2.1. *Ablative* púu *was an internal development*
        rather than a relexification

Therefore, ablative *púu* was an internal development rather than a relexification. One kind of sentence represents an earlier stage when *púu* had not yet been grammaticalized as an ablative marker: ablative sentences with *púu* as a matrix verb, in which the use of *púu* as the second verb is ungrammatical and its matrix rendition is allowed to carry the ablative semantics with its inherent meaning:

(59)   *De   tá   púu lái   (*púu) a   bóto.*
     they IMF pull cargo   LOC boat
     'They were unloading the boat.'

(60)   *De   bi   tá   púu wáta (*púu) nɛ̃ɛ̃.*
     they PAST IMF pull water   LOC.it
     'They were hauling water out of it (a boat).'

This restriction is not driven by an avoidance of semantic redundancy, given *púu*'s ample use as V2 with *hái* "to pull," as in several of the sentences in 3.1.

Rather, there would seem to be a randomly conventionalized block on the specific repetition of *púu* alone within the same VP, which also happens to preserve a stage of the language when no such V2 *púu* had yet emerged.

In any case, this means that Saramaccan's creators did not relexify the ablative marking in a Fongbe sentence such as this one (Lefebvre & Brousseau 2001: 426):

(61) Fongbe   Sɔ   kɛkɛ   ɔ   tɔn   sín   fídé
                    take   bicycle   DEF   exit   out.of   there
      Saramaccan   *Téi   dí   papíjolu kumútu   (XX)   dɛ́
      'Take the bicycle out of here.'
                                            (Höftmann & Ahohounkpanton 2003: 342)

The correct Saramaccan would be *Téi dí papíjolu púu dɛ́*. Note that Saramaccan has no adposition meaning "out of" or "away from," although Fongbe does. Lefebvre's hypothesis stipulates that creoles failed to calque items that there was no readily perceptible equivalent for in the lexifier, but it would be difficult to support this verdict for a common item like *out* (*of*), especially since Saramaccan did incorporate *for,* and Portuguese's *ku* "with," and various spatial items reconstituted as nominals postposed to the PP object such as *líba* (< Portuguese *arriba*). Meanwhile, obviously, words for *exit* were perceptible to Saramaccan's creators – given the commonly used word *kumútu* (< *come out*) today. However, Saramaccan's creators made a choice other than relexifying the Fongbe construction. (Note also another discrepancy: Saramaccan's determiner occurs on the left edge of the noun phrase rather than on the right edge as in Fongbe.)

5.3.2.2. Púu *as an example of grammar-internal change in creoles*

The significance of the independent emergence of ablative *púu* is not merely that it constitutes an exception to Lefebvre's Relexification Hypothesis. It also sheds light on a certain exotification of creole diachrony which, in its way, exemplifies the kind of essentialization contested by opponents of claims that creoles are a distinct class of language.

Most diachronic work on creole languages has focused on change due to extended contact with either substrate languages (e.g. Keesing 1988 on Melanesian Pidgin English) or lexifier languages, the typical approach here being investigations of decreolization in continuum creoles such as the English-based ones of the Caribbean. However, in work on Atlantic creoles (i.e. those born amidst the trade in African slaves), there has traditionally been little attention paid to independent internal changes (such that, for example, Bruyn's [1995] study of grammar-internal grammaticalization in Sranan is an exception, couched as a novel observation rather than as a commonplace). There would seem to be a guiding sense that as "contact" languages usually spoken in linguistically heterogenous and/or diglossic contexts, creoles' changes will typically be affected by other languages rather than emerging on their own.

However, all languages are contact languages to various extents, and yet language change specialists hardly see it as unusual that languages like Hindi have undergone significant internal changes on all levels over the millennia despite constant contact with countless other languages. Rather, with older languages it is considered unremarkable that while some change is driven by contact (Hindi's ergativity modelled on Dravidian), just as much change develops internally (no one would treat the overall transformation of Sanskrit into the modern Indo-Aryan languages as a wholescale move toward Dravidian).

I believe that the facts are the same for creoles. Specifically, after their undoubted birth as compromises between several languages, their subsequent history involves some influence from those languages if the latter continue to be spoken (as well as other ones brought later into the setting) – but also involves the same internally-driven developments that are inherent to all natural languages.

The ablative *púu* is a particularly useful example here. Saramaccan has a serial verb construction marking ablative movement not because Fongbe did, since it does not, and certainly not because English or Portuguese did, since they do not. Saramaccan has this feature for the same reason that Romance languages have a paradigm of conditional mood markers that did not exist in Latin: because internal developments created it regardless of what other languages their speakers were in contact with, or even spoke themselves.

Ablative *púu* makes an even more specific point. Actually, the usage cannot have developed in Saramaccan itself. Saramaccan is an offshoot of Sranan Creole: slaves who spoke early Sranan and worked on plantations run by Portuguese Jewish migrants partially relexified Sranan with Portuguese etyma, and then carried this early version of Saramaccan into the rain forest.[2]

---

2 At this date, I am presuming that two former hypotheses on Saramaccan's origins have been refuted by research since the 1980s and are now defunct. The first is that it began as a Portuguese contact language and was partially relexified by English (e.g. Voorhoeve 1985). This was based on the old Monogenesis Hypothesis that most or all creoles were relexifications of a Portuguese pidgin, but no creolists working at present subscribe to this, despite its frequent citation in textbooks. The second is that Saramaccan emerged and developed by itself

Because of this isolation, Saramaccan's phonology and lexicon are more deeply impacted by Fongbe (and Kikongo) than Sranan's, and because of this and the Portuguese lexical stock, Saramaccan is not intelligible with Sranan. But Saramaccan's morphology and syntax are basically a continuation of Sranan's – the creoles are about as close on this level as Spanish and Portuguese, including specific constructions and choices of etyma to express grammatical items that are too copious and similar to be due to chance, diffusion, or similar source languages.

Along these lines, ablative *púu* is not unique to Saramaccan in Surinam, but also occurs in Sranan with its cognate *puru:*

Sranan

(62) *Mofoman krabasi wiki mi **puru** na   ini   dipi sribi.*
     messenger calabash wake me pull   LOC inside deep sleep
     'The messenger's calabash wakes me from a deep sleep.'
(Sebba 1987: 47)

Sranan also passed the construction on to Ndjuka:

Ndjuka

(63) *Den e   taki ala soutu ogii wootu **puu** a   ini   den   mofu ini.*
     they IMF talk all kind bad word pull LOC inside their mouth inside
     'They spew all sorts of bad words out of their mouths.'
(Huttar & Huttar 1994: 190)

This means that ablative *púu* arose in the earliest stages of Sranan, in the few decades between the arrival of the English in Surinam in 1651 and the emergence of Saramaccan starting after 1665 when the Portuguese planters arrived. Exactly when Saramaccan emerged is controversial and perhaps unknowable: the first large rain forest settlement was in 1690, but since the grammar used there can only have been inherited from Sranan speakers on coastal plantations, we assume that Saramaccan itself had emerged

---

in the bush among slaves who had served on plantations only long enough to have acquired lexical items (e.g. Byrne 1987). On Sranan as the direct parent to Saramaccan and Ndjuka, Goodman (1987) was the first comprehensive argument for the historical facts; Smith (1987) assumes it linguistically in his historical phonological work on the creoles; I argue for it with comparative grammatical data in McWhorter (2000: 102–5); and specialists such as Migge (1998) operate on a similar assumption that there was a single Surinamese plantation creole born on coastal plantations that diverged conventionally and without interruption into today's three main varieties.

and conventionalized on Portuguese Jews' plantations sometime between 1665 and 1690 (viz. contemporary references to a Djutongo "Jew language" plantation creole distinct from Sranan).

The main point, however, is that not only is ablative *púu* an internal development rather than a product of relexification, but it did not arise, for example, in the rain forest a century or more after Saramaccan developed, such that we might see it as something that emerged long after creolization proper had occurred and faded into the past (such as Saramaccan's predicate negation construction, as traced in McWhorter 2005a: 182–98). Instead, the ablative *púu* developed at the very same time as all analysts agree that a creole – properly, Sranan – was in formation.

Substrate languages such as Fongbe were still spoken. New slaves speaking them were always arriving. Adstratal elements from Dutch were entering the language after the Dutch took over the colony in 1665. Features like the equative copula *na* (Saramaccan *da*) had yet to emerge. The earliest Sranan documents in the first decades of the 1700s suggest that there was still competition between word pairs for basic lexical concepts. In other words, creole genesis was occurring.

And yet at the very same time, this new creole was developing ablative *púu* – quite independently of the assorted languages pulling it in any number of other directions.

In reference to relexification, we see that at the exact time that Lefebvre's hypothesis proposes that Africans were simply inserting European words into their native language lemmas, there was in fact more going on: namely, internal developments, typical of all human languages, that resulted in the ample divergences between Fongbe and Saramaccan today.

It bears mentioning that although Lefebvre's hypothesis certainly acknowledges that creole genesis cannot be reduced entirely to relexification, that the "patches" she proposes are equally unable to account for the behavior of ablative *púu*. For example, as to the possibility of dialect levelling between different Gbe languages yielding a construction alien to Fongbe but present in another Gbe variety, Ewe does not use its equivalent item *ɖe* in an ablative *pull* serial either (cf. Westermann 1930b; 1973: 34). Similarly, assuming that creole creators left out native-language items with no clear equivalent in the lexifier would be inapplicable here, since the construction did not exist in Fongbe in the first place.

Finally, Lefebvre (1998: 44–5) does allow in her model for reanalysis to generate new items, but only as constrained by a particular theoretical schema, in which some substrate grammatical categories are not labelled when the creole first forms because the lexifier offers no ready equivalent. Lefebvre stipulates that the category nevertheless exists underlyingly in the grammar, and that later, a lexical item may reanalyze into a grammatical one and provide the category with an overt marker. An example she cites is the grammaticalization in Tok Pisin of adverbial *baimbai* into a future marking particle *bai,* under an assumption that the future-marker slot had been inherited without overt labelling from Tok Pisin's substrate languages, and that *baimbai*'s reanalysis was therefore driven by substrate patterns even when the languages themselves were no longer spoken. Whatever one's evaluation of this proposal, it does not apply to *púu,* since Fongbe did not present a model for it.

5.3.3. Ablative *púu* and complexity

Púu is another example that shows that there is some truth in the claim that to date, creole grammars have not always been described as thoroughly as we might like. Migge (1998) does not mention the ablative serial in Ndjuka, likely because the absence of an equivalent in Gbe languages renders it marginal to her substratist thesis. Huttar & Huttar (1994) do not mention it in their Ndjuka grammar, perhaps partly because of the constraints of the Routledge grammatical format. Byrne (1987), despite his thesis that serial verbs serve to compensate for grammatical functions performed in the lexifier by adpositions, does not mention the *púu* serial construction either, probably because the ablative does not happen to be a core grammatical function in the Government-Binding framework he was concerned with.

Yet in any case, once again, to treat *púu* simply as one more "serial verb construction" misses a larger implication that it has within the grammar. As it happens, ablative expression varies in Saramaccan according to transitivity. Like serial *túwε,* ablative *púu* is used only in transitive sentences; in intransitive sentences, when the movement away is not effected by an external actor, if a light serial verb is used, it is not *púu* but *kumútu.*

The etymology of *kumútu* suggests a simple equivalent of *come out,* and *kumútu* can be used in this meaning:

(64) *Mi kumútu a   dí   wósu.*
  I   come.out LOC DEF house
  'I left the house.'

However, more generally, *kumútu* is used as the second verb in an intransitive serial construction to indicate movement away:

(65)   *A wáka kumútu   a   dí   wósu. (*A wáka púu a dí wósu.)*
       he walk come.out LOC DEF house
       'He walked out of the house.'

(66)   *A fusí   kumútu   a   sitááfu wósu.*
       he sneak come.out LOC jail
       'He escaped from jail.'

Despite its etymology, *kumútu* does not have the specific semantics of indicating movement towards the speaker, but rather, simply, ablative semantics
regardless of perspective:

(67)   *Mi hópo kumútu   a   dí   wósu.*
       I   arise come.out LOC DEF house
       'I left the house (in response to something).'

In describing his own experience, this speaker's locus of perspective is
presumably inside the house.
    A further detail is that there is one intransitive usage of *púu,* this time as
the first verb in a serial construction with *kaí* "to fall," which signifies "to fall
accidentally":

(68)   *A púu kaí a   máũ.*
       it pull fall LOC hand
       'It fell out of my hand.'

(69)   *Dí   fuúta púu kaí.*
       DEF fruit pull fall
       'The fruit fell (down from the tree).'

In order to refer to an object, the expression must be used with a third verb
that is transitive:

(70)   *Mi púu kaí lási ɛ̃.*
       I   pull fall lose it
       'I lost it (it fell off of / out of my hand).'

In this expression, *púu* signifies "to move away from," as is clearer in sentences
in which *púu* occurs with the source entity encoded as a PP, where its semantic
contribution is obviously far removed from that of the source etymon *pull:*

(71)   *A bi   púu a   dí   papíjolu kaí ku   bándja a   gõ̃ó.*
       he PAST pull LOC DEF bicycle   fall with side   LOC ground
       'He fell off of the bike.'

                                                            (DeGroot 1977: 83)

(72) *A bi púu a líba kaí kó a gṍṍ.*
he PAST pull LOC top fall come LOC ground
'He fell off of the roof.'

(ibid. 16)

This usage of *púu* with *kaí* counts as a lexically specific idiom, however; with other verbs *púu* has not conventionalized to signify accidental occurrence:

(73) **Dí wági púu náki a dí wall.*
DEF car pull strike LOC DEF wall
'The car smashed into the wall.'

5.4. The directional paradigm

Taking together the usages we have seen, we find in Saramaccan a valency-sensitive encoding of both the ablative and the complementary distinction, the allative (movement onto; cf. Finnish *katto* "roof," *kato-lle* "onto the roof"). Saramaccan's expression of these concepts is, in fact, more elaborate than English's mere prepositional opposition between *away from / out of* and *onto / into,* which is neutral to transitivity. While I would argue that English surpasses Saramaccan in complexity overall (on grounds spelled out in, for example, McWhorter 2005a: 38–71), there is no reason that a creole might not surpass an older language in complexity in a particular area of grammar – and in fact, they often do.

Butá is the transitive allative marker, expressing that an object has reached a reference point:

(74) *Mi tá tjá wáta gó butá a dí gbóto déndu.*
I IMF carry water go put LOC DEF boat inside
'I am carrying water into the boat.'

Then, *túwɛ* encodes a more specific type of transitive allative movement, involving trajectories.

The opposite transitive action is expressed with ablative *púu:*

(75) *De tá túwe wáta púu a dí gbóto.*
they IMF throw water pull LOC DEF boat
'They were hauling water from the boat.'

Meanwhile, the intransitive ablative is expressed with *kumútu,* while the intransitive allative is encoded with the serial usages of *gó* "to go" and *kó* "to come," in this case depending on the perspective of the speaker (unlike *kumútu,* which is neutral to this distinction):

(76)   *A wáka gó a   wósu dendu.*
   he walk go LOC house inside
   'He walked into the house.'

(77)   *A   dí   dɔ́ɔ akí, a wáka kó   a   déndu.*
   LOC DEF door here he walk come LOC inside
   'He walked in through this door.'

Thus again, *gó* and *kó* play a more systematically integrated role in Saramaccan grammar than is perhaps evident in listing them simply as examples of serial verbs encoding "to" and "from" and examining, for example, whether or not they can cleft and leave a copy, take repeat tense and aspect marking, and other behaviors of interest to those speculating upon the mental representation of serial verb constructions:

Table 27. Directional expression in Saramaccan

	transitive	intransitive
ALLATIVE	**butá** (deliberate placement) **túwɛ** (projection)	**gó** (towards speaker) **kó** (away from speaker)
ABLATIVE	**púu**	**kumútu** (*púu* in idiom with *kaí*)

Just the same, the discussion is incomplete if we stop simply at the fact that yet again, we see that Saramaccan has complexity like all natural languages. Also of interest is that languages can impose a great deal more complexity upon their expression of directionality, and that there is no creole that does so to the extent that many older languages do. Here, for example, is an equivalent table for Russian:

Table 28. Directional expression in Russian (adapted from Mahota 1996: 34)

	towards	from
ILLATIVE/ELATIVE into/out of (school)	v školu	iz školy
ALLATIVE/ABLATIVE onto/off of (a meeting)	na sobranie	s sobranija
ALLATIVE/ABLATIVE towards/from (a blackboard)	k doske	ot doski

Where Saramaccan has a two-way split between transitive and intransitive in directional marking, Russian has a three-way split between finer shades of semantic distinction than Saramaccan's. Russian's marking differs according to whether the movement is into or from within (illative/elative) versus onto or off from (allative/ablative), and then within the latter distinction distinguishes whether there is telicity implied. Each of the three meanings requires a different oppositional pair of prepositions.

Also, Russian directionality is also linked to case distinctions: movement away requires the genitive while movement towards requires the accusative or, with nontelic movement towards, the dative. The chart above also gives a hint of a notorious area of arbitrariness in the language that must be learned by rote. It is not exactly universally intuitive that one goes "into" school but "onto" a meeting. The distinction is in fact semantically opaque: while *na* generally means "on" in Russian, it is also used with an arbitrary set of two-dozen-plus nouns that includes *sobranie* "meeting;" others are *vokzal* "station," *ulitsa* "street," *ostrov* "island," *rabota* "work." Then there are some random floutings of the prepositional oppositions: *vo dvor* "into the yard," but *so dvora* "out of the yard" instead of *iz dvora* (the prepositions take on an [o] by morphophonemic processes); when used with *ves'* "whole, entire," *škola* also takes *s* in the ablative: *so vsej školy*.

Added to this, recall the baroqueness of Russian's verbs of motion, with which this above machinery is used. Saramaccan directionality is complex. Russian directionality is much more complex.

5.5. Conclusion

(78) *Mi hái dí   dɔkufɔutu **púu** te   nɛ̃ɛ̃   bɛ́ɛ   déndu **túwɛ** a*
       I   pull DEF rat   pull until LOC.his stomach inside throw LOC
       táfa   líba.
       table   top
       'I pulled (with a string) the rat from all the way down in her stomach onto the table.'

This Saramaccan sentence contains both serial *túwɛ* and ablative *púu,* as well as other indications that this language has complexity. The form *nɛ̃ɛ̃* is a morphophonologically conditioned portmanteau fusing locative marker *a* and third person singular possessive *ɛ̃*. There is not only tone but (not indicated here) tone sandhi patterns in the language that are especially complex across serial verb constructions with shared objects, of the kind that *túwɛ* and *púu* occur in (Rountree 1972, Good 2004a, Kramer 2004). There is no question, then, as to whether Saramaccan has complexity.

However, the hypothesis that creoles are primarily relexifications of their substrate languages implies that Saramaccan is equal in complexity to Fongbe (as Lefebvre 2001 explicitly argues). But this particular argument that creoles are as complex as older languages cannot stand, because the data do not support the relexificationist account. The above sentence is rife with discrepancies with Fongbe structure: Fongbe uses an ablative preposition rather than a verb; Fongbe would use its *put* verb where Saramaccan uses *throw;* Fongbe's determiners are postposed to nominals rather than preposed as in Saramaccan; Fongbe has no preposed possessive markers (Lefebvre & Brousseau 2001: 67–71). A word-for-word Fongbe rendition of the Saramaccan sentence above would be not so much infelicitous as utterly misbegotten, barely even comprehensible to a speaker of the language. Crucially, the "patches" Lefebvre proposes to explain such discrepancies do not explain the problems regarding *túwɛ* and *púu* – and in McWhorter (2005a: 126–33) I show that her argumentation also cannot explain the position of Saramaccan's determiners and possessive markers.

Furthermore, while the above examples indicate ways in which Saramaccan expresses concepts in an alternate fashion to Fongbe, more commonly Saramaccan simply lacks features that Fongbe has: Fongbe has more tones, case markers, negators, complementizers, and spatial-marking nominals, and a greater number of clitic subject pronouns phonetically underivable from the full forms and/or varying for case (McWhorter 2005a: 122). Saramaccan surpasses Fongbe in complexity here and there, as one would expect by virtue of simple chance: but in fashions both seldom and slight (ibid. 112–3, 117–8).

This brings us again to the fact that creoles do not display complexity in any of their modules to a cross-linguistically *superlative* extent. Or, more precisely: I am presently aware of a single instance of a creole *possibly* presenting a feature of a cross-linguistically superlatively complex nature, and it happens to be Saramaccan. Good (2004a) shows that the Saramaccan lexicon is split between words with pitch accent and words with true tone, as the result of its heritage from both European and West African languages. He suggests that this may be the only such example among the world's languages, or at least extremely rare.

Yet Saramaccan's grammar remains, overall, strikingly less elaborated than that of a language that has existed for millennia, as I demonstrate in McWhorter (2005a: 38–71; 102–41), including a principled metric for the definition of complexity (a conclusion that Good does not present his analysis as refuting [cf. 2004b: 28–9]). And reports of *superlative* complexity for any other creole language are at present unknown to me. There remains a clear class trait among creoles on this score.

Algonquian languages have their obviative and inverse marking. Amazonian languages have their evidential marker paradigms. Semitic has its nonconcatenational morphology. Indo-European has its rich inflectional paradigms encoding a wide array of tenses as well as grammatical gender. Uralic has its consonant gradation. Sino-Tibetan languages have rich tonal systems. Mon-Khmer languages often have staggeringly large inventories of vowels. Austronesian languages have the complex derivational apparatus of Indonesian and its relatives, the notorious pragmatic focus marking system of Philippines languages, and the fine-grained possessive marking of Melanesian and Polynesian languages. Australian languages are often ergative and have pronominal paradigms richly sensitive to case and gradations of number. Niger-Congo languages tend to have either prolific noun class morphology, complex tonal systems, or both. Khoi-San languages, with their famous click sounds, often have uniquely vast segmental inventories. It is typical of an older language to have wended into superlative complexity in one area of grammar or another.

I propose that if a language has not done so – or has done so only to a slight extent identifiable only via uniquely careful analysis – then the reason for this is that the languages are not old. They are young languages, born recently of varieties that were incompletely acquired; i.e. pidginized. As we have seen in this paper, this thesis refers to languages which nevertheless display ample evidence of the *basic* complexity that is inherent to all natural languages.

Chapter 6
Complexity hotspot: The copula in Saramaccan

6.1. Introduction

I have argued that creole languages were born as structurally reduced pidginized varieties, eventually expanded into new natural languages. According to this genesis scenario, because grammatical complexity emerges in languages as the result of long-term processes of drift, we would expect creole languages to be less grammatically complex than older languages (McWhorter 2001, 2006). Furthermore, as we would expect, much of the grammatical complexity that creole grammars do display can be identified as having emerged after genesis, over the past few hundred years.

In this light, this chapter will examine an area of the grammar of Saramaccan creole that exhibits a degree of complexity unusual in the grammar as a whole, copula constructions. The question is why complexity has emerged to such a degree in the particular area of nonverbal predication, and whether the reasons for this are useful in predicting where complexity is most likely to emerge most rapidly in new grammars.

The Saramaccan data, unless otherwise indicated, were collected by the author and graduate student assistants.

6.2. Metric of complexity

My demonstration of emergent complexity in Saramaccan will be based on the metric of complexity presented in the Introduction, consisting of three aspects of grammar which contrast in degree between languages.

6.2.1. Overspecification

Languages differ in the degree to which they overtly and obligatorily mark semantic distinctions. For example, some grammars mark a finer grain of distinctions of person and number than others (as Mühlhäusler demonstrates in this volume re Norfolk English). In contrast to Indo-European languages, the Oceanic language Kwaio marks the dual and paucal, as well as an inclusivity distinction in the first person plural (Keesing 1985: 28):

Table 29. Pronouns in Kwaio

	singular	dual	paucal	plural
first person (inclusive)	(i)nau	('i)da'a	('i)dauru	gia
first person (exclusive)	('e)me'e	('e)meeru	('i)mani	
second person	(i)'oo	('o)mo'o	('o)mooru	('a)miu
third person	ngai(a)	('i)ga'a	('i)gauru	gila

There are languages that mark a "fourth person" in clauses with two third-person referents, obligatorily indicating which of the two is more prominent in the discourse. The Indo-European speaker might well marvel that a grammar would choose to mark such a distinction overtly, and indeed obviative marking is an interesting but unnecessary feature: an overspecification. Here is an example from Eastern Ojibwa (Rhodes 1990: 107):

(1)   *Maaba dash   oshkinawe o-gii-bawaad-am-**n***
       this   EMPH young.man 3-PAST-dream-3INAN-OBV
       *wii-bi-ayaa-**ini**-d*
       FUT-coming-be.at-OBV-3
       *myagi-nishnaabe-**an** x-wii-bi-nis-igo-waa-d-**in**.*
       foreign-people-OBV REL-FUT-coming-kill-INV-3-OBV
       "Then this young man dreamed that foreigners would come to kill them."

Or, in many grammars, possessive marking differs for that which belongs to one in an inherent, eternal sense, as opposed to that which is formally and less permanently owned, as in Mandinka *i faamaa* "your father" versus *i la koloŋo* "your well" (Lück & Henderson 1993:23). This distinction is hardly necessary to even nuanced communication, as is readily apparent to English speakers. It is an overspecification. The aforegoing is intended not as an exhaustive, but as a demonstrational, list of examples of overspecification.

6.2.2. Structural elaboration

An aspect of one grammar may differ from that aspect in another's in terms of the number of rules (in phonology and syntax) required to generate grammatical forms.

For example, all natural languages have morphophonemic processes. But in Celtic languages, these entail an array of consonant mutations, triggered by a range of grammatically central interfaces, in which synchronically, they are based not on assimilatory influence from preceding segments such as voicing (*leaf, leaves*) but are phonetically quite unpredictable. In Welsh, *cath* "cat" occurs in citation form with *eu* "their," but with other possessive pronouns, undergoes particular mutations:

Table 30. Welsh consonant mutations (Ball & Müller 1992: 195–6):

eu cath	"their cat"
*fy **ngh**ath*	"my cat"
*ei **g**ath*	"his cat"
*ei **ch**ath*	"her cat"

Notice that the mutation alone carries the functional load of distinguishing gender in third-person singular *gath* versus *chath*. Thus the mutations often straddle a line between phonology and morphology.

A grammar is also structurally elaborified to the extent that nominals vary in their concordial requirements and/or case markers according to phonological traits of the root. Latin is a typical example, in which concord was determined by a three-way gender distinction between masculine, feminine and neuter, while case marking varied according to five declension classes distinguished by phonetic traits.

Other examples of structural elaboration include:

a)   the tendency of clitics in some languages to seek a particular position in a clause regardless of their grammatical role. Serbo-Croatian has generally free word order, but clitics occur after the first accented constituent, and can even occur after the first accented word, intervening within a constituent:

(2)   *Taj **mi** **je**   pesnik napisao knjigu.*
      that to.me AUX poet   wrote   book
      "That poet wrote me a book."

(Spencer 1991: 355)

b)   subject-verb inversion in interrogative sentences in many European languages, a trait rare outside of Europe (Ultan 1978). Typically, languages indicate the interrogative with intonation and/or the appendage of an interrogative particle (Indonesian *apa dia sudah makan* [INT she PERF eat] "Has she eaten?" [Sneddon 1996: 311]).

6.2.3. Irregularity

Grammars differ in the degree to which they exhibit irregularity and suppletion. English's small set of irregular plurals like *children* and *people* is exceeded by the vast amount of irregularity in German plural marking: a masculine noun may take -*e* for the plural, but almost as equally will also take an umlaut: *der Arm, die Arme, der Besuch* (visit), *die Besuche* but *der Arzt* (doctor), *die Ärtze, der Gast* (guest), *die Gäste.* Similarly, a "regular" neuter is *das Jahr* (year), *die Jahre,* but then *das Buch, die Bücher, das Volk, die Völker* and even *das Floss* (raft), *die Flösse.*

Another example of irregularity in plural marking is the broken plural patterns in Arabic:

Table 31. Broken plural patterns in Arabic

singular	plural	
qalam	*'aqlām*	"pen"
bayt	*buyūt*	"house"
kalb	*kilāb*	"dog"
kitāb	*kutub*	"book"
dawla	*duwal*	"country"
šahr	*'ašhur*	"month"
wazīr	*wuzarā'*	"minister"
ṣadīq	*'aṣdiqā'*	"friend"

Then grammars differ in the degree to which they exhibit suppletion. Suppletion is moderate in English, especially evident in the verb "to be" which distributes various Old English roots across person, number, and tense: *am, are, is, was, were, been, be.* But the Caucasian language Lezgian has no fewer than sixteen verbs that occur in suppletive forms (Veselinona 2003). Elsewhere, suppletion is present in various corners of grammars, as in Spanish, where the third person indirect pronominal clitic *le,* when preceding an object clitic, transforms to *se: Le dí un libro* "I gave a book **to him**," but *Se lo dí* "I gave it **to him**" (**Le lo dí*).

6.3. The complexity of the Saramaccan copula

According to the three manifestations of complexity specified above, the way that Saramaccan expresses the concept of being is one of the most complex constructions in the grammar.

English-based New World creoles, a group within which Saramaccan is one of many members, have often been described as having a simple division of labor between an "equative" copula (generally of the shape /(d~n)a/) and a "locative" copula (generally /de/). The situation in Saramaccan is much more elaborated than this.

6.3.1. Overspecification

The default *be* verb in Saramaccan is *dέ*. It is indeed used with locative predicates:

(3) *Méíki ku wĩ́ bi dέ a táfa líba.*
milk with wine PAST be LOC table top
'Milk and wine were on the table.'

but there is nothing specifically locative in its semantics. *Dέ* is used, for example, in the existential:

(4) *A bi dέ hángi tẽ́.*
he PAST be hungry time
'There was a famine.'

and especially indicatively, even in equative constructions:

(5) *Méíki dέ wã̃ soní dí míi tá bebé.*
milk be a thing REL child IMF drink
'Milk is something that children drink.'

It is also used with adverbial predicates:

(6) *Dí kínɔ bi dέ fɔ́ júu lóngi.*
DEF film PAST be four hour long
'The film was four hours long.'

Dέ is also used with deverbal resultatives, which are expressed with a reduplicated verb:

(7) *Dí sutúu dέ boókoboóko.*
DEF chair be broken.RD
'The chair is broken.'

However, in two specific semantic contexts, the copula is *da* instead. First, in the identificational subclass of equative predicates (as opposed to the class subclass of identification in (5)):

(8)   *Mi da Gádu.*
       I   be God
       'I am God.'

Da is optionally used rather than *dé* with the other subclass of equative predicates, indicating class rather than identity:

(9)   *Méiki dé / da wǎ soní dí   míi   tá   bebé.*
       milk be be a   thing REL child IMF drink
       'Milk is something that children drink.'

Milk is one of many things a child might drink, and thus a class predicate rather than an identificational one, which it would be if milk were the only thing children drink. Thus:

(10)(a) *Mi da (*dé) dí   kabiténi.*
         I   be   DEF captain
         'I am the captain.'

   (b)   *Mi dé / da wǎ kabiténi.*
         I   be   a captain
         'I am a captain.'

Da is also used optionally with possessive predicates, although it can also be omitted:

(11)   *Dí   búku akí (da) u   mí.*
       DEF book here be for me
       'This book is mine.'

There is, therefore, an *overspecification* in the copular domain in Saramaccan compared to, for example, English, in which copular morphemes do not vary according to the semantics of the predicate.

6.3.2. Structural elaboration

The Saramaccan copulas also occasion structural elaboration of various kinds. *Da* cannot appear sentence-finally. Therefore, when the predicate is fronted, there is no copula:

(12) *Mí tatá, dísi.*
      my father this
      'This is my father.' (i.e. My father is who this is.)

(13) *Mí, dísi.*
      I   this
      'It's me.' (i.e. This is me talking to you.)

This includes in content interrogative sentences:

(14) *Ǔ   búku dí- dέ?*
      which book that
      'Which book is that?'

(15) *Andí dísi?*
      what this
      'What is this?'

although in this context it can optionally occur between the *wh*-word and the subject:

(16) *Andí da dí   búku naandé?*
      what be DEF book there
      'What is that book there (about)?'

Also, in headless relatives, there is subject-verb inversion such that *da* does not occur sentence-finally:

(17) *Mi sá'   ambέ da i. (*..ambέ i da.)*
      I   know who be you
      'I know who you are.'

in contrast to *dέ* which can occur sentence-finally in headless relatives:

(18) *Awáa mi féni naásέ a bi   dέ.*
      now I find where he PAST be
      'I finally found out where he was.'

as other verbs do:

(19) *Lúku andí i   dú!*
      look what you do
      'Look at what you did!'

Da also does not occur when predicate is marked for focus with *wε:*

(20) *(*Da) Páu wε*
             tree FOC
      'It's a *tree.*'

(21)   Dí   wómi dέ,   dáta   wε   o!
     DEF man there doctor FOC INJ
     '(Well, look here) that man is (now) a doctor!'

Da also manifests another aspect of structural elaboration, allomorphy. With possessive predicates that have been fronted, *da* occurs as an allomorph *a:*

(22)   U   mí   a   dí   búku akí. (*U mí da dí búku akí.)
     for me be DEF book here
     'This book is mine.'

Thus the appearance of *da* in Saramaccan is conditioned by a list of rules determining its absence or heterogenous position in various contexts.

    Dέ, meanwhile, also exhibits structural elaboration, in conjunction with property items. Most property items in Saramaccan are verbs; i.e. they take tense and aspect particles like verbs:

(23)   Ée i   njã́ dí   soní akí, i   ó   síki.
     if you eat DEF thing here you FUT sick
     'If you eat this thing, you will get sick.'

However, when a property item is fronted, *dέ* occurs sentence-finally although it would be ungrammatical with a property item otherwise:

(24)   Ű   bígi dí   wósu **dέ**? (*Dí wósu dέ bígi.)
     how big DEF house be
     'How big is the house?'

(Kramer 2001: 36)

6.3.3. Irregularity

The Saramaccan copulas condition a degree of irregularity which stands out in a grammar in which irregularity is minimal in comparison to, for example, an Indo-European language. *Da,* for example, is defective if analyzed as a verbal form. *Da* cannot take tense marking, in which case *dέ* occurs:

(25)   Dí   fósu líbisέmbέ   bi   dέ (*bi da) Adám.
     DEF first human.being PAST be   Adam
     'The first person was Adam.'

(26)   Mí tatá   ó   dέ dí   kabiténi.
     my father FUT be DEF captain
     'My father will be the captain.'

Da also occasions suppletion. While *dé* is negated in regular fashion with predicate negator *á,*

(27) *Mi á   dé a   wósu.*
     I NEG be LOC house
     'I am not at home.'

when negated, *da* occurs in suppletive form as *ná:*

(28) *Nɔ́ nɔ́, ná   mi. (*Nɔ́nɔ́, á da mi.)*
     no   NEG I
     'No, it wasn't me.'

Da also requires that the third person subject pronoun, normally *a,* occur in its tonic form *hɛ̃́* even when no emphasis is intended:

(29) ***Hɛ̃́** da dí   mɔ̃́ɔ lánga wã̀ a   u déndu. (*A da dí mɔ̃́ɔ lánga . . .)*
     he be DEF more tall   one LOC us inside
     'He is the tallest one among us.'

Da also fails to occur in a few contexts independently of semantic or syntactic regularity; namely, when the predicate is a day of the week:

(30) *Tidé díi-de   woóko.*
     today three-day work
     'Today is Wednesday.'

and optionally when the predicate is possessive:

(31) *Dí   búku akí (da) u   mí.*
     DEF book here be for me
     'This book is mine.'

6.4. Evidence of emergence rather than substrate transfer

The behavior of the copula in Saramaccan obviously evidences complexity. However, all evidence suggests that this complexity emerged gradually over time after the genesis of the creole in the late seventeenth century.

6.4.1. Diachronic evidence

The evidence that Saramaccan originated without a *da* copula is first that *da* is derived from no English or Portuguese copular form, but a deictic item, *dati* from *that* (preserved in Saramaccan's sister offshoot creole from Sranan, Ndjuka, although replaced in Saramaccan by *dí-dé* > "the-there"). The development of copulas from deictic items is common cross-linguistically, but requires a period during which the lexical meaning of the deictic item is bleached away and its function changes to a grammatical one. Therefore, the development of lexical *dati* to grammatical *da* is not a process that we could expect to happen in one blow at the time when Saramaccan was emerging; it can only have occurred over a long stretch of time afterward.

For example, in Archaic Chinese there was no copula:

(32)   *Wáng-Tái wù   zhě   yě.*
Wang-Tai outstanding person DEC
'Wang-Tai is an outstanding person.'

(Li & Thompson 1975: 421)

However, *shì* "this" was used as a subject in topic-comment constructions:

(33)   *Qíong   yù jiàn,   **shì** rén   zhi   sǔo   wù   yě.*
poverty and debasement this people GEN NOM dislike DEC
'Poverty and debasement, this is what people dislike.'

(ibid.)

By the first century, A.D., it had been reanalyzed as a copula, as it is used today:

(34)   *Yú **shì** sǔo   jià   fū-rén zhi   fù   yě.*
I   be   NOM marry woman GEN father DEC
'I am the married woman's father.'

(ibid. 426)

This process is common in languages, having also yielded, for example, the copular use of subject pronominal forms in Modern Hebrew (*David hu ganav* "David is a thief"). Saramaccan's *da* would have begun as the subject deictic in the comment, which itself had no copula:

[*Kobí*]	[*da*]	ø-copula	[*mí tatá*]
Kobi	that		my father
TOPIC	SUBJECT		PREDICATE

Over time, as the topic-comment structure was reinterpreted as a subject-predicate one, the topic became the subject. *Da* was retained, but edged out of its subject function and left as a mere semantically empty associative morpheme, i.e. a copula:

[*Kobí*]	[*da*]	[*mí tatá*]
Kobi	is	my father
SUBJECT	COPULA	PREDICATE

This also explains why *da* requires the tonic pronoun in subject position. When sentences with *da* were topic-comment constructions, the tonic would have been the form expected of a topic,

[*Hɛ́*]	[*da*]	ø-copula	[*mí tatá*]
him	that		my father
TOPIC	SUBJECT		PREDICATE

and persists today in that form despite being a subject, the result being a kind of Exceptional Case Marking:

[*Hɛ́*]	[*da*]		[*mí tatá*]
he	is		my father
SUBJECT	COPULA		PREDICATE

However, it is inherent to this reconstruction that there was an initial topic-comment stage, in which the copula form had yet to emerge.

Also, in terms of historical syntax, if *da* is the result of the reanalysis of a deictic subject into a particle amidst the reinterpretation of a topic-comment structure into a subject-predicate one, then it would follow that in sentences in which the predicate occurs *before* the subject, such as *wh*-questions, there would remain no copula today. This is because we can assume that such sentences occurred originally, when there was no copula yet – and now such sentences have no copula because in them, there was never a deictic item after the subject to be reinterpreted in such cases:

In addition, there is some evidence in eighteenth-century documents of Sranan, father language to Saramaccan, of equative sentences with zero-copula, such as:

Table 32. Historical development of *da* in *wh*- sentences

Stage One				Stage Two		
[*Kobí*]	[*da*]	ø-copula	[*mí tatá*]	[*Kobí*]	[*da*]	[*mí tatá*]
Kobi	that		my father	Kobi	is	my father
TOPIC	SUBJECT		PREDICATE	SUBJECT	COPULA	PREDICATE
[*Andí*]	[*dísi?*]	ø-copula		[*Andí*]	[*dísi?*]	ø-copula
what	this			what	this	
PREDICATE	SUBJECT			PREDICATE	SUBJECT	

(35) *Mi blibi   joe ø wan bon   mattie fo dem.*
      I   believe you   a   good friend for them
      'I believe you're a good friend of theirs.'

(Arends 1989: 160)

Sentences like this were a remnant of a zero-copula stage in the evolution of the grammar that developed into that of Saramaccan.[2] In an early document of Saramaccan itself, there is also evidence that at an earlier stage, *dé* was even used in the identificational context, suggesting a stage where *dé* was the only copula and *da* did not yet exist. A native speaker ends two letters he wrote with the now ungrammatical *Mi de Christian Grego Aliedja* "I am Christian Grego of Aliedja" (Arends & Perl 1995: 385, 387).

It finally bears mentioning that copulas have incontrovertible deictic sources in many other creoles; e.g. in French-based ones, *se* from *c'est* or *sa* from *ça*.

6.4.2. Synchronic evidence

The reconstruction of an original zero-copula stage is also likely given the various contexts in which *da* does not occur in modern Saramaccan's grammar where the semantics of the predicate would lead one to expect that it would; e.g. days of the week, after fronting, and with the focus marker *wɛ*. One might suppose that *da* was for some reason dropped at some point from these assorted contexts, but there is no principled reason why this would have happened.

A more systematic approach is to assume that these instances are fossilizations. For example, possessive sentences and ones referring to days of the week are heavy-usage contexts of the kind most likely to yield fossilizations, just as it is heavy-usage nouns like *man, woman* and *child* that retain irregular plurals in English.

6.4.3. Substrate inheritance?

It has commonly been argued (e.g. Migge 2003) that copulas like Saramaccan's were indeed present at the genesis of the creole, modelled on copulas in the African languages spoken by the creoles' creators. This argument is superficially attractive, given that languages of the Upper Guinea coast of Africa tend to subdivide the copular domain between equative and locative morphemes. For example, Saramaccan's grammar is modelled upon that of Fongbe, a Niger-Congo language of the Kwa group. The Fongbe equative and locative copulas are:

(36) *Ùn **nyí** Àfíáví.*
      1S be Afiavi
      "I am Afiavi."

(Lefebvre & Brousseau 2001: 144)

(37) *Wémá ɔ́   ɖ́ɔ   távò jí.*
      book DEF be.at table on
      'The book is on the table.'

(ibid. 147)

However, the resemblance here is, in the typological sense, insignificant. It is very common worldwide for languages to have equative and locative copulas. The following table shows examples from a few languages chosen for familial diversity; typically all or most of each language's group also have an equative/locative subdivision between copulas, as do a great many languages of families not represented here:

Thus the fact that both Saramaccan and Fongbe have an equative/locative split between copulas is not evidence of a causal relationship, because this trait appears idiosyncratic only from the perspective of European languages.

Importantly in this light, there are quite a few creoles with African substrates in which the equative/locative copula split of the African substrate languages is absent. In French-based creoles also created by speakers of Fongbe (and related languages), despite various transfers from Fongbe grammar, even today there is no locative copula, such as in Haitian (*Bouki anba tab-la* "Bouki is under the table"). In the Portuguese creoles of the Gulf of Guinea, while their main grammatical model was the Niger-Congo language Edo (Hagemeijer 2005) which has several distinct copulas for the equative and elsewhere (cf. Baker 2008: 28), the creoles have a single copula for the equative, locative and beyond (e.g. Principense [Maurer 2009: 95–102] and Angolar [Maurer 1995: 92–5]).

This makes it especially crucial that Fongbe's equative *nyí* evidences none of the *particular* behavioral traits of Saramaccan's *da*. *Nyí* exhibits typical verbal behavior, taking negation and tense marking (Migge 2003: 72). It is not omitted in assorted contexts as *da* is, and does not share semantic space in any context with alternate copula *ɖ́ɔ* in the way that *da* does with *dé* with class equative predicates (cf. Lefebvre & Brousseau 2001: 143–7). The sole

Table 33. Languages other than West African with separate equative and locative copulas

	Equative	Locative
Irish	*is*	*tá*
Vietnamese	*là*	*o*
Nama	*'a*	*hàa*
Hawaiian	*he*	*aia*
Chinese	*shì*	*zai*
CiBemba	*ni*	*lì*

(Sources: Stenson 1981, Thompson 1965, Hagman 1977, Hawkins 1982, Hashimoto 1969, Sadler 1964 respectively)

specific behavioral trait *nyí* shares with *da* is that it can be omitted when the focus marker *wέ* is present (*Àtín wέ* "It is a tree" [ibid. 134]), unsurprising given that Saramaccan borrowed this very focus marker.

With the resemblance between Saramaccan and Fongbe copulas revealed as a false lead, the evidence that Saramaccan's *da* emerged as a deictic element and was reanalyzed as a copula is even more significant. *Da* not only does not exhibit the behavior of *nyí,* but also has an etymology that suggests an origin in reanalysis rather than transfer.

6.4.4. Summary

Thus, while a great deal of Saramaccan's grammar is clearly modelled on Fongbe (Migge 2003, McWhorter 2008), the evidence does not suggest that the complexity of the Saramaccan copula was one of those traits. Predictably given the role of pidginization and/or second-language acquisition in creole genesis, copulas were not prioritized for transfer into the new language, as morphemes of little or no semantic content, unnecessary to what began as utilitarian, untutored, makeshift communication. In terms of the theme of this volume, omission of copulas from either the lexifier or the substrate languages has been typical of creole genesis, in line with work demonstrating that the process is one driven by principles familiar in second-language acquisition (e.g. Plag 2008).

The development of a division of labor between copular morphemes is something we would expect to occur later, when a reduced, non-native variety became a full language. Thus the modern Saramaccan copular scenario emerged when a single copular morpheme *dé* – itself not present at emergence either, as demonstrated in McWhorter 1999 – was joined by a newly reanalyzed one. This new copula subdivided the semantic domain of copular constructions, while also complicating the grammar with rules and irregularities, some immediately and others developing thereafter.

6.5. What creates complexity in Saramaccan

6.5.1. Heavy usage

What appears to unite the aspects of Saramaccan grammar in which complexity has emerged the fastest is heavy usage. Grammaticalization and reanalysis are inherently connected to conventionalization, which implies that the constructions they effect are used with especial frequency; i.e. are particularly conventional (Hopper & Traugott 1993: 103, 146).

Thus we would expect that heavily used areas of grammar would be more likely to:

1) undergo processes of grammaticalization and reanalysis that create new morphemes and constructions,
2) bear irregularities as a token of the fact that especially heavy usage also creates loci of resistance to change.

As such,

1) first in Saramaccan a new copula encroached on the domain of the original one when heavy usage encouraged a typical process of reanalysis, in which a deictic subject between a topic and a predicate becomes a copula.
2) Later, phonetic erosion created allomorphy – a kind of structural elaboration – when *da* became *a* after fronted possessive phrases (*U mí a dí búku* "The book is mine").
3) Also, irregularity was a natural outcome of the process. In its initial stage as a deictic lexical item serving as a subject rather than as a verb or copula, naturally *da* did not take negation or tense. *Da,* although now a copular item, continues not to take negation or tense although *dé* does. This aspect of *da* is a conservative feature: heavy usage discourages its complete reanalysis as a copula or verb just as the same factor preserves English plurals like *children.*

The conservative aspect of *da* can be analogized to that of the *be* verb in English. It conserves reflexes of various Old English root verbs instead of just one (*beon, sindon, wesan*), and is the only verb in English with forms that vary according to number and (in the present) person. *Be* is an unusually complex verb – according to my metric in this paper – in a language whose verbal inflection paradigms are notoriously streamlined in comparison to other languages in its Germanic family. This is because of especially heavy usage – it would be vanishingly unlikely that in a low-inflection language like English, such features would persist for verbs like *pick* or *turn*.

Another Saramaccan feature demonstrating the centrality of heavy usage to emergent complexity is its one other irregular verb. The imperfective marker in Saramaccan is *tá,* as in *Mi tá wáka* "I am walking." With the verb *gó* "to go," *tá* must occur as a prefix *nán-*, such that "I am going" is *Mi nángó.* This is the only such case with any marker on any verb, and it is not accidental that it occurs with the *go* verb, one of the most susceptible cross-linguistically to grammaticalization (Heine & Kuteva 2002). Moreover, the irregularity of *nángó* is advanced (in its boundedness) but conservative, as irregularity often is, in that the second /n/ preserves the final consonant of the source of the modern marker *tá, tan* (> *stand*), long lost otherwise.

Pointedly, there are languages in the world with only three verbs, such as Jingulu in Australia (Pensalfini 2003), and *go* and *be* are two of them. Given how central these verbs are to human expression and how heavy their usage therefore is, it is unsurprising that they are the only ones in Saramaccan ana-lyzable as irregular – i.e. to have drifted into new forms of complexity since the language's birth.

6.5.2. Topic-comment syntax

The reanalysis of topic-comment constructions into subject-predicate ones as described by Li & Thompson (1975) has been a source of emergent com-plexity in Saramaccan beyond the development of the *da* copula. In general, when the subject position in a comment phrase becomes the subject in a subject-predicate construction, the morpheme occupying this slot can un-dergo phonetic, semantic and functional transformation that adds complexity to what was at first a relatively straightforward situation.

For example, in modern Saramaccan, the predicate negator is *á: Kobí á wáka* "Kobi does not walk." The imperative is negated, however, with *ná: Ná wáka!* "Don't walk!" *Ná* is also, as shown above, the suppletive negative form of copula *da: Mi ná i tatá* "I am not your father."

However, in historical documents of eighteenth-century Saramaccan, the form of the negator with both predicates and imperatives as well as elsewhere is *no*. This, in addition to other traits in the modern grammar, shows that today's predicate negator *á* is the product of the development of topic-comment into subject-predicate structures.

Specifically, the third person subject pronominal *a* (with low tone, in contrast to the high tone of the modern predicate negator) in the comment's subject position fused with the following negator *ná* (which developed from original *no*) yielding a portmanteau morpheme *ã́* retaining the nasality of the lost /n/. (This reconstruction is supported by the fact that this remains the predicate negator form in the Upper River dialect of Saramaccan.) When the topic was reinterpreted as a subject, *ã́* was reinterpreted as a negator alone, then eventually losing its nasality, a process common in phonetically light, heavily used grammatical morphemes in the language (for further details, see McWhorter 2005: 182–98):

Table 34. The development of the predicate negator in Saramaccan

Stage 1	Stage 2	Stage 3
Kofí, **a ná** wáka	Kofí, **ã́** waka	Kofí **á** wáka.
"Kobi, he doesn't walk"	"Kobi, he doesn't walk"	"Kobi doesn't walk."

The development from topic-comment to subject-predicate, then, has created an allomorphy in Saramaccan negation where once there was none – as well one of the rare cases in the language in which tone alone marks a grammatical distinction, given that *a* with low tone persists as the third person singular pronoun.

6.6. Implications of Saramaccan for theories of complexity

6.6.1. Syntheticity is but a subset of complexity

The complexity of the copular domain in Saramaccan is a demonstration that grammatical complexity consists of a great deal more than inflectional affixation and its consequences. Investigation of the reason for analyticity in pidgins and creoles often carry an implication that low levels of inflectional affixation are in some sense a primary difference between creoles and their source languages in terms of complexity.

Worldwide, however, grammatical complexity consists of a great deal more than inflectional affixation and its consequences. Morphologically isolating languages that were *not* born a few centuries ago evidence considerable complexities even without inflections (cf. Riddle 2008), such as in the application of numeral classifiers, tonal sandhi, and in marking categories typically associated by linguists with affixation but in fact also encodable with free morphemes.

While surely this is not intended by analysts, the focus in much work on complexity carries an implication that analytic languages like Vietnamese and Yoruba are not grammatically complex, and/or that their only significant complexity is in their tonal systems. Specialists in analytic languages would disagree – relevant is the Akha sentence presented in Chapter Four, Section 5, replete with "complex" features despite the absence of inflection.

Thus our interest in the development of complexity in Saramaccan is predicated upon the fact that Saramaccan differs in degree of complexity with analytic languages like Akha, not just with Western European languages. In general, investigations of grammatical complexity in all areas, including second language acquisition and typology, would benefit from a more general acknowledgment of what complexity consists of in the larger sense, beyond well-investigated aspects such as syntheticity and clausal embedding.

6.6.2. Complexity and teleology

Many address complexity in grammars as indexed to functional imperatives of various kinds, whether this be the increase in complexity or a movement away from it. I intend this one as a demonstration that to a considerable extent, the development of complexity in a language (or not) can be unrelated to contact factors. That is, much of the process takes place as the result of the same grammar-internal processes of change familiar from historical linguistics textbooks.

The development of the two-copula system in Saramaccan, for example, was not modelled on the speakers' native language Fongbe. More obviously, European languages were not a target. Rather, the bipartite Saramaccan copula scenario happened on its own, as the result of explainable but unpredictable processes of change. Saramaccan speakers do not process the language as a variety of any European language, and thus its development of copulas – as well as negators, irregular verbs, etc. – is not couched in a dynamic relationship with a "high" superstratal language. Nor were there sociological factors affecting these processes: for example, the omission of *da* in Saramaccan, where licensed, is not indexed to sociological factors as the omission of the copula is in Black English in America.

That is, while certainly the development of grammatical complexity is linked, in many situations, to language contact factors and acquisitional factors, there is a proportion of the phenomenon linked simply to the drift of a new language's grammar over time, according to the principle of "the invisible hand" (cf. Keller 1995). I would in fact argue that in Saramaccan, essentially all of the emergence of complexity since its genesis has been grammar-internal in this fashion.

Section III
Exceptional language change elsewhere

Introduction

The chapters in this section represent extensions of my position on language contact and simplification to languages other than creoles, as least as traditionally defined.

Creole exceptionalism is but one component of a framework devoted not to the singling out of creoles for suspect or peculiar reasons, but of analyzing the difference between human language as it presumably was for the most of humans' existence, as opposed to the way many languages are now as the result – I propose – of population movements and second-language acquisition. In McWhorter (2007) I argue that English, Persian, Mandarin Chinese, the colloquial Arabics and Indonesian are all languages bearing hallmarks of adult acquisition, despite their status as standard, written languages.

Chapter Seven summarizes my response to the most challenging riposte I have encountered to creole exceptionalism at ths writing, from Indonesian specialist David Gil.

A requirement of my framework is that no language could drift into the state of the Creole Prototype just as a matter of chance, nor could a language drift randomly into a state of radically low complexity. That is, as I have stated it elsewhere (McWhorter 2007: 4–5), my thesis is that:

> In the uninterrupted transmission of a human language, radical loss of complexity throughout the grammar is neither normal, occasional, nor rare, but *impossible.* The natural state of human language is one saddled with accreted complexity unnecessary to communication. Wherever this complexity is radically abbreviated overall rather than in scattered, local fashion, this is not just sometimes, but *always* caused by a sociohistorical situation in which non-native acquisition of the language was widespread enough that grammar was transmitted to new generations in a significantly simplified form. This is true not only in the extreme case of pidgins and creoles, but also to a lesser but robust extent in many languages of the world.

I have no interest whatsoever in a "tendency" here. What makes this hypothesis worth investigating is whether it proves to be, quite simply, true. If older languages can just happen into being like creoles, then there is nothing of interest in the scientific sense. We already knew that analyticity and loss of complexity were involved to at least some extent in creole genesis. A further step would be to see if radical manifestations of these phenomena *define* creole genesis, and in less extreme but robust manifestations, are diagnostic of it.

Ten years ago, Gil apprised me of a paper he was writing on a colloquial Indonesian dialect (Gil 2001). Riau Indonesian displays the traits of the Creole Prototype, it would seem. Gil's position was that this was indeed proof that a language can wend into this "prototypical" state by chance.

After research of my own, I concluded that actually, Riau Indonesian is a product of extensive adult acquisition itself, and therefore only supports my hypothesis. To wit, the position of the dialect in its family as well as its history render it easily accounted for under my paradigm. It would surprising if it were otherwise. As Gil notes, colloquial Indonesians are almost all radically less complex than the standard language. Given that Indonesian has been used as much if not more as a second language than as a first one for over two millennia, it would be almost bizarre if the nature of these colloquial dialects were unconnected with this. Standard Indonesian is, in fact, an artificial construct based on its earlier stages as the highly codified Classical Malay, representing the language in its "untouched" rendition. The vernacular varieties, existing in a diglossic relationship with it, have long been something quite different.

Chapter Seven is an adapted version of McWhorter (2008b), with reconceived text flow, additional data I have learned of since I wrote the article, and abridgment as per changes in my thinking over time (see also below).

In seeking to make this case for dialects like Riau Indonesian, I surveyed Austronesian to confirm my hunch that no other languages in the family had drifted into mysterious analyticity. I found that my hunch was wrong. There is a handful of languages spoken on the island of Flores which are completely isolating, as well as some languages of eastern Timor that are nearly so. The conventional assumption is that these languages simply "lost their morphology." However, no specialists have proposed a mechanism for how this would have happened, and the fact that only these very few out of a thousand Austronesian languages have come to this state has suggested to me that there must be something particular about their social histories.

That is, I took these languages as challenges to my hypothesis. It could be that these languages drifted into this state by chance and therefore disconfirmed my hypothesis. However, to treat my hypothesis in the scientific sense required assessing whether these languages in fact could be revealed to be analyzable according to its dictates.

Chapter Eight outlines my conclusion, which is that these languages can indeed be accommodated within my proposal. These languages of Flores and Timor show evidence of a massive interruption by adult learners, in the form of extremely unusual aspects of their lexicons which would otherwise be, from what I can tell, quite inexplicable.

The article version of Chapter Seven originally included a preliminary analysis from elsewhere of the situation in Timor which I have now disavowed, and a mere description of the Flores data, with analysis tabled as future work. That section, which has archival value only, is therefore omitted from Chapter Seven. My current views on Timor and Flores are here contained in Chapter Eight.

Chapter Nine is an analysis of none other than English. The placement of English in Box 4 of the language contact typology in the Introduction, as a saliently simplified member of its Germanic subfamily, can be seen to refute any possible impression that my aggressive taxonomization of creoles as defined by simplification entails any sense of my native language as somehow "normal." It is not, as I have outlined extensively in McWhorter (2005a: 267–311), and spread the word to the general public in McWhorter (2008a).

In Chapter Nine I make a case that English is even less "normal" than specialists in its diachrony have typically supposed. English grammar is deeply impacted by Celtic in a way that no other Germanic language is, such that depending on where one draws the proverbial line, it could be seen as both moderately simplified as well as moderately *mixed,* and therefore belonging in Box 5 as a semi-creole along with Afrikaans and Reunionnais French. This chapter represents a "director's cut" version of the article it is based on, which was abridged somewhat for length (however, the chapter is not, in my view, lengthy to any unwieldy degree!).

At this writing, the Celtic Hypothesis on English diachrony would appear to be at a tipping point. In reference to recent arguments from adherents, Minkova (2009:900fn) announces in *Language* that "the profession is listening," a statement unimaginable just ten years before. Chapter Nine is intended as a spur for further listening. As language change goes, English's pathway has been, like that of creoles, exceptional – and not merely in terms of lexical mixture, but in a vast streamlining and hybridization of its grammar.

Chapter 7
Why does a language undress?
The Riau Indonesian problem

7.1. Introduction

Gil (2001 and elsewhere), in response to my argument that languages do not radically simplify without extensive adult acquisition, has presented the nonstandard Indonesian dialect of Riau province in Sumatra as an exception. Gil certainly shows Riau Indonesian to be an almost counterintuitively telegraphic form of natural language. It is essentially pro-drop. Its word order is free. There are no copulas, complementizers, or relativizers. There is no possessive marker according to Gil's analysis. While in Standard Indonesian, use of tense and aspect markers is optional, in Riau they are even less conventionalized. Numeral classifiers are an areal feature and used in Standard Indonesian, but rarely in the Riau variety (ibid. 343–57).

Riau Indonesian also recasts Standard Indonesian's voice-marking morphology – agent-oriented *meN-* and object-oriented *di-* – into optional pragmatic markers of agent and patient (Gil 2002). Thus whereas in Standard Indonesian, *di-* marking connotes a passive reading, in Riau Indonesian it only lightly highlights patienthood (OO = object-oriented):

(1) *Aku **di**-goreng.*
     I   OO-fry
     Standard: 'I was fried.'
     Riau: 'I fried it.' (or by my reading of Gil, "I fried the thing.")

The Riau variety is but one of several colloquial Indonesians that Gil calls attention to in which the situation is similar, such as one in southern Sulawesi, Kuala Lumpur, and Irian Jaya (which makes barely any use of either voice marker). Overall, Standard Indonesian is the "high" member in a diglossia, an artifically constructed language few speak casually. Gil describes Indonesian as it has actually evolved as a spoken language almost everywhere that it is spoken.

This implies that grammars may naturally opt to shed massive amounts of complexity just as a matter of course. Gil (2005) states that "the accretion of complexity cannot be construed as an inexorable monotonic process," since apparently "at some stage between Proto-Austronesian and Riau Indonesian, the accretion of complexity must have been reversed." But when he notes that this leaves a question as to "why more languages could not have taken the same path, and leaves it at that "I have no answer to this question," I propose that the reason is that no languages have taken this path – that is, without extensive non-native use.

The idea that grammars can simplify vastly just by chance is conditioned in large part by the development from earlier Indo-European languages to modern ones, such as Old English to Modern English and Latin to Romance. However, in McWhorter (2007), I stress that these cases are in fact due to non-native acquisition themselves. These languages' central role in linguistic discussion is an epiphenomenon of the fact that academic inquiry is a product of civilizations borne of large-scale population movements, such that linguistic research has been spearheaded and dominated by speakers of languages with heritages in such sociohistorical developments, and languages of this type have tended to be recorded most in writing over time.

More illustrative of how conservative of complexity grammars are under normal conditions is a bird's-eye view of the world. There exists no mysteriously analytic Algonquian language. No Chinese language lacks tones. The only Semitic variety that eschews the family's hallmark triliteral consonantal template is, significantly, Nubi *Creole* Arabic.

I stipulate that any grammar that 1) has developed without a significant degree of non-native acquisition and 2) is starkly less grammatically complex than its sister languages constitutes counterevidence to my thesis. In this chapter I will argue that Riau Indonesian is not such a case.

7.2. Why would a language undress?

Before addressing the Indonesian cases in question, it will be useful to be somewhat more specific as to my motivations for stipulating that grammars do not, under ordinary conditions, drift into vastly less complexity. The fact is that an unmediated, grammar-internal drift into analyticity manifests *no theoretically documented process of language change.*

7.2.1. Pidginization

Usually when a grammar changes in this way, linguists trace it to some kind of abrupt interruption in transmission due to population movements. For example, here is a sentence in an indigenous variety of the Bantu language Kikongo and then in the contact variety Kituba, developed amidst speakers of various divergent Kikongo dialects amidst the upheavals of Belgian colonization. There is no Bantu variety in eastern or southern Africa remotely as isolating as Kituba – other than Fanakalo, a pidginized Zulu, or some varieties of Lingala, which is, again, a lingua franca that emerged amidst non-native acquisition (of the Ngala dialect complex):

(2)(a) (*Yándi*) *ka- ku- zól- elé.*
     he/she AGR-2SOBJ-like-NEAR.PERFECT

  (b) *Yándi zóla ngé.*
     he/she like 2S
     'He/she likes you.'

(Mufwene 1990: 176)

In the Mesoamerican language Pipil, future marking in the living language was inflectional: *Ni-panu-s* I-pass-FUT "I will pass"). As spoken by today's last elderly speakers, the future is periphrastic:

(3) *Ni-yu ni-k-chiwa.*
   I-go I-it-do
   'I'm going to do it.'

(Campbell & Muntzel 1989: 192–3)

Scholars of language death associate such processes with interruption in transmission due to speakers failing to pass a grammar on fully to new generations.

7.2.2. Maintenance of complexity

Meanwhile, certainly grammars lose inflections to phonetic erosion. But they also develop new ones via grammaticalization and reinterpretation of phonetic segments. One might object, for instance, that Old Chinese was an analytic language, and that since the development of affixes is an inevitable process in language change, and Old Chinese was a stage of transformation quite long after the emergence of human language several tens of millennia before, that here was a language that apparently shed all of its affixation as an internal development. However, the affixes did not simply sheer away, but left new complexity in their wake in the form of tonal alternations.

For example, certain tonally marked derivations in Middle Chinese and beyond have been traced to effects of the erosion of a final -*s* before Old Chinese, in which language the alternations remained as segmental distortions intermediate between the -*s* and tones (cf. Norman 1988: 84–5). The reconstruction of other analytic Sino-Tibetan languages is replete with processes of this kind. Simplification left complexity, as happens so often in language change worldwide.

What factor, precisely, would condition a generation of speakers to reject a mass of, rather than just occasional, living features in the grammar they are exposed to as children *with no erosional sign left of the material shed?* If we suppose that the process occurred over several generations, then the question remains as to what would lead a first generation to reject even a good bundle of the living features their parents used? And then, if they for some reason did, why would the succeeding generation take this as a "trend" and continue this rejectional orientation towards their native grammars, to a degree significant or even slight? What theoretically constrained factor would prevent this succeeding generation from simply reverting back to "normal" and reproducing the grammar as they learned it?

One might imagine English speakers tossing out strong verb ablaut to mark the past: certainly the system has faded around the edges over time, but then new forms continually develop by analogy (e.g. *wore, spat, dove*). Dahl (2004: 269–74) notes that Germanic strong verb ablaut has persisted in all members of the family in robust form for millennia. Certainly, no single generation would begin using *only* weak forms (*I comed, I seed, I conquered*), and if such a thing did occur over several generations, we would suspect that the grammar was not being transmitted fully; i.e. that a critical mass of learners were not children.

Of course, an alternate-universe scenario could eliminate the strong verb ablaut via natural development: if English's phonological evolution happened to make the distinctions between the relevant vowels so fine as to impede processibility to new generations. We could imagine, for example, that a critical mass of ablaut patterns came to entail alternations between vowels distinguished only by tenseness (for instance, *sit*/*sat* > [sɛt]/[set]) or close in other ways such as [ɑ] and [ɔ]. Certainly, here it is conceivable that the ablaut distinction would leach away entirely, just as unaccented final vowels' fragility surely has much to do with why Germanic has abbreviated a degree of Proto-Indo-European suffixation.

But the crucial fact is that while such processes occur, normally new constructions are emerging. For example, in an English losing strong verb ablaut, in its timeline there would still be the grammaticalization of *will* as a future marker, which in modern English has yielded a clitic *'ll* (*That boy that came here yesterday'll found out*), *will's* past form *would* as a conditional and its corresponding clitic *'d* (*That boy over there'd know*), and a fine-grained array of future markings that challenge adult learners (*I am going* [tomorrow], *I will go, I am going to go*). In modern American teen speech, *all* is used to indicate indirect speech in sentences like *And she was all "I'm going to tell your father!"* If English were spoken by an obscure tribe and the conservatism of written norms did not cast this usage of *all* as "slang," then there would be a new quotative marker in the description of the grammar. We could even propose that in a much later stage of this "tribal English," the origin of the construction in a copular one would be synchronically opaque, and there was a paradigm of quotative markers indexed to person and number according to what were once the final consonants of the *be*-verb allomorphs, such that the first-person singular reflex would be [mɔl] (from *I'm all*), the third-person singular one [zɔl] (from *she's all*), and the plural reflex [rɔl]. Things come as things go.

Then – if English evolved into an entirely analytic language, all theories of language change would identify non-native learning as the reason – and indeed, the only descendants of English with, for example, no inflection at all are creole languages in Surinam like Sranan and Saramaccan.

Thus the question that languages mysteriously more analytic and less grammatically complex than their sister languages raises is precisely what step-by-step process would have created such a situation, other than one mediated by non-native acquisition? At this point in the development of diachronic linguistic theory, I am not aware that such a process has been identified.

7.2.3. A phonological explanation?

I am aware of but one systematic account of how a grammar might transition from syntheticity to analyticity independently of language contact, Hyman's (2004) hypothesis regarding the analyticity of West African branches of Niger-Congo in contrast to the prolifically agglutinative typology of most Bantu languages. A natural assumption would be that if some Niger-Congo languages like Yoruba are highly analytic:

(4) *Mo mú ìwé wá fún ẹ.*
     I   take book come give you
     'I brought you a book.'

then this was the original state of Proto-Niger-Congo, and that typical Bantu verbal constructions like East African Yao's:

(5) *taam-uk- ul- igw- aasy- an- il- a*
     sit- IMP- REV-PASS-CAUS-REC-APPL-V
     'to cause each other to be unseated for"

must be a result of free words falling into morphologization.

But Hyman proposes that Proto-Niger-Congo was an agglutinative language along the lines of today's "classic" Bantu, and that languages like Yoruba developed when agglutinative ancestors took on phonological templates that restricted verbs' syllable count, such that only bi- or trisyllabic words were allowed. As such, Niger-Congo languages in Cameroon, West Africa, and along the northern boundary of the Niger-Congo realm are, if not as strictly monosyllabic as Yoruba, limited to less syllabically prolific phonological templates. Thus take Yao's capacity:

Table 35. Morphology of the Yao verb

taam-a	"sit"	
taam-ik-a	"seat"	impositive
taam-ik-ul-a	"unseat"	reversive
taam-ik-ul-igw-a	"to be unseated"	passive
taam-ik-ul-igw-aasy-a	"cause to be unseated"	causative

An Edoid language of Nigeria like Degema has no verb monsters like Yao, but allows a causative marker cognate with Yao's *-assy-*, as in *tul* "to reach," *tul-ese* "to cause to reach." The Ubangian language Banda-Linda of the Central African Republic has a reversive marker cognate with Yao's (with an alternation of Yao's lateral consonant to a rhotic): *ʒe* "bubble, overflow, belch," *ʒè-rɔ* "deflate, take a final breath, shove into, go down."

Along these lines, we could consider whether Riau Indonesian is an "unravelled" version of an inflectional ancestor.

But Hyman's analysis leaves a question: if it is so natural for a language to develop a phonological template so incommensurate with its typology that its entire grammatical structure is transformed, then why has no Bantu language in southern or eastern Africa drifted into such a phonology over the 3000 years since Bantu speakers started migrating from Cameroon? Not a single one has, amidst a notoriously vast proliferation of hundreds of languages. Where is the weirdly analytic Bantu language in Mozambique? For that matter, we also seek similar examples in agglutinative languages around the world, i.e. the Turkic or Eskimo-Aleut language that limits affixation to one or two morphemes per root.

There is also no reason to suppose that this phonological recasting would only occur in agglutinative languages. We must ask why fusional typology would necessarily put a break on such a change. Why no Indo-European languages that submitted to such a transformation? As fusional languages they typically have, for example, verbal suffixes that connote both tense and person (Portuguese *fal-o* "I speak"). But if templatic structure can drift into analyticity, then why could not, for example, an Iberian dialect separate present-tense/person/number markers as free morphemes? We could even imagine that the morphemes would take with them the final consonant of the verb root, such that there would be new verb classes distinguished by paradigms of post-verbal subject pro-nominal clitics differing in their initial consonant. Thus, in a hypothetical Iberian dialect, *fa lo* "I speak," *fa las* "you speak;" but from *andar* "to walk," *an do* "I walk," *an das* "you walk." Obviously, however, there is not even a single such Indo-European language of this kind – after eight millennia or more.

And again, it is difficult to imagine why a certain generation would begin contracting the number of syllables a word was allowed to have: the process is easier to describe than to actually explain – especially as presumably oc-curring in hundreds of languages (or at least dozens, unless we posit a single early language as the source for an areal phenomenon).

It is more graceful to suppose that Niger-Congo was indeed more like Yoruba and that Bantu languages are a particular branch in which an extreme degree of agglutinativity has developed. This, after all, would have happened via familiar processes of grammaticalization – i.e. it is clear and documented how this kind change would occur across generations. Crucially, it is equally understandable why once this agglutinativity had emerged, it would persist in hundreds of languages over millennia.

We imagine that the next natural step would be not phonological undoing of boundedness, but fusional typology; i.e. boundedness increasing to the point of phonetic collapses. For example, some agglutinative morphemes would erode – but not into the ether, but leaving behind vocalic alternations upon other morphemes, yielding constructions like the ablaut patterns in families like Indo-European, much older than Bantu. And then a further, or alternate, step would be the development of tonal morphology as in Chinese.

In sum, the idea of a language losing all of its morphology just as a mat-ter of course is perhaps easy to imagine in a passing sense, but devilishly challenging to conceive of a precise mechanism for. In that light, I will now propose the following arguments for the position that Riau Indonesian does not constitute a puzzle for this position. In other words, Riau Indonesian undressed for a reason.

7.3. There are no varieties of Indonesian's relatives that are reduced like Riau Indonesian

If the nature of Riau Indonesian plus several other colloquial Indonesian varieties were a typical result of uninterrupted transmission, then it would be nothing less than common to find similarly reduced varieties of languages closely related to Indonesian like Javanese, Sundanese, Madurese, Minangkabau and Iban. Given that these languages have similar grammars to Indonesian's, then surely happenstance would exert like effect upon at least a few varieties of some of these languages.

This is, to my knowledge at this writing, unknown. A relevant example is Smith-Hefner's (1988) and Conners' (2008) descriptions of the Javanese of Tengger, differing from the standard in minor elisions and collapsings of morphology, but hardly to the extent of Riau Indonesian from the standard.

Importantly, we would not need to assume that all such cases would be, like the spoken Indonesians, socially unacknowledged colloquial levels of more complex standard languages, difficult to smoke out without fluent command of the language and thus unsurprisingly undocumented today. Since the vast majority of Indonesian languages are small, unwritten ones, if Riau Indonesian's nature is a natural development, then we would expect that a map of Sumatra or Sulawesi would be dotted with at least occasional highly analytic languages that had happened along the same pathway, with no artificially preserved written variety to mask the spoken reality.

At our current state of knowledge, there are no such varieties. I submit that this is because under conditions of full transmission, natural languages *never* evolve in such a direction.

In an ingenious study, Gil (2007) proposes that Indonesian's close relatives Minangkabau and Sundanese can be shown to have indeed reached a radical degree of reduction despite not having histories in which they were learned more by adults than children. Gil's metric is the freedom of interpretation of items under association. In a language like English, association is highly constrained by rules such as subjects normally preceding objects, such that if an English-speaking subject is presented with the sentence *The bird is eating* and then shown one picture showing a bird eating and the other showing a cat eating a bird, he or she will point to the former picture. However, if a Sundanese speaker is given the equivalent sentence *Manuk dahar* 'bird eat,' then they will accept both pictures as illustrating the sentence, because it could also mean "He (the cat) eats the bird." The absence of case or inflectional affixation constraining the interpretation makes this possible in Sundanese.

Testing sixteen sentences, Gil shows that of eleven languages, Minangkabau and Sundanese have the freest association according to this metric – and, by implication, parallel Riau Indonesian, whose freedom of associational semantics Gil has examined elsewhere.

It is certainly true that compared to the hundreds of other languages of the Western Malayo-Polynesian subdivision of Austronesian, Minangkabau and Sundanese stand out as relatively low in grammatical complexity, lacking, for example, tense and aspect affixes or concordial affixes on the head. However, internal evolution is not the only possible cause here. In this, Minangkabau and Sundanese parallel Standard Indonesian, and in McWhorter (2007: 237–42) I suggest that this is an areal trait due to the intimate contact with Indonesian that these languages (as well as Javanese and Madurese) have had over the eons. The associational freedom that Gil analyzes can be seen as due to this reality.

Moreover, the fact remains that this associational freedom is but one aspect of what grammatical complexity can consist of, and in many other areas of grammar, Minangkabau and Sundanese surpass Riau Indonesian. For example, they parallel Indonesian's battery of derivational morphology complete with morphophonemic complications in their surface realization (something the sentences in Gil [2007] do not happen to cover). Meanwhile, Minangkabau surpasses even Standard Indonesian in grading distance more finely and in the number of numeral classifiers (Moussay 1981). Sundanese has the same traits, as well as productive infixation with *-ar-*, a negative existential marker, a high yogh vowel along with the typical vowel inventory of languages of its Malayo-Javanic group, and other features (Müller-Gotama 2001).

In the same way, Javanese has imperative morphology ("write" *nulés, nulisô!*), suppletive noun plurals such as *wet, witwitan* "tree" and a subjunctive suffix *-a* (Horne 1961). There do not even seem to be dialects of languages related to Indonesian that are as reduced as Riau Indonesian and similar varieties. As noted, Tengger Javanese is not such a case. Meanwhile, the Mualang dialect of Iban has inalienable possessive marking:

(6)(a) *Anak tu' **mpu** ku.*
     child this POSS 1S
     'This child is mine.'

  (b) *Uma   tu' **nu'** ku.*
     rice.field this POSS 1S
     'This rice field is mine.'

(Tjia 2007: 128)

and a four-way demonstrative distinction (*tu'* "this,"*nya'* "that," *nyin* "that over there" and *nyun* "that way over there" [ibid. 61]), as well the dual pronoun well known from the Sarawak variety.

Thus I accept Gil's argument that his study shows that a language can drift into extreme simplicity in a particular area – as well as that in this case, Minangkabau and Sundanese clearly surpass even creoles like Saramaccan. However, in that my interest is in overall complexity, it would seem that the study does not, in itself, demonstrate that Minangkabau, Sundanese and related languages have by chance drifted into the *overall* degree of simplicity of Riau Indonesian.

7.4. The grammar of Riau Indonesian gives no concrete indication of transfer from other languages

Gil also argues that Riau Indonesian's nature is due to a Sprachbund feature typical of Southeast Asia, a tendency to allow considerable ellipsis of arguments. However, the fact remains that languages with this tendency can be inflected nevertheless, such as the Philippines languages and so many other Austronesian languages, or even if analytic, have ergativity (like Polynesian languages) or massive lists of numeral classifiers (common in Southeast Asia in general). Our question, then, is why Riau is so naked of complexity even beyond its tendency to elide arguments unnecessary to comprehension?

The question is why Riau Indonesian apparently incorporated only this abbreviational feature of surrounding languages, rather than concrete additions from them. A contrasting case is Acehnese, the result of a language closely related to Indonesian mixing with Mon-Khmer:

(7) *Na si-droe-ureueng-ladang geu-jak lam-uteuen geu-jak koh kayee.*
    be one-CL-person-farm   he-go in-forest   he-go cut wood
    'There was a farmer who went into the forest to cut wood.'
    (Durie 1985: 192)

The mixture here is unequivocal. The phonetic inventory is unlike that in any related language. Orthographically, *eu* represents unrounded back vowel [ɯ]; *eue* represents a diphthong with a schwa offglide ([ɯə]); *oe* represents [ɔə]. These are clear parallels to typical sounds in Mon-Khmer languages. The *droe* classifier comes from the use of this word as "self" (cf. Indonesian *diri*), but Indonesian's cognate is not used in this function. The syntax departs from Indonesian as well, with its obligatory subject-marking clitics and absence of voice-marking prefixes (*di-* and *meN-* have no cognates or equivalents in Acehnese).

Importantly, however, there is nothing especially "simplified" about Acehnese overall, a well-inflected and overspecified grammar. Here, then, is a relative of Indonesian's in which mixture has created a language sharply different from any form of Indonesian itself. Riau Indonesian, obviously, is not mixed to anything approaching this extent. It differs from Standard Indonesian in its radical simplification.

Similarly, the Urak Lawoi' variety of Indonesian spoken in Thailand has Thai-style sentence-final particles:

(8) *Buwac rumah balay jadi   tuhat kami   dah tə   lə.*
     make house shrine become God   we.INCL PAST EMPH EMPH
     'We made a shrine house to become our God.'

                                                         (Hogan 1999)

as well as serial verbs as in Thai:

(9) *Pi atac ka? lawoc lər   bri ɲa haɲɔc pi buwak.*
     go send to   sea   EMPH let it float go finally
     'They send it off to sea; so that it floats right away.'

                                                             (ibid.)

Then there are colloquial Indonesian varieties that display concrete evidence of mixture, but remain strikingly simplified compared to Standard Indonesian and the contact language. They show that even when unambiguous, mixture can leave a colloquial Indonesian variety still strikingly simplified, and thus cannot explain these varieties' difference from the standard.

Baba Malay (throughout, "Malay" will be used as a synonym of "Indonesian" where convention uses "Malay" in names of language varieties) of Malaysia and Singapore is typical. It was developed by Hokkien (Min) Chinese speakers, and as a result has some Hokkien-derived features such as phonemic nasal vowels, some pronouns and a comparative construction, and, possibly, extensions of the use of the *ada* existential, the use of *kena* "give" for the passive, and the *punya* possessive (Ansaldo & Matthews 1999). For example, an example of the latter case follows, in which the *punya* marker is used as an associative marker along the lines of a Hokkien marker:

(10) *betol **punia** hap*
      good POSS match
      'a good match!'

along the lines of Hokkien:

(11)   *khăq tuā é   cābò*
        more old PART woman
        'an older woman.'

But Ansaldo & Matthews present only a scattered and shallow seven features, with the above being perhaps the most sharply divergent from Indonesian. If Baba Malay were simply a mixture of Bazaar Malay and Hokkien, then we would expect it to display, if not seven or eight lexical tones like Min Chineses, then at least three or four (for example, Western Cham of Vietnam, an Austronesian-Mon-Khmer hybrid related to Achenese, has five). We might also expect a healthy system of grammaticalized serial verb constructions, multiple semantically specific negators, or a reflection of Hokkien's multiple complementizers.

Instead, the dominant factor in the emergence of Baba Malay was not mixture but structural reduction, contrasting it sharply in complexity with both Standard Indonesian and Hokkien. Importantly, Baba Malay has been classified as a creole, as I think Riau Indonesian and similar varieties should be (McWhorter 2001c: 407–8).

Another example is the colloquial Indonesian of Roti island. Here, mixture is more unequivocally evident than in Baba Malay, with even borrowing of grammatical items from the Rotinese language (data from Fox 1982: 312, rearranged):

(12)   Roti variety   *Beta*   *su*   *pi*   *ma*   *lu*   *sonde*   *ada.*
       Standard Malay   *Saya*   *sudah*   *pergi* *tapi* *kamu*   *tidak*   *ada.*
                        I   PERF   go   but   you   NEG   be
                        'I went but you weren't there.'

The mixture here is in the form of borrowings: *lu* from Hokkien; *sonde* is from Dutch *zonder* (Kumudawati & Setjadiningrat 2001: 78); *ma* from Dutch *maar* reinforced by a Rotinese conjunction of similar shape. *Su* and *pi* are shortened forms of the standard ones. Yet again, simplification has been central, as the complexities of the source languages are not incorporated. The perfective marker is not, as in Hokkien, postposed and as such, contravening the usual word order for verb modifiers. Rotinese's subject-marking inflectional prefixes are nowhere in evidence.

7.5. Theories of grammar-internal change do not predict the fate of voice markers in colloquial Indonesians

The drifting of semantic markers into more optional and less regularized pragmatic ones also goes against the strong tendency that grammaticalization specialists recognize in the other direction. This renders the fate of *di-* and *N-* in colloquial Indonesians peculiar – until we recall that non-native acquisition can lead to precisely this kind of reversal.

In creoles, for example, categories obligatorily and even redundantly expressed in source languages are very often marked in a smaller range of contexts, and often only for explicitness. Palenquero Creole Spanish inherits the *ma-* plural affix from Kikongo. But whereas Kikongo marks the plural categorically as does Spanish, Palenquero, besides "loosening" the affix into the less bounded status of a clitic, often omits it when context supplies the inference:

(13)(a)   *Kasi   to **ma** moná di ayá la   baho*
          almost all PL girl   of there there below
          'Almost all the girls from down there'

     (b)   *Ese ea   ɵ mamá puñera-ba   re akí.*
          that be.PAST   mother boxing-PAST of here
          'Those were the boxing women here.'

                                          (Schwegler 1998: 289)

In cases like pidginization and creolization, "unravelling" of this kind is ordinary. In uninterrupted language change, it is anomalous.

7.6. Summary

On the basis of the above observations, I suggest that Riau Indonesian is not a natural development that Indonesian grammar would take, and that explaining this grammar as a Sprachbund phenomenon is only partially useful in the explanatory sense. Riau Indonesian gives all evidence of being what happens when Indonesian is acquired widely enough non-natively that the complexities of its grammatical machinery start falling away in cases where context can easy convey their meaning or function. Hence the voice markers devolved into optional pragmatic ones; numeral classifiers contracted into extreme optionality; derivational machinery atrophied; etc. – these are hallmarks of the dissolution of a language, not its normal transformation over time.

Jakarta Malay is reduced in a fashion similar to in Riau Indonesian, with:

a)   *sama* as multifunctional preposition
b)   virtually no *meN-* prefix
c)   collapse of transitivizing *-kan* and *-i* to *-in*

d)   negator *bukan* generalized over *tidak*
e)   no exclusive 1PL *kami*

Grijns (1991: 4) concludes that it "developed from Malay as a second language into a Malay-based first language," noting that in the 1800s under Java's period of Dutch rule, vast numbers of domestic slaves from various regions and assorted speakers of Chinese varieties were shifting to Malay as first language. In that light, it is important that as Gil notes (2001: 330–4), even today one in four Riau Indonesian speakers grew up in homes where at least one parent was not a native Indonesian speaker, and that "the present-day Riau province was the venue of substantial language contact over much of the last 2000 years," that "various contact varieties of Malayic must have arisen during this lengthy period," and that "such contact varieties constitute plausible ancestors for what is now Riau Indonesian." In general, only 7% of Indonesians speak Indonesian as a first language (Prentice 1987: 915).

To be sure, Grijns' proposal is only that; there exists no sociohistorical data remotely detailed enough to decisively conclude that it is accurate. In the same fashion, Gil (p.c.) notes that his one-in-four figure is based on his informal investigation, and that sociohistorical documentation on the development of Riau Indonesian is likely unavailable. However, my proposal is that Grijns' deduction is likely correct, and that what Gil discovered in his survey can be plausibly taken as germane to the uniquely streamlined nature of the grammar. This is because, precisely, that there is no known diachronic mechanism that would yield such results other than extensive second-language acquisition.

Specifically, I consider Riau Indonesian to be a creole language, under a definition of creolization as simplification of a radical degree. There are no more lines between *none, moderate* and *radical* than there are between *child, teenager* and *adult,* and as such, I can offer no specific measurement as a justification for my classification. The very endeavor to create one would be not just futile but nonsensical.

However, Riau Indonesian can be seen as representing not just one but two waves of adult acquisition. The typical Austronesian language is as cluttered with overspecification, structural elaboration and irregularity as the Sulawesi language Tukang Besi:

(14)   *No-to-   pa-   ala- mo   na   iai-su   te   kau.*
        3R-PASS-CAUS-fetch-PERF NOM younger.sibling-my CORE wood
        'My younger sibling was made to fetch some wood.'

(Donohue 1999: 297)

This contrasts with, for example, Standard Indonesian, in which affixation is largely limited to a few derivational affixes such as *di-* and *meN-*:

(15) *Zainal **di**-pukul   Ali kemarin.*
Zainal OO-strike Ali yesterday
'Zainal was struck by Ali yesterday.'

(Prentice 1987: 933)

Note that the difference between Tukang Besi and Indonesian here is not a mere matter of isolating and affixal typology. Indonesian does not encode a great deal of what Tukang Besi does in any way, such as Tukang Besi's grammaticalized realis distinction, its specific marker of passive, its obligatory marking of tense or aspect, and its distinction of nouns between nominative and "core." Even Standard Indonesian is uniquely streamlined among Austronesian languages (cf. McWhorter 2007: 197–221), because of its long history as a lingua franca.

Riau Indonesian, compared to Standard Indonesian, has undergone yet another "pass" of reduction, with even *di-* and *meN-* largely eliminated or reconceived as pragmatic markers, and free word order, no copulas, barely any tense or aspect marking, no complementizers or relativizers, and barely any use of numeral classifiers. As such, it is a language even less overspecified and structurally elaborated than Saramaccan Creole. This degree of grammatical simplification in comparison to source languages is one I consider salient enough to need a label, and the label I choose is *creole*. Riau Indonesian would be one.

Note that I do not consider the typical plantation creole life-cycle to be in any way defining of the term creole. Creoles have been born in countless settings: plantations (Saramaccan), displaced military bodies (Nubi Creole Arabic), orphanages (Unserdeutsch Creole German), missionary settlements (Tayo Creole French), Native American reservations (Grande Ronde Chinook Jargon creole), and others. Therefore, the fact that Riau Indonesian was not created by plantation slaves is irrelevant to the creole definition, as is the fact that there was likely no stable "pidgin" variety that preceded the "creole" stage. Creole, under my typology, refers to a degree of simplification. There are various pathways to that mountaintop, of which Malay has apparently followed several.

Chapter 8
Affixless in Austronesian: Why Flores is a puzzle and what to do about it

8.1. Introduction: The problem

The Austronesian family is notoriously large and multifarious. Yet a defining grammatical feature of the family is that Austronesian languages are affixal, of agglutinative and often fusional typology.

8.1.1. Austronesian is affixal

Typical are the Philippines languages such as Tagalog, with its allomorphic focus marking on verbs and even pronouns:

(1) *Na-kita   mo   siya   kahapon.*
    PT.PERF-see 2S:ACTOR 3S:TRIGGER yesterday.
    'You saw him yesterday.'

                    (Schachter 1987: 941) (PT = patient trigger)

Among "Indonesian-type" languages, there is derivational marking of subject- and object-orientation, as in Indonesian:

(2) *Zainal **di**-pukul Ali kemarin.*
    Zainal OO-strike Ali yesterday
    'Zainal was struck by Ali yesterday.'

                                        (Prentice 1990: 933)

In the languages of Sulawesi, often both focus and many other categories are affixally marked, as in Tukang Besi:

(3) *No-to- pa-   ala- mo   na   iai-su   te   kau.*
    3R-PASS-CAUS-fetch-PERF NOM younger.sibling-my CORE wood
    'My younger sibling was made to fetch some wood.'

                                        (Donohue 1999: 297)

Affixation is less copious in the Central Malayo-Polynesian languages, but typically robust nonetheless, as in Leti, in which the following typical sentence includes inflections marking the indicative and evidentiality:

(4)   *Ra-mtïètan-nòr-e*   *kadèr-o*.
      3PL-sit-INSTR-EVID chair-IND
      'They use a chair to sit on.'

(Van Engelenhoven 2004: 235)

Meanwhile, Melanesian languages are also well affixed, as in Kwaio, with robust marking of transitivity and arguments coreferenced with affixes on the head:

(5)   *Lauta ku aga-si-a   boo a-na   i   langa'a a-gu   nau*
      if   1S see-TR-3S pig POSS-3S LOC garden POSS-1S   I.EMPH
      ta-ku   'ui'a.
      FUT-1S shoot-3S
      'If I see his pig in my garden then I'll shoot it.'

(Keesing 1985: 118)

Meanwhile, Polynesian languages, although lacking inflectional affixation, have derivational affixation, as in Maori:

(6)   *A te tae-**nga**   mai   o   ngaa moni* . . .
      at the arrive-NOM to-here GEN the.PL money
      'When the money arrives . . . '

(Bauer 1993: 278)

Also, to the extent that "inflection" can be treated as a grammatical process realizable with or without affixation (cf. Kihm 2003), while almost all languages have free morpheme "inflection" of the *inherent* variety in Booij's (1993) terminology, marking tense and aspect, Polynesian languages have free morpheme "inflection" of the *contextual* variety, marking syntax-dependent features such as case and ergativity. Tongan is an example:

(7)   *'oku tamate '**e**   he   fefine '**a**   e   tangatá.*
      PRES kill   ERG DEF woman ABS DEF man
      'The woman kills the man.'

(Tchekhoff 1979: 409)

8.1.2. What happened in Flores?

It is in this light that a few languages of the central part of the island of Flores must be seen. They are completely isolating, with no affixation at all. One example is Keo:

(8)   *Ho ghonggé   ndé, dima 'imu mélé ka   'uru   né'é kara*
      oh grope-in-hole that arm   3S stuck PERF because have bracelet

'When she was groping in the hole, her arm got stuck because she had a shell bracelet.'

(Baird 2002: 491)

Keo does not, like Polynesian languages, mark case (i.e. contextual inflection) with free morphemes instead, or mark focus in grammaticalized fashion with free morphemes as Philippines languages do (e.g. Tagalog *ang*). Its grammar is, compared to that of the Austronesian languages listed above, strikingly telegraphic. This is also true of Ngadha (Arndt 1933, Djawanai & Grimes 1995), the close relatives Li'o and Ende (McDonnell 2006), Rongga, and Keo's close relative Nage.

Given that these languages belong to a family of roughly one thousand languages with ample affixation, the question is why this handful of Floresian languages are isolating – and radically so.

To most analysts this would appear not to qualify as a question at all. A common assumption is apparently that these languages simply "lost their morphology" at some point, in an unremarkable fashion.

However, there is, in fact, no regular process that scholars of language change have identified in which a grammar sheds not just some, but all of its affixation just as a matter of chance. It is one thing to observe an affixless language today and imagine that its affixes were simply "lost" – but another to conceive of what the actual stepwise process would have been to lead to such a state.

Grammars are passed from one generation to another. Why would one generation opt to eliminate an affix used by the previous one – or even to use it significantly less? And crucially, to the extent that we might propose an answer referring to a single affix in a particular set of circumstances, what kind of explanation could we propose for the total elimination of all affixation from a grammar? That is, what could explain the specific problem of the difference between Tukang Besi and Keo?

The difference between the Central Floresian languages and their Austronesian relatives is a puzzle, suggesting that something irregular occurred in their history. This chapter will propose an explanation as to what that remarkable process was.

8.2. How languages go analytic: extensive second-language acquisition

8.2.1. Pidginization and creolization

In language change theory, what is known to shear all or most of a language's affixation is pidginization and creolization.

Importantly, creoles are low on inflectional affixation even when their source languages are not, contrary to a common misimpression that most creoles have little inflection simply because so many are compromises between analytic Kwa Niger-Congo languages and inflection-light English and colloquial French. For example, Palenquero Creole Spanish of Colombia was created by speakers of Kikongo, a highly inflected agglutinative language with obligatory tense marking and noun phrase concord. Its lexifier language Portuguese is highly fusional, also with obligatory tense marking and concord both nominal and verbal. Palenquero, however, is largely an isolating language:

(9)   *Nunka suto poné brabo nu.*
      never 1P   put   brave NEG
      'We never fought rough.'

(Schwegler 1998: 288)

Also relevant is the creolized variety of Chinook Jargon on the Grand Ronde reservation in Oregon. The source languages were various highly inflected Native American languages; the creole was isolating:

(10)   *Na čáku háya hayu   wáwa áwa   wáwa.*
       I   come big   FREQ talk   Indian talk
       'When I was growing up, I spoke the Indian language.'

(Grant 1996: 237)

Considering the Flores puzzle, then, requires that we at least consider that these languages' grammars were incompletely acquired at some point in their history. This is a known cause of analyticity, whereas the idea of generations of first-language speakers "dropping" *all* of the affixes used by previous ones is peculiar at best and implausible at worst.

8.2.2. Pidginization Lite: extensive second-language acquisition and affixal erosion

The assumption that a grammar actually may shed radical amounts of its affixation grammar-internally without external cause is based, it would seem, on a schema of language change represented by Latin's development into Romance and Old English's development into Modern English.

However, besides that these developments did not entail the stark abbreviation typical of pidginization and creolization and embodied by the difference between Tukang Besi and Keo, the sense of the development from Latin to French as typical is more problematic than traditionally realized.

I have argued (McWhorter 2002, 2007, 2008) that the cases just mentioned and others (Classical Arabic to the modern colloquial varieties, Old Persian to Modern, Old Chinese to Mandarin) were due to extensive acquisition of these languages by adults at certain points in their history, simplifying them to an extent that would have been unlikely or impossible if there had not been interference in transmission. Kusters (2003) is a monograph making a similar argument for several languages including Norwegian and Swahili; cf. also De Dardel & Wüest (1993) and Goyette (2000) on Romance. Relevant to Austronesian, I argue in McWhorter (2007, 2008) that the near-isolating varieties of Malay and Indonesian such as Riau Indonesian highlighted extensively by David Gil (e.g. 2001) achieved their state due to the long-term and widespread usage of Malay as a second-language throughout its history.

In support of this framework is that there seem to be: 1) no languages unusually analytic in comparison to others in their family without extensive second-language acquisition in their history, and 2) no languages highly inflected in comparison to others in their family *with* extensive second-language acquisition in their history.[1]

In this light, Thurston (1987) distinguishes *esoteric* grammars, rarely acquired by non-native speakers, in which sound change is free to create allomorphy and suppletivity – inherent to inflections – and materials are recruited to mark ever more fine semantic distinctions (often via inflections) from *exoteric* grammars, subjected to extensive non-native acquisition. Adults, with their ossified capacity for acquiring languages, tend to substitute sounds harder to acquire, simplify morphological opacities, and eliminate semantic distinctions and syntactic constructions tangential to conveying urgent aspects of meaning or difficult to glean for the non-native – much of which entails eliminating inflections.

The implication of Thurston's argument is that "esoteric" languages are a natural state, an argument more recently fleshed out by Wray & Grace (2007). Similarly, Kusters (2003: 41–4) distinguishes between Type 1 languages, spoken mainly as first languages, and Type 2 languages, spoken mainly as second languages and, as a result, less inflectionally rich than Type 1 languages.

---

1 This analysis applies to languages spoken before the advent of widespread literacy and standardization, which retard change and deflect the effects of second-language acquisition because of the presence of a frozen model on the page, often taught formally. For example, Russian retains its rich inflection despite use as a lingua franca across the former Soviet Union because it spread as a written language taught formally in schools.

Under this analysis, the normal condition of language change is conservative, such as Icelandic in contrast to English, and Slavic in contrast to Romance. Proto-Slavic, rich in affixation, has developed into Slavic languages similarly rich in affixation; the reconstructed Proto-Algonquian language is highly inflected, and all of its modern descendants are as well. In such cases the famous "drift" towards analyticity typical of a few subfamilies in Western Europe is not in evidence – there are no mysteriously affixless Slavic or Algonquian languages. More to the point, worldwide, the kinds of cases just listed are typical of language change, rather than that of Latin to French. Note, for example, how little indication there would seem to be of analytic "drift" in the large body of Australian languages, home to hundreds of highly inflected languages for tens of thousands of years.

Pointedly, there do exist Bantu languages that court analyticity – but not "mysteriously." Generally, the hundreds of Bantu languages are richly agglutinative after three millennia. The only ones that aren't are the ones that have arisen as vehicular lingua francas among speakers of disparate languages or dialects, such as Kituba, shown here in an example repeated from Chapter Seven. The source language (a) is Kikongo; (b) is Kituba:

(11)(a)   *(Yándi) ka-   ku-   zól- elé.*
        he/she   AGR-2SOBJ-like-NEAR.PERFECT

   (b)   *Yándi zóla ngé.*
       he/she like 2S
       'He/she likes you.'

(Mufwene 1990: 176)

8.2.3. Affixation otherwise: fecund, persistent and disruptive

Otherwise, language change theory stipulates that in inflected languages, while natural processes of phonetic erosion and the operations of analogy wear away some affixation, new affixation is always developing via grammaticalization and other processes of reinterpretation. The Romance languages lost Latin's future-marking suffixes, but developed new ones from the verb *habere* (Latin *amare habeo* 'love-INF have-1S' > Italian *amerò* "I will love"). Importantly, all Romance languages nevertheless retain an ample proportion of Latin's suffixation. Or, while Bantu languages mark tense with both prefixes and suffixes, Swahili has lost most of the suffixes – but has innovated the perfect prefix *-me-* via grammaticalization of a verb "to finish." Swahili also retains most of the Bantu affixal inheritance in the meantime.

In general, what is ordinary in grammar-internal change is for affixal processes to contract in their usage rather than disappear entirely. Classical Aramaic nominal morphology marked a distinction between the absolute and the emphatic; in modern Western Aramaic, this distinction has contracted into use only with adjectives, and transformed into a definite/indefinite contrast – but still varying according to number and gender (Jastrow 1997):

Table 36. Definite and indefinite marking in Aramaic

	indefinite	definite
masc. sing.	*if̱ker*	*f̱kīra*
fem. sing.	*f̱kīra*	*f̱kīrča*
masc. pl.	*f̱kīrin*	*f̱kīrō*
fem. pl.	*f̱kīran*	*f̱kīrōθa*

Finally, when affixation is lost, it typically leaves behind evidence of its erstwhile existence, in the form of morphophonemic processes, umlaut and ablaut, or frozen segments. For example, the plural suffix -*i* no longer exists in English, but in bringing preceding vowels forward, left behind irregular plurals such as *feet* ([foti] > [føti] > [fit]). Plural-marking -*s* has been lost in French at the end of noun phrases, but in NP-medial concordial usage, lingers as "liaison" in word-initial segments on vowel-initial roots: *les grandes arbres* [le gʁɔ̃ zaʁbʁ] "the big trees."

To be sure, related languages differ somewhat in the extent to which they retain ancestral affixation due to sheer chance. That Slovenian is the only Slavic language retaining dual marking poses no challenge to the theory of language change: things happen. Within Austronesian, for example, Crowley (2000) reported that between the close Erromangan relatives Sye and Ura, Ura is less richly inflected despite no significant usage as a second language. In Sye, for verbs with which pronominal objects occur as suffixes, the suffixes occur in two or more allomorphs in all persons and numbers (except first person singular) according to phonological conditioning factors. In Ura, pronominal objects occur as suffixes only in the third person plural, in an invariant form, while elsewhere pronominal objects occur as invariant free morphemes (or zero in the third person singular) (Crowley 2000: 183), see Table 37.

However, Ura remains overall an inflected language typical of its relatives – and note that the third person singular suffix -*i* still productive in Sye has in Ura been generalized in fossil form to all persons and numbers rather than simply vanishing. Typically, affixal loss leaves footprints.

Table 37. Verb conjugation in Sye and Ura

	Sye	Ura		Sye	Ura
1S	*yokil-yau*	*yocori you*	1P (incl.)	*yokil-coh*	*yokori qis*
2S	*yokil-oc*	*yocori qa*	1P (excl.)	*yokol-cam*	*yocori gimi*
3S	*yokil-i*	*yocori*	2P	*yokil-cum*	yocori gimi
			3P	*yokil-or*	*yocori-l*

Cases such as these are ordinary in language change. For a language to become completely isolating, and with no significant phonological or fossil evidence left behind, is not ordinary in language change of the uninterrupted, grammar-internal sort. The contrast between the languages of central Flores and the rest of Austronesian is parallel to that between creoles and their source languages, suggesting an interruption in the regular transmission of the languages to new generations.

8.2.4. The continuum nature of the Flores puzzle

Language contact processes occur in varying degrees. In an English-based creolophone society such as Jamaica, for example, there is a creole continuum ranging from a basilect, deeply imprinted by African grammatical features and classifiable as essentially a different language from English, to mesolectal varieties classifiable as a lightly Africanized English dialect. In Turkey, there are Greek varieties so mixed with Turkish as to motivate an analyst to state that "the body has remained Greek, but the soul has become Turkish" in Cappadocia, and others mixed with Turkish to a robust but lesser degree in Sílli and Phárasa (Thomason & Kaufman 1988: 216).

In the same fashion, the Flores peculiarity exhibits itself in degrees. Keo and its relatives are completely isolating, while their neighbor languages to the west and east are slightly less so – but contrast markedly nevertheless with the affixal norm in the subfamily they belong to, Central Malayo-Polynesian.

The typical Central Malayo-Polynesian language has, for example, paradigmatic allomorphy conditioned by word shape, such as the plural marking in Serua of the southern Moluccas (Van Engelenhoven 2003: 53) (Table 38). This allomorphy can also condition metathesis, another hallmark of Central Malayo-Polynesian (Klamer 2002) occuring in various grammatical contexts:

Table 38. Plural marking in Serua

	sing.	pl.
stone	*watu*	*wat-ru*
banana	*wia*	*wia-ra*
child	*wakoi*	*wako-ri*

Table 39. Metathesis in Serua plural marking

	sing.	pl.
bamboo	*temra*	*temar-a*
forest	*letna*	*letan-ra*

In Serua, metathesis also occurs in nominals modified by adjectives: /ina lapna/ > [ian lapna] "big boat" ('boat big'); /usna lapna/ > [usan lapna] "big fish" ('fish big').

Serua also has the typical Central Malayo-Polynesian distinction between alienable and inalienable possession, with postposed marking for the former (*ina-ku* "my mother," *ina-mu* "your mother"), and preposed for the latter, in which case the marking varies according to whether the referent has a single initial consonant: *mu wroa* "your boat," *m-ruma* "your house" (Van Engelenhoven 2003: 54).

Central Malayo-Polynesian languages also tend to have subject-marking prefixes, varying allomorphically according to phonological factors. In Roti, for example, subject prefixation varies according to whether the verb's initial segment is a consonant, a high vowel, a mid-front vowel, or a low vowel or glottal stop (Fox & Grimes 1995: 616–7):

Table 40. Subject prefixation in Roti

	fada "speak"	*inu* "drink"	*eni* "bring"	*ʔa* "eat"
1S	a-fada	inu	u-ni	u-a
2S	ma-fada	m-inu	mu-ni	mu-a
3S	na-fada	n-inu	n-eni	na-a
1PL (excl.)	ma-fada	m-inu	m-eni	mi-a
1PL (incl.)	ta-fada	t-inu	t-eni	ta-ʔa

(Continued)

Table 40. Subject prefixation in Roti (*Continued*)

	fada "speak"	*inu "drink"*	*eni "bring"*	*ʔa "eat"*
2PL	ma-fada	m-inu	m-eni	mi-a
3PL	la-fada	l-inu	l-eni	la-ʔa

Roti also has an array of verbal prefixes of a type common in Central Malayo-Polynesian, demonstrating the descent of these languages from inflected languages of the Tukang Besi type – i.e., marking them as typically Austronesian: *ma-* stative, *ka-* causative, *sa-*, *pa-* and *la-* verbal, *fa-* durative, *ŋa-* iterative, *ta-* agentless passive (ibid. 618).

The languages immediately contiguous to the central Floresian ones, although not totally isolating, are markedly less so than the Central Malayo-Polynesian norm. Immediately eastward of the completely isolating languages of Flores is Sika, in which subject-prefix allomorphy is limited to a few irregular verbs (Lewis & Grimes 1995: 605–6):

Table 41. Subject prefixation in Sika

	bano "go"	*gita "see"*	*raʔit "sew"*
1S	pano	ʔita	ʔraʔit
2S	bano	gita	raʔit
3S	bano	gita	raʔit
1P (exclusive)	bano	gita	raʔit
1P (inclusive)	pano	ʔita	raʔit
2P	bano	gita	raʔit
3P	pano	gita	raʔit

Meanwhile, west of the isolating languages is Manggarai, in which inflection is limited to a single set of object suffixes and possessive suffixes neutral to alienability (Verheijen & Grimes 1995: 588–9):
Riung and Rembong appear to be similar in this regard based on Rosen (1983), while Arka (2007) suggests the same of Waerana.

Thus while what most urgently requires explanation is why there are completely isolating Austronesian languages on Flores, a solution must also address the fact that the factor responsible for this exerted itself to a lesser but significant degree on contiguous languages.

Table 42. Suffixes in Manggarai

		obj.	poss.
1S	aku	-k	-g
2S	hau	-h	-m
3S	hia	-i/-y	-n
1PL (excl.)	ami	-km	-gm
1PL (incl.)	ite	-t	-d
2PL	meu	-m	-s
3PL	ise	-s	-d

Arka (2007) is correct that the culprit cannot have been contact with the languages spoken on Flores before the arrival of Austronesian speakers. Papuans from the east and likely Negritos from the west inhabited all or most of the islands of eastern Indonesia for millennia before the Austronesians arrived (cf. Bellwood 1995: 105), and the result in all locations was various degrees of grammatical (Klamer 2002) and lexical mixture without any unusual grammatical simplification, evidence of typical language shift. Our question is specific: what happened on Flores?

8.3. Towards a solution: The Timor factor

A solution to the Flores puzzle must also address that there are also near-analytic languages on the eastern half of Timor.

The Tetun Dili variety of Tetun, productive affixation is largely confined to the causative *ba-* (Williams-Van Klinken, Hajek & Nordlinger 2002). This is easily traceable to the variety's usage as Timor's lingua franca. In general, in fact, the claim in this chapter is not that all analyticity in Austronesian challenges language change theory: Alorese, an offshoot of the amply affixal Flores language Lamaholot (cf. 4.3.3.), only has some vestiges of affixiation, and Klamer (2010) convincingly attributes this to long-term lingua franca usage.

That kind of explanation does not apply, however, to the fact that in eastern Timor, the indigenous language Tokodede is no more affixal than Tetun Dili, while Mambai and Waimaha are only slightly more so (Hull 1998: 166; 2001b:101). These three languages have no history as regional lingua francas: they are *esoteric* languages in Thurston's terminology.

Table 43. They stole my buffalo and killed it in four Timorese languages (from Hull 2001: 163)

Tetun Dili	Sira	na'ok	ha'u	nia	karau,	roho	tiha.
Tokodede	Ro'o	mana'o	aka'u		karbau,	hora	bali.
Mambai (Maubisse)	Sirá	fnao	au		arbau,	sa	te.
Waimaha	Sire	hile	au		karabau	hige	lo
	they	steal	my	POSS	buffalo	kill	PERF

Meanwhile, even the other East Timor languages, while hardly completely analytic, lack the degree of affixation typical of Central Malayo-Polynesian. Subject-marking prefixes generally appear only before vowels or *h,* or in many of the languages not at all (Hull 2001: 153–4). The battery of derivational prefixes still robust in, for example, Roti as described above generally survives in abbreviated and partly fossilized form in East Timor, and often barely at all (ibid. 149–51). Tense and aspect are marked with free morphemes, while in the especially isolating languages, affixal marking of inalieable possession is reduced to the single suffix *-n* (ibid.118–20). Overall, languages in East Timor occupy a range of affixation from a tad more than Keo to, roughly, that of Manggarai.

Antoinette Schapper (p.c.) usefully notes that in Waimaha, there is evidence of subject prefixes having been fossilized rather than shed, arguing that this belies an argument for abbreviation of the grammar, rather than ordinary development over time. For example, while *tuu* means "knife handle," the verb "stab" is /tʰuu/, the aspiration of the /t/ derived from what began as a plural subject prefix *h-*. However, for one, this argument applies only to this one prefix, leaving the question as to the fate of the singular prefixes – why are Waimaha verbs not variant according to person and number via assorted phonetic variations of the initial consonant conditioned by the erosion of other prefixes? It would appear that these prefixes were indeed eliminated rather than fossilized – upon which we return to the question as to why this kind of elimination has happened to such a lesser degree in Roti (or less radically analytic languages of East Timor such as those Schapper presents).

More generally, fossilization, when so rampant as to render a grammar almost completely isolating, is as much a sign of extensive second-language acquisition as the elimination of affixes. For example, in French-based plantation creoles, French definite articles and partitive-marking *de* are very often fossilized on nouns, no longer processed as morphemes: *latab* "table" from *la table, dilo* "water" from *de l'eau,* etc., with definiteness indicated with a postposed determiner (Mauritian Creole French *latab-la* "the table"). In these creoles this is not an occasional happenstance but a prevalent phenomenon, such as occurring with 637 nouns in Mauritian according to the tabulation of Grant (1995:156). This kind and degree of agglutination occurs in no vernacular dialect of French and only in French creoles – and to some significant degree, in all of them. It is a symptom – amidst, elsewhere, massive elimination of affixation – of incomplete acquisition of French, amidst which the function of articles and partitive markers was not perceived while their phonetic form was retained.

This, then, is also what the echoes of erstwhile affixation are traceable to in Waimaha, as well as like instances in other analytic East Timor languages; cf. also rampant fossilizations of Lamaholot morphology in Alorese (Klamer 2010). Certainly affixes fossilize as an ordinary language process, as noted in 2.3. on Germanic umlaut and French liaison. The question is why this would happen to such an extent as to render a language of a robustly affixal family like Austronesian all but analytic – when this is so vastly rare amidst the one thousand members of the family. German has umlaut but also ample affixation; French liaison exists in a grammar nowhere near analytic.

A comparison: French verb conjugation is, as the result of phonetic erosions, much less rich than that in Spanish. However, there is no Romance language in which verbs are invariant for person and number entirely, with perhaps voicing or aspiration of verbs' final consonants traceable to the disappearance of some segment. No Romance variety even appears on its way to such a state after 2000 years, while only Romance-based *creoles* have invariant verbs.

Flores languages exhibit similar cases of fossilization which also indicate, given the comparative peculiarity of their overall analyticity compared to their Austronesian relatives, incomplete acquisition rather than natural development. In Sika, for example, Arka (2007) notes fossilized, unproductive nominal marking in *lorung* "woven thing" versus *loru* "weave."

Neither this nor the analyticity and fossilizations in East Timor suggest natural development – if it did, we would see similar "natural" developments in assorted Austronesian languages of the Philippines, Borneo, Sulawesi, the Moluccas, Melanesia, etc. It appears that something interrupted generational transmission of language in East Timor. Given the proximity of Timor to Flores plus the fact that these are the only two Austronesian loci, to my knowledge, of starkly isolating languages with histories neither as lingua francas (like Riau Indonesian and other colloquial Indonesians [cf. McWhorter 2008], Tetun Dili, or Alorese) or as long-term mixtures with isolating languages as are the Chamic varieties with Mon-Khmer ones (Thurgood 1999), it is appropriate to seek a single factor that affected both islands.

8.4. What more do Flores and Timor have in common?

8.4.1. Hull's thesis

8.4.1.1. The central Moluccan invasion

Hull (1998, 2001) argues that the reason for the analytic cast of the languages of East Timor is invasions by Central Moluccans from Ambon and nearby islands. Specifically, he reconstructs that in approximately 1200 AD, invaders from this region disrupted language transmission in East Timor and left the languages pidginized to an extent. The linguistic evidence for this is about 100 items traceable to these languages including some grammatical items. Evidence beyond the linguistic includes that Timorese origin myths correspond to lore connected with the Moluccan aristocracy; that Rotinese tales of origin describe inmigration by a band of Ceramese over 400 years before the arrival of the Portuguese; and that speakers of the Timoric language Galoli recount that in antiquity, men from the Central Moluccan Nusa Laut arrived and married local women (ibid. 161–4). Especially indicative of intimate interactions between Timor and Ambon is that six place-names on Ambon correspond to Timorese groups.

Hull (1998) and (2001) are fascinating works, based on exhaustive research and ingenious argumentation. For that reason in McWhorter (2008) I espoused Hull's explanation of the East Timor analyticity. However, after further reflection and research on the Flores question I left as a question mark in that paper, in this one I revise that verdict. The Central Moluccan invasion is a tempting explanation for why the East Timor languages are so light on affixation, but becomes less compelling to the extent that it leaves the even starker analyticity in Flores, so close by, unexplained.

I believe that many of Hull's observations, recast in the light of additional data and perspectives, provide a springboard for a unified explanation for the analyticity on both islands. However, under this new explanation, the Central Moluccan influence on Timoric languages is a mere adstratal matter. The Moluccan speakers left many words in Timoric languages, but did not pidginize them to any perceptible degree.

After all, robust lexical borrowing does not necessarily entail grammatical simplification, as is clear from the German component in the Estonian lexicon, the Chinese one in the Vietnamese, or the rampant lexical borrowing among Australian languages as described in sources such as Heath (1981).

8.4.1.2. Cognate matches between Sulawesi and southward

In broader view, Hull proposes that the languages of Timor and Flores (as well as the Southern Moluccas) are not Central Malayo-Polynesian at all, but rather are direct descendants of Western Malayo-Polynesian as spoken on the southeastern peninsula of Sulawesi. He argues for this claim on the basis of a core of ninety words common to all or most languages of Timor, showing that in Tukang Besi and others in southeastern Sulawesi, the percentage of cognate matches with this Timorese set as opposed to replacement items is 80%, in contrast to Sulawesi languages as nearby as the southwestern peninsula such as the 64% match with Buginese and 46% match with Macassarese. Working from this likeness, Hull also notes that in Flores the percentage of cognates with the southeast Sulawesi set rather than replacements is much higher than elsewhere in the region: 77%, in contrast to the average of 63.6% with the Central Moluccan languages (and concordances with individual languages in this group as low as 40.6% for Manumbian [114–5]).

The implications Hull draws from cognate matches are a useful basis for a further engagement with the lexical data in question, which leads to conclusions inspired by, but different from, Hull's.

8.4.2. Lexicons on Timor and Flores: frozen in time?

Archaeology and genetics suggest that the Lesser Sunda Islands and the Moluccas were settled from Sulawesi (Tryon 1995b, Spriggs 2003), approximately 3500 years ago. We can thus assume that the languages of Sulawesi and those of the Moluccas have been separated for 3000 years at the least.

Typically, word list comparisons correspond with this time split. For example, below is a word list of Tukang Besi compared with the same words in three languages of the southern Moluccas.[2]

---

2 The lexical data are from Hull (1998: 178–200), supplemented by data from Tryon (1995), Blust (2008), Baird (2002), the on-line Basic Austronesian Vocabulary Database, and for Rongga, the dictionary available at this writing at http://rspas. anu.edu.au/linguistics/projects/iwa/Web-Pages/RonggaDictionary2007.pdf and for the word for "yawn," Wayan Arka, p.c. Feb. 2010. Italics signify a non-cognate. The lexical items chosen are an unsystematic sampling of those of Austronesian provenance in Hull's Tukang Besi list. I have limited the list in order to illustrate the comparisons in visually processible fashion. However, a wider sampling of the

Table 44. Lexicon sample of Tukang Besi and southern Moluccan languages

	T. Besi	Kei	Yamdena	Dobel
come	mai	maa	ma	'a-ma
dead	mate	enmaat	mat	'a-kʷoy
fish	ika	*vuut*	ian	si'a
fowl	manu	manut	manik	*toru*
liver	ate	yatan	ati	sata
new	wo'ou	vait	*beberi*	*tu'bay*
pig	wawu	vaav	babi	ɸaɸi
rain	usa-	*doot*	udan	kʷusan
red	meha	*wulwul*	memeye	*kʷudi*
sea	tai	tahit	tasik	tay
skin	kuli	ulin	kulit	'ala-m
snake	sa'a	*rubai*	*kasi*	yakʷa
stone	watu	vaat	bati	ɸatu
sugar cane	towu	tev	tefu	*kʷuŋar*
be thirsty	moro'u	nebroo	*manges*	ma'raw-ni
tree	hu'u	*vuak*	*katutun*	'ay
wood	kau	ai	kai	'ay
worm	ulo	uar	ule	*kʷaytuba*
yawn	moma'a	enkamoat	maup	'a-maɸu

The genetic relationship is obvious. However, for one, in line with Hull's observations, cognate correspondence is approximate: quite often where Tukang Besi has a particular Austronesian root, a Moluccan language has a different Austronesian root, or a root from one of the "Papuan" languages spoken by the original inhabitants of Eastern Indonesia. These are, of course, ordinary results of semantic drift and language contact over long periods of time.

---

languages' lexicons reveals the same degrees of likeness and unlikeness between the relevant languages, as the interested reader can ascertain from the sources I have referred to, and as I assume Austronesianists familiar with these languages will understand and intuit. In some comparisons I have abbreviated the list somewhat due to gaps in the available data.

However, cognate correspondences are not the only feature indicating time depth in such comparisons. A second indication of the 3000-year separation is degree of sound change. Not a single one of these lexical items is the same between Tukang Besi and these languages. Rather, in all cases there has been some degree of phonetic change, including accretion of segments due to fossilizations. The developments that have led to "pig" as *wawu* in Tukang Besi, *vaav* in Kei, *babi* in Yamdena and *ɸaɸi* in Dobel are analogous to "hand" as French [mɛ̃], Spanish [mano], Portuguese [mãu] and Romanian [minə].

The comparison is similar with Central Moluccan languages: ample cognate replacement and phonetic evolution (such that, e.g. Tukang Besi's *kuli* is *uritol* in Nusa Laut):

Table 45. Lexicon sample of Tukang Besi and central Moluccan languages

	T. Besi	Asiluluan	Nusa Laut
come	mai	*kawae*	*tawae*
dead	mate	matate	mata
fish	ika	íane	yano
fowl	manu	manu	manuo
liver	ate	*wélua*	ata-
new	wo'ou	helu	huruil
pig	wawu	hahu	hahul
rain	usa-	úlane	*kialo*
red	meha	*rau*	*kau*
sea	tai	*sawa*	*sawaol*
skin	kuli	*usa*	uritol
snake	sa'a	*nyia*	*nial*
stone	watu	hatu	hatul
sugar cane	towu	tehu	tohul
be thirsty	moro'u	*letasele*	amalael
tree	hu'u	úwene	*aiwonyo*
wood	kau	ai	ainyo
worm	ulo	*salálene*	*retal*
yawn	moma'a	mawa	*makakoa*

These perfectly ordinary differences between lexical items in related but distinct languages render quite striking the comparison between Tukang Besi and the languages of East Timor:

Table 46. Lexicon sample from Tukang Besi and eastern Timor languages

	T. Besi	Tetun	Tokodede
come	mai	mai	mai
dead	mate	mate	mate
fish	ika	ikan	ika
fowl	manu	manu	manu
liver	ate	aten	ate
new	wo'ou	foun	veu
pig	wawu	fahi	vavi
rain	usa-	udan	ura
red	meha	meran	mio
sea	tai	tasi	tasi
skin	kuli	kulit	kluta
snake	sa'a	sa-	sa-
stone	watu	fatuk	vatu
sugar cane	towu	tohu	tevu
be thirsty	moro'u	hamrook	broo
tree	hu'u	hun	puu
wood	kau	ai	kai
worm	ulo	ular	ula
yawn	moma'a	maas	mava

In this word list there are no cognate replacements, and phonetic evolution is generally anomalously modest, as Hull (1998: 150) notes, compared to that between Tukang Besi and the Moluccan languages. There are certainly cases such as "red" being *mio* in Tokodede as opposed to *meha* in Tukang Besi – but even more where, for example, the words for "come" and "dead" are identical in all three languages, or the Timor language's word differs from the Tukang Besi one in only one segment, such as *tasi* "sea." The comparisons are similar with all of the languages of East Timor.

The analogy is less with the distance between the Romance languages than between dialects of one of them, such as "come" in Italian being *venire* in the Tuscan standard, *vegnì* in Milanese, *venì* in Neapolitan, and *vnì* in Piedmontese. This is hardly what we would expect of languages from distinct subfamilies – especially when the comparison between Tukang Besi and other Central Malayo-Polynesian languages is very much what one would expect of languages of distinct subfamilies.

Except in the case of Flores. The comparison of Tukang Besi with Sika alone is noteworthy, similar to the one with Timor languages: no cognate replacements and modest phonetic evolution:

Table 47. Lexicon sample of Tukang Besi and Sika

	T. Besi	Sika
come	mai	mai
dead	mate	mate
fish	ika	iang
fowl	manu	manu
liver	ate	wateng
new	wo'ou	warun
pig	wawu	wawi
rain	usa-	uran
red	meha	merak
sea	tai	tahi
skin	kuli	ulit
snake	sa'a	sawaria
stone	watu	watu
sugar cane	towu	tewu
be thirsty	moro'u	mara
tree	hu'u	puhun
wood	kau	ai
worm	ulo	ule
yawn	moma'a	moa

With other Flores languages, there are some cognate replacements, but what is especially unexpected is that phonetic evolution is similarly moderate, nothing approaching the gulf between words in Tukang Besi and Dobel or Nusa Laut – despite that the separation between the languages in all cases has been of roughly the same length: 3000+ years:

Table 48. Lexicon sample of Tukang Besi and central Flores languages

	T. Besi	Sika	Ende	Ngada	Rongga	Keo
come	mai	mai	mai	mai	mai	ma'i
dead	mate	mate	mata	mata	mata	mata
fish	ika	iang	ika	ika	ika	'ika
fowl	manu	manu	manu	manu	manu	manu
liver	ate	wateng	ate	ate	até	'até
new	wo'ou	warun	wi'u	*muzi*	*muri*	*muri*
pig	wawu	wawi	wawi	wawi	wawi	wawi
rain	usa-	uran	ura	uza	nura	'ura
red	meha	merak	mera	*toro*	*toro*	*to*
sea	tai	tahi	*ae-mësi*	*məsi*	mbata	'ae-mesi
skin	kuli	ulit	u'i	*huki*	*huki*	uwa
snake	sa'a	sawaria	*nipa*	*nipa*	nggala	*nipa*
stone	watu	watu	watu	vatu	watu	watu
sugar cane	towu	tewu	tëwu	təvu	tewu	tewo
be thirsty	moro'u	mara	moa	moa	mara	moa
tree	hu'u	puhun	puu	pu'u	pu'u	pu'u
wood	kau	ai	kaju	pu'u-kaǰu	kaju	kaju
worm	ulo	ule	ure	ulé	ula	udé
yawn	moma'a	moa	moa sodho	moa-paa	muapa	

The contrast is sharp with the phonetic distance and drift in cognate assignment between two Austronesian languages separated for much less time: Malagasy and Ngaju, its presumed Borneo ancestor. Estimates for the separation range from approximately 1800 years to only a thousand: in either case, the result has been:

Finally, we must compare the closeness of the lexical items of Tukang Besi and the central Flores languages and East Timor ones to the same ones in two Bantu languages, Kikuyu of Kenya and Zulu of South Africa (data from Barlow & Benson 1975 and Doke, Malcolm & Sikakana 1971).

Considering that Bantu is thought to have arisen approximately 3000 years ago in Nigeria and Cameroon, we can assume that Kikuyu emerged at least several centuries after this if not more, and that therefore Kikuyu and Zulu represent developments separated by much less than 3000 years. Yet the gulf between their lexicons is vast, as shown here, where I have tried to adduce cognates in cases where there are several words for a meaning:

Table 49. Lexicon sample of Ngaju and Malagasy

	Ngaju	Malagasy
come	dumah	avy, tonga, tamy
dead	matei	maty
fish	laok	tondro
liver	atei	aty
new	taheta	vaovao
rain	ujan	orana
red	randang	mena
sea	tasik	ranomasina, riaka
skin	upak	hoditra
snake	handipe	bibilava
stone	batu	vato
worm	handalai	kankana

Table 50. Lexicon sample of Tukang Besi and Sika compared with one for Kikuyu and Zulu

	T. Besi	Sika	Kikuyu[1]	Zulu
come	mai	mai	ũka	za
dead	mate	mate	kua	fa
fish	ika	iang	tega	inhlanzi
fowl	manu	manu	ngũkũ	inkuku
liver	ate	wateng	ini	isibindi
new	wo'ou	warun	erũ	sha
pig	wawu	wawi	ngũrũe	ingulube

(*Continued*)

Table 50. Lexicon sample of Tukang Besi and Sika compared with one for Kikuyu and Zulu (*Continued*)

	T. Besi	Sika	Kikuyu[1]	Zulu
rain	usa-	uran	mbura	imvula
red	meha	merak	tune	bomvu
sea	tai	tahi	iria	ulwandle
skin	kuli	ulit	ikonde	isikhumba
snake	sa'a	sawaria	njoka	inyoka
stone	watu	watu	ihiga	itshe
sugar cane	towu	tewu	kigwa	umoba
be thirsty	moro'u	mara	nyota	ukoma
tree	hu'u	puhun	mũtĩ	umuthi
yawn	moma'a	moa	meũka	zamula

1 In Kikuyu the nasal symbol is an orthographic convention indicating tense mid vowels (ũ = [o], ĩ = [e]); *njoka* means "intestinal worm" but serves here as a cognate for Zulu's "snake" word.

Why are the lexical items in the languages of Flores and East Timor, Central Malayo-Polynesian languages, so modestly divergent phonetically from their cognates in Tukang Besi, a Western Malayo-Polynesian language? One need not subscribe to the inappropriate rigidities of strict glottochronology to find the parallels between these languages peculiar in comparison to that between Kikuyu and Zulu, Ngaju and Malagasy, or countless other comparisons in language families worldwide.

8.4.3. An account

Our problem is that the lexicons of these Flores and Timor languages appear not to have transformed to the degree we would expect them to have after over 3000 years. It is as if words from Tukang Besi were transferred into these languages at a relatively recent date, and have only been developing on their own since then.

8.4.3.1. *My proposal*

In fact, a solution to this puzzle entails exactly this – while also explaining the stark paucity or absence of affixation. Two factors in combination, the lexical correspondence and the grammatical simplification, suggest that at some point much later than 3000 years ago, speakers of Tukang Besi and/ or related languages migrated to Flores and Timor in large numbers and acquired the local languages incompletely amidst language shift.

This incomplete acquisition would have had two results. First, there was a great deal of relexification, with Tukang Besi words replacing their Flores/ Timor cognates, typical when shifting speakers are sociologically dominant (Thomason & Kaufman 1988: 116). Second, there was considerable grammatical simplification, as predictable from rapid adult acquisition, explaining the loss of affixation.

Written history does not exist for the ancient stages of the histories of Sulawesi, Flores, and Timor. However, we can interpret the linguistic data as evidence indicating this migration, as it would be difficult to interpret the data in any other way.

The process described is hardly unusual as language contact scenarios go. It is precisely what happened to Old English amidst the Scandinavian invasions starting in the ninth century, A.D.: a massive incursion of Danish and Norse lexicon accompanied by a considerable abbreviation of the Old English inflectional system. Similarly, the relatively low volume of inflection in Norwegian is due to contact with first Low German and then Danish, resulting in extensive lexical influence from those languages and a reduction in affixation compared to the more conservative Icelandic and Faroese (Kusters 2003: 191–5).

We do not observe the Norse-derived items in English and assume that they were actually English-internal developments that morphed by chance into shapes identical or virtually so to their Norse cognates. Rather, we assume that these words parallel Norse ones because they were inherited from Norse at a latterly date. Our evaluation standard ought be the same for Eastern Indonesia as it is in Germanic – especially when the recipient languages display the same kind of affixal abbreviation as English and Norwegian.

8.4.3.2. Creole vs. NCSL

My claim is not that the affixless languages of Flores and the near-affixless ones of Timor are "creoles," to the extent that creolization represents the sharpest kind of break in transmission (Thomason & Kaufman 1988) and the most radical degree of grammatical simplification in natural language (McWhorter 2001). Affixation is but one kind of grammatical complexity; these languages contain ample amounts of other kinds.

Ngadha, for example, has an object marker used when emphasis is connoted:

(12)   *Sazi vela **go** radza.*
       3S   kill OBJ king
       'He murdered the *king*.'

(Arndt 1933:9)

as well as third person pronouns used when a sympathetic note is desired (*laki* [sing.], *emu-laki* [pl.]) (Djawanai & Grimes 1995: 598). Ngadha also distinguishes alienable from inalienable possession (Arndt 1933: 8), and has grammaticalized pragmatic modal particles like German's (ibid. 27) (see Chapter Four, Section 5). Ngadha also has 19 sortal classifiers (ibid. 6–7), some of semantically arbitrary assignment: *vid'a* is used with books, trees, and pieces of meat; *mata* is used with fields, (water) springs, and tree trunks (ibid. 6).

Ngadha, despite its analyticity, bears ample hallmarks of being an ancient language, as do the other affixless or affix-light languages under discussion. Thus by affixless I do not intend "pidgin" or "creole."

Typically, significant grammatical simplification is associated with creoles, in which the simplification is also accompanied by grammatical mixture. However, grammatical simplification does not always occur to the degree that it does in creoles, and also hardly requires the grammatical mixture. There are ample cases of languages that have undergone significant but not extreme simplification, and without their grammars becoming mixed ones. The theory of language contact has lacked a term or taxonomic place for such cases, and in McWhorter (2007), I designate them Nonhybrid Conventionalized Second-Language varieties – NCSLs – a class including English, Mandarin Chinese, the modern colloquial Arabics, Malay, and Persian. Under the analysis in this chapter, I include in this class Ngadha, Keo, Nage, Ende, Li'o, Rongga, and the languages of East Timor.

8.4.3.3. Supporting evidence: exceptions that prove the rule

If the affixless and affix-light Austronesian languages of Flores and Timor are the result of relexification amidst second-language acquisition, and if language contact effects occur to differing extents in different locations (cf. 2.4.), then we would expect that in languages of Flores and Timor, the ones that retain significantly more affixation would also have lexicons less akin to that of Tukang Besi and other Sulawesi languages. This is the case.

In Lamaholot, spoken on the eastern end of Flores and nearby Solor island, fewer than half of its lexicon is cognate to the Timorese core that matches Tukang Besi's so closely (Hull 1998: 107) – and its grammar is replete with inflectional and derivational affixes, giving no evidence of a disruption in acquisition at any point in its recent history. It marks concord not only on verbs but adjectives and even numerals:

(13)   *inamǝlake belv-na*
　　　man　　　big-3S
　　　'the big man'

(Nishiyama & Kelen 2007: 98)

(14)   *Ra rua-ka bǝrin tite tǝlo-te.*
　　　3P two-3P hit　　1P three-1P
　　　'They two hit us three.'

(ibid. 39)

Lamaholot also has seven derivational affixes including an infix: *pet* "bind," *met* "belt;" *pasak* "shoot," *bǝpasak* "shooter;" *hǝgak* "replace," *pǝnǝgak* "re-placement;" etc. The meanings that the affixes contribute are often semantically arbitrary: *hupǝk* "cover," with *nupǝk* as "a cover" but *tenupǝk* "a lid," or with the *-ǝn-* infix, *tika* "divide" *tǝnika* "piece" but *tien* "to open," *tǝnie'en* "open (state)."

This battery of derivational affixes is clearly an inheritance from the analogous affixes in Western Malayo-Polynesian, and in the overlapping and often unpredictable semantics among them, reveals itself as ancient and uninterrupted – i.e. these are not newly grammaticalized innovations in the language. This also highlights for us, again, that Flores (along with East Timor) is indeed a puzzle. Via what mechanism would a language simply "lose" *all* of an array of inflection and derivation such as this one in Lamaholot? Clearly, an intervening factor removed these affixes from certain earlier languages in Flores and Timor while leaving them intact in others.

In Manggarai, which retains a certain amount of affixation in contrast to the central Flores languages, the lexicon is more phonetically distinct from Tukang Besi cognates than in those languages, as highlighted in these cases:

Table 51. Lexicon sample of Tukang Besi, central Flores languages and Manggarai

	T. Besi	Sika	Ende	Manggarai
fowl	manu	manu	manu	manuk
pig	wawu	wawi	wawi	ǝla vai

(*Continued*)

Table 51. Lexicon sample of Tukang Besi, central Flores languages
and Manggarai (*Continued*)

	T. Besi	Sika	Ende	Manggarai
red	meha	merak	mera	ndérén
be thirsty	moro'u	mara	moa	masa
worm	ulo	ule	ure	ular
yawn	moma'a	moa	moa sodho	ŋoap

Kambera, of Sumba just south of Flores, is also a well-affixed language, for example marking subjects with the accusative in impersonal constructions, thus rendering an absolutive distinction in a language otherwise nominative/accusative:

(15) *Jàka   nda   nyumu, meti-ya.*
      CONJ NEG you   die-3S.ACC
      'Without you, we would die.' (one would have died)

                                                  (Klamer 1998: 161)

As we would expect, its lexicon in comparison to Tukang Besi's has more replacements and greater phonetic distance than, for example, Sika (e.g. *eti* "liver," *we* "pig," *tesi* "sea," *tibu* "sugar cane"):

Table 52. Lexicon sample of Tukang Besi, Sika and Kambera

	T. Besi	Sika	Kambera
come	mai	mai	mai
dead	mate	mate	mate
fish	ika	iang	yang
fowl	manu	manu	manu
liver	ate	wateng	eti
new	wo'ou	warun	*bidi*
pig	wawu	wawi	we
rain	usa-	uran	urang
red	meha	merak	*rara*
sea	tai	tahi	tesi
skin	kuli	ulit	*manula*

(*Continued*)

Table 52. Lexicon sample of Tukang Besi, Sika and Kambera (*Continued*)

	T. Besi	Sika	Kambera
snake	sa'a	sawaria	*kataru*
stone	watu	watu	watu
sugar cane	towu	tewu	tibu
be thirsty	moro'u	mara	madau
tree	hu'u	puhun	pingi-ai
wood	kau	ai	ai
worm	ulo	ule	ula
yawn	moma'a	moa	*yai*

In Dawanese (a.k.a. Timorese) of West Timor, there are two sets of subject prefixes, syllabic ones and ones consisting of only a single consonant, with it unpredictable which set a given verb takes (Steinhauer 1993: 133–4). Verbs in Dawanese change shape in several fashions including metathesis. Thus with no object, "I cut" is *qau qòt,* but with a fronted object the verb occurs with a suffix:

(16) *Nuif qi qau **qote***
      bone this I   cut
      'This bone I cut.' (142)

The same shape occurs if a following object begins with a cluster:

(17) *Hò m-**qote** qfulaq.*
      you 2S-cut flower
      'You cut flowers / a flower.'

But otherwise, a following object triggers metathesis:

(18) *Hò m-**qoet** nuif?*
      you 2S-cut bone
      'Do you cut bones?' (141)

Predictably Dawanese is also an outlier amidst the lexicons of Timorese languages: for example, the first five numbers are (*m*)*esa, nua, tenu, haa, nima* – of which only *haa* "four" is found in any other Austronesian language on the island (from Hull 1998: 184), in contrast to the relatively minor variation that these words exhibit in the other languages of Timor (as well as in Central Malayo-Polynesian in general).

These languages are analogous to southwestern dialects of English after the Scandinavian invasions in the northeast, which until the spread of standard English via widespread literacy and media were 1) much less permeated by Scandinavian words, retaining *his, here* and *hem* for *they, their* and *them, stone* for *stane, church* for *kirk,* etc., and correspondingly 2) much more grammatically conservative, retaining grammatical gender and richer verb conjugation paradigms as recently as the nineteenth century.

8.5. What we know about how analyticity happened in Flores and Timor

First, the geographical distribution of the languages in question clearly shows that on Flores, the main impact was in the central region, that there was a lesser impact immediately westward (Manggarai) and eastward (Sika) (cf. 2.4.), and that there was little or none further in both directions. From data available at present, this is clear in the east from Lamaholot as well as Kedang (Samely 1991); westward, a language like Bima on Sumbawa has tense-specific subject-marking prefixes (Wayan Arka, p.c. 2006):

(19)   *Nahu **ka**-hade   sawa kamau   ake.*
      1S   1S.FUT-kill snake rice.field that
      'I will kill this python.'

as well as tense-specific passive bound morphemes:

(20)   *Ngao ede **ra**-hade   ba sia.*
      cat   that PASS.PERF-kill by 3S
      'The cat has been killed by him/her.'

Sumbawa's other language, Sumbawa itself, is similar in this regard (Wouk 2002: 301, 304). The impact also did not spread southward across to Sumba, where subject-marking prefixes are retained by all languages (Klamer 2002: 373) and Kambera exemplifies ample affixation. On Timor, the impact was only in the east; on the western part of the island the languages are typical Central Malayo-Polynesian ones like Dawanese and Roti. (However, the most extremely analytic East Timor languages do not occupy any single "epicenter" within the region.)

Second, we know that the lexical peculiarity and the analyticity on both islands were not a mere instance of wave theory-style "diffusion." Certainly language relationships do not conform to a strict tree model. Scholars of language change are familiar with the fact that a realistic model of language change must incorporate diffusion between languages and dialects despite its inherent "messiness." Central Malayo-Polynesian itself notoriously appears to constitute more a cluster of tendencies than an efflorescence from a single ancestor.

However, wave theory cannot explain the contrast between Tukang Besi and Keo. While we might propose that the lexical likenesses between Sulawesi and two islands southwards are due to random diffusion due to geographical proximity, diffusion cannot explain the grammatical aspect of our puzzle: a highly affixal language such as a Sulawesi one would clearly not occasion a "wave" of analyticity.

What requires accounting for in our situation, then, does not lend itself to wave theory analysis. What happened was not borrowing (of words and typology), but language shift by a group from Sulawesi to languages spoken on Flores and Timor (cf. the distinction between borrowing and shift in Thomason & Kaufman 1988). The result was heavy lexical retention from the Sulawesi language and incomplete acquisition of the Floresian and Timorese grammars.

8.6. Three garden paths

Three explanations for the Flores anomaly (and the Timor one) seem especially prone to occur to linguists presented with them. None, upon examination, are as useful as they appear.

8.6.1. Isolating lingua francas were not the culprit

We cannot propose that the relevant Flores and Timor languages are analytic because of contact with colloquial varieties of Malay and Indonesian, along the lines of Hull's argument (1998: 166) that contact with Ambonese Malay, one of the many "creolized" morphologically reduced Malays of Indonesia, has also been responsible for the analyticity in Timor.

For one, countless languages in Indonesia have been in contact with similarly inflection-light Malay and Indonesian varieties for several centuries without coming to resemble them typologically: e.g. why no completely analytic languages in Borneo or the Moluccas? More to the point, on Flores, why Keo but not Lamaholot, or on Timor, why Tokodede but not Dawanese?

Moreover, in the cross-linguistic sense, widespread use of a less inflected lingua franca does not regularly simplify indigenous languages. If it did, then we would observe a drift toward analyticity among the hundreds of languages of Papua New Guinea whose speakers use Tok Pisin as a lingua franca.

Similarly, Africans who use the vehicular, affix-light varieties Sango, Lingala, and Kituba do not transfer its analyticity into their Bantu vernaculars.

This also applies to a temptation to suppose that the analyticity of Tetun Dili would cause the analyticity of other languages of eastern Timor – again, humans can speak at the same time analytic languages and synthetic ones with minimal "bleeding," and this is clear on Timor itself. A claim, for example, that Tokodede is isolating because Tetun Dili is leaves the question as to why Kemak and other languages of eastern Timor are so much less isolating – as well as why central Flores languages are all completely isolating despite the absence of any indigenous isolating lingua franca variety there.

The evidence suggests, I argue, that something else, beyond Indonesian or Tetun Dili, was responsible for the two peculiar "outbreaks" of analyticity in question.

8.6.2.　Isolating Papuan languages?

One might propose that the central Flores languages became isolating in contact with now-extinct Papuan languages that were also isolating. This is reasonable – but a scientific dead end. Papuan languages are no longer spoken on Flores, and the presumably closest living relatives of those that once were, the Timor-Alor-Pantar group, are by no means analytic (cf. Schapper in this volume on those of Timor). These hypothetical isolating Papuan languages of Flores could only remain, therefore, an unverifiable surmise, whereas this chapter is an attempt to assign a more systematic and refutable explanation to the facts. The surmise would be even less useful in that there are isolating languages on Timor despite the Papuan languages there *not* being isolating.

8.6.3.　Tukang Besi as "Old Timorese"?

Hull's (1998) proposal is that an entire language, both lexicon and grammar, was transported to Timor from Sulawesi, and another related one to Flores, and that in both places the language was pidginized. Hull's idea is that in Timor one pidginizing factor was the Ambonese invasion (cf. 4.1.1.) and that in both Timor and Flores, the analyticity of colloquial Malay was an additional spur. Upon that, my argument in 6.1. is germane.

In general, however, it is reasonable to suppose that the lexical parallels between Tukang Besi and the Flores and Timor languages could signal that what happened was not the pidginization of the Flores and Timor languages, but Floresians and Timorians pidginizing an imported Tukang Besi. Despite its initial plausibility, there are two problems with that scenario.

8.6.3.1. The Flores and Timor languages are typically Central Malayo-Polynesian

First, an account transporting a Sulawesian language leaves unexplained why despite their low-to-absent affixation, the relevant languages of Timor and Flores remain typical Central Malayo-Polynesian in their overall typology. This includes vestiges of metathesis, the famous verbal parallelism (e.g. in Roti, synonyms *soku* and *ifa* for "carry" used sequentially in formulaic fashion established within a mortuary chant), the absence of focus marking machinery typical of Western Malayo-Polynesian, and verb-medial syntax (cf. Klamer 2002). To propose that Sulawesi languages were transported southwards and then picked all of these features up via "diffusion" from nearby Central Malayo-Polynesian languages would be *ad hoc*. Relexification and grammatical simplification are a more economical approach.

However, a precise definition of what "Central Malayo-Polynesian" typology consists of has been elusive, and it could be argued that the Flores and Timor languages' lack of focus marking and their verb-medial syntax could also be symptoms of pidginization only accidentally akin to that in other Central Malayo-Polynesian languages. Under this analysis the focus marking could be a mere abbreviation of complexity, while SVO order would be typical of creolization (e.g. Berbice Creole Dutch's SVO order despite its source languages Dutch and Eastern Ijo being SOV). In that vein, the verb pairs could be seen as a cultural feature easily surviving pidginization. The second problem with the Sulawesian import account is more conclusive, however.

8.6.3.2. The Flores languages are not Tukang Besi pidgins

Definitive evidence that the central Flores languages are not incompletely acquired Tukang Besi is that they give no evidence of being based on its grammatical items, as is diagnostic of pidginization and intermediate degrees of incomplete acquisition of a target language.

Tukang Besi has three paradigms of demonstrative pronouns, with one indicating referentiality and the "presentative" used when explicitly and physically presenting an object (Donohue 1999:137):

Table 53. Demonstratives in Tukang Besi

	actual	referential	presentative
this	ana	meana'e	kaana'e
that	atu	meatu'e	kaatu'e
yonder	iso	measo'e	kaaso'e

While under incomplete acquisition of Tukang Besi it would hardly be expected that these three paradigms be retained, the Keo forms – *té* "this," *ké* "that," and *kéra* "that further way" (Baird 2002: 371) – give no evidence of derivation from any of the forms.

Keo's aspect markers are (ibid. 150):

Table 54. Aspect markers in Keo

négha	persistent perfect	ma	progressive
ka	persistent perfect with inevitability	dhatu	imperfective continuative
da'é	imperfective incompletive	mo'o	prospective

Assuming that amidst incomplete acquisition Tukang Besi's aspectual affixes would be bypassed, a presumed source for Keo's aspect markers would Tukang Besi's preverbal auxiliaries used in conjunction with its aspect-marking affixes. These, however, are (Donohue 1999: 170, 176):

Table 55. Aspect markers in Tukang Besi

ako	future	mina	ever
pasi	already	sagaa	a little
la'a	just	ane	is still
po'oli	after		

These morphemes offer not a single source for the Keo aspectual paradigm, and to the extent that amidst incomplete acquisition aspect is often indicated via periphrastic constructions with *be, have,* or *stand,* these items in Tukang Besi are *ane, hoto,* and *tade* respectively, again providing no model for the Keo items.

Similarly, while the Tukang Besi predicate negator is *mbea(ka),* Keo's is *mona;* the third person singular and plural pronouns in Tukang Besi are *ia* and *amai* (ibid. 113), but are *'imu* and *'imu-ko'o* (or *sira*) in Keo (Baird 2002: 110).

The central Flores languages, then, are not renditions of Tukang Besi minus affixation, or even more disrupted acquisitions of Tukang Besi. They are central Floresian languages, with typical Floresian grammatical items (and typology), but with a strikingly large battery of lexical items tracing to Tukang Besi. We seek, then, an explanation for the analyticity that can account for, at the same time, 1) a strange parallelism between these languages' content morphemes and those of Tukang Besi, 2) a strangely analytic structure, and 3) both of these despite no evidence of the pidginization of Tukang Besi's particular grammatical apparatus.

This is by no means an unusual language contact relationship. It is precisely that between Old English and Old Norse, in which case we do not reconstruct, despite the massive lexical component from Old Norse in English and the significant affixal loss that accompanied it, that Middle English was a new Scandinavian language, rather than simply English with a massive inheritance of Norse words.

8.7. Two additional differences between Hull's proposal versus mine

8.7.1. The Southern Moluccas were normal

My account also contrasts with Hull's in that I do not consider the Southern Moluccas to have undergone the relexification that Flores and Timor did. Hull notes that the languages of these islands replace Sulawesi cognates at rates similar to those in Flores and Timor (Hull 1998: 114). However, cognate matches alone are not a basis for designating a direct mother-daughter relationship between languages. Equally relevant is the phonetic difference between cognates in these languages with those in, for example, Tukang Besi, which is much greater than in Flores and Timor (cf. 4.2.). Moreover, as Hull (1998: 137) notes himself, there is no notable grammatical simplification in these languages in terms of the Central Malayo-Polynesian norm. In terms of amount of description necessary, a grammar such as Van Engelenhoven's (2004) of Leti contrasts sharply with, for example, Baird's (2002) of Keo. The Southern Moluccan languages would appear to have undergone regular processes of internal change grammatically, and their Austronesian lexical stock has drifted from its cognates in older Austronesian languages to a typical extent.

Overall, Hull's account has it that languages from Sulawesi were imported to Flores, Timor, and the Southern Moluccas and that inmigrants from the Central Moluccas simplified East Timor's languages – but leaves unexplained why languages were simplified in Flores, and why they were not in the Southern Moluccas. Under my proposal, a Sulawesi exodus simplified languages in both Flores and Timor, but did not reach the southern Moluccas, leaving its grammars unaffected.

8.7.2. The Sulawesi Exodus in question did not introduce Austronesian to Flores and Timor

Hull's formulation also supposes (168) that Austronesian had yet to reach Flores and Timor before the Sulawesi exodus under examination (under his thesis, as recently as one thousand years ago). This, too, however, would require that once settled on the islands, these Sulawesi varieties would have taken on their Central Malayo-Polynesian typology. This would have been even less likely if languages of this type were only spoken across the water on faraway islands – and vanishingly unlikely if they were only spoken as far north as the Central Moluccas, under Hull's proposition that the Austronesians also had yet to reach the southern Moluccas until this time.

There is also the question as to why Austronesian speakers would not have reached Flores and Timor by 1000, A.D., or simply why they would have settled them last, while having long ago occupied the Moluccas and passed on to New Guinea and eastward. As Hull notes, archaeological evidence has yet to confirm when Austronesian speakers, specifically, reached Flores or Timor. However, the general outlines of linguistic, anthropological and archaeological evidence indicate that Austronesian speakers had certainly progressed northwards and far eastward of Flores and Timor by roughly 3500 years ago (cf. Spriggs 2003: 63–4). Why would they have steered clear of these two islands, or even their general area?

The only way to avoid this question would be to assume that the reason the Flores languages' lexicons correspond so closely to Tukang Besi's is the original Austronesian population movement 3500 years ago. But this would leave an unsuitably long three millennia-plus during which lexical items between Sulawesi and these islands would have stayed implausibly similar, strangely immune to natual processes of drift.

It is more graceful to suppose that there were two crucial migrations, with Austronesian first reaching Flores and Timor from Sulawesi when traditionally supposed, about 3500 years ago, but with a second migration from Sulawesi much later, exerting a profound effect upon the Austronesian languages long established there.

8.8. When? In search of historical evidence

Historical documentation of population movements between Sulawesi and islands to the south is essentially nonexistent. Historiography of the islands largely begins with the accounts of the Portuguese and the Dutch starting in the sixteenth century, in the wake of which earlier patterns of rule and conquest among indigenous groups were in the process of dissolution. Before this, archaeological evidence cannot shed light on anything as specific as the migration of Tukang Besi speakers to Flores and Timor.

However, in the light of these realities, our question is not "Is there historical evidence demonstrating that large numbers of Tukang Besi speakers migrated to Flores and Timor within the last thousand years?" The answer is, inevitably, no: the events would have occurred among people without writing.

The aim of this chapter is to show that the *linguistic* evidence tells the story. We search not for historiographical confirmation which could never have existed, but for evidence that the proposal based on linguistic analysis is compatible with what historical evidence there is.

Anthropological data suggests that it is, in that there is ample evidence that Flores and Timor peoples have ancestry much more recently than 3500 years ago in Sulawesi – with the caveat that it points not to southeastern but southwestern Sulawesi. The Gowa empire of southwestern Sulawesi controlled the Manggarai region of Flores from 1658 to 1750, and many Manggarai trace their ancestry to migrations from Gowa (Erb 1999: 85–6). One of the ancestor stories of the Nage involves invaders from Gowa as well (Forth 1998: 230), and their cosmology traces them in general to either Sulawesi or "Bugis bonerate" (the Bugis kingdom was also on southwestern Sulawesi).

Manggarai and Nage people also trace ancestry to the Minangkabau (Erb 1999: 85, Forth 1998: 81), but Van Bekkum (1944) documented the alternate term "Bonengkabau," suggesting that "Minangkabau" here may be a folk distortion of an actual descent from the more geographically plausible region of the Gulf of Bone between the southwestern and southeastern legs of Sulawesi. This was home of the Luwu kingdom, thought to have emerged around 1300 A.D.

Meanwhile, on Timor, Tetun Terik speakers' origin myth involves a Sulawesi crocodile "rai-Makasar" sailing east and becoming the island of Timor (the Macassar kindgom was on southwestern Sulawesi), while speakers of the East Timor language Kemak recount original settlers coming through Sulawesi (Hull 1998: 150).

Recasting the hypothesis with southwestern Sulawesi as the source region is as inappropriate as it would seem tempting. Its languages provide nothing approaching the lexical similarities motivating the argument – only half of the cognates in Macassarese match with the Flores and Timor languages, for example, and phonetic differences in both Macassarese and Buginese entail stopping (/v/, /w/ > /b/; /r/ > /d/) and nasalizations (Buginese *pong* for "tree") atypical in Tukang Besi and the Flores and Timor languages:

Table 56. Lexicon sample of Tukang Besi, Sika, Tokodede and SW
            Sulawesi languages

	T. Besi	Sika	Tokodede	Macassarese	Buginese
come	mai	mai	mai	*batu*	*pole*
dead	mate	mate	mate	mata	mata
fish	ika	iang	ika	*juku'*	*bale*
fowl	manu	manu	manu	manu	manuk
liver	ate	wateng	ate	ate	*bas*
new	wo'ou	warun	veu	*isah*	beru
pig	wawu	wawi	vavi	bawi	bai
rain	usa-	uran	ura	*bosi*	*bosi*
red	meha	merak	mio	*eja*	*cəlla*
sea	tai	tahi	tasi	*tamparang*	tasi
skin	kuli	ulit	kluta	bukuleng	uli
snake	sa'a	sawaria	sa-	sawa	ula
stone	watu	watu	vatu	batu	batu
sugar cane	towu	tewu	tevu	tabu	tæbu
be thirsty	moro'u	mara	broo	*turere*	madəka
tree	hu'u	puhun	puu	*bonang*	pong
wood	kau	ai	kai	*bombang*	*duri*
worm	ulo	ule	ula	olo'bulu	*cambulu*
yawn	moma'a	moa	mava	*anganga*	*mangangale*

The importance of the above table remains the uncanny likeness between the Lesser Sunda languages and Tukang Besi, as opposed to their divergence from languages of the very same island just across a narrow gulf, which differ from them as we would expect they would after 3500 years of separation – to a degree akin to Romance languages rather than dialects of a single Romance language.

In that light it must be borne in mind that the Timorese, at least, use "Makassar" as a generic reference to Sulawesi as a whole (Hull 1998: 150), and this could well have been true among Floresians of the terms Gowa and Bugis in the past. Whatever caused migrations from southwestern Sulawesi could well have exerted influence on peoples of the peninsula across the gulf as well – and to people of Flores and Timor, exactly which regions of Sulawesi its emigrants were from would have been of little interest.

Nevertheless, I suggest that confirmation of a specifically southeastern Sulawesi source for Floresian and Timorian peoples will come from genetic comparison. In fact, given that on Sumba, genetic evidence has been shown to correlate in striking lockstep with the degree to which subjects' languages are influenced lexically by pre-Austronesian languages (Lansing et al., 2007), it would not be surprising if degree of genetic likeness to southeastern Sulawesians were highest, specifically, among central Floresians and eastern Timoreans.

8.9. Homo floresiensis

Finally, it must be noted that Flores happens to be where local descriptions of "wildmen," usually described as short, hairy, and elusive, are more explicit and realistic than anywhere else in Indonesia (Forth 2008: 12–89).[3] The *ebu gogo* are described by the Nage, for instance, as having lived on the outskirts of society until as recently as 200 years ago when they were exterminated for a tendency to thievery. They are treated as separate from the realm of spirits and other mythical creatures. The only primate models on Flores are small macaque monkeys rather than human-like apes, and the *ebu gogo* are discussed with the human classifier (*ga'e*) rather than the animal one (*éko*). Furthermore, the *ebu gogo* are recalled as capable of speech, specifically a child-like rendition of Nage.

The danger in dismissing the *ebu gogo* conception as complete fantasy is evident in cases such as the Lele of Africa's description of the pangolin, a "scaly anteater" which turned out to exist, and the assorted indigenous myths that correspond to the occurrence of a massive flood in the Middle East 7000 years ago. In this light, remains of a possible additional species of hominid in a cave in the Manggarai-speaking region of Flores, smaller than *Homo sapiens* but evidently using tools, may be concrete evidence of the source of

---

3 On Sumba, directly south, the equivalent descriptions are so similar that they are almost certainly due to the slave trade between Flores and Sumba that thrived until the recent past.

the *ebu gogo* conception (the remains happen to date back 12,000 years, but this hardly rules out the survival of the species later).

Interestingly, recall of *ebu gogo*-like creatures of this nonfantastical variety are found not just on Flores in general, but only where the languages are completely analytic, among Nage and Li'o speakers. In the Manggarai region, the descriptions are more of the mythical variety, and in the east where Sika and Lamaholot are spoken, there is no lore equivalent to the *ebu gogo* description at all. Could it be that the analyticity of these particular Flores languages is due to second-language rendition by a second species of *Homo?*

The problem with this speculation is that all descriptions of *ebu gogo* and like beings describe them as outliers living apart, interacting with other humans only briefly – and nothing in the *Homo floresiensis* remains discovered thus far sheds any light on whether these people interacted with *Homo sapiens*. However, given what an oddity the analyticity of these languages is, further discoveries related to *Homo floresiensis* ought be of a certain amount of interest to Austronesianists and language contact specialists in general.

8.10. Conclusion

If the languages of central Flores and East Timor were analytic and there were nothing about them that seemed out of the ordinary as language change goes, then we would have grounds for treating them as evidence that grammars can shed all of their afiixation as a mere matter of chance.

The problem is that even then, more properly we would have to enshirine this dozen-odd languages out of the world's 6000 as having wended down a path none of the others ever have, except amidst extensive acquisition by language-challenged adults. This – languages that let go of all or virtually all of their affixes just "because" – would be as newsworthy as the discovery of OVS languages like Hixkaryana in South America.

However, the languages in question do harbor something out of the ordinary. Their core lexicons seem only slightly evolved from that of a language that they split off from several millennia ago. This suggests an encounter with that language much more recently, of a kind which, according to the tenets of language contact theory, provides an explanation for why they lost their affixes.

Future linguistic and archaeological research will shed further light on what interrupted the normal transmission of the languages of central Flores and East Timor. If the reader is convinced at least that something did, then this chapter has served its main purpose.

Chapter 9
A brief for the Celtic hypothesis: English in Box 5?

9.1. Introduction

In McWhorter (2002), I argued that English inherited less of the Proto-Germanic legacy than any other Germanic language, and that this contrast with its sisters is stark enough to demand an explanation in interrupted acquisition at some point in its time line. My proposal was that Scandinavian Viking invaders acquired an incomplete version of English, reducing or eliminating features such as grammatical gender (entirely absent in no other Indo-European language in Europe but English), directionally marked adverbs (*here* / *hither*), V2 syntax, and inherent reflexive marking (German *sich erinnern* "to remember"), and that this rendition was prevalent enough to be passed on to future generations of native English speakers.

Various scholars, however, while concurring that the grammatical contrast between English and its sisters is too vast to be a mere matter of chance, argue that the intervening factor was the Celtic languages spoken by the original inhabitants of Britain. In contrast to traditional arguments that the indigenous Celts were largely eliminated by the Germanic-speaking invaders, adherents of the Celtic Hypothesis (henceforth CH) suppose that Old English was deeply transformed when used as a second language by speakers of Brythonic Celtic languages, specifically Welsh, Cornish, and possibly the extinct and sparsely documented Cumbric. These scholars point to numerous grammatical parallels between Celtic and English that do not exist between Celtic and other Germanic languages, such that English would be a deeply Celticized Germanic language just as Indo-Aryan languages are agreed to be imprinted by Dravidian.

Signature arguments begin with early work by scholars such as Keller (1925), Dal (1952), G. Visser (1955), and especially Preusler's (1956) broad-ranging argument, and continue with a modern revival school exemplified by Poussa (1990), Klemola (1996, 2000), Tristram (1999), Filppula (2003), Hickey (1995), Vennemann (2000, 2001), Van der Auwera & Genee (2002), White (2002), and Poppe (2003). The contributions of Hamp (1975) and even J.R.R. Tolkein (1963) have also been useful.

The CH has been regularly dismissed by most scholars of English dia-chrony. A major objection has been that the purported Celtic influences do not appear in the historical record until the Middle English period despite contact with Celts beginning several centuries before this. Another has been that English has so few Celtic lexical items. I myself was convinced by such objections when writing McWhorter (2002). However, upon further engage-ment with the CH literature, I have been moved to revise my views.

My reading of the evidence is that what drew English grammar away from the Proto-Germanic template was two developments. One was that Norse-speaking invaders simplified the grammar. The second was that Celtic speak-ers infused the grammar with new constructions as the result of language shift over time.

I will focus this presentation on a single construction, periphrastic *do,* which is especially useful in demonstrating that the usual objections to the CH fail upon examination. For reasons of space and focus, I will refrain from presenting a full typology of auxiliary do constructions in English, for which Van der Auwera (1999) and Jäger (2006) will be useful. Our interest will be in *do*-support: the use of *do* as a semantically empty carrier of tense in negated and interrogative sentences:

I walk.
I do not walk.
Do I walk?

As ordinary as these sentences are in English, one would be hard pressed to name a language one had learned or was even aware of that used *do* in this particular way. That is, unless one is a speaker of, or familiar with, a Celtic language, in which case one is confronted with a close parallel.

The intended contribution of this presentation is to reinforce other CH accounts of periphrastic *do* by calling attention to the urgency of the CH argument in view of cross-linguistic facts, by bolstering counterarguments to the objections about issues of timing of occurrence and lexical contribu-tion, and by showing that traditional accounts of periphrastic *do*'s emer-gence cannot be seen as preferable to a CH account in the scientific sense. I will conclude that the evidence suggests an even stronger conclusion than that of Van der Auwera & Genee (2002), that there was a reinforcing influ-ence between English and Celtic that created the modern periphrastic do. I will build a case that the decisive force was influence of Celtic upon English.

9.2. Celtic models for periphrastic *do*

Various CH adherents have pointed to Welsh and Cornish models for periphrastic *do* (Preusler 1956, Poussa 1990, Klemola 1996, Van der Auwera &
Genee 2002). Their tendency has been to designate Cornish as the most likely
source specifically, given that periphrastic *do* appears first in southwestern
texts dated to about 1300 and Cornish is the Celtic language that was spoken
in this region.

Cornish's auxiliary *do* presents a thoroughly plausible model for English's
periphrastic *do,* and not simply in its auxiliary status – plenty of grammars
use *do* as an auxiliary – but in using this auxiliary in semantically neutral
fashion as a syntactic place-filler with all verbs.

Do in Cornish is used both in finite form and in a complex with the verbal
noun, in which *do* occurs in the third-person singular form after a particle
(PT in the glosses):

(1)(a) **gwrav** *vî cara*
        do. 1S I   love.VN

  (b) *mi a*   **wra**   *cara*
       I   PRT do.3S love.VN
       'I (do) love.'

(Jenner 1904: 136, 116)

and in the negative and the interrogative:

(2) *Ni* **wrigav**   *vî dha*   *welas.*
     NEG do.PRET.1S I   you.POSS see.VN
     'I did not see you.'

(Jenner 1904: 160)

(3) **Gwra** *cara?*
     do.2S love.VN
     'Do you love?'

(Jenner 1904: 117)

The *do* auxiliary occurs not only in the present but the past:

(4)(a) **gwrîgav**   *vî   cara*
        do.PAST.1S you love.VN

  (b) *tî   a*   **wrîg**   *cara*
       you PRT do.PAST.3S   love.VN
       'You (did) love.'

(Jenner 1904: 137, 116)

The usage of auxiliary *do* conveys little or no semantic difference (George 1993: 454). In fact, Jenner (1904: 117) documents the *do* auxiliary as used not just alternately, but usually, in the first- and second-person singular. Cornish's *do* is also the usual choice in dependent clauses:

(5)   ..*mar **qwressa**   an   dên cara.*
      if   do.COND.3S DEF man love.VN
      '..if the man would lozve.'

(Jenner 1904: 117)

Of course our interest must be in Cornish as it was encountered in its earlier stages. The fact is that even the earliest substantial attestations of Cornish, termed the Middle Cornish stage, already display the same auxiliary usages of *do* as later Cornish. Middle Cornish used auxiliary *do* in the present:

(6)   *My a   **ra**   y   dybry.*
      I   PRT do.3S him eat.VN
      'I eat him.'

in the negative:

(7)   *Omma ny   **wreugh** why tryge.*
      here   NEG do.2P   you stay.VN
      'You do not stay here.'

in the interrogative:

(8)   *Pwy a   **rwa**   coul   dreheuel ol   the chy?*
      who PRT do.FUT.3S whole build.VN entirely your house
      'Who will finish building your whole house?'

and in dependent clauses:

(9)   ..*mar a   **cruk**   donfen...*
      if   PRT do.PRET.3S send.VN
      '..if he sent . . . '

(Lewis 1990: 46)

As such, the usage of auxiliary *do* as model for English's periphrastic *do* in Modern Cornish was ancient.

Welsh, on the other hand, presents a slightly less close parallel to English. As in Cornish, the *do* verb occurs with the verbal noun, conveying no significant semantic difference from constructions without *do:*

(10)(a)   *agor-es   i*
          do.VN-1S I

(b) ***nes***   *i agor?*
     do.PRET.1S I open.VN
     "I open."

(King 2003: 189)

The *do* auxiliary is used in Welsh in the negative and interrogative as well:

(11) negative   *agor-es i **ddim** nes i **ddim** agor* "I didn't open"
     interrogative *agor-es i?*   *nes i agor?*   "Did I open?"

But in Modern Welsh the similarity to English's periphrastic *do* fades beyond the present tense. Welsh does not use *do* as an auxiliary in the past (rather, only in the northern dialect, *ddaru* "to happen" is used thus [King 2003: 189–90]). Then, in the future, *do* is used only when a specific meaning of intentionality (in King's terminology) is intended, rather than as semantically neutral:

(12) ***Nawn***   *ni siarad â   fo   nes ymlaen.*
     do.FUT.1P we speak with him later
     'Let's speak to him later.'

(King 2003: 193)

As it happens, this incongruity of distribution regarding tense was somewhat lesser in Middle Welsh. Like Cornish, it used the *do* auxiliary in a semantically identical alternate construction with a particle, and here, *do* occurred in the past as well:

(13) *Eistedd a   **wnaeth***
     sit.VN PT do.PAST.3S
     'He sat.'

(Watkins 1993: 327)

(Today this construction is a less semantically central one, connoting emphasis.) However, only Cornish, early and modern, prefers auxiliary *do* in dependent clauses, or has entrenched it even further in using auxiliary *do* semantically neutrally in the imperative: ***Gwra** cara* "Love!" (Jenner 1904: 141).

Thus while Welsh would hardly be an implausible source for English's periphrastic *do,* Cornish is the closer match, which is one of many suggestions that the English construction's origin in the Cornish-speaking region was due to transfer from Cornish.

9.3. CH Criticism Number One: Celtic's auxiliary *do* was due to contact with English

Given that Cornish and English have existed in contact for a very long time, we must consider whether English developed periphrastic *do* internally and then passed the construction on to Cornish speakers using English bilingually.

To be sure, strictly speaking, attestations allow us to trace Cornish's usage of auxiliary *do* only so far back. The Middle Cornish stage began in 1200, and the aforegoing citations date to the 1400s or later. Thus technically, there is still room for the surmise that Cornish before this had no auxiliary *do,* and that *do* developed on its own into an auxiliary in English around, as attested, 1300, with Cornish merely inheriting the construction subsequently from contact with English.

As it happens, the history of Celtic gives us a window on its grammatical nature long before its substantial attestations, and precisely when Germanic speakers invaded England in the middle of the 400s. Namely, Celtic speakers migrated from southern England to northwestern France in the 400s and 500s, seeding what is now the Breton-speaking community. As such, grammatical features that Breton shares with Cornish, tracing back to the last time they were the same language, must be taken as evidence of the nature of Cornish just when the Angles, Saxons and Jutes would have encountered it.

If English lent periphrastic *do* to Cornish, then we would expect that Breton would be a language with nothing resembling periphrastic *do* – like most of the world's languages. This is not what we find. Modern Breton uses auxiliary *do* in the same fashion as Welsh and Cornish, such as in the affirmative:

(14) *Selaou   a   **rit**   an   avel.*
      listen.VN PRT do.2S DEF wind
      'You listen to the wind.'

(Press 1986: 128)

It also uses it in the negative, but only for emphasis according to Press (1986):

(15) *Kousket   ne   **rin**   ket.*
      sleep.VN NEG do.1S NEG
      'I shall not sleep.'

(Press 1986: 128)

McKenna (1988) cites it in the interrogative:

(16)   *Debo   mad e   **ret**?*
       eat.VN well PRT do.2P
       'Do you eat well?'

(McKenna 1988: 151)

However, it bears mentioning that Stephens (1993: 394–5) specifies that in Breton it occurs only in the affirmative, and that McKenna (1988: 150) states that auxiliary *do* occurs in the interrogative but not in the negative.

Meanwhile, Middle Breton sources only give us affirmative citations, such as:

(17)   *Da   pidy   a   **graff**.*
       you.POSS swear.VN PRT do.1S
       'I swear to you.'

(Lewis 1990: 41)

Breton, then, allows two possible interpretations as to the presence of auxiliary *do* in Cornish when Anglo-Saxon speakers arrived.

One is that when Breton branched off from Cornish, auxiliary *do* occurred in the affirmative, negative and interrogative as it does in Modern Cornish, and that today, Breton's negative and interrogative usages are pragmatically or dialectally restricted because Breton speakers have long been bilingual in French, which has no analogue of auxiliary *do* and thus may have led to the narrowing of the construction's grammatical application.

Alternately, we might take a more parsimonious route and suppose that the evidence shows that when Breton offshooted from early Cornish, that auxiliary *do* only occurred in the affirmative. This would mean that the Cornish spoken when Germanic speakers invaded England used auxiliary *do* only in the affirmative.

The fact is, though, that this alone would have been a plausible model for English's current use of *do*. In its first stage as an auxiliary in English, *do* was used in the affirmative as well as the negative and interrogative; i.e., as the *do* alternately treated as causative, habitual, perfective, etc.. Only later did its affirmative usage disappear, leaving only the negative and interrogative usages. If Cornish provided a model only for an affirmative usage, then it is unproblematic to reconstruct that English first incorporated this usage, and then generalized auxiliary *do* into the negative and interrogative in line with the syntactic nature of auxiliaries: it is not usual that a syntax bars the expression of an auxiliary in the negative and interrogative.

Relevant also is that periphrastic *do* occurs in English first in the affirmative, with negative and interrogative usages some decades later (Denison

1993: 265). While this may be an accident of documentation, it would also be compatible with Cornish's having only the affirmative usage when English encountered it – or even by the 1300s, such that we could allow that its occurrence in Cornish sources in the negative and interrogative in the 1400s and afterwards were due to influence from English's having generalized periphrastic *do* to these contexts. Crucially, however, the "default" affirmative usage was established in Cornish before English speakers came to Britain.

In sum, however interpreted, the evidence does not allow that Cornish began as a language without a periphrastic *do* construction and only later inherited it from English, leaving a mistaken impression to modern observers that Cornish was the borrower. Cornish had, at the very least, a periphrastic usage of *do* in the affirmative, which would have been a ready model for an English equivalent that was used in negative and interrogative sentences as well. And then, only the marginality or absence of periphrastic *do* in the negative and interrogative in Breton suggests the possibility that Old Cornish lacked these: Middle Cornish uses periphrastic *do* in all relevant contexts, and thus so may have Old Cornish.

This suggests that a scientifically responsible version of the CH on periphrastic *do* need not leave the pathway of influence flexible and reconstruct a general Sprachbund of which *do*-periphrasis is one trait, with its family of origin unknowable due to the sparseness of its documentation in Old Celtic sources, as Tristram (1997) has it and Van der Auwera & Genee (2002) concur with. Given that Breton split from Cornish starting in the 400s, then even in the absence of copious texts in Old Brythonic varieties, Breton's usage of periphrastic *do* confirms that Celtic spoken in the south at that time had already developed a periphrastic *do* before contact with English speakers.

9.4. CH Objection Number Two: Periphrastic *do* is a Germanic family trait

It has also been claimed that English's periphrastic *do* is less a local oddity than an unremarkable development, found in many Germanic varieties (e.g. Tieken-Boon Van Ostade 1988). For example, in nonstandard German dialects *tun* "to do" is used in sentences such as (rendered with Standard German lexical forms):

(18)   *Er **tut**   das schreiben.*
       he do.3S that write
       'He writes that.' (Abraham & Conradie 2001: 83)

Similar constructions with *do* are found in nonstandard Dutch dialects (Cornips 1994), earlier stages of Frisian (Van der Auwera & Genee 2002: 287), Old Norse (Ellegård 1953: 27), and elsewhere.

However, English's periphrastic *do* behaves quite differently than these nonstandard Germanic usages. For one, German's usages appear to be more restricted in terms of tense than English's *do*. Abraham & Conradie (2001:83) note that it is not used in the past, for example:

(19) **Er tat   das schreiben.*
      he do.PAST.3S that write
      'He wrote that.'

To be sure, Eroms (1998) claims on the contrary that periphrastic do is indeed used in the past in Bavarian, but Abraham & Conradie's analysis suggests that it is, at least, used less freuqently in the past, in contrast to its obligatory status in both past and present in English.

Overall, while English's *do* is a syntactic place-filler, Abraham & Conradie (2001: 80–93), in a discussion more extended than the brief flaggings of the German and Dutch *do*-sentences in descriptions of nonstandard varieties, analyze nonstandard German's *tun*-construction as primarily a pragmatic strategy encoding focus:

(Leipzig dialect)

(20) *Ich **due**   da   dän dsädl filai   an   bäsdn dser<u>rubm</u>.*
      I   do.1S 2S.DAT your scrap maybe PREP best   tear.up
      'Maybe I'd better tear up your piece of paper.' (translation mine)

(ibid. 86)

(Standard German: *Ich tue dir deinen Zettel am besten zer<u>reisen</u>.*)

Bavarian:

(21)(a) *I **tua**   vielleicht den <u>Sack</u> aufschnaidn.*
         I do.1S maybe   DEF bag   cut.open
         'Maybe I'll (just) cut the bag open.'

   (b)   *I **tua**   vielleicht den Sack aufschnaidn.*
         I do.1S maybe   DEF bag   cut.open
         'Maybe I'll (just) cut the bag open.' (translations mine)

(ibid. 87)

Importantly, we cannot treat this usage as a potential precursor to English's periphrastic *do,* despite that nothing would rule this out as a plausible grammatical development. This is because *do* was never used in this pragmatic fashion in any earlier stage of English; i.e. no analyst has ever proposed such an analysis of early occurrences of auxiliary *do* in English. Germanic languages that use *do* in this way have come to do so independently of English.

The pragmatic analysis does not cover the entire domain of the usage of auxiliary *do* in nonstandard Germans, in that the *tun*-construction's usage in some dialects has been analyzed differently, such as in Hessian where it serves as an analytic subjunctive:

(22)   *Isch **deed**'s   ned   mache.*
       I   would.do.it NEG do
       'I wouldn't do it.'

(Durrell & Davies 1990: 235)

(Thuringian makes a similar usage [Spangenberg 1990: 284]). Yet this is also a usage quite distinct from that of English's periphrastic *do*.

One might nevertheless suppose that these represent a mere difference in grammatical outcomes in different languages: certainly we would not expect *do*'s usage as an auxiliary to be identical from one sister language to another. One might propose that Proto-Germanic lent an auxiliary usage of *do* that had differing fates in the daughter languages, including English.

However, it must be recognized that the *particular* fate of auxiliary *do* in English is, in the cross-linguistic sense, extremely peculiar. To be sure, because of the general nature of its semantics, it is hardly uncommon for *do* to be generalized into semantically bleached functions. Commonly, for example, grammars can express many verbal concepts with compounds composed of *do* and a nominal element. Persian, for example, has only a few hundred simple verbs, otherwise making heavy use of combinations of nominals with *kardan* "to do": *u-rā bidār **kard*** "he woke him up" (Windfuhr 1987: 538). Similar is Japanese's use of *suru:*

(22)   *Taroo ga   Tokyo ni ryokoo o   **suru**.*
       Taroo NOM Tokyo to travel   ACC do
       'Taroo travels to Tokyo.'

(Miyamoto 1999: 1)

the usage of which can be so semantically distant from its core meaning of "to do" as to encode possession and existentiality:

(23)   *Taroo ga   kega   o   **suru**.*
       Taroo NOM wound ACC do
       'Taroo has a wound.'

(ibid. 5)

(24) *Hen-na   nioi   ga   **suru**.*
strange-ASSOC smell NOM do
'There is a strange smell.'

(ibid. 4)

Yet in neither Persian nor Japanese has *do* extended to usage with all verbs and become a purely syntactic place-filler. We could say that this is barred in these languages because morphology makes it clear in both that the nominals are not verbs, whereas the barrier is lesser in English given its poor inflectional apparatus. This inflectional poverty is precisely what motivates Garrett (1998) to propose that English's periphrastic *do* began as a habitual-marking *do* occurring with deverbal nominals (*folc reste **dede*** "people rested" lit. "people did resting," from original verb *resten*) and that *do*'s modern occurrence in conjunction with verbs traces to when inflectional erosion left the verbal sources of the nominals formally identical with their deverbal progeny (i.e. *reste* now meant both "resting" and "to rest"), such that speakers reinterpreted nominals used with *do* as verbs (*reste dede* "did resting" > "did rest$_V$").

But this only raises another question: why no periphrastic *do* in Germanic varieties almost as inflectionally denuded as English, like Dutch, Swedish, Norwegian or Danish? The question is especially urgent given that all of these languages include numerous nonstandard varieties, often significantly divergent grammatically from the standard ones, in which we would expect that over so many centuries sheer chance would create a periphrastic *do* in at least some of them. Indeed, *do* occurs as a place-filler in Mainland Scandinavian in cases of inversion and topicalization, as in Danish:

(25) *Læse **gør**   han aldrig.*
read do.3S he   never
'As for reading, he never does it.'

(Allan, Holmes & Lunskær-Nielsen 1995: 511)

But this is what English diachrony specialists typically term "substitutive *do*," plausibly treated as a Germanic family trait – but our question is whether Germanic languages typically recruit *do* as a required dummy auxiliary element in negative and *all* inverted sentences such that interrogative ones are subsumed. More precisely: why no English-style periphrastic *do* in *just one* of the dialects of these several languages? Again, English's usage of *do* is extremely odd.

Many Australian languages have a usage more similar to English's periphrastic *do,* in occurring with verbs instead of nominals, and not in substitutive function. In these languages, *do* is one of as few as three simple verbs, and verbal concepts other than these few are obligatorily expressed in coverbial constructions with the simple ones. In Jingulu, for example, *do* is used thus:

(26)   *Ngaba-nga-ju karnarinymi.*
        hold-1S-do   spear
        'I have a spear.'

(27)   *Ngaja-nya-ana-ju.*
        see-2S-me-do
        'You can see me.'

(Pensalfini 2003)

But even here, *do* is not the only verb with this behavior, in contrast to periphrastic *do*'s unique status in English as applying to all negated and interrogative sentences. In Jingulu, *come* and *go* exhibit the same behavior; meanwhile, in many Australian languages, this set of simple verbs is as large as thirty (Dixon 2001: 71), and in none of them is there only a single such verb, *do* or any other.

Thus worldwide, certainly *do* is uniquely ripe for grammaticalizations of various kinds, and for lexicalizations in verbal compounds with nominals. This is predictable from its cognitively central semantics as denoting basic, unspecified action. However, a search for languages in which *do* has devolved into *semantically empty syntactic conjunction with all verbs* is challenging indeed. Surely it is significant, then, that Celtic languages like Cornish – precisely the languages spoken by the indigenous inhabitants of Britain who adopted English – are among the precious few of the world's languages that use *do* in just this way.

9.5. CH Objection Number Three: Periphrastic *do* emerged via ordinary processes of internal change

The sheer weirdness of English's periphrastic *do* in the cross-linguistic sense sheds light on the various accounts of its origin by traditional specialists in English diachrony. These authors suppose that periphrastic *do* can be traced to ordinary processes of internal grammaticalization, but upon analysis, their accounts raise as many questions as they answer. Fifty years after Ellegård's (1953) foundational crack at the problem, the origin of periphrastic *do* remains unclear, with analysts undecided as to which account is most appropriately subscribed to. Traugott's (1972: 141) assessment that "the debate still continues and may never be resolved" remains resonant decades later – while the simple fact that the Celtic languages English was in contact with had their own periphrastic *do* sits dismissed.

9.5.1. Earlier accounts

I will assume that certain earlier accounts have been conclusively refuted. For example, Ellegård proposed that periphrastic *do* has its roots in the causative usage of *do* (*Henry . . . þe walles **did** doun felle* "Henry felled the walls"), with *do* developing a semantically empty interpretation because of cases where verbs were used with causative meaning without *do,* such as in the second clause of the aforegoing citation: *Henry . . . þe walles did doun felle, þe tours ø bette he doun.* But Denison (1993: 278) notes that causative *do* is too rarely attested to be a viable candidate for a grammatically central development like periphrastic *do.* Moreover, Ellegård's proposal that periphrastic *do* was entrenched because of its prosodic utility in poetry requires that rarified registers deeply imprint casual speech, a notion less plausible in view of advances in sociolinguistic theory as yet unknown when Ellegård wrote. This is especially given that *gin* "begin" was used in prosodic function in poetry at the same time (*þus þe bataile **gan** leste long* "Thus the battle went on a long time" [Fischer 1992: 265]) but remained, as we would suppose intuitively, largely restricted to that register (used only in poetry, for example, by Chaucer rather than in his prose).

Finally, we might add that Ellegård's account does not square well with grammaticalization theory as it developed decades after he wrote. He stipulated that a causative *do* became interpreted as semantically empty because there were bare verbs with causative meaning – but his account did not scientifically explain why it could not have been that causative *do* was *generalized* to such unmarked verbs as a redundant but semantically contentful marker. While redundancy is rife in grammars, grammaticalization theory has little or no room for the conventionalization of zero-marking.

Similarly, Visser's (1963–73: §1413–4) account based on the generalization of "substitutive *do*" fails in that, as Denison (1993: 277) notes, there are too few citations of the relevant construction, *do* used in conjunction with an infinitive.

9.5.2. Habituality?

However, to derive periphrastic *do* from more recent presentations is similarly difficult. For example, Garrett (1998) proposes that *do* was first recruited as a habitual marker, used first with deverbal nominals (*do reste* "do some rest") which were reinterpreted as verbs when their verbal sources (here, *resten*) were phonetically eroded such that they were identical with their deverbal derivates (i.e. the verb, too, was now *reste*).

However, the problem is why once the nominals were reinterpreted as verbs, habitual *do* devolved into a syntactic place-filler instead of retaining its habitual semantics. Garrett proposes a semantic reanalysis beginning in *do* used in negated sentences. The immediate connotation of a sentence like *Cows do not eat nettles* is the habitual one, that eating nettles is something that cows do not do. But it could also be taken as meaning that not eating nettles is something typical of cows – a descriptive rather than durative statement. Under Garrett's analysis, when negation acquires scope over the entire proposition (*neg*-raising) in this way, it left the habitual marker semantically empty: now the sentence simply negated the concept of cows eating nettles, with habituality left by the wayside. Thus sentences that were "assertions of general nonexistence," Garrett states, "were strengthened to become assertions of nonexistence" (317).

Garrett's account, formalized in principles of theoretical semantics, is ingenious and elegant in itself. Yet, it does not explain why this is not a typical pathway of habitual markers worldwide, much less why it seems to have only happened in English. Crucially, it does not explain why it could not have been that the new *neg*-raising interpretation could not have preserved the habitual semantics of *do* regardless, such that a sentence like "We do not eat dinner early on Saturday" would be reinterpreted to mean the still habitual "It is not the case that we are in the habit of eating dinner early on Saturday" rather than the habituality-neutral "The act of our eating on Saturday does not exist." Why, that is, did *do* not retain habitual semantics in such sentences even if subsumed to negation? Garrett's analysis seems to imply a certain inherent evanescence of habitual marking, which is perhaps tempting from the perspective of Modern English in which its indication in the present affirmative is a zero-marker (*We eat dinner early on Saturday*), but would be less so from the perspective of other languages that have overt habitual markers clearly and eternally central within their batteries of aspectual morphemes.

In that light, we also wonder why the habitual semantics of *do* in the affirmative, robust despite whatever tendencies threatened the negative usage, would not have *blocked* its semantic bleaching in the negative. Presumably, while *neg*-raising semantics were threatening *do* in the negative, in affirmative sentences, semantically central to human expression, *do*'s habitual semantics would still have been transparent and reinforced by constant usage.

Also, Garrett's analysis does not conclusively demonstrate that early auxiliary *do* was in fact a habitual marker. He acknowledges that out of the

195 pre-1400 citations of periphrastic *do* that he bases his argument upon, no fewer than 39 percent of them (i.e. virtually 40 percent, which could be parsed as ominously close to half) are not habitual. Even after accounting for some of the exceptions by surmising that conditional sentences carry an inherent negative inference that would encourage a similar reanalysis of *do,* and sidelining others as idiosyncratically advanced ones already behaving like modern periphrastic *do* in negative, interrogative and inverted sentences, the volume of exceptions remains problematic. Garrett notes that "almost 75 percent" are not (320), but then it could also be put that one in four of the citations in his corpus do not fit his hypothesis – for reasons that he leaves to "future research."

Finally, on the subject of habitual *do,* Garrett's supporting proposition that *do* is also used habitually in German dialects must be seen as founded upon too brief a reference to the data to be conclusive. He notes this Low German sentence as "apparently habitual":

(28)   *Sei   dain   em   Nats on heitn.*
       they do.PAST.3P 3S.DAT Nats PT call.INF
       'They used to call him Nats.'
                        (Grimme 1922: 126, cited in Garrett 1998: 313)

But this is only one sentence. And while his citing habitual descriptions of the usage of auxiliary *do* in two other German dialects must be acknowledged, these are passing comments in sources written at the turn of the previous century. In this light, it bears mentioning that while *do* in these dialects gives ready appearance of being a habitual marker upon passing analysis of the kind that these early grammarians lent the construction, more extended and concentrated studies such as Abraham & Conradie (2001), as well as modern descriptions of the dialects such as those in Russ (1990), give no indication that a habitual analysis captures the essence of the behavior of German dialects' auxiliary *do.* Garrett does not engage modern sources on German dialects' usage of *do,* and in general only addresses the issue briefly.

There looms, then, a possibility that the nexus between negative habitual and universal semantics, and the theoretical plausibility that the latter could have overtaken the former, were in fact not the source of periphrastic *do.* Rather, it is equally plausible theoretically that periphrastic *do* was modelled on, for example – periphrastic *do* already existing in another language such as Cornish.

Importantly, if the rendition in English of Cornish's *do* did have even a leaning towards habitual semantics, this by no means belies its source in transfer from a Celtic item whose behavior was determined by syntax.

Transfer, after all, is almost never precise between languages. Cushitic languages have a causative double suffix; Ethio-Semitic, influenced by Cushitic acquirers, has a causative double *prefix* (Thomason & Kaufman 1988: 135). Nguni Bantu languages like Xhosa and Zulu have click consonants inherited from Khoi-San languages, but never in remotely the proliferation as in the latter. As to a syntactic construction being rendered in a borrowing language as a semantic one as English would have rendered a Celtic periphrastic *do* as a habitual marker, Saramaccan Creole's rendition of the Niger-Congo Kwa language Fongbe's reduplication is an analogue. In Fongbe, property items (adjectival concepts) are syntactically obliged to occur in reduplicated form when used attributively:

(29)(a)   sáki ɔ̀ **wì**
           bag DEF black
           'The bag is black.'

   (b)   sáki **wìwì**   ɔ̀
          bag black.black DEF
          'the black bag.'

                                (Lefebvre & Brousseau 2002: 358–9)

Saramaccan, with a syntax deeply parallel to Fongbe's given that a preponderance of its creators spoke that language natively, has reduplicated verbs as attributive adjectives as well, but only as a *semantic* construction. In Saramaccan, with stative verbs the reduplication encodes counterexpectational semantics, such that *dí **baákabaáka** sáku* would mean "the blackened bag" (as by fire), i.e. "that bag that is, against what you would expect, black." "The black bag" is simply *dí **baáka** sáku,* whereas in Fongbe this unreduplicated usage would be ungrammatical given that the reduplication is syntactically required of property items when occurring in the attributive.

   Here then, is a living example of a mechanism via which English would incorporate Cornish's periphrastic *do* that is both theoretically plausible – like Garrett's account – but also cross-linguistically typical, which Garrett's account is not. We could propose that English took on Cornish's periphrastic *do* with a semantic leaning, but only that, towards habituality – encouraged by the action-focused semantics of the verb *do,* although the particular Cornish rendition happened not to be colored by such and was solely syntactically conditioned. We must choose between Garrett's ingenious but studied semantic pathway to periphrastic *do* – unparalleled anywhere else among the world's languages – and an account that stipulates that English simply incorporated periphrastic *do* from a language that *had it already.*

9.5.3. Perfectivity?

Denison's (1985, 1993) account of periphrastic *do* as a semantic bleaching of what began as a perfective marker leaves similar questions. Denison (1993: 264) refers to sentences such as *His sclauyn he dude dun legge* "He laid down his pilgrim's-cloak" as indicating this perfective function, but like Garrett, is faced with quite a few exceptions. Namely, in his corpus of references, 30 sentences are activities or states as against about 400 that conform to his analysis (Denison 1985: 54), such that its support in the 1200s and 1300s qualifies in his own estimation as only "broad" (Denison 1993: 281). Interestingly, the exceptional 30, with their imperfective semantics, could support Garrett's habitual analysis instead, and in general, the historical data's amenability to accounts based on aspectual concepts as distinct as the habitual and the perfective can be taken as suggesting that the very quest to treat early auxiliary *do* as expressing any single aspect is futile. We return to the case that English's usage of *do* was simply modelled on the semantically empty usage in Cornish.

In any case, Denison otherwise appeals to speculations that are theoretically questionable. An example is his claim (1993: 281) that *do* developed its perfective function as compensation for English's loss of Germanic derivational prefixes like *be-*, *for-* and *ge-* that had carried considerable functional load in expressing aspectual distinctions. This is a brilliant analysis – except that as Denison readily indicates, we must reconstruct that this perfective usage of *do* for some reason did not last, and devolved into the semantically neutral periphrastic one that concerns us. Denison supposes that *do*'s compensation for the loss of the prefixes was a passing "experiment" – but we must ask just why it was. That is, why didn't *do* remain a perfective marker until today? There is no theoretical basis in the tenets of diachronic syntax or semantics for a process in which constructions arise as "experiments" only to mysteriously evanesce. The derivational prefixes did not return, and as such we wonder what general principle would have motivated that *do,* purportedly entrenched among certain generations of English speakers as a perfective marker, would then strangely bleach into a semantically empty syntactic place-filler even though the derivational prefixes remained gone forever. Just why did the "experiment" fail? Importantly, Denison, unlike Garrett, does not propose a theoretical semantic pathway via which this devolution would have been predictable or even natural.

Also relevant: Old Norse also lost the derivational prefixes, and while in Mainland Scandinvian, they were restored by contact with Low German (Braunmüller 2002: 1037–8), Icelandic and Faroese remain lacking them.

And yet *do* has not compensated for their loss in these languages by becoming a perfective marker, despite Old Norse having used its *do*-verb as an auxiliary in other uses (albeit not analogously to periphrastic *do*).

Denison, perhaps aware of such problems, brings in a reinforcing factor, proposing that the causative usage of *faire* "to do" in French influenced English's *do* (Denison 1993: 279). However, this contravenes the magisterial argumentation of Thomason & Kaufman (1988: 306–15) that French speakers were never numerous enough, or in intimate enough contact, with most English speakers to affect English grammatically. Namely, for French grammar to have affected English, there would have to have been a critical mass of Francophones mastering English incompletely and passing on their rendition to the Anglophone masses. There is no evidence that this was the case: rather, French was spoken by a small elite rarely encountered by most English speakers, such that this elite's renditions of English, however incomplete, would have had no appreciable effect upon English grammar over time.

Thomason & Kaufman are mainly concerned with refuting the idea that French speakers developed an English creole, but their argumentation also refutes that French speakers could have had even less dramatic influence on English grammar. Sociohistorical circumstances in Norman-ruled England were not ones that would have conditioned language-shift effects; rather, French affected English only in the superficial layer of lexical incursion, and this largely via the written medium. Denison developed his analysis before Thomason & Kaufman's study existed (and given the realities of academic publishing, even his 1993 article would have been written long before a book released in 1988 would have become an established reference). But the fact remains that today, French influence must be judged as incapable of supporting an account of English grammatical diachrony.

9.5.4. A reinforcement for SVO order?

Kroch, Myhill & Pintzuk's (1982) explanation for the emergence of periphrastic *do* has a potential explanatory power less evident in Garrett's and Denison's presentations – but still runs up against cross-linguistic generality. They propose an explanation for why in modern English periphrastic *do* is limited to negated and inverted sentences. This is useful, in addressing an important discrepancy between Brythonic Celtic and Modern English: e.g. Cornish uses *do* in affirmative sentences as well. While Kroch et al. are not concerned with the CH, the eclipse of the affirmative usage stands as a question under the CH, and their account offers a solution.

Namely, they propose that *do*'s usage in the negative and interrogative brought the relevant sentences in line with the SVO order that became regular in Middle English in contrast to Old English's SOV order in subordinate clauses and frequent VS order elsewhere. As such, in a newly SVO language, *do*-support in negative and interrogative sentences would iron out the cognitive dissonance of sentences like *Alas wherefore lighteth me the sonne?* (462), by displacing the main verb after the subject (*Alas, why does the sun light me?*). We might suppose that English first inherited Cornish's use of periphrastic *do* across the board, but then trimmed its usage to the negative and interrogative for reasons of processability amidst the grammar's transition into SVO word order.

As useful as this idea is, the question still remains: why was a semantically empty dummy *do* available for such recruitment in the first place? If this account were valid by itself, then presumably, worldwide, there would be various languages which, after a transition from SOV to SVO word order, would have brought a *do*-verb (or maybe a *be*-verb?) into such a usage. For example, Latin was primarily SOV. Wouldn't we expect, then, that *just one* of the countless grammars that have evolved from it, all of them today SVO, would have a reflex of Latin's *facere* as a dummy place-filler in negated and inverted sentences? Yet none of them, not French or Spanish, not the most nonstandard dialect of Portuguese on the Iberian peninsula or the obscurest and most untutored dialect of Romanian, and in no village dialect of Occitan or Catalan and in no mountain variety of Italian or Rhaeto-Romance in between, display any such thing. The author is aware of a single glimmer of such: in the Monnese dialect of Italian, *do* is used as a place-filler, but only in interrogative sentences, and even here, only in non-subject ones (Beninca & Poletto 2004). The famous SOV-SVO transition in West Africa (Hyman 1975) yielded no languages documented to date that English diachrony specialists could point to as showing that *do* typically becomes a syntactic place filler due to exigencies created by word order change.

Kroch, Myhill & Pintzuk's argument alone is, then, a just-so story. It "explains" only a particular situation via what, very technically, could have been, rather than what actually tends to be.

The argument instead can be taken as, in fact, entailing that English was in contact with another grammar in which *do* had already become, by chance, a dummy auxiliary. To put it another way, the fact that Cornish already had such a place-filler cannot be taken as irrelevant to English's developing one, nor can it be taken as a mere "possible factor" – rather, it must be seen as a crucial factor. This is because innumerable grammars making the transition from SOV to SVO do not bring in *do* to *obligatorily* disambiguate syntactic patterns that disturb SVO order – this including not some but *all* Germanic grammars except English. More to the point, it would appear that nowhere in the world have, or do, languages recruit their *do* verb in this fashion as a processing strategy except in the British Isles. Clearly, Celtic was the reason that English did.

It is true that English may have been especially ripe for *do* to be recruited this way given the general Germanic tendency for *do* to lose a certain amount of lexical content and serve in assorted grammatical, pragmatic and place-filling roles. However, again, English was the only one in which the process resulted in the uniquely meaningless and purely syntactic function of peri-phrastic *do:* mirrored in the languages indigenous to its island. Celtic, again, played the decisive role, not a marginal one.

The question becomes: what scientific basis justifies dismissing Cornish as the source of this recruitment of *do,* or even marginalizing it as merely a "possible influence"? What other factors qualify as more or even equally possible? Which other factors are so theoretically compelling as to disqualify Cornish as anything less than pivotal to the scenario? These questions, and the argumentation in this section, apply to any accounts of periphrastic *do* that have appealed, or will in the future, to processing problems in the wake of changes in English auxiliaries and word order during Middle English.

Obviously English did not incorporate all of Celtic's grammatical features. Kroch, Myhill & Pintzuk's article can be taken as a principled explanation of why English incorporated one of them, periphrastic *do.* It is hardly unsci-entific to propose that periphrastic *do* was useful for processing reasons in a language moving from SOV to SVO. But this also requires that we treat Cornish as the source of the construction.

The idea that Cornish and Welsh borrowed periphrastic *do* from English is well entrenched among English specialists who have occasion to assess the Celtic hypothesis. As for the existence of periphrastic *do* in Breton, one might observe that there were extensive contacts between Cornish and Breton people over the centuries, such that just perhaps, Cornish lent Breton periphrastic *do.* However, this English-to-Celtic hypothesis is highly strained given the full range of the evidence.

My hypothesis is that the reason English is the only Germanic language with periphrastic *do* as an obligatory place-filler is because it developed in contact with Celtic languages which have this kind of construction as well. That Welsh, Cornish and Breton share this usage of periphrastic *do* is, I as-sume along the lines of traditional historical linguistic analysis, that their an-cestral language had this trait, and that therefore the three modern languages have had the trait since their origin.

The English-to-Celtic hypothesis stipulates the following:

> Most Germanic languages use periphrastic *do* only to a limited extent. Only in English did *do* happen, by chance, to become an obligatory syntactic place-filler. This trait then passed into Welsh and Cornish. Breton was at first unaffected, but eventually, Cornish lent the construction to Breton across the English Channel.

This analysis is, quite simply, less economical than my own and that of other adherents of the CH. It relies infelicitously on chance; to an unseasoned observer of work on the history of English, it would appear curious that this analysis was considered traditional or ordinary.

For example, it is quite natural that Cornish and Breton people remained in contact over time. However, we have no independent reason to suppose that this contact was intimate enough to lend Breton a new syntactic construction. For example, Tristram (1995) argues that retroflex *r* crossed the channel into Breton: however, uvular *r* is well-known to have spread throughout much of Europe without being accompanied by syntactic disruption. Humans regularly, after all, speak a second language with phonological features of their native language, the most difficult level of natively-acquired language for adults to erase in acquiring a new one, while rendering the grammar quite accurately.

9.6. CH Objection Number Four: Periphrastic *do* appears too late to have been modelled on Celtic

Periphrastic *do* first appears in Early Middle English, in southwestern texts of c. 1300. English speakers had first encountered Brythonic-speaking Celts in the 400s, almost a thousand years before, and yet there is no evidence of periphrastic *do* in the vast Old English literature.

This has been seen by many as counterevidence to a Celtic account. As Ellegård (1953: 119) had it regarding Celtic influence, "I do not see any reason why it should have been stronger in the 13th century than during all the previous centuries that the races had been in contact."

The observation is well-taken, but various CH adherents have argued that we can expect that constructions like periphrastic *do,* if developed by Celtic speakers, could easily have been restricted to the vernacular register for a long period, considered "low" speech unsuitable for the print medium. An especially succinct rendition was by Dal (1952: 113), for which, because it was written in German, I offer a translation:[1]

> However, the primary justification for our take on the issue is that the sociohistorical relationships in question indicate that we would, precisely, *not* expect ample usage of syntactic Celticisms in the Old English literature. The Celts were the oppressed group; to the extent that they expressed themselves in the English language, this carried the stigma of the speech of the vulgate, of a sort that was to be avoided in refined literary language. Certainly, then, it is hardly unexpected that constructions of the quotidian language of the masses could thrive for centuries without appearing in the written register.

(See also Vennemann 2001; Klemola 2002: 207.) In this section I would like to flesh out this point: Dal was correct that if Celts contributed periphrastic *do,* then its delayed appearance in texts was nothing short of ordinary. For it to have occurred in Old English texts would have been a stark contradiction of sociolinguistic realities typical of written languages worldwide since time immemorial.

9.6.1. Dating periphrastic *do* to 1100: The nature of Early Middle English texts

In assessing whether Celts contributed periphrastic *do* to English on the basis of the documentation, it must be held front and center that Early Middle English texts are an especially approximate reflection of the reality of the spoken language at the time, such that periphrastic *do* may very well have been widespread, at least in a certain region of Britain, earlier than 1300. Namely, the nature of the texts of the period in no sense establish that the construction existed only by 1300, and indicate nothing implausible in the construction's occurring at least as far back as the beginning of the Middle English period in 1100.

First, documentation of English from 1100 to 1300 is notably sparse (Laing 2000: 103–4). This means that to the extent that periphrastic *do* first appears

---

1 Original version:

Das Hauptargument für unsere Auffasung der Sache ist aber, dass wir wegen der historischen und sozialen Verhältnisse keine reiche Verwendung von syntakischen Keltizismen in der altengl. Literatur erwarten *können.* Die Kelten waren das unterdrückte Volk, ihre Syntax, soweit sie in englischer Sprache zur Ausdruck kam, trug das Gepräge von Vulgarismus, der von der gepflegten Literatursprache vermieden werden musste. Es is gewiss keine Seltenheit, dass Konstruktionen der vulgären und alltäglischen Sprache Jahrhunderte lang leben können, ohne in der Schriftsprache zu erscheinen.

in two 1300 texts, it could easily have been accidental that no text was written, or survived, in which the construction occurred as early as 1100.

In addition, English documents at this time are highly variable in terms of dialectal diversity (Dobson 1962, Milroy 1992, Smith 2000). English was re-emerging as a written medium after centuries of replacement by French, and its transcription reflected the changes that the spoken language had undergone during this time (and likely, as agreed upon by all analysts in reference to extent of inflectional erosion, even during the Old English period). As with all primarily oral languages spoken over vast distances, there was considerable dialectal divergence, and Middle English would only be standardized starting in the 1400s. This means that if periphrastic *do* emerged in a particular dialect or dialect group, then its attestation at all in a multi-dialectal corpus from 1100 to 1300 is a matter of chance. Its absence in texts written before 1300 in other dialects cannot be taken as indication it had not yet arisen in the southwest before this.

9.6.2. Dating periphrastic *do* to the fifth century, A.D.: The conservativity of the written medium

The next question is why periphrastic *do* is entirely absent in Old English texts. Here is where observations such as Dal's are relevant. The nut of the case is that writing the way you talk is a modern idea: for Old English speakers, writing was an elite, codified and static activity.

We have concrete evidence of this in that even when written English was "reborn" as Early Middle English, the centuries-deep tradition of Old English writing exerted a conservative pull on how the language was rendered on the page. Middle English between 1100 and 1300 varies between the new variety reflecting spoken norms and more antique varieties reflecting the Old English tradition. In fact, *most* Early Middle English is distinctly conservative (Laing 2000: 105, Sweet 1892: 211). The *Owl and the Nightingale* text of c. 1200 retains grammatical gender marking on definite articles and nouns; the *Ancrene Visse* text of c. 1215 retains Old English features such as the genitive plural, present-tense plural and infinitive endings.

However, the general tendency in Middle English is for English to be written reflecting realities of regional variation to an extent vastly surpassing that in the Old English corpus. This was because Middle English represents the revival of writing in English after a 150-year "blackout" period during the Norman takeover. As Norman control receded starting in the 1200's and English was again written in on a regular basis, the chain had been broken in ancient scribal traditions. The scene was set for a more honest transcription of the language onto paper. This, then, is exactly when we would expect a feature like a periphrastic *do,* previously barred from writing as a "colloquialism," to appear on the page.

Thus arguments such as Dal's and others' that Celtic features could have been established in spoken English for centuries before they were used in written English should be received not as particular and athletic surmises referring to English alone, but as applying to English diachrony a typical phenomenon of register differentiation in language use worldwide since the invention of writing. The differentiation has always been especially robust in societies that have not known the democratic impulses in the wake of the Reformation and the Enlightenment, which encouraged the ushering of vernacular varieties into the written realm.

It could be ventured that specialists in the history of English are skeptical of the "delay" hypothesis of CH adherents partly because they live in societies in which, because of these very democratic impulses, a relatively close correspondence between spoken and written language is ordinary. In contrast, in Early Middle English speakers' world, speakers of what we know today as the Romance languages still encountered Latin on the page as the closest written equivalent to their everyday speech – while as often as not, the English speaker found on the page (if in an essentially pre-literate society they ever engaged writing at all) an inflection-heavy tongue alien to what they had learned on their mother's knee.

In this light, in a rigidly hierarchical pre-Magna Carta England in which writing was restricted to formal subjects and literacy was the province of a small elite, a gulf between spoken and written language equivalent to that between Moroccan and Modern Standard Arabic would not be a surprise: that the gap was lesser almost qualifies as a quandary.

For example, Persian is another language whose middle stage of attestation reflects the emergence in writing of what had previously been relegated to the spoken register. Old Persian was a typical early Indo-European language, bristling with three genders, six case inflections dividing into declensional paradigms and displaying complex ablaut patterns, a proliferation of tenses and aspects expressed with conjugational paradigms, and so on. But just three centuries after the last attestations of this language whose grammar was akin to Sanskrit's, in the 300s B.C. Middle Persian attestations begin, in a language as anomalously light on inflection and other complexities as English is in comparison to its sisters (Khanlari 1979: 231). Certainly a change this vast did not occur in a mere three hundred years, before which the language had retained a typical Indo-European morphological battery for countless eons.

Iranian specialists suppose that these changes had already begun during the Old Persian period, but that the highly formal contexts in which Old Persian had been written discouraged the transcription of the spoken reality. Indeed, late Old Persian reveals the very beginnings of the breakdown of the case system (Schmitt 1989: 60), although nothing remotely approaching the vast simplifications evident in Middle Persian. It is assumed that the cracks in the dam evident in the latest Old Persian data were due to transcribers by then writing Old Persian as a different language, their everyday language being an inflectionally light one like Middle Persian. This latter kind of Persian only appears in writing in full bloom after a profound sociological dislocation, when an empire had been overthrown by a new regime. There is no reason to suppose that the situation was different between Old and Middle English.

After all, in many modern languages there is a gulf between written and spoken language that reflects the situation before the emergence of Middle Persian and Middle English; i.e, the very definition of diglossia. The classic case here is the relationship between Swiss and High German in Switzerland as outlined in Ferguson's classic article (1972). However, it bears reviewing how thoroughly typical such splits are, occurring in languages less generally familiar than German or Italian.

The standard Indonesian used in writing and formal, public contexts contrasts with the vernacular varieties most of its speakers use as everyday speech, which vastly simplify the standard language's derivational machinery (Gil 2002). Standard Finnish is spoken everyday by no one: the colloquial language includes various "evolved" constructions such as (Karlsson 1999: 245–8):

(30)
vienkö minä > vienks mä "Shall I take?"
he tulevat > ne (those) *tulee* (sing. ending) "they come"
autolla > autol "by car"
me sanomme > me sanotaan (passive) "we say"

The last construction above, in which the colloquial version is an alternative (a passive usage) rather than a phonetic erosion is useful as a transition to showing that spoken language can differ from written not only in abbreviations, but in substitutions – of the kind such as, in Early Middle English, using auxiliary *do* plus a main verb as an alternate to sentences with matrix verbs alone.

In the Finnish case, we see the passive, not a simplification but a substitution, used in place of the indicative. This involves variation between constructions available within a single language. But elsewhere, we get closer to our proposition re a Celtic-induced periphrastic *do:* "substitution" modelled on a substrate language, never reaching print except in academic linguistic publications.

An example is the influence of Quechua on Spanish in Ecuador. The most prominently covered language variety here is Media Lengua, a "mixed" or "intertwined" language that uses Spanish lexical items with Quechua morphological affixes, phonology, and syntax. However, Ecuadorians also speak Spanish dialects with varying degrees of influence from Quechua less extreme than in Media Lengua (*ocupado estoy* busy I-am "I'm busy," reflecting Quechua's SOV word order [Lipski 1994: 251]; *de Juan su sombrero* 'of John his hat' based on Quechua *Huwan-pa ch'uku-n* Juan-GEN hat-his) – Spanish with moderate grammatical interference from Quechua. These varieties reach the page only in academic works by linguists: in the consciousness of Ecuadorians they are strictly spoken language, with no written presence over countless centuries.

Another example is the impact of Berber languages on the spoken Arabic of Morocco. Berber nomads relocated to this area soon after Arabic speakers reached it, to the extent of constituting a majority of the population of settlements there, and Berber dynasties ruled from the end of the tenth century into the fifteenth (Abun-Nasr 1987; Versteegh 1997). Today, Moroccan Arabic contrasts with other colloquial (i.e. largely unwritten) Arabic dialects in its especially pronounced loss of short vowels and reduction of long ones. This is surely due to influence from the notoriously vowel-shy Berber languages (Kaye & Rosenhouse 1997: 265). Yet, this variety of Arabic, the native language of millions for a millennium-plus, is and always has been all but absent from the written medium.

We might imagine a thought experiment, in which at some point in the future, in Morocco Moroccan Arabic replaces Modern Standard Arabic as the written variety. It is plausible that sociological reality would at first mean that for many or most writers, writing Moroccan Arabic would mean nudging the dialect towards standard – that is, purportedly "good" – Arabic by restoring vowels that Berberization has eliminated, out of a lay sense that the elided vowels were "sloppy" subtractions. This would be entirely plausible given the lay assumption that language is words rather than grammar. It is equally plausible that over time, as public memory of the earlier place of Modern Standard Arabic faded and the relentless spoken reality of Moroccan Arabic had its effect, that this "revocalization" would gradually disappear. As such, Moroccan Arabic would only come to be written in phonetically accurate form long after contact with Berber speakers conditioned that very variety, before which a Berber-influenced Arabic had been spoken as a living home language for centuries.

In which case: imagine future linguists supposing that this meant that the elided vowels were not conditioned by Berber because they appeared in documents so long after Berber speakers encountered Arabic. Naturally many linguists would craft deft accounts via which the vowel elisions were internal developments – but leaving as a question why this did not happen in colloquial Arabics elsewhere, and neglecting that Moroccan Arabic was created by speakers of languages notoriously given to reducing and eliding vowels.

Examples continue: in a thousand years, linguists could easily be unaware that the Mandarin Chinese of Singapore has a fifth tone because of influence from Min Chinese (Chen 1983), or that Taiwanese Mandarin is replete with Min features (Kubler 1985). Written documentation of these varieties is minimal to nonexistent. The argument that prescriptivism barred Celtic features from written English for a very long time is not a nimble feint, but a thoroughly typical historical reconstruction.

To wit: if Celtic influence were rife as early as Old English texts, then this would be so peculiar as to be nothing less than problematic for the CH. Faced with grammatical Celticisms in Old English documents, a reasonable strategy would be to search for evidence that the Celtic influence had occurred in Northern Europe via continental Celts, before Anglo-Saxon was brought to Britain. Pushing the Celtic influence back to this extent would allow for a typical extended period during which vernacular varieties are considered "bad" speech, which would be the only coherent reason that by the time it was put on the page, Old English would already have Celtic grammatical influence. That is, we would suppose that English's transplantation to British soil would have encouraged an honest rendition of a variety that in Northern Europe had long been considered "tainted" by aliens. The last thing we would expect is that in Britain, an indigenized, non-native rendition of English that emerged on that island would have been readily transcribed on the page as soon as it emerged.

9.7. CH Objection Number Five: There are too few Celtic loanwords in English

Certainly a natural expectation is that if Celts significantly affected English grammar, then they would also have affected its lexicon, lexicon being the most readily exchanged feature in language contact. As such, it would appear problematic for the CH that, for example, Kastovsky (1992: 318–9) lists only fourteen Celtic borrowings in English – most obsolete – beyond place names and mostly defunct ones introduced by Christian missionaries from Ireland.

However, the problem is in fact illusory. When speakers shift to a new language, they may well incorporate L1 lexical items in their rendition – but they may just as well do so to only a marginal extent, acquiring the L2 lexicon essentially in its entirety. As Thomason & Kaufman (1988: 117) have it:

> We can be confident about only one retrospective generalization in this area: if the language of a shifting population did *not* contribute lexicon to the target language, other than a few words for local natural and cultural items, then we can conclude that the shifting population did not enjoy much social or political prestige.

Put another way, of course, this is to say that a group without prestige (i.e. the Celts under English rule) can *not* contribute significant lexicon. This has been the case with various languages that are the product of language shift.

For example, the Uralic influence on Russian grammar is uncontroversial, although opinions differ on specifics. Yet there are only a couple of dozen Uralic loanwords in Russian, most of them marginal (Kiparsky 1969: 23). Similarly, despite the rich Dravidian influence on Indo-Aryan grammar, while the contact situation lent many Dravidian loanwords in early Sanskrit, the number decreases in later Sanskrit, is even lower in Sanskrit's descendant Prakrit, and then, despite a millennium of subsequent contact between Dravidian languages and Modern Indo-Aryan ones, there have been almost no new Dravidian loanwords (Burrow 1955: 380–6).

Thus: Russian marks objects as genitive in negative sentences just as Finnish marks objects in negative sentences as partitive; the Russian possessive is a nonverbal one marking the possessor as an oblique (*u menja kniga* 'at me book' "I have a book") just as in Finnish (which uses the dative) while other Slavic languages use a *have* verb; and so on. The Uralic impact on Russian's grammar cannot be denied. Yet there is no significant battery of Finnic or Uralic lexical items in Russian.

This means that it is theoretically unproblematic that English could have Celtic grammatical influence, such as periphrastic *do,* without a battery of Celtic loanwords. The useful schema is Russian/Uralic versus English/Celtic. The CH stipulates that the extent of grammatical influence is equivalent, and in evaluating that, we must keep in mind that the Russian/Uralic relation entails no significant lexical influence. If we accept that Russian contains grammatical peculiarities due to Uralic despite having little Uralic lexical influence, then we cannot dismiss the CH because of the paucity of Celtic loanwords in English.

Finally, Celtic loanwords beyond the "cultural" have not been as utterly rare in English as traditionally implied. Breeze (2002 and elsewhere) compellingly presents hitherto neglected Celtic etymologies of numerous words such as *brag, brat, curse,* and *baby.* It must be mentioned that these four are among the very few of the words Breeze adduces that lasted beyond Middle or even Old English: he refers mostly to archaisms now unknown. What Breeze attributes this mysterious evanescence of Celtic borrowings to, in contrast to the hardiness of most Scandinavian lexical items in English, is unclear. However, to the extent that one is skeptical that language shift could leave essentially no loanwords of significance at all, Breeze's findings will be useful: at least in the past, English picked up plenty of Celtic words beyond names of towns.

There is also a Celtic lexical contribution in regional dialects of English that conclusively indicates Celts shifting to English but retaining in their rendition words especially resistant to translation: "sheep-scoring" numbers, actually less for counting sheep than in children's games, knitting, and nursery rhymes. They have been recorded in northern areas, mostly in the 1800s, and are clearly from a Celtic variety closely related to Welsh (Barry 1969, Klemola 2000). Here, for example, are the numbers from one to twenty compared with modern Welsh ones:

	Welsh		Welsh
1 aina	un	11 aina-dig	un-ar-ddeg
2 peina	dau	12 peina-dig	deuddeg
3 para	tri	13 para-dig	tri-ar-ddeg
4 pedera	pedwar	14 pedera-dig	pedwar-ar-ddeg
5 pump	pump	15 bumfit	pymtheg
6 ithy	chwech	16 aina-lumfit	un-ar-bymtheg
7 mithy	saith	17 peina-bumfit	dau-ar-bymtheg
8 owera	wyth	18 para-lumfit	deunaw
9 lavera	naw	19 pedera-bumfit	pedwar-ar-bymtheg
10 dig	deg	20 giggy	ugain

These numbers prove that Celtic speakers did not mysteriously vanish upon the appearance of Germanic speakers, but instead survived and mastered English over time. Their retention of Brythonic numerals for culturally entrenched practices is hardly surprising – and it would actually be unexpected that their rendition of English would retain only this remnant of their native tongue.

We might imagine speakers of whatever our own native language happens to be, of foreign heritage, speaking our language indistinguishably from ourselves except for mysteriously reverting to foreign numbers when counting certain animals or engaging in word play. Readily we suppose that at some earlier stage of contact, these people's ancestors would have not only used these numbers, but rendered our language with an accent – i.e., that there was at least phonological interference from their native language. And then, it would be hard to conceive of a reason that the same people would not have rendered the language with some morphological or syntactic interference from that native language as well.

9.8. Why not just Celts?

Of course, the strongest version of the CH is that both the simplification and the mixture were due to Celtic influence: many CH arguments note Proto-Germanic features lacking in English that also happen to be absent or weak in Celtic grammar (e.g. Vennemann 2001 on the external possessor construction, Tristram 2002 on inflection). However, this kind of widespread *elimination* of features absent in the L1 is not, actually, typical of cases of language shift over long periods of time. Supposing so perhaps underestimates the capability of shifting speakers to acquire unfamiliar L2 features, especially given that such cases occur over multiple generations amidst rich opportunites for exposure.

For example, Dravidian languages mark biological gender and animacy but not grammatical gender. Indo-Aryan languages are replete with features inherited from Dravidian to an extent that indicates that Dravidian speakers acquired Indo-Aryan varieties in vast numbers. Yet Indo-Aryan languages tend strongly to retain grammatical gender despite its absence in Dravidian, with Marathi being an Indo-Aryan language that retains three genders despite eons-long contact with Dravidian Kannada to the south. That is, Dravidian speakers acquired Indo-Aryan grammatical gender. Or: Altaic languages have no tones, and yet indigenized varieties of Mandarin that its speakers have created are richly tonal (cf. Lee-Smith 1996).

Widespread *abbreviation* of grammatical machinery is typically associated, rather, with rapid acquisition within a single generation. Pidginization is the most extreme example, but the parallels between pidginization and fuller but still incomplete acquisition are well-known (Andersen 1983, Veenstra 2003). Here, the Scandinavian invaders fit the profile, being newcomers who rapidly assimilated into the pre-existing society. The Celts, indigenous inhabitants coping with Anglo-Saxon settlement over several centuries while retaining their natuve tongues, do not. Rather, we would expect that they would have acquired English in relatively full form, but infusing it over generations with Celticisms in *additional* fashion, creating an Anglo-Celtic hybrid along the lines of the blending of Australian languages described by Heath (1978) or Amazonian languages as described by Aikhenvald (1999).

In addition, what is known about the emergence and spread of the features distinguishing English from its sisters further supports that the Norse speakers subtracted from the grammar while the Celts added to it. It is well established that the elimination of grammatical gender began in the north and spread southwards. This has also been demonstrated for the loss of V2 syntax (Kroch & Taylor 1997) and there is suggestive evidence along the same lines for some other constructions (McWhorter 2002: 255–6). There is known to me no argument that a case of simplification proceeded from any region but the north.

In contrast, Celtic impact on English traces to various regions, and conditioned additions rather than subtractions. The emergence of *do* as an auxiliary is agreed to have begun in the southwest by all specialists, regardless of their position on the CH. But the Northern Subject Rule (in which third-person plural agreement [i.e. zero-marking] occurs only with a) the subject pronoun rather than full NPs and b) only when the pronoun and the verb are adjacent, such that *Birds flies* but *They peel and boils them*) occurs to this day only in northern Englishes.

This is exactly what we would expect of Celts shifting gradually to English across a vast expanse of space: sociohistorical and even fortuitous particularities establishing different L1 transfers in different locations. An analogy would be Finnic influence on Russian: northern Russian dialects have inherited a syllable-initial stress pattern, but central and southern ones instead likely inherited a different Finnic feature, the *akan'je* transformation of [o] to [a] or [ə] in unstressed syllables from Finnic languages of that area (Thomason & Kaufman 1988: 241; 244–5). What would be peculiar in Britain is if the transfers all occurred in a single region and spread from there, in which case the question would arise as to what suppressed L1 transfer in all but that given region.

We would expect, then, that if Celts were the sole or principal agents in the transformation of English, then the result would have been a Britain-wide hybrid of Germanic and Celtic grammar with no significant degree of simplification in comparison to languages of either original family. When Ethio-Semitic was influenced by Cushitic languages, the result was not that Amharic, Tigrinya et al. were oddly grammatically streamlined compared to Arabic and Hebrew. The grammatical mixture described in South America by scholars like Aikhenvald (1999) does not yield languages less grammatically complex than that of their relatives.

What actually resulted in English suggests two processes. One group was infusing the grammar with L1 strategies, creating, as it were, a Celticized Anglo-Saxon variety, while another group equally influential, the Scandinavian invaders, was acquiring and passing on an incomplete rendition of the grammar.

I am skeptical, therefore, of the longer lists of proposed Celtic inheritances in English that include things *absent* both in Celtic and in English. It is not impossible that Celts learning English may have eliminated an English feature they were unfamiliar with here and there. But general tendencies in language contact suggest that these cases would have been exceptions. Cases in which Celts transferred an L1 feature into English are therefore more compelling in arguments for the CH.

9.9. Standard of proof: what's good for the Balkan Sprachbund . . .

Attempts to trace periphrastic *do* to ordinary internal changes have been deeply considered and impressively deft, but in the end they all can be analyzed as suffering from an infelicitous degree of ad hocness. Meanwhile, resistance to the CH account on the basis of the late appearance of periphrastic *do* in the documentation is based on a misunderstanding of the relationship between spoken and written language in most human societies.

This leaves us with the simple fact that the use of *do* as a semantically empty syntactic carrier of tense is extremely peculiar cross-linguistically, and that the only Germanic language that displays this use of *do* is the one that has been in historically documented close contact with semantically-empty *do*-happy Celtic languages for its entire history. Moreover, it can be concluded that the Celtic languages had the construction before English did, refuting the possibility that English developed periphrastic *do* on its own and passed it on to Celtic.

The evidence makes a strong case that English's periphrastic *do* is based on the transfer of a similar usage of *do* from a Brythonic language, most likely Cornish. Moreover, as White (2002) valuably notes, to the extent that contact accounts such as the Balkan Sprachbund are accepted despite ever lingering questions and ambiguities, the evidence allow more than that Celtic "may have" been "an influence." It was the direct cause.

For instance, in the Balkan Sprachbund, the replacement of infinitives with dependent constructions begins in Greek as far back as the Hellenistic koine and is also found as far afield as German (*Ich will, dass er geht* "I want him to go"). It is considered sound to venture that the Sprachbund may once have extended further, albeit without direct evidence of such. Kinks in the Celtic-English situation are hardly more damaging to the CH, in view of the weight of evidence pointing to a single conclusion.

For example, Garrett (1998: 295–6) argues that the CH account of periphrastic *do* is refuted by the fact that Celtic lexical influence is strong in the southwest only in the small region of the West Cornwall finger. For him, since in the southwest beyond this, lexical influence is slight, this means that certainly we would not expect deeper influence of a grammatical nature, such as the incorporation of an auxiliary *do*.

But as we have seen, grammatical transfer can occur without significant lexical influence. We can reasonably propose that Cornish speakers could have lent their English a periphrastic *do* even without retaining Celticisms such as *whidden* for "smallest pig of a litter," and that the retention of such items in West Cornwall was due to its relative geographical isolation. Crucially, to the extent that this could probably never be proven conclusively, our verdict on the CH account must be based on the other lines of evidence that point in one direction. Why don't traditional analysts of periphrastic *do*'s history have several languages around the world to refer to as models for the development of such an item? *Precisely why* would we not trace English's development of such a peculiar construction to its presence in the languages of the peoples its speakers encountered?

Similarly, while even affirmative *do* has been attested as surviving in regional English of much of the southwestern region (Cornwall English *Th' Queeryans **do** s'poase th' boanses **ded** b'long to a helk* "The Antiquarians suppose that the bones belonged to an elk" [Hancock 1994: 103]), it has been more rarely found in Devon (viz. Klemola 2002: 201–2). One might treat this as evidence that Cornish cannot be seen as the source of English's periphrastic *do*. But Klemola points out that Celtic-derived place-names are also strikingly sparse in Devon, and that it would seem that Celts were largely exterminated from this region or left it in massive numbers (cf. White 2002: 161). Again, documentational historical proof will likely never surface. But the important fact is that the grammatical anomaly in Devon does correlate with a lexical anomaly, and that the two facts together lend themselves to a plausible sociohistorical account (i.e. this would not be the case if instead, what was unusual about Devon was that its English devoiced final consonants).

Periphrastic *do* emerged eons ago in a society in which writing was an elite activity. Thus our sources constitute an approximate refraction of the spoken reality of their times. Moreover, their sparseness means that they have left to us little but whispers of local sociohistorical specifics. Inevitably, then, we will encounter odd wrinkles in the data that lend themselves to various interpretations. Our interest, then, will be in whether English and Brythonic's likenesses are likely to be accidental in light of their typological oddness. To the extent that we do not consider the Balkan Sprachbund a dubious case short of demographic and linguistic data obviously lost to history, we must allow that a CH account be deemed to stand under equivalent conditions.

9.10. Conclusion

It is reasonable, therefore, to assume a direct line of influence from Celtic to English. That is, without the Celtic model, English could easily make no use of *do* as an auxiliary at all, or would use *do* in the fashion of German dialects, probably in substitutive or perhaps habitual function, and quite possibly as a permanently nonstandard feature, varying in its usages across dialects.

The thesis suffers in no way from the fact that English happened to lose the usage of periphrastic *do* in the affirmative while this lives on in Brythonic Celtic. What is important is that the affirmative usage (and likely the others) were transferred at a given time. That after the point of transfer English grammar wended in a different direction than the Brythonic ones is normal: what would be strange is if after so much time, English mysteriously preserved in amber precisely the periphrastic *do* configuration it had nearly a millennium ago. After all, neither Welsh nor Cornish do.

Technically, to subscribe to the CH account of *do* leaves an important question: why would this be the only significant grammatical parallel between Brythonic and English? Put otherwise, if periphrastic *do* is a borrowed construction, then we must *predict* that Celtic contributed other constructions. Under this analysis, CH accounts of other features merit more attention than they have traditionally received.

The traditional diachronic account of English is that a West Germanic language was imported to Britain where it mysteriously shed most of its inflections and took on an awful lot of new words, and meanwhile developed some new constructions on its own like all grammars do.

The evidence, however, can be taken as indicating that a West Germanic language was imported to Britain where it was rendered much simpler grammatically when acquired by large numbers of North Germanic speakers, while at the same time it was infused with a degree of Celticisms that pulled its grammar even further from its origins – and then meanwhile was taking on an awful lot of new words.

English diachrony under this analysis included a fascinatingly wide range of language contact processes in interaction. It remains to be seen whether we need go so far as to treat English as virtually another Celtic grammar, as some CH accounts imply, and I for one doubt that this conception will prove valid. However, we must question the outright rejection of the CH – which includes allowing that Celtic may have had merely "some" influence, where this means – in practice – continuing to document the diachrony of English with Celtic playing anything less than a crucial role.

Rather, it seems reasonable to assume that Celtic mixture in English is modest but robust – robust enough that English could be classified as a language slightly simplified and slightly mixed. This, in terms of the typology of language contact proposed in Chapter One, would place English as, of all things, a semi-creole, in Box 5. As counterintuitive as this may seem in terms of conventions of terminology, under which creoles and semi-creoles are associated with Africans and/or plantation slavery, in the comparative sense the classification of English as semi-creole is quite ordinary. The difference between French and the semi-creole French of Reunionnais is, in gramd scheme, quite qualitatively similar to that between Old English and Modern English, as is that between Dutch and Afrikaans.

Table 57. Typology of language contact with English relocated

	lexicon only	lexicon and syntax	lexicon, syntax, morphology, phonology
no simplification	1. Germanic in Finnish	2. Romanian and other Balkan Sprachbund languages	3. Media Lengua Ancient language areas (Amazon, Australia)
some simplification on all levels	4. Persian, Indonesian, Mandarin, New Arabic, Swahili, Abun	5. **English**, Afrikaans Réunionnais French Singapore English	6. Shaba Swahili
extreme simplification on all levels	7. Hawaiian Creole Chinook Jargon creole	8. most creoles	9. Saramaccan Tok Pisin Berbice Creole Dutch

I remain agnostic as to whether resistance to the CH is rooted in British chauvinism (cf. German 2000). I might note that my new embrace of the CH is not based on any previous commitment to Celtic languages or culture. In that light, my Celtic surname is an inheritance from a nineteenth-century slaveowner; I am a black American, not Irish.

It is more empirically obvious that dismissal of the CH is sparked especially by the fact that periphrastic *do* and other proposed Celticisms do not occur in Old English texts. It is also encouraged by the sheer familiarity of core linguistic concepts such as habitual aspect and the INFL node, which founds so much work on English diachrony.

I submit that in view of the actual nature of the evidence for the CH, this dismissal qualifies as unscientific.

References

Aboh, Enoch and Umberto Ansaldo 2007 The role of typology in language creation: a descriptive take. In: Umberto, Matthews & Lim, 39–66.

Abraham, Werner and C. Jac Conradie 2001 *Präteritumschwund und Diskursgrammatik*. Amsterdam: John Benjamins.

Abun-Nasr, Jamil M. 1987 *A History of the Maghrib in the Islamic Period*. Cambridge: Cambridge University Press.

Adelaar, K. Alexander and David J. Prentice (with Cornelis D. Grijns, Hein Steinhauer and Aone van Engelenhoven) 1996 Malay: its history, role and spread. In Stephen. A. Wurm, Pieter Mühlhäusler & Darrell T. Tryon (eds.), *Atlas of Languages of Intercultural Communication in the Pacific, Asia, and the Americas* (Vol. II:1), 673–693. Berlin: Mouton De Gruyter.

Agheyisi, Rebecca 1986 *An Edo-English Dictionary*. Benin City: Ethiope Publishing Corporation.

Aikhenvald, Alexandra Y. 1999 Areal diffusion and language contact in the Içana-Vaupés basin, north-west Amazonia. In: Robert M.W. Dixon and Alexandra A. Aikhenvald (eds.), *The Amazonian Languages*, 385–416. Cambridge: Cambridge University Press.

Aikhenvald, Alexandra Y. 2001 Areal diffusion, genetic inheritance, and problems of subgrouping: a North Arawak case study. In: Alexandra Aikhenvald and R.M.W. Dixon (eds.), *Areal Diffusion and Genetic Inheritance*, 167–94. New York: Oxford University Press.

Aissen, Judith 2003. Differential object marking: iconicity vs. economy. *Natural Language and Linguistic Theory* 21.435–483.

Allan, Robin, Philip Holmes and Tom Lunskær-Nelson 1995 *Danish: A Comprehensive Grammar*. London: Routledge.

Andersen, Roger 1983 *Pidginization and Creolization as Language Acquisition*. Rowley, MA: Newbury House.

Ansaldo, Umberto 2008 Sri Lanka Malay revisited: genesis and classification. In: David Harrison, David Rood and Arienne Dwyer (eds.), *A World of Many Voices: Lessons from Documented Endangered Languages*, 13–42. Amsterdam: John Benjamins.

Ansaldo, Umberto and Stephen J. Matthews 1999 Creolization and the Hokkien substrate in Baba Malay. *Journal of Chinese Linguistics* 27: 38–68.

Ansaldo, Umberto and Stephen J. Matthews 2001 Typical creoles and simple languages: the case of Sinitic. *Linguistic Typology* 5.3/4.311–325.

Ansaldo, Umberto, Stephen Matthews and Lisa Lim (eds.) 2007. *Deconstructing Creole*. Amsterdam: John Benjamins.

Arends, Jacques 1989 Syntactic developments in Sranan. University of Nijmegen dissertation.

Arends, Jacques 2001 Simple grammars, complex languages. Linguistic Typology 5: 180–2.

Arends, Jacques and Matthias Perl (eds.) 1995. *Early Suriname Creole Texts: A Collection of 18th-Century Sranan and Saramaccan Documents.* Frankfurt: Vervuert.

Arends, Jacques, Pieter Muysken and Norval Smith (eds.) 1995 *Pidgins and Creoles: An Introduction.* Amsterdam: John Benjamins.

Arka, W. 2006 A note on numerals and classifiers in Rongga. Paper delivered at 10-ICAL.

Arka, W. 2007 Creole genesis and extreme analyticity in Flores languages. Paper presented at the East Nusantara conference, Kupang Indonesia.

Arndt, Peter P. 1933 *Grammatik der Ngad'a Sprache.* Bandung: A.C. Nix. (*Verhandelingen: Koninklijk Bataviaasche Genootschap van Kunsten en Wetenschappen* 72:3)

Aronoff, Mark 1976 *Word Formation in Generative Grammar.* Cambridge, MA: MIT Press.

Bakker, Peter and Mikael Parkvall 2011 Creoles versus languages with little morphology. MS.

Baird, Louise 2002 A grammar of Kéo: a language of East Nusantara. Australian National University PhD dissertation.

Baker, Mark C. 2008 *The Syntax of Agreement and Concord.* Cambridge: Cambridge University Press.

Baker, Philip 1987 Historical developments in Chinese Pidgin English and the nature of the relationships between the various pidgin Englishes of the Pacific region". *Journal of Pidgin and Creole Languages* 2: 163–207.

Baker, Philip 1999 Investigating the origin and diffusion of shared features among the Atlantic English creoles. In: Philip Baker and Adrienne Bruyn (eds.), *St. Kitts and the Atlantic Creoles,* 315–64. London: University of Westminster Press.

Baker, Philip and Anand Syea 1991 On the copula in Mauritian Creole, past and present. In Byrne and Huebner, 159–175.

Baker, Philip (ed.) 1995 *From Contact to Creole and Beyond.* London: University of Westminster Press.

Bakker, Peter 2003 The absence of reduplication in pidgins. In Kouwenberg, 37–46.

Bakker, Peter, Norval Smith and Tonjes Veenstra 1995 Saramaccan In Arends, Muysken and Smith, 165–78.

Bakker, Peter, Aymeric Daval-Markussen, Mikael Parkvall and Ingo Plag. 2011 Creoles are typologically distinct from non-creoles. *Journal of Pidgin and Creole Languages* 26: 5–42.

Ball, Martin J. and Nicole Müller 1992 *Mutation in Welsh.* London: Routledge.

Ball, Martin J. and Nicole Müller with James Fife (eds.) 1993 *The Celtic Languages.* London: Routledge.

Baptista, Marlyse 2003 Reduplication in Cape Verdean Creole. In Kouwenberg, 177–184.

Barlow, A. Ruffell and T.G. Benson 1975 *English-Kikuyu Dictionary.* Oxford: Clarendon Press.

Barry, M.V. 1969 Traditional enumeration in the North Country. *Folk Life: Journal of Ethnological Studies* 7: 75–91.

Bauer, Laurie 1988 *Introducing Linguistic Morphology.* Edinburgh: Edinburgh University Press.

Bauer, Winifred 1993. *Maori.* London: Routledge.

Bellwood, Peter 1995 Austronesian prehistory in Southeast Asia: homeland, expansion and transformation. In Bellwood, Fox and Tryon, 96–111.

Bellwood, Peter, James L. Fox and Darrell Tryon (eds.) 1995 *The Austronesians: Historical and Comparative Perspectives.* Canberra: Australian National University.

Beninca, Paola and Cecilia Poletto 2004 A case of *do*-support in Romance. *Natural Language and Linguistic Theory* 22: 51–94.

Bentley, W. Holman 1887 *Dictionary and Grammar of the Kikongo Language.* London: Trübner & Co.

Berry, Keith and Christine Berry 1999 *A Description of Abun.* Canberra: Pacific Linguistics.

Bickerton, Derek 1981 *Roots of Language.* Ann Arbor: Karoma.

Bickerton, Derek 1984. The Language Bioprogram Hypothesis. *The Behavioral and Brain Sciences* 7: 173–88.

Blake, Norman (ed.). 1992. *Cambridge History of the English Language (Volume II).* Cambridge: Cambridge University Press.

Blust, Robert 2008 Is there a Bima-Sumba subgroup? *Oceanic Linguistics* 47: 45–113.

Booij, Geert 1993 Against split morphology. In: Geert Booij and Jaap van Marle (eds.), *Yearbook of Morphology 1993,* 27–49. Dordrecht: Kluwer.

Braunmüller, Kurt 2002 Language contact during the Old Nordic period I: with the British Isles, Frisia and the Hanseatic League. In: Oskar Bandle, Kurt Braunmüller, Ernst Håkon Jahr, Allan Karker, Hans-Peter Naumann, and Ulf Teleman (eds.), *The Nordic Languages: An International Handbook of the History of the Nordic Germanic Languages, Vol. I,* 1028–39. Berlin: Mouton De Gruyter.

Breeze, Andrew 2002 Seven types of Celtic loanword. In Filppula, Klemola and Pitkänen, 175–81.

Brustad, Kristen E. 2000 The Syntax of Spoken Arabic. Washington, DC: Georgetown University Press.

Bruyn, Adrienne. 1995. *Grammaticalization in Creoles: The Development of Determiners and Relative Clauses in Sranan.* Amsterdam: IFOTT.

Burrow, Thomas 1955 *The Sanskrit Language.* London: Faber & Faber.

Byrne, Francis X. 1987 *Grammatical Relations in a Radical Creole.* Amsterdam: John Benjamins.

Byrne, Francis X. and Thom Huebner (eds.) 1991 *Development and Structure of Creole Languages.* Amsterdam: John Benjamins.

Cadely, Jean-Robert 1994 Aspects de la phonologie du créole haïtien. Université du Québec à Montréal PhD dissertation.

Campbell, Lyle and Martha C. Muntzell 1989 The structural consequences of language death. In Nancy Dorian (ed.), *Investigating Obsolescence: Studies in Language Contraction and Death,* 181–96. Cambridge: Cambridge University Press.

Carter, Hazel 1987 Suprasegmentals in Guyanese: some African comparisons. In Gilbert, 213–263.

Chappell, Hilary 2001 Language contact and areal diffusion in Sinitic languages. In Aikhenvald and Dixon, 328–57.

Chen, Chung-Yu 1983 A fifth tone in the Mandarin spoken in Singapore. *Journal of Chinese Linguistics* 11: 92–119.

Colarusso, John 1992 *A Grammar of the Kabardian Language.* Calgary: University of Calgary Press.

Comrie, Bernard (ed.) 2009 *The World's Major Languages,* second edition. London: Routledge.

Comrie, Bernard 1989 *Language Universals and Linguistic Typology.* Chicago: University of Chicago Press.

Conners, Thomas 2008 Tengger Javanese. Yale University PhD dissertation.

Corbett, Greville G. 2005 Number of genders. In Haspelmath, Dryer, Gil and Comrie, 126–129.

Corne, Chris 1995 A contact-induced and vernacularized language: how Melanesian is Tayo? In Baker, 121–48.

Corne, Chris 2000. Na pa kekan, na person: the evolution of Tayo negatives. Processes of language contact: studies from Australia and the South Pacific, ed. by Jeff Siegel, 293–317. Montreal: Fides.

Cornips, Leonie 1994 De hardnekkige vooroordelen over de regionale *doen*+infinitief-constructie. *Forum der Letteren* 35: 282–94.

Croft, William 1990 *Typology and Universals.* Cambridge: Cambridge University Press.

Crowley, Terry 1990 *From Beach-la-Mar to Bislama: The Emergence of a National Language in Vanuatu.* Oxford: The Clarendon Press.

Crowley, Terry 2000 Simplicity, complexity, emblematicity and grammatical change. In Siegel, 175–93.

Crowley, Terry 2004 *Bislama Reference Grammar.* Honolulu: University of Hawaii Press.

Culicover, Peter and Ray Jackendoff 2005 *Simpler Syntax.* New York: Oxford University Press.

Daeleman, Jan 1972 Kongo elements in Saramacca Tongo. *Journal of African Languages* 1: 1–44.

Dahl, Östen 2004 The *Growth and Maintenance of Linguistic Complexity.* Amsterdam: John Benjamins.

Dal, Ingerid 1952 Zur Entstehung des englischen Participium Praesentis auf-*ing*. *Norsk Tidsskrift for Sprogvidenskap* 16: 5–116.

De Dardel, Robert and Jakob Wüest 1993 Les systèmes casuels du proto-roman: les deux cycles de simplification. *Vox Romanica* 52: 25–65.

DeGraff, Michel 1993 A riddle on negation in Haitian. *Probus* 5: 63–93.

DeGraff, Michel 1999 Creolization, language change, and language acquisition: An epilogue. In DeGraff, 473–543.

DeGraff, Michel (ed.) 1999. *Language Creation and Language Change*. Cambridge, MA: The MIT Press.

DeGraff, Michel 2001 On the origin of creoles: a Cartesian critique of Neo-Darwinian linguistics. *Linguistic Typology* 5.2/3: 213–310.

DeGraff, Michel 2003 Against creole exceptionalism. *Language* 79: 391–410.

DeGroot, Anton 1977 *Woordregister Nederlands-Saramakaans*. Paramaribo.

Denison, David 1985 The origins of periphrastic *do:* Ellegård and Visser reconsidered. In Roger Eaton, Olga Fischer, Willem Koopman and Freferike van der Leek (eds.), *Papers from the 4th International Conference on English Historical Linguistics,* 45–60. Amsterdam: John Benjamins.

Denison, David 1993. *English Historical Syntax: Verbal Constructions*. London: Longmans.

Déprez, Viviane 1992 Is Haitian Creole really a pro-drop language? *Travaux de Recherche sur le Créole Haïtien* 11: 23–40.

Diagana, Ousmane Moussa 1995 *La langue Soninkée*. Paris: L'Harmattan.

Dimmendaal, Gerrit J. 2001 Areal diffusion versus genetic inheritance: an African perspective. Areal diffusion and genetic inheritance. In Aikhenvald and Dixon, 358–92.

Dixon, R.M.W. 1979 Ergativity. *Language* 55: 59–138.

Dixon, R.M.W. 1997 The rise and fall of languages. Cambridge: Cambridge University Press

Dixon, Robert M.W. 2001 In Aikhenvald and Dixon, 64–104.

Djawanai, Stephanus and Charles E. Grimes 1995 Ngada. In Tryon, 593–9.

Dobson, E.J. 1962 The affiliations of the manuscripts of *Ancrene Wisse*. In Norman Davis and C.L. Wrenn, *English and Medieval Studies, Presented to J.R.R. Tolkein,* 128–63. London: Oxford University Press.

Doke, C.M., D. McK. Malcolm and J.M.A. Sikakana 1971 *English-Zulu Dictionary.* Johannesburg: Witwatersrand University Press.

Donohue, Mark 1999 A Grammar of Tukang Besi. Berlin: Mouton de Gruyter.

Du Feu, Veronica 1996 *Rapanui.* London: Routledge.

Durie, Mark 1958. *A Grammar of Acehnese on the Basis of a Dialect of North Aceh.* Dordrecht, Holland: Foris.

Durrell, Martin and Winifred V. Davies 1990 Hessian. In Russ, 210–40.

Elbert, Samuel H. 1988 *Echo of a Culture: a Grammar of Rennell and Bellona.* Honolulu: University of Hawaii Press.

Ellegård, Alvar 1953 *The Auxiliary do: The Establishment and Regulation of Its Use in English*. Stockholm: Almqvist & Wiksell.

Erb, Maribeth 1999 *The Manggarais.* Singapore: Times Editions.

Eroms, Hans-Werner 1998 Periphrastic *tun* in present-day Bavarian and other German dialects. In: Ingrid Tieken-Boon Van Ostade, Marijke van der Wal and Arjan van Leuvensteijn (eds.), *Do in English, Dutch and German: History and Present-day Variation,* 139–67. Amsterdam: Stichting Neerlandistiek / Nodus.

Farquharson, Joseph 2007 Creole morphology revisited. In Ansaldo, Matthews and Lim, 21–37.

Ferguson, Charles A. 1971 Absence of copula and the notion of simplicity. In Dell Hymes (ed.), *Pidginization and Creolization of Languages,* 141–150. Cambridge: Cambridge University Press.

Ferguson, Charles A. 1972 (orig. 1959). Diglossia. In Pier Paolo Giglioli (ed.), *Language and Social Context,* 232–51. Harmondsworth, England: Penguin Books.

Ferlus, Michel 1992 Essai de phonétique historique du khmer (du milieu du premier millénaire de notre ère à l'époque actuelle). *Mon-Khmer Studies* 21: 57–89.

Ferraz, Luis Ivens 1979 *The Creole of Sao Tomé.* Johannesburg: Witwatersrand University Press.

Ferraz, Luis Ivens 1987 Portuguese creoles of West Africa and Asia. In Gilbert, 337–357.

Filppula, Markku 2003 More on the English progessive and the Celtic connection. In Tristram, 150–68.

Filppula, Markku, Juhani Klemola and Heli Pitkänen (eds.) 2002 *The Celtic Roots of English.* Joensuu, Finland: University of Joensuu Faculty of Humanities.

Fischer, Olga 1992 Syntax. In Blake, 207–408.

Foley, William A. 1986 *The Papuan Languages of New Guinea.* Cambridge: Cambridge University Press.

Forth, Gregory 1998 Beneath the volcano. Leiden: KITLV.

Forth, Gregory (ed.) 2004 Guardians of the land in Kelimado (trans. from MS by Louis Fontijne). Leiden: KITLV.

Forth, Gregory 2008 *Images of the Wildman in Southeast Asia.* London: Routledge.

Fox, James J. 1982 The Rotinese chotbah as a linguistic performance. In: Amran Halim, Lois Carrington and Stephen A. Wurm (eds.), *Papers from the Third International Conference on Austronesian Linguistics* (Vol. 3), 311–8. Canberra: Pacific Linguistics.

Fox, James J. and Charles E. Grimes 1995 Roti. In Tryon, 611–22.

Friedlaender, Jonathan S., Françoise R. Friedlaender, Floyd A. Reed, Kenneth K. Kidd, Judith R. Kidd, Geoffrey K. Chambers, Rodney A. Lea, Jun-Hun Loo, George Koki, Jason A. Hodgson, D. Andrew Merriwether, and James L. Weber 2008 The genetic structure of Pacific Islanders. *PLoS Genetics* 4(1): e19. doi:10.1371/journal.pgen.0040019.

Gair, James W. 1998 *Studies in South Asian Linguistics.* New York: Oxford University Press.

Garrett, Andrew 1998 On the origin of auxiliary *do. English Language and Linguistics* 2: 283–330.

George, Ken 1993 Cornish. In Ball, 410–68.

German, Gary D. 2000 Britons, Anglo-Saxons and scholars: 19th century attitudes towards the survival of Britons in Anglo-Saxon England. In Tristram, 347–74.

Gil, David 2001 Creoles, complexity, and Riau Indonesian. *Linguistic Typology* 2/3: 325–71.

Gil, David 2002 The prefixes *di-* and *N-* in Malay/Indonesian dialects. In Wouk and Ross, 241–83. Canberra: Pacific Linguistics.

Gil, David 2005a Numeral classifiers. In Haspelmath, Dryer, Gil and Comrie, 226–229.

Gil, David 2005b Isolating-Monocategorial-Associational language. In: Henri Cohen and Claire Lefebvre (eds.), *Categorization in Cognitive Science,* 347–79. Amsterdam: Elsevier.

Gil, David 2007 Creoles, complexity and associational semantics. In Ansaldo, Matthews and Lim, 67–108.

Gil, David 2008 How complex are isolating languages? In Miestamo, Sinnemäki and Karlsson, 109–31.

Gilbert, Glenn G. 1987 *Pidgin and creole languages.* Honolulu: University of Hawaii Press.

Goldsmith, John 1987 Tone and accent, getting the two together. *Proceedings of the 13th Annual Meeting of the Berkeley Linguistics Society,* 88–104. Berkeley, CA: Berkeley Linguistics Society.

Good, Jeff 2004 Tone and accent in Saramaccan: charting a deep split in the phonology of a language. *Lingua* 114: 575–619.

Good, Jeff 2004b Split prosody and creole simplicity: The case of Saramaccan. *Journal of Portuguese Linguistics* 3: 11–30.

Gooden, Shelome 2003 Prosodic contrast in Jamaican creole reduplication. In Plag, 193–208.

Goodman, Morris F. 1987 The Portuguese element in the American creoles. In Gilbert, 361–405.

Goyette, Stephane. 2000. From Latin to Early Romance: a case of partial creolization? In McWhorter, 103–131.

Grant, Anthony P. 1995 Article agglutination in Creole French: a wider perspective. In Baker, 149–76.

Grant, Anthony P. 1996 The evolution of functional categories in Grande Ronde Chinook Jargon: ethnolinguistic and grammatical considerations. In: Philip Baker and Anand Syea (eds.), *Changing Meanings, Changing Functions: Papers Relating to Grammaticalization in Creole Languages,* 225–42. London: University of Westminster Press.

Grant, Anthony P. 2003 Reduplication in Chinook Jargon. In Kouwenberg, 319–22.

Grijns, Cornelis D. 1991 *Jakarta Malay: a Multidimensional Approach to Spatial Variation.* Leiden: KITLV Press.

Grimme, H. 1922 *Plattdeutsche Mundarten.* Berlin: Mouton de Gruyter.

Grinevald, Collette and Frank Seifart 2004 Noun classes in African and Amazonian languages: towards a comparison. *Linguistic Typology* 8: 243–85.

Hagemeijer, Tjerk 2005 The origins of serialization in the Gulf of Guinea creoles. Paper presented at Creole Language Structure: Between Substrates and

Superstrates conference, Max Planck Institute of Evolutionary Anthropology, Leipzig, Germany, 2005.

Hagman, Roy S. 1977 *Nama Hottentot Grammar.* Bloomington: Indiana University Publications.

Hall, Robert A., Jr. 1943 *Melanesian Pidgin English: Grammar, Texts and Vocabulary.* Baltimore, MD: The Linguistics Society of America.

Ham, William H. 1999 Tone sandhi in Saramaccan: A case of substrate transfer? *Journal of Pidgin and Creole Languages* 14:45–91.

Hamp, Eric 1975 On the disappearing English relative particle. In Gaberell Drachman (ed.), *Akten der Salzburger Frühlingstagung für Linguistik,* 297–301. Tübingen: Gunter Narr.

Hancock, Ian F. 1993 Componentiality and the creole matrix: the southwest English contribution. In Michael Montgomery (ed.), *The Crucible of Carolina,* 95–114. Athens, GA: University of Georgia Press.

Hansson, Inga-Lill 1976 What we think we know about Akha grammar. Paper presented at the Ninth International Conference on Sino-Tibetan Languages and Linguistics, Copenhagen.

Hansson, Inga-Lill 2003 Akha. In: Graham Thurgood and Randy J. LaPolla (eds.), The *Sino-Tibetan Languages,* 236–51. London: Routledge.

Hashimoto, Anne Yue 1969 The verb "to be" in Modern Chinese. In: John W.M. Verhaar (ed.), *The Verb "Be" and Its Synonyms: Philosophical and Grammatical Studies,* 72–111. New York: Humanities Press.

Haspelmath, Martin, Matthew Dryer, David Gil & Bernard Comrie (eds.) 2005 *World Atlas of Language Structures.* Oxford: Oxford University Press.

Hawkins, Emily 1982 A *Pedagogical Grammar of Hawaiian: Recurrent Problems.* Honolulu: University Press of Hawaii.

Heath, Jeffrey 1978 *Linguistic Diffusion in Arnhem Land.* Canberra: Australian Institute of Aboriginal Studies.

Heath, Jeffrey 1981 A case of intensive lexical diffusion. *Language* 57: 335–67.

Heine, Bernd and Tania Kuteva 2002 *World Lexicon of Grammaticalization.* Cambridge: Cambridge University Press.

Hesseling, Dirk C. 1905 *Het Negerhollands der Deense Antillen: Bijdrage tot de Geschiedenis der Nederlandse Taal in Amerika.* Leiden: A.W. Sijthoff.

Hetzron, Robert (ed.) 1997 *The Semitic Languages.* London: Routledge.

Hickey, Raymond 1995 Early contact and parallels between English and Celtic. *Vienna English Working Papers* 4: 87–119.

Höftmann, Hildegard and Michel Ahohounkpanton 2003 *Dictionnaire Fon-Français avec une esquisse grammaticale.* Cologne: Rüdiger Köppe.

Hogan, David W. 1999 *Urak Lawoi'* (prepared by Stephen Pattemore). Munich: Lincom Europa.

Hogg, Richard M. (ed.) *The Cambridge History of the English Language (Vol. I).* Cambridge: Cambridge University Press.

Holm, John 1988 *Pidgins and Creoles,* Vol. I. Cambridge: Cambridge University Press.

Holm, John 1989 *Pidgins and Creoles,* Vol. II. Cambridge: Cambridge University Press.

Holm, John and Peter Patrick 2007 *Comparative Creole Syntax: Parallel Outlines of 18 Creole Grammars.* London: Battlebridge.

Hopper, Paul and Elizabeth Closs Traugott 1993 *Grammticalization.* Cambridge: Cambridge University Press.

Horne, Elinor C. 1961 *Beginning Javanese.* New Haven: Yale University Press.

Huddelston, Rodney and Geoffrey K. Pullum (eds.) 2002 The Cambridge Grammar of the English Language. Cambridge: Cambridge University Press.

Huffman, Franklin E. 1970 *Modern Spoken Cambodian.* New Haven: Yale University Press.

Hull, Geoffrey 1998 The basic lexical affinities of Timor's Austronesian languages: a preliminary investigation. *Studies in the Languages and Cultures of East Timor* 1: 97–174.

Hull, Geoffrey 2001a *Baikenu Language Manual for the Oecussi-Ambeno Enclave (East Timor).* Winston Hills, Australia: Sebastia~o Aparício da Silva Project.

Hull, Geoffrey 2001b A morphological overview of the Timoric Sprachbund. *Studies in Languages and Cultures of East Timor* 4: 98–205.

Hurles, M.E., J. Nicholson, E. Bosch, C. Renfrew, B.C. Sykes and M.A. Jobling 2002 Y chromosomal evidence for the origins of Oceanic-speaking peoples. *Genetics* 160: 289–303.

Huttar, Mary and George Huttar 1994 *Ndjuka.* Newbury, MA: Routledge.

Huttar, Mary and George Huttar 1975 On the change from SOV to SVO: evidence from Niger-Congo. In Charles N. Li (ed.), *Word Order and Word Order Change,* 113–47. Austin, TX: University of Texas Press.

Hyman, Larry M. 2004 How to become a Kwa verb. *Journal of West African Languages* 30: 69–88.

Igessen, Oliver 2005 Number of cases. Haspelmath, Dryer, Gil and Comrie, 202–205.

Jacq, Pascale and Paul Sidwell 2000 *A Comparative West Bahnaric Dictionary.* Munich: Lincom Europa.

Jäger, Andreas 2006 *Typology of Periphrastic 'do' Constructions.* Bochum: Brockmeyer.

James, Winthrop 2003 The role of tone and rhyme structure in the organisation of grammatical morphemes in Tobagonian. In Plag, 165–190.

Jastrow, Otto 1997 The Neo-Aramaic languages. In Hetzron, 334–77.

Jenner, Henry 1904 *A Handbook of the Cornish Language.* London: David Nutt.

Jurafsky, Dan 1996 Universal tendencies in the semantics of the diminutive. *Language* 72: 533–78.

Kapanga, André Mwamba 1993 Shaba Swahili and the processes of linguistic contact. In Byrne and Huebner, 441–58.

Karlsson, Fred 1999 *Finnish: An Essential Grammar.* London: Routledge.

Kastovsky, Dieter 1992 Semantics and vocabulary. In Hogg, 290–408. Cambridge: Cambridge University Press.

Kaye, Alan and Judith Rosenhouse 1997 Arabic dialects and Maltese. In Hetzron, 263–311.

Kazenin, Konstantin 2009 Discontinuous nominals, linear order, and morphological complexity in languages of the North Caucasus. *Linguistic Typology* 13: 391–416.

Keesing, Roger M. 1985 *Kwaio Grammar.* Canberra: Pacific Linguistics.

Keesing, Roger M. 1988 Melanesian Pidgin and the Oceanic Substrate. Palo Alto, CA: Stanford University Press.

Keller, Rudi 1995 On *Language Change: The Invisible Hand In Language.* London: Routledge.

Keller, Wolfgang 1925 Keltisches im Englischen Verbum. *Anglica: Untersuchungen zur englischen Philologie (Vol. I: Sprache und Kulturgeschichte),* 55–66. Leipzig: Mayer & Müller.

Khanlari, Parvis N. 1979 A History of the Persian Language. Delhi: Idarah-i Adabiyat-i Delli.

Kihm, Alain 1989 Lexical conflation as a basis for relexification. *Canadian Journal of Linguistics* 34: 351–76.

Kihm, Alain 2003 Inflectional categories in creole languages. In Plag, 333–363.

Kihm, Alain and Claire Lefebvre (eds.) 1993 *Aspects de la grammaire du fongbe.* Paris: Peeters.

King, Gareth 2003 *Modern Welsh: A Comprehensive Grammar.* London: Routledge.

Kiparsky, Valentin 1969 *Gibt es ein Finnougrisches Substrat im Slavischen?* Helsinki: Suomalainen Tiedeakatemia.

Klamer, Marian 1998 *A Grammar of Kambera.* Berlin: Mouton de Gruyter.

Klamer, Marian 2002 Typical features of Austronesian languages in Central / Eastern Indonesia. *Oceanic Linguistics* 41: 363–83.

Klamer, Marian 2010 Papuan-Austronesian language contact in Alor Pantar: Aloese grammar in areal perspective. Paper presented at the Workshop on Papuan Languages II: Melanesian Languages on the Edge of Asia, Past, Present and Future, Manokwari, Papua.

Klein, Wolfgang and Clive Perdue 1997 The basic variety. *Second Language Research* 13: 301–47.

Klemola, Juhani 1996 Non-standard periphrastic *do:* a study in variation and change. University of Essex PhD dissertation.

Klemola, Juhani 2000 The origins of the northern Subject Rule: a case of early contact? In Tristram, 329–46.

Klemola, Juhani 2002 Periphrastic *do:* dialectal distribution and origins. In Filppula, Klemola and Pitkänen, 199–210.

Koefoed, Geert and Jacqueline Tarenskeen 1996 The making of a language from a lexical point of view. In: Herman Wekker (ed.), *Creole Languages and Language Acquisition,* 119–38. Berlin: Mouton de Gruyter.

Kouwenberg, Silvia 1995 Berbice Dutch. In Arends, Muysken & Smith, 233–243.

Kouwenberg, Silvia 2003 *Twice as Meaningful: Reduplication in Pidgins, Creoles and Other Contact Varieties.* London: Battlebridge.

Kouwenberg, Silvia 2010 Creole studies and linguistic typology, Part 1. *Journal of Pidgin and Creole Languages* 25: 173–86.

Kouwenberg, Silvia, Darlene LaCharité and Shelome Gooden 2003 An overview of Jamaican Creole reduplication. In Kouwenberg, 105–110.

Kouwenberg, Silvia, Darlene LaCharité and Shelome Gooden 2001 Substrate transfer in Saramaccan Creole. University of California, Berkeley PhD dissertation.

Kramer, Marvin 2004 High tone spread in Saramaccan serial verb constructions. *Journal of Portuguese Linguistics* 3: 31–53.

Kroch, Tony and Ann Taylor 1997 Verb movement in old and Middle English: dialect variation and language contact. In: Ans van Kemenade and Nigel Vincent (eds.), *Parameters of Morphosyntactic Change,* 297–325. Cambridge: Cambridge University Press.

Kroch, Tony, John Myhill and Susan Pintzuk 1982 Understanding *do.* In Kevin Tuite, Robinson Schneider and Robert Chametzky (eds.), *Papers from the Chicago Linguistics Symposium 18,* 282–94. Chicago: Chicago Linguistics Society.

Kubler, Cornelius C. 1985 *The Development of Mandarin in Taiwan: A Case Study of Language Contact.* Taipei: Student Book Co.

Kumudawati, Ratri and Theresa W. Setjadiningrat 2001 Distinguishing features of Ambon and Kupang Malay. *Studies in Languages and Cultures of East Timor* 4: 61–98.

Kusters, Wouter 2003 *Linguistic Complexity: The Influence of Social Change on Verbal Inflection.* Utrecht: Landelijke Onderzoekschool Taalwetenschap (Netherlands Graduate School of Linguistics).

Ladhams, John, Tjerk Hagemeijer, Philippe Maurer and Marike Post 2003 Reduplication in the Gulf of Guinea creoles. In Kouwenberg, 165–176.

Lafage, Suzanne 1985 *Français écrit et parlé en pays éwé Sud-Togo.* Paris: SÉLAF.

Laing, Margaret 2000 *Never the twain shall meet:* Early Middle English – the East-West divide. In Taavitsainen, Nevalainen, Pahta and Rissanen, 97–124.

Langacker, Ronald W. 1987 *Foundations of Cognitive Grammar: Theoretical Prerequisites.* Stanford: Stanford University Press.

Languages of Suriname: Sranan-English dictionary (at http://www.sil.org/americas/suriname/Sranan/English/SrananEngDictIndex.html)

Lansing, J.S., M.P. Cox, S.S. Downey XXXX. 2007 Coevolution of languages and genes on the island of Sumba, eastern Indonesia. *Proceedings of the National Academy of Sciences* 105: 11645–50.

Lefebvre, Claire 1998 *Creole Genesis and the Acquisition of Grammar.* Cambridge: Cambridge University Press.

Lefebvre, Claire 2000 What do creole studies have to offer to mainstream linguistics? *Journal of Pidgin and Creole Languages* 15: 127–53.

Lefebvre, Claire 2001 What you see is not always what you get: apparent simplicity and hidden complexity in creole languages. *Linguistic Typology* 5: 186–213.

Lefebvre, Claire and Anne-Marie Brousseau 2001 *A Grammar of Fongbe*. Berlin: Mouton de Gruyter.

Le Gleau, René 1973 *Syntaxe du Bretonne moderne*. La Baule: Éditions La Baule.

Le Page, Robert B. and David DeCamp 1960 *Jamaican Creole: Creole Studies I*. London: Macmillan.

LePage, Robert and Andre Tabouret-Keller 1985 *Acts of Identity*. Cambridge: Cambridge University Press.

Lee-Smith, Mei W. 1996 The Tangwang language. In Stephen A. Wurm, Peter Mühlhäusler and Darrell T. Tryon (eds.), *Atlas of Languages of Intercultural Communication in the Pacific, Asia, and the Americas (Volume II.2)*, 875–92. Berlin: Mouton de Gruyter.

Lehmann, Christian 1985 Grammaticalization: synchronic variation and diachronic change. *Lingua e Stile* 20: 303–18.

Lewis, E. Douglas and Charles E. Grimes 1995 Sika. In Tryon, 601–9.

Lewis, Henry 1990 *Handbuch des Mittelkornischen*. Innsbruck: Insbrucker Beiträge zur Sprachwissenschaft. (German translation by Stefan Zimmer.)

Lewis, Henry and J. R. F. Piette 1990 *Handbuch des Mittelbretonischen*. Innsbruck: Insbrucker Beiträge zur Sprachwissenschaft. (German translation by Wolfgang Meid.)

Li. Charles N. and Sandra A. Thompson 1975 A mechanism for the development of copula morphemes. In: Charles N. Li (ed.), Word Order and Word Order Change, 419–44. Austin: University of Texas Press.

Lipski, John 1994 *Latin American Spanish*. London: Longman.

Lück, Marlies and Linda Henderson 1993 *Gambian Mandinka*. Banjul, Gambia: WEC International.

Ludwig, Ralph, Sylviane Telchid and Florence Bruneau-Ludwig (eds.) 2001 *Corpus créole*. Hamburg: Helmut Buske.

Luffin, Xavier 2005 *Un créole arabe: le kinubi de Mombasa, Kenya*. Munich: Lincom Europa.

Lupyan, Gary and Rick Dale 2010 Language Structure is Partly Determined by Social Structure. *PloS One* 5:1.

Magner, Thomas 1966 *A Zagreb Kajkavian Dialect*. University Park: Pennsylvania State University.

Mahota, William J. 1996 *Russian Motion Verbs for Intermediate Students*. New Haven: Yale University Press.

McKenna, Malachy 1988 *A Handbook of Modern Spoken Breton*. Tübingen: Max Niemeyer.

Manessy, Gabriel 1994 *Le français en Afrique noire*. Paris & St-Denis: L'Harmattan/ Université de la Réunion.

Manessy, Gabriel 1995 *Créoles, pidgins, variétés véhiculaires: procès et genèse*. Paris: CNRS.

Matthews, Peter H. 1974 *Morphology*. Cambridge: Cambridge University Press.

Matthews, Stephen and Virginia Yip 1994 *Cantonese: A Comprehensive Grammar.* London: Routledge.

Matisoff, James A. 1973 Tonogenesis in Southeast Asia. In Larry Hyman (ed.), *Consonant Types and Tone,* 73–95. (*Southern California Occasional Working Papers in Linguistics no. 1*) University of Southern California Linguistics Department.

Matisoff, James A. 1991 Areal and universal dimensions of grammaticization in Lahu. In Elizabeth Traugott and Bernd Heine (eds.),*Approaches to Grammaticalization* (Volume II), 383–453. Amsterdam: John Benjamins.

Maurer, Philippe 1995 *L'angolar: un créole afro-portugais parlé à São Tomé.* Hamburg: Helmut Buske.

Maurer, Philippe 2009 *Principense.* London: Battlebridge.

McDonnell, Bradley J. 2006 Possessive structures in Ende: a language of Eastern Indonesia. Paper presented at Tenth International Conference on Austronesian Linguistics, January 2006. Puerto Princesa City, Philippines.

McWhorter, John H. 1992 *Towards a New Model of Creole Genesis.* New York: Peter Lang.

McWhorter, John H. 1998 Identifying the creole prototype: vindicating a typological class. *Language* 74: 788–818.

McWhorter, John H. 1999 Skeletons in the closet: anomalies in the behavior of the Saramaccan copula. In: John R. Rickford and Suzanne Romaine (eds.), *Creole genesis, attitudes and discourse,* 121–42. Amsterdam: John Benjamins.

McWhorter, John H. 2000 *The Missing Spanish Creoles: Recovering the Birth of Plantation Creole Languages.* Berkeley, CA: University of California Press.

McWhorter, John H. (ed.) 2000. *Language Change and Language Contact in Pidgins and Creoles.* Amsterdam: John Benjamins.

McWhorter, John H. 2001a The world's simplest grammars are creole grammars. *Linguistic Typology* 5.3/4: 125–156.

McWhorter, John H. 2001b What people ask David Gil and why. *Linguistic Typology* 5.3/4: 388–412.

McWhorter, John H. 2001c Defining Creole as a synchronic term. In: Ingrid Neumann-Holzschuh and Edgar Schneider (eds.), *Degrees of Restructuring in Creole Languages,* 85–123. Amsterdam: John Benjamins.

McWhorter, John H. 2002 What happened to English? *Diachronica* 19: 217–272.

McWhorter, John H. 2004a Saramaccan and Haitian as young grammars: the pitfalls of syntactocentrism in creole genesis research. *Journal of Pidgin and Creole Languages* 19: 77–138.

McWhorter, John H. 2004b Review of Migge (2003). *New West Indian Guide* 78¾: 368–371.

McWhorter, John H. 2005a *Defining Creole.* New York: Oxford University Press.

McWhorter, John H. 2005b Review of *Issues in the Study of Pidgin and Creole Languages,* by Claire Lefebvre. *Journal of Pidgin and Creole Languages* 20: 211–8.

McWhorter, John H. 2007 *Language Interrupted: Signs of Non-native Acquisition in Standard Language Grammars*. New York: Oxford University Press.

McWhorter, John H. 2008a *Our Magnificent Bastard Tongue: The Untold History of English*. New York: Gotham Books.

McWhorter, John H. 2008b Why does a language undress?: strange cases of Indonesia. Miestamo, Sinnemäki and Karlsson, 167–90.

McWhorter, John H. and Mikael Parkvall 2002 Pas tout à fait du français: une étude créole. *Études Créoles* 25: 179–231 (special book-length edition ed. by Albert Valdman: *La créolisation: à chacun sa vérité*).

Melzian, H. J. 1937 A *Concise Dictionary of the Bini Language of Southern Nigeria*. London: Kegan Paul, Trench, Trubner & Co.

Mendoza-Denton, Norma 1999 Turn-initial No: collaborative opposition among Latina adolescents. In: Mary Bucholtz, A.C. Liang and Laurel A. Sutton (eds.), *Reinventing Identities: The Gendered Self in Discourse,* 273–92. New York: Oxford University Press.

Miestamo, Matti, Kaius Sinnemäki and Fred Karlsson (eds.) 2008 *Language Complexity: Typology, Contact, Change*. Amsterdam: John Benjamins.

Migge, Bettina M. 1998 Substrate influence in the formation of the Surinamese Plantation Creole: A consideration of the sociohistorical data and linguistic data from Ndyuka and Gbe. Ohio State University PhD dissertation.

Migge, Bettina M. 2003 *Creole Formation as Language Contact: the Case of the Surinamese Creoles*. Amsterdam: John Benjamins.

Mihalic, F. 1971 The Jacaranda Dictionary and Grammar of Melanesian Pidgin English. Milton, Queensland: The Jacaranda Press (1986 edition).

Miller, D. Gary and Kathryn Leffel 1994 The Middle English reanalysis of *do*. *Diachronica* 11: 171–98.

Milroy, James 1992 Middle English dialectology. In Blake, 156–206.

Minkova, Donka 2009 Review article: Elly van Gelderen, *A History of the English Language;* Richard Hogg and David Denison (eds.), *A History of the English Language;* Lynda Mugglestone (ed.), *The Oxford History of English. Language* 85: 893–907.

Miyamoto, Tadao 1999 *The Light Verb Construction in Japanese: The Role of the Verbal Noun*. Amsterdam: John Benjamins.

Moravcsik, Edith A. and Jessica R. Wirth 1986. Markedness: an overview. In Fred R. Eckman, Edith A. Moravcsik & Jessica R. Wirth (eds.), *Markedness,* 1–11. New York: Plenum.

Moussay, Gerard 1981 *La langue minangkabau*. Paris: Archipel.

Mufwene, Salikoko S. 1990 Kituba. In Thomason, 173–208.

Mufwene, Salikoko S. 1996 The Founder Principle in creole genesis. *Diachronica* 13: 83–134.

Mühlhäusler, Peter 1985 The scientific study of Tok Pisin: language planning and the Tok Pisin lexicon. In: Stephen A. Wurm and Peter Mühlhäusler (eds.), Handbook of Tok Pisin (New Guinea Pidgin),595–664. Canberra: Australian National University.

Mühlhäusler, Peter 1997 *Pidgin and creole linguistics* (expanded and revised edition). London: University of Westminster.

Müller-Gotama, Franz 2001 *Sundanese*. Munich: Lincom Europa.

Mustanoja, Tauno F. 1960 *A Middle English Syntax (Part I)*. Helsinki: Societé Néophilologique.

Muysken, Pieter 1994a Column: the first seven years, fat or lean? *Journal of Pidgin and Creole Languages* 9: 103–7.

Muysken, Pieter 1994b Saramaccan and Haitian: a comparison. *Journal of Pidgin and Creole Languages* 9: 305–14.

Nagaraja, K.S. 1985 *Khasi: A Descriptive Analysis*. Deccan College Post-Graduate & Research Institute: Pune 6.

Naro, Anthony and Maria Marta Pereira Scherre 2000 In McWhorter, 235–255.

Neumann, Ingrid 1985 *Le créole de Breaux-Bridge, Louisiane: étude morphosyntaxe, textes, vocabulaire*. Hamburg: Helmut Buske.

Newmeyer, Frederick J. 2005 *Possible and Probable Languages: A Generative Perspective on Linguistic Typology*. New York: Oxford University Press.

Nordhoff, Sebastian 2009 *A Grammar of Upcountry Sri Lanka Malay*. Utrecht: LOT, 2009.

Norman, Jerry 1988 *Chinese*. Cambridge: Cambridge University Press.

Ogie, Ota 2003 About multi-verb constructions in Edo. In: Dorothee Beermann and Lars Hellan (eds.), Proceedings of the Workshop on Multi-Verb Constructions (Trondheim Summer School 2003). (On-line publication at edvarda.hf.ntnu.no/ling/tross/)

Owens, Jonathan 1991 Nubi, genetic linguistics, and language classification. *Anthropological Linguistics* 33: 1–30.

Owens, Jonathan 1997 Arabic-based pidgins and creoles. In Thomason, 125–72.

Parkvall, Mikael 2008 The simplicity of creoles in a cross-linguistic perspective. In: Miestamo, Sinnemäki and Karlsson (eds.), *Language Complexity. Typology, Contact, Change*, 265–285.

Paauw, Scott 2007 A North Papua linguistic area? Paper presented at the Workshop on the Languages of Papua, Manokwari.

Pensalfini, Robert 2003 *A Grammar of Jingulu*. Canberra: Pacific Linguistics.

Plag, Ingo (ed.) 2003. *Phonology and Morphology of Creole Languages*. Tübingen: Niemeyer.

Plag, Ingo 2008a Creoles as interlanguages: inflectional morphology. *Journal of Pidgin and Creole Languages* 23: 114–135.

Plag, Ingo 2008b Creoles as interlanguages: syntactic structures. *Journal of Pidgin and Creole Languages* 23: 307–28

Poppe, Erich 2003 Progress on the progressive? A report. In Tristram, 65–84.

Post, Marike 1995 Fa d'Ambu. In Arends, Muysken & Smith, 191–204.

Poussa, Patricia 1990 A contact-universals origin for periphrastic *do,* with special consideration of OE-Celtic contact. In Sylvia Adamson, Vivien Law, Nigel Vincent and Susan Wright (eds.), *Papers from the 5th International Conference on English Historical Linguistics, Cambridge, 6–9 April 1987,* 407–34. Amsterdam: John Benjamins.

Premsrirat, S. 2001 Tonogenesis in Khmu dialects of SEA. *Mon-Khmer Studies* 31: 47–56.

Prentice, David J. 1987. Malay (Indonesian and Malaysian). In Comrie, 913–35.

Press, Ian 1986 A *Grammar of Modern Breton.* Berlin: Mouton de Gruyter.

Preusler, Walther 1956 Keltischer Einfluss im Englischen. *Revue des Langues Vivantes* 22: 322–50.

Price, Richard and Sally Price 1991 *Two Evenings in Saramaka.* Chicago: University of Chicago Press.

Price, Richard and Sally Price n.d. (Transcriptions of folktales obtained from Val Ziegler, recorded in the 1970s.)

Quirk, Randolph, Sidney Greenbaum, Geoffrey Leech and Jan Svartvik (eds.) 1985 *A Comprehensive Grammar of the English language.* London: Longman.

Rabel-Heyman, Lili 1977 Gender in Khasi nouns. *Mon-Khmer Studies* 6: 247–272.

Rhodes, Richard 1990 Obviation, inversion, and topic rank in Ojibwa. In David J. Costa (ed.), *Proceedings of the Berkeley Linguistics Society* 16, 101–15. Berkeley: University of California, Berkeley.

Riddle, Elizabeth M. 2008 Complexity in isolating languages: elaboration versus grammatical economy. In Miestamo, Sinnemäki and Karlsson, 133–51. Amsterdam: John Benjamins.

Rivera-Castillo, Yolanda 1998 Tone and stress in Papiamentu: the contribution of a constraint-based analysis to the problem of creole genesis. *Journal of Pidgin and Creole Languages* 13: 1–28.

Rivera-Castillo, Yolanda and Lucy Pickering 2004 Phonetic correlates of stress and tone in a mixed system. *Journal of Pidgin and Creole Languages* 19: 261–284.

Roberts, Ian. 1999. Verb movement and markedness. In DeGraff, 287–327.

Roberts, John R. 1988 Amele switch-reference and the theory of grammar. *Linguistic Inquiry* 19: 45–63.

Roberts, Sarah J. 1998 The genesis of Hawaiian Creole and diffusion. *Language* 74: 1–39.

Roberts, Sarah J. 2000 Nativization and the genesis of Hawaiian Creole. In McWhorter, 257–300.

Roberts, Sarah J. 2003 Reduplication and the formation of Pidgin Hawaiian. In Kouwenberg, 307–318.

Roberts, Sarah J. and Joan Bresnan 2008 Retained inflectional morphology in pidgins: a typological study. *Linguistic Typology* 12: 269–302.

Rosen, Joan M. 1983 Rembong and Wangka: A brief comparison of two dialects. In: John W.M. Verhaar (ed.), *Miscellaneous Studies of Indonesian and Other Lan-*

guages in Indonesia, Part VII, 50–68. Jakarta: Badan Penyelenggara Seri NUSA & Universitas Katolik Indonesia Atma Jaya.

Rountree, S. Catharine 1972 Saramaccan tone in relation to intonation and grammar. *Lingua* 29:308–25.

Russ, Charles V.J. (ed.) 1990 *The Dialects of Modern German.* London: Routledge.

Sadler, Wesley 1964 Untangled CiBemba. Kitwe, N. Rhodesia: The United Church of Central Africa in Rhodesia.

Salmons, Joseph 1992 *Accentual Change and Language Contact.* Palo Alto, CA: Stanford University Press.

Samarin, William J. 1997 The creolization of pidgin morphophonology. In: Arthur Spears and Donald Winford (eds.), *The Structure and Status of Pidgins and Creoles,* 175–216. Amsterdam: John Benjamins.

Samarin, William J. 2000 The status of Sango in fact and fiction. In McWhorter 301–33.

Sampson, Geoffrey 2006 Does Simple Imply Creole? *A Man of Measure: Festschrift in Honour of Fred Karlsson on his 60th Birthday* (special supplement to *SKY Journal of Linguistics,* Vol. 19), 362–374. Turku: The Linguistic Association of Finland.

Sampson, Geoffrey David Gil and Peter Trudgill (eds.) 2009 *Language Complexity as an Evolving Variable.* Oxford: Oxford University Press.

Samely, Ursula 1991 *Kedang (Eastern Indonesia): Some Aspects of Its Grammar.* Hamburg: Helmut Buske.

Schachter, Paul 1987 Tagalog. In Comrie, 936–58.

Schaefer, Ron and Francis Egbokhare 2002 On Emai's causative motion parameters. *Journal of African Languages and Linguistics* 23: 63–76.

Schmitt, Rüdiger 1989 Altpersisch. In Rüdiger Schmitt (ed.), *Compendium Linguarum Iranicarum,* 56–85. Wiesbaden: Ludwig Reichert.

Schuchardt, Hugo 1888 Kreolische Studien. VIII. Über das Annamito-französische. *Sitzungsberichte der Kaiserlichen Akademie der Wissenschaften zu Wien* 116: 227–34.

Schumann, C.L. 1783 Neger-Englisches Wörterbuch (at http://www.sil.org/americas/suriname/Schumann/National/SchumannGerDict.html)

Schwartz, Bonnie and Rex A. Sprouse 1996 L2 cognitive states and the full transfer/full access mode. *Second Language Research* 12: 40–72.

Schwegler, Armin 1998 El palenquero. In: Matthias Perl and Armin Schwegler (eds.), *América negra: panorámica actual de los estudios lingüísticos sobre variedades criollas y afrohispanas,* 219–91. Frankfurt: Vervuert.

Schwegler, Armin 1993 Rasgos (afro-) portugueses en el criollo del Palenque de San Basilio (Colombia). In: Carmen Díaz D. Alayón (ed.), *Homenaje a José Perez Vidal,* 667–96. La Laguna, Tenerife: Litografía A. Romero S. A.

Schwegler, Armin 1996 *Chi ma nkongo, chi ma ri Luango: cantos ancestrales afrohispanos del Palenque de San Basilio (Colombia).* Frankfurt: Vervuert.

Sebba, Mark 1987. *The Syntax of Serial Verbs: An Investigation Into Serialisation in Sranan and Other Languages.* Amsterdam: John Benjamins.

Sebba, Mark 1997 *Contact Languages: Pidgins and Creoles.* New York: St. Martin's.

Shanks, Louis (ed.) 1994 *A Buku fu Okanisi anga Ingiisi Wowtu (Aukan-English dictionary).* Paramaribo, Suriname: Summer Institute of Linguistics.

Sidwell, Paul 2000 *Proto South Bahnaric: a Reconstruction of a Mon-Khmer language of Indo-China.* Canberra: Pacific Linguistics.

Siegel, Jeff 2000a Substrate influence in Hawai'i Creole English. *Language in Society* 29: 197–236.

Siegel, Jeff (ed.) 2000b *Processes of Language Contact: Studies from Australia and the South Pacific.* Montreal: Fides.

Siegel, Jeff 2006 Transmission and transfer. In: Ansaldo, Matthews and Lim, 167–201. Amsterdam: John Benjamins.

Singler, John 2006 Children and creole genesis. *Journal of Pidgin and Creole Languages* 21:157–73.

Smith, Jeremy 2000 Standard language in Early Modern English? In Taavitsainen, Nevalainen, Pahta and Rissanen, 125–39.

Smith, Kenneth D. 1972. A *Phonological Reconstruction of Proto-North-Bahnaric.* Santa Ana, CA: Summer Institute of Linguistics

Smith, Norval 1987 The genesis of the creole languages of Surinam. University of Amsterdam dissertation.

Smith, Norval 2001 Voodoo Chile: differential substrate effects in Saramaccan and Haitian. In: Norval Smith and Tonjes Veenstra (eds.), *Creolization and Contact,* 43–80. Amsterdam: John Benjamins.

Smith-Hefner, Nancy J. 1988 Cara Tengger: notes on a non-standard dialect of Javanese. In: Richard McGinn (ed.), *Studies in Austronesian Linguistics,* 203–33. Athens, OH: Ohio University Center for International Studies.

Sneddon, James Neil 1996 *Indonesian: A Comprehensive Grammar.* London: Routledge.

Spangenberg, Karl 1990 Thuringian. In Russ, 265–89.

Spencer, Andrew 1991 *Morphological Theory.* Oxford: Blackwell.

Spriggs, Matthew 2003 Chronology of the Neolithic transition in Island Southeast Asia and the Western Pacific: a view from 2003. *The Review of Archaeology* 24: 57–80.

Stahlke, Herbert F. 1970 Serial verbs. *Studies in African Linguistics* 1: 60–99.

Steinhauer, Hein 1993 Notes on verbs in Dawanese (Timor). In: Ger P. Reesink (ed.), *Topics in Descriptive Austronesian Linguistics,* 130–58. Leiden: Vakgroep Talen en Culturen van Zuidoost-Azië en Oceanië.

Stenson, Nancy 1981 Studies in Irish Syntax. Tübingen: Günter Narr.

Stephens, Janig 1993 Breton. In Ball, 349–409.

Stewart, John M. 1967 Tongue root position in Akan vowel harmony. *Phonetica* 16: 185–204.

Stolz, Thomas and Pieter Stein 1986 Social history and genesis of Negerhollands. *Amsterdam Creole Studies* 9: 103–122.

Sweet, Henry 1892 *A New English Grammar, Logical and Historical, Part I: Introduction, Phonology and Accidence.* Oxford: Oxford University Press.

Taavitsainen, Irma, Terttu Nevalainen, Päivi Pahta and Matti Rissanen (eds.) 2000 *Placing Middle English in Context.* Berlin: Mouton de Gruyter.

Talmy, Leonard 1985 Lexicalization patterns. In: Timothy Shopen (ed.), *Language Typology and Syntactic Description* (Vol. III: Grammatical categories and the lexicon), 57–149. Cambridge: Cambridge University Press.

Tchekhoff, Claude 1979 From ergative to accusative in Tongan: an example of synchronic dynamics. In: Frans Plank (ed.), *Ergativity: Towards a Theory of Grammatical Relations,* 407–80. London: Academic Press.

Thomas, David D. 1971 *Chrau Grammar.* Honolulu: University of Hawaii Press.

Thomas, Dorothy M. 1969 Chrau affixes. *Mon-Khmer Studies* 3: 90–107.

Thomason, Sarah J. 1997 Contact Languages: A Wider Perspective. Amsterdam: John Benjamins.

Thomason, Sarah J and Terence Kaufman 1988 *Language Contact, Creolization, and Genetic Linguistics.* Berkeley: University of California Press.

Thompson, Laurence C. 1965 *A Vietnamese Grammar.* Seattle: University of Washington Press.

Thompson, R. Wardlaw 1958 Let's take Hong Kong's word. *The China Mail,* 9/13 and 9/20.

Thongkum, Therapan L. 1981 The distribution of the sounds of Bruu. *Mon-Khmer Studies* 8: 221–293.

Thurgood, Graham 1999 *From Ancient Cham to Modern Dialects: 2000 Years of Language Contact and Change.* Honolulu: University of Hawaii Press.

Thurgood, Graham 2002 Vietnamese and tonogenesis: revising the model and the analysis. *Diachronica* 19: 333–63.

Thurston, William R 1987 *Processes of Change in the Languages of Northwestern New Britain.* Canberra: Australian National University.

Tieken-Boon Van Ostade, I. 1988 The origin and development of periphrastic auxiliary do: a case of destigmatization. *Dutch Working Papers in English Language and Linguistics* 3.

Tjia, Johnny 2007 *A Grammar of Mualang.* Utrecht: LOT.

Tolkein, J.R.R. 1963 English and Welsh. *Angles and Britons* (O'Donnell Lectures), 1–41. Cardiff: University of Wales Press.

Tottie, Gunnel 1983 The missing link or, why is there twice as much negation in spoken English as in written English? In: Sven Jacobson (ed.), *Papers from the Scandinavian Symposium on Syntactic Variation, Stockholm, May 15–16, 1982,* 67–74. Stockholm: Almqvist & Wiksell.

Traugott, Elizabeth C. 1992 Syntax. In Hogg, 168–289. Cambridge: Cambridge University Press.

Trépos, Pierre 196 *Grammaire Bretonne.* Rennes: Simon.

Tristram, Hildegard L.C. 1995 Zaos and Zomerset: linguistic contacts across the English Channel. In Wolfgang Viereck (ed.), *Verhandlungen des Internationalen*

Dialektologenkongresses, Bamberg 1990 (Vol. IV), 276–98. Stuttgart: Franz Steiner.

Tristram, Hildegard L.C. 1997. *Do*-periphrasis in contact? In: Heinrich Ramisch and Kenneth Wynne (eds.), *Language in Time and Space: Studies in Honor of Wolfgang Viereck on the Occasion of his 60*th *Birthday*, 401–17. Stuttgart: Franz Steiner.

Tristram, Hildegard L.C. 1999 *How Celtic is Standard English?* St. Petersburg: Nauka.

Tristram, Hildegard L.C. (ed.) 2000 *The Celtic Englishes II.* Heidelberg: C. Winter.

Tristram, Hildegard L.C. 2002 Attrition of inflections in English and Welsh. Filppula, Klemola and Pitkänen, 111–49.

Tristram, Hildegard L.C. (ed.) 2003 *The Celtic Englishes III.* Heidelberg: C. Winter.

Tryon, Darrell T. and Jean-Michel Charpentier (eds.) 2004 *Pacific Pidgins and Creoles: Origin, Growth and Development.* Berlin: Mouton de Gruyter.

Trudgill, Peter 1989 Contact and evolution in linguistic change. In: Leiv Egil Brevik and Ernst Håkon Jahr (eds.), *Language Change: Contributions to the Study of Its Causes*, 227–37. Berlin: Mouton de Gruyter.

Trudgill, Peter 1996 Dialect typology: isolation, social network and phonological structure. In: Gregory Guy, Crawford Feagin, Deborah Schiffrin and John Baugh (eds.), *Towards a Social Science of Language, Vol. I: Variation and Change in Language and Society*, 3–21. Amsterdam: John Benjamins.

Trudgill, Peter 2001 Contact and simplification: historical baggage and directionality in linguistic change. *Linguistic Typology* 5:371–4.

Tryon, Darrell 1995 Proto-Austronesian and the major Austronesian subgroups. In Bellwood, Fox and Tryon, 17–38.

Tryon, Darrell (ed.) 1995 *Comparative Austronesian Dictionary, Part I, Fascicle I.* Berlin: Mouton de Gruyter.

Tuldava, Juhan 1994 *Estonian Textbook.* Bloomington, IN: Research Institute for Inner Asian Studies.

Ultan, Russell 1978 Some general characteristics of interrogative systems. In: Joseph Greenberg (ed.), *Universals of Human Language* (Vol. IV), 211–48. Palo Alto: Stanford University Press.

Valdman, Albert 1978 *Le créole: Structure, statut et origine.* Paris: Klincksieck.

Van Bekkum, W. 1944 Warloka-Todo-Pongkor: een brok gescheidenis van Manggarai. *Cultureel Indie* 6: 144–52.

Van der Auwera, Johan 1999. Periphrastic 'do': typological prolegomena. In: Guy A.J. Tops, Betty DeVriendt and Steven Geukens (eds.), *Thinking English Grammar: To Honour Xavier DeKeyser, Professor Emeritus*, 457–70. Leuven: Peeters.

Van der Auwera, Johan and Inge Genee 2002 English *do:* on the convergence of languages and linguists. *English Language and Linguistics* 6: 283–307.

Van Diggelen, Miep 1978 Negro-Dutch. *Amsterdam Creole Studies* 2: 69–100.

Van Engelenhoven, Aone 2003 Language endangerment in Indonesia. In: Mark Janse and Sijmen Tol (eds.), *Language Death and Language Maintenance: Theoretical, Practical and Descriptive Approaches,* 49–80. Amsterdam: John Benjamins.

Van Klinken, Catharina L. 1999 *A Grammar of the Fehan Dialect of Tetun.* Canberra: Pacific Linguistics (The Australian National University).

Veenstra, Tonjes 1996 *Serial Verbs in Saramaccan.* The Hague: Holland Academic Graphics.

Veenstra, Tonjes 2003 What verbal morphology can tell us about creole genesis: the case of French-related creoles. In Plag, 293–313.

Veiga, Manuel 2000 *Le créole de Cap-Vert.* Paris: Éditions Karthala.

Vennemann, Theo 2000 English as a "Celtic" language: Atlantic influences from above and below. In Tristram, 399–406.

Vennemann, Theo 2001 Atlantis Semitica: structural contact fetaures in Celtic and English. In Laurel Brinton (ed.), *Historical Linguistics 1999,* 351–69. Amsterdam: John Benjamins.

Verhaar, John W.M. 1995 Towards *a Reference Grammar of Tok Pisin: An Experiment in Corpus Linguistics.* Honolulu: University of Hawaii Press.

Verheijen, J.A.J. and Charles E. Grimes 1995 Manggarai. In Tryon, 585–92.

Versteegh, Kees 1997 *The Arabic Language.* New York: Columbia University Press.

Veselinona, Ljuba 2003 Suppletion in Verb Paradigms. University of Stockholm PhD dissertation.

Visser, G. 1955 Celtic influence in English. *Neophilologus* 39: 276–93.

Visser, F. Th. 1963–73 *An Historical Syntax of the English Language.* Leiden: E.J. Brill.

Voorhoeve, Jan 1962 *Sranan Syntax.* Amsterdam: North-Holland Publishing Co.

Voorhoeve, Jan 1973 Historical and linguistic evidence in favor of the relexification theory in the formation of creoles. *Language in Society* 2: 133–45.

Westermann, Diedrich 1930a *Gbesela yeye or English-Ewe Dictionary.* Berlin: Dietrich Riemer.

Westermann, Diedrich 1930b *A Study of the Ewe Language.* London: Oxford University Press.

Westermann, Diedrich 1973. *Evefiala or Ewe-English dictionary / Gbesela Yeye or English-Ewe-Dictionary.* Nendeln, Liechtenstein: Kraus Reprint.

White, David L. 2002 Explaining the innovations of Middle English: what, where, and why. In Filppula, Klemola and Pitkänen, 153–74.

Wiesemann, Ursula 1991 Tone and intonational features in Fon. *Linguistique Africaine* 7: 65–90.

Williams-Van Klinken, Catharina, John Hajek and Rachel Nordlinger 2002 *Tetun Dili: A Grammar of an East Timorese Language.* Canberra: Pacific Linguistics (The Australian National University).

Windfuhr, Gernot L. 1987 Persian. In Comrie, 523–46.

Wittmann, Henri 1998 Les créolismes syntaxiques du français magoua parlé aux Trois-Rivières. In: Patrice Brasseur (ed.), *Français d'amérique: variation, créolisation, normalisation,* 219–248. Avignon: Université d'Avignon, Centre d'études canadiennes.

Wouk, Fay 2002 Voice in the languages of Nusa Tenggara Barat. In Wouk and Ross, 285–309.

Wouk, Fay and Malcolm Ross (eds.) 2002 *The History and Typology of Western Austronesian Voice Systems.* Canberra: Pacific Linguistics.

Wray, Alison and George W. Grace 2007 The consequences of talking to strangers: evolutionary corollaries of socio-cultural influences on linguistics form. *Lingua* 117: 543–78.

Wurm, Stephen A. and Peter Mühlhäusler (eds.) 1985 *Handbook of Tok Pisin (New Guinea Pidgin).* Canberra: Australian National University.

Zhou, Minglang 1998 Tense/aspect markers in Mandarin and Xiang dialects. *Sino-Platonic Papers* 83. (University of Pennsylvania, Department of Asian and Middle Eastern Studies)

Zsiga, Elizabeth C. 1997 Features, gestures, and Igbo vowels: an approach to the phonology-phonetics interface. *Language* 73: 227–74.

Index